ARCHAEOLOGY AND LANGUAGE I

ONE WORLD ARCHAEOLOGY
Series Editor: P. J. Ucko

ARCHAEOLOGY AND LANGUAGE I

Theoretical and methodological orientations

Edited by

Roger Blench and Matthew Spriggs

London and New York

First published 1997
by Routledge
11 New Fetter Lane, London EC4P 4EE

Simultaneously published in the USA and Canada
by Routledge
29 West 35th Street, New York, NY 10001

Typeset in Bembo by Florencetype Ltd, Stoodleigh, Devon

Printed and bound in Great Britain by
Biddles Ltd, Guildford and King's Lynn

British Library Cataloguing in Publication Data
A catalogue record for this book is available from the British Library.

Library of Congress Cataloging in Publication Data
A catalog record for this book has been requested.

ISBN 0-415-11760-7

Cum remotae gentium origines historiam transcendant, linguae nobis praestant veterum monumentorum vicem.

Gottfried Wilhelm Leibniz, De originibus gentium

There is no tracing the connection of ancient nations but by language; and therefore I am always sorry when any language is lost, because languages are the pedigree of nations. If you find the same language in distant countries, you may be sure that the inhabitants of each have been the same people; that is to say, if you find the languages are a good deal the same; for a word here and there the same will not do.

Samuel Johnson, quoted in Boswell, 1785

If we possessed a perfect pedigree of mankind, a genealogical arrangement of the races of man would afford the best classification of the various languages now spoken throughout the world; and if all the extinct languages, and all intermediate and slowly changing dialects had to be included, such an arrangement would, I think, be the only possible one . . . this would be strictly natural, as it would connect together all languages extinct and modern, by the closest affinities, and would give the filiation and origin of each tongue.

Charles Darwin, On the Origin of Species

To seek, by the multiple routes of anatomy, physiology, history, archaeology, linguistics and even palaeontology, what have been in historic times and in the ages which preceded the most ancient remains of humanity, the origins, the affiliations, the migrations, the mixtures of the numerous and diverse groups which make up the human species.

Paul Broca, 'La linguistique et l'anthropologie'

Contents

Figures

Tables

Contributors

Lidia Ashikhmina, Syktyvkar, Komi Science Centre of the Russian Academy of Sciences, Glavpochtamt, Syktyvkar, Komi Republic, Russia.

Bernard H. Bichakjian, Department of French, Catholic University of Nijmegen, The Netherlands.

Roger Blench, CISPAL, Cambridge, UK.

Paul A. Bouissac, Victoria College, University of Toronto, Toronto, Ontario, Canada.

Joseph Eboreime, National Commission for Museums and Monuments, National Museum, Benin City, Nigeria.

Daniel Frimigacci, 195 bis rue Raymond Losserand, 75014 Paris, France.

José Garanger, 49 rue du Dr Jean-Vaquier, 93160 Noisy-Le-Grand, France.

Gabór Györi, Janus Pannonius University, Hungary.

Irén Hegedüs, Janus Pannonius University, Hungary.

James P. Mallory, Department of Archaeology, School of Geosciences, Queens University, Belfast, N. Ireland.

Johanna Nichols, Department of Slavic Languages and Literatures, University of California at Berkeley, California, USA.

Marcel Otte, Université de Liège, Service de Préhistoire, Liège, Belgium.

Jon Patrick, Massey University, Palmerston North, New Zealand.

Ilia Pejros, Department of Linguistics, University of Melbourne, Parkville, Australia.

Anand Raman, Massey University, Palmerston North, New Zealand.

Lawrence A. Reid, Social Science Research Institute, University of Hawaii.

Colin Renfrew, McDonald Institute, University of Cambridge, Downing Street, Cambridge, UK.

Malcolm Ross, Department of Linguistics, Research School of Pacific Studies, ANU, Canberra, Australia.

Margaret Sharpe, N. Department of Aboriginal and Multicultural Studies, University of New England, Armidale, NSW, Australia.

Victor Shnirelman, Institute of Ethnology and Anthropology, Leninskij Prospekt, Moscow, Russia.

Matthew Spriggs, Department of Archaeology and Anthropology, Faculty of Arts, ANU, Canberra, Australia.

Jerry Taki, Department of Linguistics, Research School of Pacific Studies, ANU, Canberra, Australia.

Dorothy Tunbridge, N. Department of Aboriginal and Multicultural Studies, University of New England, Armidale, NSW, Australia.

Darrell Tryon, Department of Linguistics, Research School of Pacific Studies, ANU, Canberra, Australia.

Inger Zachrisson, Riksantikvariea'mbetet, Statens historiska museer, Stockholm, Sweden.

Preface

The relation between the present volumes and the Third World Archaeological Congress, held in New Delhi in December 1994, is complex. Events at the Congress have been described in some detail (e.g. Colley 1995; Hassan 1995; Golson 1995; Bernbeck and Pollock 1995) and need not be further touched upon. Some of the chapters were presented as papers in the Congress, as part of a five-day session containing some eighty papers on Language and Archaeology, while others were commissioned for the present volumes. In some cases, scholars who presented papers at the Conference have substantially revised their work or even divided it into several chapters. The object has been to develop as comprehensive a coverage as is practical of the issues raised in this area, both geographically and methodologically. These books should therefore not be regarded as proceedings, but as ideas stimulated following that meeting.

Issues of nomenclature, style of data presentation and editorial principles are dealt with below. The introduction[1] is divided into two parts: a generic introduction, dealing with the broad issues raised by the interface of archaeology and language, and an introduction specific to the volume in hand.

TERMINOLOGY AND METHOD: SOME EDITORIAL PRINCIPLES

Terminology

An issue thrown into sharp relief by pulling together chapters that in principal undertake the same enterprise in very different intellectual traditions is the wide variety of terminology used to describe the same phenomena. This is nowhere more apparent than in the case of language subgrouping. The terms 'phylum', 'stock', 'family', 'branch', 'section', 'group', 'subgroup', 'language', 'lect', 'communalect' and 'dialect' are thrown freely around without any clear definition that could assist someone in another region to apply them consistently. This is not to say that the literature is not well-endowed with

Table 1 Definitions of language groupings

Term	Percentage range
Phylum	5–12
Stock	13–28
Family	29–45
Subfamily	46–78
Language	79–81
Dialect	above 81

Source: from Wurm and McElhanon (1975: 152)

attempts to define these categories. The most common of these are in terms of lexicostatistics. Lexicostatistics provides mathematical definitions of the relations between one language and another and therefore would seem very suitable for concrete definitions. For example, one well-known use of this system was applied to the languages of Papua New Guinea (Table 1).

The use of a table such as Table 1 depends heavily on the faith of individual linguists in lexicostatistics. If it is possible for languages to be 'mixed' – i.e. to draw a significant proportion of basic vocabulary from two or more unrelated languages – then lexicostatistics will give contradictory results. It used to be denied that mixed languages existed; then, when this view became untenable, that they were very rare. Mbugu (Ma'a) in Tanzania appears frequently in the literature exemplifying this sort of rarity (Mous 1994). However, Oceania has supplied some of the most striking examples of 'mixed' languages, such as Maisin or Magori, which create problems in applying the lexicostatistic method. Since the work of Thomason and Kaufmann (1988) it is increasingly accepted that this type of language-mixing may in fact be quite common. The effect of a synchronic perspective on language description is that extraneous elements in the lexicon have been assimilated and are no longer evident. If we identify a mixed language in the present it is because we can still identify its components. Assuming that these types of language mixture occurred in the past (and probably did with greater frequency) it may well be that many languages today are 'mixed' but that their elements are no longer so easily discerned.

As more syntheses of world languages appear (notably, Ruhlen 1991), a consensus on terminology is slowly emerging. The most important of these is the use of 'phylum', now applied to the large well-known and reasonably established families of languages such as Indo-European or Uralic, but more controversially extended to any language grouping whose external affiliations are not well established or remain highly controversial. This can mean that an individual language may represent a phylum; thus Japanese/Ryukyuan is generally considered an isolate and is usually referred to as 'Japonic'. Indeed NE Asia represents an intriguing cluster of either very small language groups or individual isolates; these are generally considered to be phyla (see Janhunen, Volume II).

The term 'stock' has remained in discussions of Pacific, especially Papuan, languages but has not been widely adopted outside; most linguists probably use 'family' as the next level of relationship below phylum. Indeed, Indo-European scholars, the most conservative subgroup of historical linguists, remain unused to referring to Indo-European as a phylum. Between stock and language something of a free-for-all obtains; branch, section, group, subgroup are used quite freely, and no fiat from individual scholars is likely to change this situation. 'Language' is generally considered to be a group of speech-forms whose speakers can all understand one another without considerable effort. Below 'language' in the hierarchy of classification either dialect or communalect are commonly used. However, recently, the term 'lect' has been adopted to capture the ambiguity between language and dialect and in part also to avoid the pejorative overtones of dialect.

Reconstructions and conventions

A focal point of historical linguistics are reconstructions, usually denoted by an asterisk (*) and often referred to as 'starred forms'. These are abstract forms, derived from attested languages that were supposedly part of a hypothetical proto-language. Thus an author citing * plus a formula for a word is implying that it formed part of the proto-language spoken by the particular reconstructed group. Terms such as proto-Indo-European are common enough to be standard terminology. However, not all authors use the same standards of evidence to derive these proto-forms. Problems arise:

(a) when the dataset is defective, i.e. lexical attestations are known only from some languages in the proposed subgroup;

(b) when a reconstruction is built indirectly, i.e. on the back of other reconstructed forms whose status is doubtful.

Proto-forms can be cited for defective datasets; this is an inevitable part of hypothesis building. Problems arise when speculative reconstructions of this type are quoted as solid results by specialists from another area.

In some domains of African language research a distinction has been adopted between a 'pseudo-reconstruction' and a 'regular reconstruction' (e.g. in Bendor-Samuel 1989). Pseudo-reconstructions are essentially well-informed guesses as opposed to regular reconstructions which are based on a thorough analysis of historical sound-correspondences. Pseudo-reconstructions are marked '#' in contrast to regular reconstructions which retain the asterisk *. This distinction is difficult to enforce as authors are inevitably touchy about the reality of their reconstructions. This is particularly true of deep-level reconstructions such as the hypothetical Nostratic; the claim by Hegedüs (Ch. 4, this volume) that it is based on regular sound correspondences would be disputed by many historical linguists. However, as variations arise in the reconstruction and subgrouping of the language phyla of the world, historical linguists will gradually be compelled to become more critical of proposed reconstructions.

Phonetic characters and orthographic conventions

These books make no apology for making use of the technical conventions of linguistics; unless authors can back up their results in a way credible to other linguists their assertions will remain speculative. As far as possible, authors have been encouraged to shift their data tables to an appendix and to establish a clear flow of argument independent of these. However, where argument and data are inextricably intertwined the tables have been left in place.

In an ideal world, all linguists would switch to a standard set of conventions for representing phonetic characters and these would be internationally agreed upon and developed or expanded as research continues. The conventions of the IPA (International Phonetic Association) largely serve this function in the case of basic phonetic research and often in the description of undescribed languages. However, where an old-established research tradition exists, as in Indo-European, Kartvelian or Sino-Tibetan, phylum-specific conventions have been established and writers are often loath to break away from these and shift their whole dataset to IPA. In addition, orthographies that have been developed in this century for mission or other literacy purposes often reflect the technology of the period. Where authors were expecting to produce primers or Bible translations they developed conventions that are effective on typewriters. In some cases these have been well-established and, now that printed materials are produced by computer, word-processors have to mimic these.

In the chapters that follow most authors use IPA phonetic symbols, but in the case of well-established traditions they follow disciplinary orthographic conventions. Where these might be obscure they are explained in endnotes.

Editorial policy

Approximately half the contributions in these volumes were written by scholars whose first language is not English. These books are not intended to present a façade of ideological homogeneity; indeed as an overview of the field they include many contradictory points of view. A particular effort has been made to include research by Russian and East European scholars, the importance of whose work is only gradually being recognized. This has involved the editors in very extensive rewriting in places and it is not always easy to ensure that the full meaning of the original has been retained. An endnote following each chapter indicates the extent of the changes that have been made. Some of the flavour of Russians writing in English has been maintained, partly because it is also important to understand the parameters of what is a strikingly different style of argumentation.

NOTES

1   I would like to thank Kevin MacDonald, Matthew Spriggs, Malcolm Ross, Mark
    Thomas and Peter Ucko for commenting on this introduction.

REFERENCES

Bendor-Samuel, J. (ed.) 1989. *The Niger-Congo languages*. Lanham: University Press
   of America.
Bernbeck, R. and S. Pollock. 1995. Ayodhya, archaeology and identity. *Current
   Anthropology*, Volume 37 Supplement: 138–42.
Colley, S. 1995. What really happened at WAC-3? *Antiquity* 69(26), 15–8.
Golson, J. 1995. What went wrong with WAC 3 and an attempt to understand why.
   Australian Archaeology, 41, 48–54.
Hassan, F. 1995. The World Archaeological Congress in India: politicizing the past.
   Antiquity 69(266), 874–7.
Ruhlen, M. 1991. *A Guide to the World's Languages*. Volume I. Stanford: Stanford
   University Press.
Thomason, S.G. and T. Kaufman. 1988. *Language Contact, Creolization and Genetic
   Linguistics*. Berkeley: University of California Press.
Wurm, S.A. and K. McElhanon. 1975. Papuan language classification problems. In
   Papuan Languages and the New Guinea Linguistic Scene, S.A. Wurm (ed.), 145–64.
   Pacific Linguistics C-38. Canberra: ANU.

General introduction

ROGER BLENCH

PRINCIPAL THEMES IN ARCHAEOLOGY AND LANGUAGE

The relationship between linguistics and archaeology has been affected by both the internal dynamic of the disciplines in question and external political and social trends. Many archaeologists still feel that archaeology and linguistics do not share much common ground; some of the reasons for that are internal to archaeology, others can be traced to the sometimes startling misuse of these linkages by earlier scholars.

Three major threads in the history of this dialogue can be distinguished:

1   Theories of language affiliation developed without the use of a critical or orthodox methodology to reconstruct human history.
2   The use of language grouping to promote nationalist ideologies.
3   The use of the results from mainstream historical linguistics to interpret prehistory and archaeological findings.

These three volumes represent the best of the research falling into category 3. Unfortunately, in the past, archaeologists have often been influenced by publications which would fall under 1 and 2.

Another reason that these disciplines have been kept apart has been the internal development of archaeological theory, in particular the purist version that is referred to as processualism. This has acted to exclude data from multiple sources:

> Yet there is little general awareness of the value of combining the study of archaeological data with that of historical linguistics, oral traditions, historical ethnography and historical records although it is clear that many archaeological problems can be resolved in this way ... the resistance seems to come from the view, widely held by processual archaeologists, that their discipline must be based as exclusively as possible on the study of material culture.
>
> (Trigger 1989: 356)

A further aim of these volumes is to suggest to archaeologists and linguists the value of combining their disciplines.

THREE STREAMS IN LINGUISTIC PREHISTORY

Tlon, Uqbar, Orbis Tertius

As the epigraphs on p. v indicate, the view that historical linguistics has something to contribute to the history of peoples has been present for more than two centuries. Indeed Johnson appears to be already reacting to an aspect of historical linguistics that has often caused it to be regarded with the gravest suspicion by other disciplines: the tendency for some of its practitioners to develop unusual models of world prehistory based on apparent links between geographically remote languages.

One of the earliest theories to develop along these lines was the version of Amerindian history that claimed the inhabitants of the New World to be the Lost Tribes of Israel. This interpretation was advanced as early as 1650 when Menasseh ben Israel published his account of the traveller Aaron Levi who reported that he had encountered Hebrew-speaking Amerindians in the mountains near Quito. This type of linguistics is often broadly referred to as Voltairean linguistics from his famous characterization 'Etymology is a science in which the vowels count for nothing and the consonants for very little.'[1]

This type of theorizing, usually the province of amateurs, is quite often linked with bolder cultural hypotheses that generally involve long-distance migration and often have a religious or political agenda. It is easily caricatured and may often provide a well-founded excuse for archaeologists and prehistorians to avoid this type of excursus. Such theories are, of course, not exclusively based on linguistic evidence, but lexical connections are always claimed to support comparison of material culture. Two key themes of this body of scholarship relate to specific regions of the world: Ancient Egypt and the Pacific.

The notion that civilization was somehow invented in Ancient Egypt and spread out through the remarkable navigations of its inhabitants has at least a nineteenth-century pedigree and the ascription of Egyptian origins to African peoples was well under way by the beginning of the twentieth century. Johnson (1921, but manuscript prepared in 1897) wrote an influential history of the Yoruba, arguing against an Arabian origin for the Yoruba and promoting their migration from Egypt. Such theorizing continues today in the works of the followers of Cheikh Anta Diop and is often promulgated in luxuriously produced handbooks of hieroglyphics. However, claims for such land migrations were relatively restrained compared with the deepwater navigation proposed in classics such as Perry's (1923) *Children of the Sun*. Elliot Smith, and later Thor Heyerdahl, was an eloquent proponent of long-distance migrations, and much curious scholarship was adduced in support of such hypotheses.

There has been a substantial literature on pre-Portuguese trans-Pacific contact originating as early as the seventeenth century (Wauchope 1962: 83ff.). Although recent DNA research suggests that such contacts did indeed occur at least sporadically, this is far from accepting that some of Kublai Khan's ships were driven eastwards to the New World after a failed invasion of Japan (Ranking 1827, quoted in Wauchope 1962), or that fragments of the fleet of Alexander the Great reached the Americas in 323 BC (Gladwin 1947).

Exponents of such ideas are typically aggrieved when the predictably cautious academic establishment fails to take on board their ideas. One of the advocates of trans-Pacific contact took a robust view of their caution;

> All the lights in the House of the High Priests of American Anthropology are out, all the doors and windows are shut and securely fastened (they do not sleep with their windows open for fear that a new idea might fly in); we have rung the bell of Reason, we have banged on the door with Logic, we have thrown the gravel of evidence against their windows; but the only sign of life in the house is an occasional snore of dogma.
>
> (Gladwin 1947)

There is probably a useful distinction to be drawn between fringe ideas that draw the attention of more cautious scholars to possible previously unsuspected connections and similarities (Heyerdahl, for example), and those which are nothing more than an encumbrance to scholarship (Atlantis, Von Daniken, Velikovsky). Keep the windows open but look out through them rather than simply sleeping by them.

Links with nationalist ideologies

One of the more troubling aspects of the history of this discipline has been its links with nationalist ideologies. Linguistic nationalism still engenders a rich emotional harvest at present, often for good reason, since the suppression of minority languages is commonly a prominent feature of totalitarian governments. Democracies sometimes encourage voluntary euthanasia among minorities through neglect. None the less, when a national language is linked to a national culture it is a short step to linking that to archaeological entities and thence to broader historical claims on territory and political authority (see Kohl and Fawcett 1995).

Throughout the nineteenth century these ideas would have been considered acceptable by many researchers, and the links between nationalist ideologies and scientific research were unproblematic. However, somewhere in the early twentieth century, a split developed between the rationalist, academic tradition and the promotion of certain types of archaeology in support of nationalist goals. This has been well-documented in Germany and the former Soviet Union, where linguistic ideologues developed theories of the relation between particular language groups and specific types of material culture, and were ruthless with those tempted to disagree (Trigger 1989).

None the less, evidence is mounting that there is a European-wide tradition of rewriting the past in pursuit of nationalist goals (Díaz-Andreu and Champion 1996).

Nikolay Marr (1865–1934) has been called the 'Lysenko of anthropology' in Russia and had a comparable influence on all types of linguistic, ethnographic and archaeological research in his tenure as Director of the Russian Academy of Material Culture. His career and influence are described in Slezkine's (1994) account of Russian imperial relations with the minority peoples of Siberia. Central to Marr's ideas were evolutionary or 'Japhetic' theories of language, whereby languages developed in stages from 'primitive' to advanced. Primitive societies had 'mollusc-like' speech forms which had to develop 'upwards', until at the conclusion of history all language would merge into a single Communist speech. This eventually led him to the conclusion that both ethnography and archaeology were anti-Marxist, and therefore these were formally condemned at the All-Russian Conference on Archaeology and Ethnography in 1932. The practical consequence of Marr's tenure of authority was the destruction of much of the academic infrastructure around these subjects: museums, journals and learned societies were disbanded and non-Marxist teachers persecuted. Marr's work was explicitly rejected by no less a figure than Stalin who wrote an essay in 1950 examining the relation of Marxism to linguistics (Slezkine 1994: 314). Shnirelman, who describes the Russian 'linguoarchaeology' in Ch. 10 of this volume, warns that links with nationalist ideologies are still alive today, although their structure is less formalized than in an era of centralized state control.

German linguists played an important role in the development of Indo-European scholarship, and as early as the mid-nineteenth century Jacob Grimm was to explain the distribution of various sound changes by referring to the ethnic character of speakers. Gustaf Kossinna (1858–1931) whose principal work, *Die Herkunft der Germanen*, published in 1911, became a key text in Nazi Germany, provided an important ideological plank for territorial expansion. He argued that specifically Germanic material culture could be identified in archaeological sites, and that where such material was found this was evidence of the original extent of Germany.

The positivist tradition

It is easy to dismiss both marginal historical linguistics and nationalist ideology as forgotten errors of a past epoch. However, they have had an important historical influence on archaeologists, making them wary of all types of correlation with linguistic theories, no matter how carefully couched.

Another more sceptical tradition of historical linguistics has existed for several centuries and indeed persisted through a long period of neglect. For example, precursors to historical linguistics exist, both among the Sanskrit grammarians and in the works of the rabbinical grammarians. Most striking is the work of Yehuda Ibn Quraysh, who lived in Fez, Morocco in the tenth century and was the first to compare the phonology and morphology of

Hebrew, Aramaic and Arabic in his book ʿRisāla (Téné 1980). Such precursors seem to have had little influence on their successors, and an intellectual tradition only developed after historical linguistics was put on a more scientific footing. This event is conventionally attributed to Sir William Jones's famous lecture in 1786 demonstrating the links between Sanskrit and the classical languages of Europe, but it has become clear in recent years that Jones's perception was far from original. Bonfante (1953) quotes a reference to an unpublished manuscript by Marcus Boxhorn (1612–53) hypothesizing a 'Scythian' origin for all the major languages of Europe, while in Saumasius's *De Hellenistica*, published in 1643, reconstructed proto-forms for European numerals are proposed. The concept of reconstruction of an Indo-European proto-language appears as early as 1713 in the works of the English divine, William Wotton:

> My argument does not depend on the difference of Words, but upon the Difference of Grammar between any two languages; from whence it proceeds, that when any Words are derived from one Language into another, the derived Words are then turned and changed according to the particular Genius of the Language into which they are transplanted. [. . .] I can easily suppose that they might both be derived from one common Mother, which is, and perhaps has for many Ages been entirely lost.
>
> (Wotton 1730 [1713]: 57)

Wotton had related Icelandic ('Teutonic'), the Romance languages and Greek, which are certainly as convincing a demonstration of Indo-European affinities as Jones's demonstration of the links of classical languages with Sanskrit. Moreover, Wotton developed some estimates of the speed of language change and was concerned about the apparent contradiction with the widely accepted 'Biblical' age of the earth. Jones, in contrast, erroneously believed that Egyptian, Japanese and Chinese were part of Indo-European while Hindi was not, which suggests that his method was flawed (Muller 1986).

Outside Indo-European, Uralic classification had been virtually completed prior to Jones. As Ruhlen observes:

> The basic structure of the Uralic family had thus been roughly worked out at least six years before William Jones's celebrated address, which opened the era of I-E [Indo-European] studies.
>
> (Ruhlen 1991: 66)

The nineteenth century was a major period for the development of historical linguistics and indeed most of the debates which still characterize the discipline today have their origin in the work of scholars of the previous century. Throughout the nineteenth century there was a strong conviction that language could be analysed to establish historical results. Donaldson commented in the 1830s:

> There is in fact no sure way of tracing the history and migrations
> of the early inhabitants of the world except by means of their
> languages; any other mode of enquiry must rest on the merest
> conjecture and hypothesis. It may seem strange that anything so
> vague and arbitrary as language should survive all other testimonies,
> and speak with more definiteness, even in its changed and modern
> state, than all other monuments however grand and durable.
>
> (Donaldson 1839: 12)

and Craik in the 1860s:

> Each language has a life of its own, and it may be made to
> tell us its own life, so to speak, if we set the right way to work
> about it.
>
> (Craik 1861: 1)

Just as Finno-Ugric (i.e. Uralic) and Indo-European were earliest on the
scene in terms of historical reconstruction, so they began the tradition of
reconstructing history through lexical reconstruction. Early attempts to do
this, such as Pictet[2] (1859–63) evolved convoluted theories of the migrations
of the Aryan race that we should now consider highly suspect; however, this
should not distract attention from the significance of the enterprise.

These efforts continued throughout the late nineteenth century, and they
served to establish the conventions which were to be adopted and developed
elsewhere in the world. Historical linguistics of this type requires a certain
density of research to be credible; without adequate lexical materials for
language classification and reconstruction no amount of methodological
sophistication will fill the lacuna.

The pattern of research

Research concentrations are often reflections of political accessibility and
funding. Research on the Andamanese and Nicobarese languages has remained
largely static due to the refusal of the Indian government to issue research
permits. Although they co-exist in the same part of the world, Papuan has
lagged far behind Austronesian due to the inaccessibility of many Papuan
languages. Comparative Australian has taken off following the efforts of relatively few highly motivated individuals. Bantu is far better known than
Niger-Congo due to early interest in the topic, accessibility of many of the
languages and relatively unproblematic transcription.

Despite these problems, a global picture of the disposition and relations of
language phyla is slowly beginning to emerge. The pattern of phyla in the
world appears to be relatively stable (although the analysis of macrophyla is
highly controversial; see next section). Data is beginning to be less of a
problem than collating it. Few regions of the world are entirely without
archaeology, although the density of excavated sites is highly variable. In
consequence, crackpot theorizing and promotion of nationalist ideologies have

largely been shed and the volume of papers and books exploring the links between language and archaeology is on the increase. The major threat to this area of scholarship is probably now its allegiance to an old-fashioned empiricism and a positivist commitment to data; to avoid strangulation at the hands of the post-modern devotees of Kali it will have to develop more sophisticated public relations. Lenin is reputed to have said that the express train of history cannot be stopped; all that revolutionaries can do is grease the wheels.

THEMES IN THE INTERACTION OF LINGUISTICS AND ARCHAEOLOGY

Historical linguistics, lexicostatistics and glottochronology

The single most important theme of these books is the interaction of histor- ical linguistics with archaeology. Historical linguistics may be defined as the analysis of the relationship between two or more languages that are assumed to be genetically related (that is, to 'have sprung from some common source'), such as English and German. Linguists are concerned to develop testable rules by which specific languages can be related to one another, relating to phonology, morphology and lexicon. These rules should generally be able to predict the patterns of relationship between 'new' vocabulary and thus generate a tree-like genetic structure which allows modelling of the relative antiquity of splits between different languages. Proto-forms predicted by the rules that relate two or more languages and a sequence of proto-languages can be recon- structed for nodal points in the genetic tree.

Lexicostatistics, the counting of cognate words in a standardized list and assigning a numerical degree of relationship, seems to have been first used in the early nineteenth century. Dumont d'Urville (1834) compared a number of Oceanic languages (which would today be called Austronesian) and proposed a method for calculating a coefficient of relationship. He extended his comparison to some Amerindian languages and concluded that there was no evident relationship with the Oceanic languages in his sample. Hymes (1983) provides a detailed history of the further development of lexicostatis- tics in the nineteenth and twentieth centuries.

Another aspect of historical linguistics is glottochronology. Writers such as Wotton (1730) believed that it was possible to calculate how rapidly languages change by comparing ancient texts of known date with the modern form of languages. Robert Latham (1850) was probably the first author to sketch the possibility of assigning a precise date to the split of two languages through applying a mathematical algorithm. Hymes (1983: 73ff.) cites other tentative experiments in the nineteenth century, but these seem not to have been developed until Swadesh (1952).

Lexicostatistics and glottochronology have the attractive aspect of quan- tification; they seem to represent a scientific approach to the dating and genetic classification of languages. However, very few historical linguists now accept the premises of such approaches. In part this may reflect a wave of criticism of the mathematics underlying these methods (see discussion in Hymes 1983: 75). More important, however, has been the realization that languages undergo a variety of changes in interacting with one another, and lexicostatistics inevitably assumes a lexical purity that allows languages to change at a regular rate (especially of core vocabulary). Using the methods of historical linguistics that are generally accepted, only relative dating is possible; for absolute dating linguists now turn to archaeology.

Historical linguistics as a discipline

Whereas archaeology is taught as a method that can be applied to any situation (rather like economics), and although archaeologists divide into theoretical schools and schools develop their own terminologies, this is usually not location-specific. Indeed, within a single institution different methods may well be propagated by individual scholars. In other words, the archaeology of Japan or Australia does not appear to have a large technical vocabulary that would not be immediately comprehensible to a regional outsider.

Although theoretical linguistics has many of the same intellectual subdivisions there is only a limited interface between historical linguists and the larger linguistic establishment. This is partly because historical linguistics remains a minority interest in a world dominated by syntax, phonology and, to a lesser extent, socio-linguistics. Historical linguists are often partly self-taught or take their cue from individual teachers. The consequence is that there can be striking disagreements over method and standards of evidence; this debate is most apparent in the case of the sometimes bitter disputes that have raged over macrophyla (see p. 10).

Scholars of the older-established phyla often take a patronizing attitude to results from those phyla more recently recognized. This is particularly striking in the case of Indo-European, where the conviction that the phylum is well-founded and that its reconstructions are accurate and convincing appears to be widespread among its adherents. A darkly humorous version of this can be seen in the comments of Hopper (1989), reviewing Thomason and Kaufman, who contrasted the 'factually established genetic categories' such as Indo-European with 'broad-based guesses' such as Niger-Congo, Afroasiatic and Nilo-Saharan. The view taken in these volumes is that the major language phyla of the world that are accepted by the scholarly community are all equally well-founded.

The Indo-Europeanist habit of ignoring what are strangely called 'minor languages' has resulted in a virtual lacuna in research on Indo-European languages of India with only small numbers of speakers. One of the more evident tendencies in Indo-European linguistics is to give primacy to written languages, such as Sanskrit. Thus, reconstruction of the Indo-Aryan languages is in terms of relating the present-day forms to attested Sanskrit (cf. Turner 1966) rather than subjecting the body of Indo-Aryan languages to the usual procedures of historical linguistics. The consequence has been a striking inadequacy of fieldwork to describe the more than 300 unwritten Indo-European languages spoken in the India–Pakistan region today (see the assessment of research needs in Grimes 1992). The conventional practice of historical linguistics in the region is thus in a rather backward state. Applying the standards of proof common, say, among Austronesianists, would of course reduce Indo-European to a 'broad-based guess'.

Geographical coverage

All types of research have a patchy coverage when considered globally, but linguistics and archaeology have proved to be especially sensitive to political and economic constraints (see pp. 6–7). Different disciplinary traditions also lead to uneven emphases with particular regions. For example, although East Asian archaeology is well represented in terms of excavated sites, specific digs seeking the origins of food production are few and far between. The incidence of monuments can be in inverse relationship to an emphasis on economic prehistory. Countries with a dominant culture often discourage work on regional languages for fear of encouraging local aspirations. Until recently the languages of China were poorly known, and research on minority languages unaccountably spoken by peoples not part of an officially recognized minority was strongly discouraged (Ramsey 1992: 162ff.).

In addition, intellectual traditions and the organization of scholarship affect interdisciplinary work. Countries with National Research Centres that unite scholars from different intellectual areas, such as France, the former Soviet Union and Australia, are far more likely to produce interdisciplinary scholarship than England and America, where experts are ghettoized in university departments. Generally speaking, where careers depend on publications, and where only publications in a specific discipline are highly valued, there is every incentive to concentrate on one intellectual area to the exclusion of others. Indeed, in both linguistics and archaeology, intellectual justifications for excluding other approaches have been explicitly developed, as witness the examples of generativism (Chomsky 1988).

The consequence has been that both historical linguistics and its combination with archaeology are developed to very different degrees in different parts of the world. The areas where the focus has been most significant are Eurasia and Oceania: Eurasia because of the Indo-Europeanist tradition and its remarkable survivals in the former Soviet Union, and Oceania because of fortunate support for this type of approach in a few key institutions. India represents a curious lacuna in Eurasia since, despite its importance in the early decades of the twentieth century and the production of the massive 'Linguistic Survey of India' during the 1920s, restrictions on research permits have led to an almost complete cessation of research by outside scholars on its some 500 unwritten languages. The New World and Africa have been marked by a relatively small amount of research. In Africa this may be due to nothing more than time-depth (convincing amounts of data have only recently become available) and lack of dedicated institutions. In the case of the Americas, however, despite the all-embracing traditions of cultural anthropology which conjoined archaeology, anthropology and linguistics, the absence of a major tradition of syntheses suggests that the reality has been academic isolationism.

Texts and pretexts

One of the earliest interfaces between archaeology and language has remained distinct from the type of historical linguistics discussed here: the interpretation of ancient written documents and the decipherment of scripts. This story has been rehearsed too many times (e.g. Simpson 1985) to need further recounting, beginning with the decipherment of hieroglyphics and cuneiform, through to Hittite and other epigraphic languages of the Ancient Near East. In this century, decipherment has been extended to India, China and Central America and continues today with recent proposals for the decipherment of the Olmec script of the Yucatan (Wichmann, Volume II). Epigraphy is also equipped with its own eccentric fringe; a Harvard professor of Zoology tells us that inscribed rocks in Texas record the journey of migrant Zoroastrians from Iberia some 2,000 years ago (Fell 1980: 164).

Interpreting epigraphy and relating it both to known historical events and to excavated sites has been a major theme of archaeology, especially in the Near East. Indeed, the prominence accorded to written texts has obscured other types of interpretation of linguistic data. Thus a considerable body of work exists translating, transcribing and interpreting ancient texts in a variety of Semitic languages; overall models of the evolution and dispersal of this language family barely exist. An example of this is the attempt by Zohar (1992) to interpret the spread of Semitic in the Near East. African Semitic languages (which are considerably more numerous and diverse than those of the Near East) are referred to as 'minor languages' in the text and excluded entirely from the family tree of Semitic (Zohar 1992: Figure 1).

There is a strong argument for supposing that much of the most innovative work in using historical linguistics has been brought about by the *absence* of ancient texts. Just as North American archaeology developed innovative analytic techniques to analyse the sites of hunter-gatherer communities, so in regions of the world where there are no early texts, modelling in historical linguistics has been stimulated.

Testable hypotheses

One of the attractive aspects of linking historical linguistics with archaeology is that it is possible to generate testable hypotheses. Linguists are usually way ahead of archaeologists in their speculations. Finding an informant for a language is easier and far less costly than mounting an archaeological expedition to search, for example, for the origins of food production. An experienced linguist can often elicit a range of basic and key cultural vocabulary in a few hours, whereas excavations often take years. Historical linguists are often tempted to throw off hypotheses on the origins of food production far more quickly and perhaps more casually than would be permissible within other academic frameworks.

However, when a prediction is made then it can at least be tested. So, for example, if a historical linguist claims that certain species of domestic animal can be reconstructed back to the proto-language of a particular phylum, and at the same time makes a proposal for the homeland of the speakers of the proto-language, then excavations should ideally be able to confirm the presence of those species. An example of such a correlation is presented in the chapter by Green and Pawley (Volume III), where linguistics is used both to pinpoint a proposed homeland of Oceanic languages and to suggest the features of house-forms that should be present. Archaeology suggests that house structures of the predicted type are indeed present. Such correlations are rare in practice, especially when only a small number of sites have been identified, but as the density of sites increases, hypotheses can be subjected to a reasonable test.

Phyla and macrophyla

There are some language phyla whose existence is generally accepted, such as Indo-European or Austronesian, as a result of the weight of scholarly opinion. In a few cases, such as Nilo-Saharan, a body of scholarly comment exists questioning either its unity as a phylum or the families that compose it. In addition, there are regions of the world where a large number of languages exist which show common features but which have not been shown to be related to the satisfaction of most researchers. These 'geographical' names are often shown as phyla in works of synthesis. The most important of these are Papuan, Australian and Amerind: groups of languages whose relationship can be demonstrated but where overall genetic relations have proved resistant to the methods of historical linguistics. Similarities of phonology or other features do suggest a common origin, but it is possible that they have so far diversified from a common proto-language that proof will remain a chimera. Finally, in one case, Andamanese, inadequate data makes any final judgement impossible at present. Table 2 sets out the language phyla of the world and their status in this hierarchy.

It is not possible to order the class of 'accepted' phyla by degree of acceptance. In recent years, numerous publications have advanced the case for macrophyla; that is, the uniting of several accepted phyla into one genetic group. The best-known example is Nostratic, a macrophylum that brings together most of the phyla of the Eurasian land mass, whose membership varies according to different authors. The journal *Mother Tongue* has published the speculations of 'long-rangers' who wish to promote continent-spanning comparisons. With increasing awareness of the traditions of such scholarship in the former Soviet Union and the publication of some major texts (e.g. Bomhard 1994) this type of large-scale comparison has reappeared. Other more controversial proposals include Indo-Pacific and Amerind, pioneering

Table 2 Language phyla of the world and their status

Phylum	Usual acronym	Where spoken	Status/comment
Niger-Congo	NC	Western, Central and Southern Africa	Accepted
Afroasiatic	AA†	NE Africa and the Middle East	Accepted
Indo-European	IE	Eurasia	Accepted
Uralic	U	Eurasia	Accepted
Kartvelian	K	Caucasus	Accepted
North Caucasian	NC	Caucasus	Accepted
Chukchi-Kamchatkan	CK	Siberia	Accepted
Yeniseic	Y	Siberia	Accepted
Dravidian	DR	India	Accepted
Sino-Tibetan	ST	Central Asia	Accepted
Miao-Yao	MY	China	Accepted
Daic (=Tai-Kadai)	D	SE Asia	Accepted
Austroasiatic	AS†	SE Asia	Accepted
Austronesian	AN	Pacific	Accepted
Eskimo-Aleut	EA‡	Bering Strait	Accepted
Na-Dene	ND‡	North America	Accepted
Khoisan	KH	Eastern and Southern Africa	Usually accepted
Nilo-Saharan	NS	Eastern and Central Africa	Usually accepted
Altaic	AT	Eurasia	Usually accepted although the affiliation of Korean is debated
Papuan	PP‡	Papua	Consists of a large number of accepted groups but their unity is not considered proven
Australian	AU‡	Australia	Consists of a large number of accepted groups but their unity is not considered proven
Amerind	AM‡	Americas	Consists of a large number of accepted groups but their unity is not accepted
Andamanese	AD‡	Andaman islands	Inadequate data makes effective historical linguistics impractical

Notes: This table excludes a number of well-known isolates such as Basque, Burushaski, Ghilyak, Ainu and Japanese, as well as African isolates (see Blench, Volume III), and problematic languages of Asia such as Nahali and Kusunda.

† AA is unfortunately used for both Afroasiatic and Austroasiatic. AS is adopted here for Austroasiatic to eliminate confusion. PN is applied to Polynesian, hence the use of PP for Papuan here.

‡ Proposed acronym

hypotheses (e.g. Joseph Greenberg 1987) and Sino-Caucasian from the Soviet School, especially Starostin (e.g. Shevoroshkin 1992). These proposals have excited considerable scepticism, although most linguists do not command the vast range of data that would be necessary to give them a full evaluation. Ruhlen (1991: 270ff.) gives a lengthy bibliography of 'alleged connections between families usually assumed to be unrelated', which suggests that almost any two or more of the world's language phyla have been related by some researcher.

Behind such enterprises is an intriguing and controversial agenda: the reconstruction of proto-World or 'Proto-Sapiens' as Ruhlen (1994: 192) has it. The hypothesis that all human language has a common origin is certainly emotionally persuasive; the myth of the Tower of Babel still exerts a powerful pull. However, conviction is not proof and enthusiasm not demonstration. Although one of the most eloquent advocates of proto-World, Vitaly Shevoroshkin, has recited poems in this remarkable language on the media, this cannot yet conjure it into reality.

The exploration of long-range comparison has aroused considerable opposition; historical linguists working on a smaller scale are frequently outraged at the misuse of language data by non-specialists. Trask (1995), for example, has recently analysed in considerable detail the evidence for a traditional hypothesis linking Basque to Caucasian languages and concludes that it depends in almost every case on a misuse or defective analysis of the Basque language materials. Thurgood (1994) has shown that the hypotheses, such as Benedict's Austro-Tai, that link together the major language phyla of SE Asia are based on ancient loanwords.

Between near-global hypotheses and accepted phyla stand more modest proposals that link together two phyla that already have a history of observed similarities. Two recent examples are Austric (linking the Austronesian and Austroasiatic phyla; Reid 1994) and Niger-Saharan (Niger-Congo with Nilo-Saharan; Blench 1995). The linking of Japanese (or Japonic) to the Altaic phylum has a venerable pedigree but still continues to generate controversy and cannot be regarded as accepted.

Intriguing as these planet-spanning proposals are, they remain to be critically evaluated by the body of historical linguists and thus cannot easily be used by archaeologists. Indeed there are still few wholly convincing models to explain the origin and diversification of accepted phyla; to interpret the more doubtful macrophyla would be over-egging an already rich pudding.

Linguistics and genetics: 'The New Synthesis'

An aspect of the reconstruction of prehistory that has come to the fore since the mid-1980s is the use of evidence from genetics, especially from analysis of mitochondrial DNA. However, the reputations of traditional biological anthropologists stand presently at an all-time low following analyses such as that of Gould (1982) who accurately skewered the underlying racial preoccupations of the supposedly scientific physical anthropologists of the nineteenth and early twentieth centuries. It should be noted that osteometrics remain acceptable in many European traditions, especially in France, as witness a standard text on human remains in the Sahara (Dutour 1989).

However, a major break with traditional biological anthropology occurred with the development of modern techniques of DNA analysis – both because DNA could be effectively recovered from archaeological material and because DNA analysis seemed to offer a way of relating present human populations to one another and to past materials. Linguistic classifications of human populations seemed to offer a way beyond simple racial models; more abstract, they seemed to provide an ideal analogue to the classificatory trees from DNA. If DNA trees and language trees were to correspond then this would provide striking mutual confirmation for models of human prehistory. Indeed the links between them were enthusiastically promoted at the end of the 1980s and into the early 1990s as 'The New Synthesis' (see, for example, Cavalli-Sforza et al. 1988; Renfrew 1992). The culmination of this trend was the appearance of *The History and Geography of Human Genes* (Cavalli-Sforza et al. 1994), which promotes a major revision of the methodology for exploring human history.

More recently there has been a distinct withdrawal from some of the claims of this type of work. The 'fit' between language trees and DNA results has been seen not to be quite as close as suggested in earlier publications. Chen et al. (1995: 610) compare genetic and language trees on a global basis and conclude: 'The consensus between language trees and genetic trees is low . . . so low as to make the trees incomparable.' This will probably remain the case on the scale of phylic and macrophylic relations. With very large land masses such as Eurasia, language shift is an extremely common process, as the disappearance of Basque-related languages suggests. To find a people speaking their 'original' language may prove to be the exception. In contrast, much of the Pacific has seen expansion of populations into otherwise un-inhabited territory. Almost certainly Oceania will again prove an important testing-ground for the methods of DNA analysis, as it has with linguistics and archaeology, because the parameters of population movement and contact can be simplified.

CONCLUSIONS: AN AGENDA PAST 2000

The process of synthesizing linguistics and archaeology has largely shaken off its historically negative image. Processual archaeology will no doubt continue to collect adherents, but a larger body of scholars are increasingly interested in what multi-disciplinary research has to offer. The potential to construct and distribute large databases of linguistic information has made confidence in the broader results of historically minded scholars more credible. At the same time, the allure of results from DNA analyses and other types of genetic data has the potential to attract those seeking the credibility of 'hard science'.

Although such eclecticism has a certain congruence with post-modern positions, the potential testability of hypotheses should align it more with an empiricist platform.

As with all types of scientific change, paradigm shifts occur over time, though with a less revolutionary time-scale than that advocated by Kuhn (1962). Non-synthetic traditions in archaeology will not be argued away. Universities and academic institutions have been able to keep dominant schools of method coherent through control of publishing and because a relatively small circle of individuals were in power. As these institutions increasingly fragment, publishing becomes cheaper and easier of access and research takes place outside the academy.

With this added diversity of approach, it can be predicted that the current unfortunate distinction between prehistory and history should lessen or even disappear. Both the study of the archaeological evidence of the past and the modelling of social change through historical linguistics will be considered valid approaches to the past. The result should be the study of the broad outlines of a human history which allows for a complexity in the past that is so evident in the present.

NOTES

1   Although quoted in Leonard Bloomfield's 'Language' (1935: 6), the direct source in Voltaire's writings has yet to be uncovered, and there is more than a suspicion that this is a piece of convenient linguistic folklore.
2   Pictet also first used the expression 'linguistic palaeontology', often attributed to more recent authors.

REFERENCES

Blench, R.M. 1995. Is Niger-Congo simply a branch of Nilo-Saharan? In *Proceedings: Fifth Nilo-Saharan Linguistics Colloquium, Nice, 1992*, R. Nicolai and F. Rottland (eds), 83–130. Köln: Rudiger Köppe.

Bloomfield, L. 1935. *Language*. London: Allen & Unwin.

Bomhard, A. 1994. *The Nostratic Macrofamily*. Berlin and New York: Mouton de Gruyter.

Bonfante, G. 1953. Ideas on the kinship of the European Languages from 1200 to 1800. *Cahiers d'Histoire Mondiale* 1, 679–99.

Broca, P. 1862. La linguistique et l'anthropologie. *Bulletin de la Société d'Anthropologie de Paris*, pp. 264–319.

Cavalli-Sforza, L.L., A. Piazza and P. Menozzi *et al.* 1988. Reconstruction of human evolution: bringing together genetic, archaeological and linguistic data. *Proceedings of the National Academy of Science, USA* 85, 6002–6.

Cavalli-Sforza, L.L., A. Piazza and P. Menozzi. 1994. *The History and Geography of Human Genes*. Princeton, N.J.: Princeton University Press.

Chen, J., R. R. Sokal and M. Ruhlen. 1995. Worldwide analysis of genetic and linguistic relations of human populations. *Human Biology* 67(4), 595–612.

Chomsky, N. 1988. *Language and Problems of Knowledge. The Managua Lectures.* Cambridge, Mass.: MIT Press.

Craik, G. L. 1861. *A Compendious History of English Literature and of the English Language.* London: Griffin, Bohn & Co.

Darwin, C. 1859. *On the Origin of Species.* London: John Murray.

Díaz-Andreu, M. and T. C. Champion. 1996. *Nationalism and Archaeology in Europe.* London: UCL Press.

Donaldson, J.W. 1839. *The New Cratylus.* Cambridge: Deighton.

Droixhe, D. 1990. Le voyage de *Schreiten*: Leibniz et les débuts du comparatisme finno-ougrien. In *Leibniz, Humboldt and the origins of comparativism*, T. de Mauro and L. Formigari (eds), 3–30. Amsterdam: Benjamins.

Dumont d'Urville, Jules S.C. 1834. *Philologie, par M. D'Urville. Seconde Partie. Les autres vocabulaires de langues ou Dialectes océaniens recueillies durant la votage, et le Vocabulaire comparatif des languages françaises, madekass, malaio, mawi, tonga, taiti et hawaii, suivis de quelques considérations générales sur ces langues.* Paris: Ministère de la Marine.

Dutour, O. 1989. *Les hommes fossiles du Sahara.* Marseille: CNRS.

Fell, B. 1980. *Saga America.* New York: Times Books.

Gladwin, H.S. 1947. *Men out of Asia.* New York: McGraw Hill.

Gould, S.J. 1982. *The Mismeasure of Man.* New York: Norton.

Greenberg, J. 1987. *Language in the Americas.* Stanford: Stanford University Press.

Grimes, B.F. 1992. *Ethnologue.* Edition 12. Dallas: SIL.

Hopper, P.J. 1989. Review of *Language Contact, Creolization and Genetic Linguistics*, by S.G. Thomason and T. Kaufman. *American Anthropologist* 91: 817–18.

Hymes, D.H. 1983. Lexicostatistics and glottochronology in the nineteenth century (with notes towards a general history). In *Essays in the History of Linguistic Anthropology*, D.H. Hymes (ed.), 59–113. Amsterdam and Philadelphia: John Benjamins.

Johnson, S. (Revd) 1921. *The History of the Yorubas.* Lagos: CMS (Nigeria) Bookshops.

Kohl, P.L. and C. Fawcett 1995. *Nationalism, Politics and the Practice of Archaeology.* Cambridge: Cambridge University Press.

Kuhn, T.S. 1962. *The Structure of Scientific Revolutions.* Chicago: University of Chicago Press.

Latham, R.G. 1850. *The Natural History of the Varieties of Man.* London: John van Voorst.

Mous, M. 1994. Ma'a or Mbugu. In *Mixed languages*, P. Bakker and M. Mous (eds), 175–200. Amsterdam: IFOTT.

Muller, J.-C. 1986. Early stages of language comparison from Sassetti to Sir William Jones (1786). *Kratylos* 31(1), 1–31.

Perry, W.J. 1923. *Children of the Sun.* London: Methuen.

Pictet, A. 1859–63. *Les origines indo-européennes, ou les Aryas primitifs: essai de paléontologie linguistique.* Paris: Chetbuliez.

Ramsey, S.R. 1992. *The Languages of China.* Princeton: Princeton University Press.

Reid, L. 1994. Morphological evidence for Austric. *Oceanic Linguistics* 33(2), 323–44.

Renfrew, C. 1992. Archaeology, genetic and linguistic diversity. *Man* 27(3), 445–78.

Ruhlen, M. 1991. *A Guide to the World's Languages.* Volume I. Stanford: Stanford University Press.

Ruhlen, M. 1994. *The Origin of Language.* New York: John Wiley & Sons.

Shevoroshkin, V. (ed.) 1992. *Nostratic, Dene-Caucasian, Austric and Amerind.* Bochum: Brockmeyer.

Simpson, G. 1985. *Writing Systems, a linguistic introduction.* Stanford: Stanford University Press.

Slezkine, Y. 1994. *Arctic Mirrors.* Ithaca and London: Cornell University Press.

Swadesh, M. 1952. Lexicostatistic dating of prehistoric ethnic contacts. *Proceedings of the American Philosophical Society* 96, 453–62.

Téné, D. 1980. The earliest comparisons of Hebrew with Aramaic and Arabic. In *Progress in Linguistic Historiography*, K. Koerner (ed.), 355–77. Amsterdam: John Benjamins.

Thurgood, G. 1994. Tai-Kadai and Austronesian: the nature of the relationship. *Oceanic Linguistics* 33(2), 345–68.

Trask, R.L. 1995. Basque and Dene-Caucasian: a critique from the Basque side. *Mother Tongue* 1, 3–82.

Trigger, B.G. 1989. *A History of Archaeological Thought*. Cambridge: Cambridge University Press.

Turner, R. 1966. *An Indo-Aryan Comparative Dictionary*. London: Oxford University Press.

Wauchope, R. 1962. *Lost Tribes and Sunken Continents*. Chicago and London: University of Chicago Press.

Wotton, W. 1730. *A Discourse Concerning the Confusion of Languages at Babel*. London: Austen & Bowyer.

Zohar, M. 1992. Pastoralism and the spread of the Semitic languages. In *Pastoralism in the Levant: archaeological materials in anthropological perspectives*, O. Bar-Yosef and A. Khazanov (eds.), 165–80. Madison, Wis.: Prehistory Press.

Introduction

ROGER BLENCH

Theory plays a major role in modern archaeology, especially that practised in academic institutions. Indeed the growth of the heritage industry and the broader economic potential of antiquities and monuments has only acted to emphasize an already deep split between academic archaeology and excavation; in some cases these have become opposed to one another. However, in the area of language and prehistory the opposition of theory and practice has remained within the academy, since the interchange between language and prehistory rarely lures tourists.

Linguistics is a broadly defined discipline and it is worth noting that only small sub-areas of it regularly come into contact with prehistory. The major effort in the second half of the twentieth century has been in the development of syntactic theory, with Chomsky and other generativists setting the agenda. Even those who oppose generativism have allowed it to set the terms of the debate. Linguistic controversies are very much couched in specific jargons and have become so detailed that entire conferences may now be devoted to a small point of syntax. Little of this has made any impact on historical linguistics, and indeed the classificatory genetic enterprise has frequently been dismissed by generativists.

The other major theme of linguistics has been socio-linguistics; an enterprise that might be expected to have more impact on modelling past societies than has in fact been the case. Some authors (e.g. Ross, Ch. 13, this volume) have made extensive use of synchronic studies of sound-change, for example the works of Labov and Milroy. Work on creoles, bilingualism and language shift has important implications for modelling ethnic and cultural interaction and change. Too often, however, this work is written in a dense particularist language that outsiders find hard to interpret. As important, however, is that in many parts of the world, data-gathering and basic genetic work is still in progress; researchers often feel that socio-linguistic modelling is a second phase when a baseline has been laid down.

The balance between general articles on theory and actual practice remains strongly weighted in favour of data-oriented articles. The editors have encouraged authors to support their cases with actual data or direct reference to where such data may be consulted. There are, however, some important themes where speculation is allowed freer play and where empirical confirmation of the hypotheses advanced must inevitably be sketchy, to say the least. The two most important areas are language origins and deep-level (macrophylum) reconstruction.

LANGUAGE ORIGINS

The origins of language have been the subject of speculation for almost as long as linguistics has been a subject of academic inquiry. Indeed, an oft-repeated piece of academic folklore is the prohibition of the topic as a subject for discussion by the Linguistic Society of Paris as far back as 1886. The expansion of brain research and increased knowledge about human evolution have given a boost to this topic in the last few years. Indeed, one of the most important attempts to 'scientize' the evolution of language are the technical articles by Pinker and Bloom (e.g. 1990), and Pinker's (1994) more popular text *The Language Instinct* which argues that Universal Grammar (i.e. Chomskyan principles of syntax) has its correlate in brain DNA. This is discussed in some detail in the chapter by Bichakjian who argues that such a universal grammar is an artefact of the generativist school. Universal grammar is not an empirical result of a survey of the world's languages, but rather a postulate essential to the Chomskyan enterprise. Bichakjian cites evidence for a unidirectional movement of certain syntactic changes and adduces new evidence from child language learning to argue that language and language change are culturally determined. He shows that this type of 'innatist' model, where grammar is hard-wired into the brain, is in conflict with recent scientific findings. If his critique is correct, then the evolution of language must be linked to human culture rather than classified as basic to human biology.

In his chapter, Györi attacks a similar problem from a slightly different perspective: that of 'cognitive archaeology', defined as 'the search for biological-cognitive constraints that may become embodied in organisms as a result of their interaction with the environment during evolution'. This is effectively an attack on the generativist position from biology. Chomsky (1988) argued for a 'macro-mutation' to explain the human capacity to deal with language acquisition. Györi shows that this is a problematic hypothesis in terms of adaptation in evolutionary biology and that the cognitive modelling that language makes possible extends beyond the human species. He argues that it is the unique ability to manipulate cognitive symbols that sets apart human language and that this can be analysed as having adaptive value in the classic Darwinian sense.

Bouissac's chapter moves on from language evolution to another very controversial topic: the evolution of writing. Writing systems are like language as a whole; we can never see intermediate phases. Just as we cannot encounter

humans speaking some precursor to fully formed language[1] we cannot see
writing systems evolving. This is not to say that the graphic systems encountered in archaeological contexts are not clear precursors of writing; both in
Egypt and China candidates for such 'pre-writing' exist (Postgate *et al.* 1995).
Indeed the complexity of some of the graphic systems in West Africa illustrates how the precursors of writing might develop into a fully fledged
orthographic system (Griaule and Dieterlen 1951).

The diversity of palaeolithic art suggests that something more than representation is at work, and this is usually argued to be a symbolic system.
Indeed, the interpretative enterprise among specialists in rock-art goes far
beyond the empiricist notions that underlie most of the rest of archaeolinguistics and may be better seen as a branch of art history. Bouissac claims,
as have some other specialists, that we can see proto-writing or 'scriptoids'
in various examples of rock art. He explores the matrix patterns that can be
derived from hand prints and 'ships' apparently represented in major regions
of European rock-art, and suggests that we move away from the language
of motifs and patterns to regarding these images as proto-scripts.

Bouissac's claim is interlinked with recent hypotheses on deep-level linkages and macrophyla; these suggest a greater antiquity for language than has
previously been admitted by specialists on individual phyla. The claim that
'the brain sciences, evolutionary biology and cultural archaeology . . . lead to
a notion of "archaic language" far more ancient than previously assumed –
on the order of two million years' will still be resisted by historical linguists
working on a more recent era.

There is no doubt that macrophyla hypotheses have recently become important after a long period in the background. Genetic linguistics in the former
Soviet Union remained almost unknown to western traditions of scholarship
until the frontiers began to open. A concern with large-scale language groupings and long-range comparison has been the thrust of much of this tradition.
Since 1985 there has been a physical diaspora; some Russian researchers have
posts in the West; others can present their ideas in English at conferences.
Although many of the actual results of these researches are treated with scepticism by scholars in the western tradition, these ideas have been firmly placed
back on the agenda of linguists.

Hegedüs's chapter, 'Principles for Palaeolinguistic Reconstruction', is a
manifesto for this school, as well as a presentation of results widely accepted
among Eastern European/former Soviet Union researchers but which have
so far found limited assent outside. This is an agenda for deep-level reconstruction based on entities such as Nostratic and Sino-Caucasian and proposes
to push back the time-limits of reconstruction deep into the Palaeolithic.
Many of the categories are still very controversial, but they represent a useful
summary of more than half a century of intense scholarly effort within a
particular tradition.

Otte (Ch. 5) tackles the question of the evolution of modern languages
of Europe from an archaeological point of view. Otte argues that there has

been a striking technological continuity in Eurasia from the Palaeolithic onwards, and that the real discontinuity was much earlier than proposed in theories of Indo-European attributed to Gimbutas and Renfrew. He opposes the common dogmas of Indo-European as either incoming horse pastoralists or as the diffusion of agricultural technology.

The themes in Renfrew's interpretation of Indo-European prehistory which have been a fruitful starting point for many contributors are expanded on a global basis in his chapter. This takes a Greenberg/Ruhlen view of world language phyla and attempts to interpret it in population terms, in particular distinguishing Pleistocene and post-Pleistocene phases. The suggestion, also referred to in the chapter by Peter Bellwood (Volume II) is that agricultural dispersals have been an important mechanism of dispersal, not just for Indo-European but in many of the world's language phyla. Renfrew's arguments are referred to in many other contributions, either in this version or in Renfrew (1992), and this provides an up-to-date statement of his position.

METHODS

One of the major focuses of historical linguistics has been to determine the homeland of particular language phyla, to establish the geographical region in which the proto-language was spoken. A long-time opponent of Renfrew's interpretation of Indo-European has been J.P. Mallory, whose iconoclastic approach to the homelands problem has been situated in the methods section because of its sceptical approach to an issue where there is often perceived to be a consensus. Mallory's chapter provides a useful short view of the more delightful fringe theories of Indo-European, such as arguing for a Baltic homeland on the basis of phonaesthetic similarities between Indo-European velars and the cries of sea-birds. In a more serious vein he examines the four major theories of the Indo-European homeland that have gained credence in the literature and illustrates the problems encountered with entirely accepting any of these. This may have important implications for the long-term future of 'homeland' research in general. Perhaps when the density of research on other language phyla approaches that of Indo-European the case for differing and contradictory solutions will be equally compelling.

Johanna Nichols's chapter takes a novel approach to the question of the Indo-European homeland and comes up with a very different solution from those previously mentioned. Following an approach deriving partly from her own work on linguistic geography (see Nichols 1992 and Volume II) and from the chronological and geographic implications of loans between neighbouring phyla, she argues for a homeland in the Central Asia grasslands; a locus of 'interaction between nomads of the Central Asian grasslands and the settled farmers of the oasis towns'. This bold new approach to an old problem will eventually be expanded to a monograph-length argument.

Pejros's chapter examines the general problem of correlating linguistics and archaeology at a more philosophical level. In contrast to the general thrust of these volumes, he gives a rather negative account of the potential for correlating archaeological data with the accounts that linguistics provides from material culture terminology. Pejros distinguishes 'deep' and 'surface' representations of material culture in a community; reconstructions of proto-lexicons may be liable to simplistic equations with the archaeological record.

Victor Shnirelman puts a positive gloss on the situation with his chapter describing the development of 'linguoarchaeology' in the Soviet period. This account of results derived from conjoining linguistics and archaeology within the Soviet research tradition promotes the innovatory aspects of this method. Over-enthusiastic language/prehistoric culture identifications by Soviet archaeologists have been called into question for lack of a coherent methodology, and Shnirelman proposes some standard techniques to test hypotheses in this field. The chapter summarizes the results of co-operative projects in Russia on the reconstruction of the Afroasiatic and Dravidian language phyla and the potential implications for homeland proposals. Shnirelman also sounds some useful warnings about both over-precise reconstructions of plant species and the possible misleading implications for homeland identification. In addition he points to links between this apparently 'objective' linguistic research and modern nationalist arguments.

Shnirelman's chapter also puts in a bid for a name for the discipline espoused in these three volumes. Elsewhere its inversion, 'archaeolinguistics', has been proposed, although Hegedüs has used this for one of her phases of deep-level reconstruction. No doubt a consensus terminology will emerge during the next decade.

Another type of methodological problem is raised by Blench in his chapter on the terminology of crabs, turtles and frogs in Africa and their relevance for models of prehistory. The riverine fauna here appear as an example of a more general problem for historical linguistics: the problem of sound-symbolism for genetic linguistics. Certain lexemes of quite specific phonological shapes seem to have an Africa-wide, and in some cases a world-wide, distribution. These have frequently and erroneously been used as part of the arguments for genetic affiliation. However, their widespread occurrence is either an argument for Ruhlen's proto-Sapiens or, more likely, for the global operation of phonaesthetic processes that are still little understood. In either case there may be a connection with very deep-level human subsistence strategies and a reflection of the 'archaeolinguistics' proposed by Hegedüs.

The next two chapters deal with sociological aspects of data interpretation and historical linguistics. The case of the Tasaday in the Philippines, discussed by Lawrence Reid, represents a strange case history that illuminates both romantic fantasies about peoples supposedly cut-off in the Stone Age and the incredible speed with which speech-forms mutate among a very small number of speakers. The main conclusions that can be drawn are:

1   That reports of isolated groups of people living in an archaic lifestyle
    can be subject to political interference. Linguists and anthropologists
    should be sceptical about both positive and negative reports on the
    reality of such groups. Archaeologists should be wary of assuming that
    reports of Stone Age people, 'living fossils' etc., have direct relevance
    for their work.

2   That even if a group of people do appear to be living in a techno-
    logically backward state *vis-à-vis* their immediate neighbours, this is no
    necessary evidence they have always been like that. Survivals from the
    Stone Age have to be taken *cum grano salis,* even though the Tasaday
    have proved to be a distinct ethnolinguistic group.

3   That small isolated groups with a fragile language community can easily
    lose their language and culture. It is plausible that a people who had
    been speaking their own language all day everyday less than 25 years
    ago would still recall it fluently, even after they stopped speaking it.
    But self-perception turns out to be of crucial importance; where it is
    fluid, so is speech itself. Language data can be influenced by the socio-
    political context of elicitation, something generativists ignore to their
    peril.

Malcolm Ross approaches a broader field in his discussion of social networks
and their linkages with categories of speech-community event. A fundamental
issue in interpretations of the genesis of speech forms and ethnic communities is rhizotic versus cladistic models. In other words, the models that
essentially treat the development of peoples and languages as the fission of
older 'higher-order' groups as against 'multi-genetic' models supposing that
every entity has multiple origins. Represented visually this is the difference
between the tree diagram and the interlocking polygons of a Venn diagram.
Ross has no truck with such simple oppositions and his chapter outlines a
theory of the 'Speech Community Event' using a variety of diagrams to illustrate the rich complexity of such events. The argument is that we must get
away from the positions that have characterized cladistic versus rhizotic
'wave'[2] models and look in much more detail at the network structure of
communities speaking these languages or lects. The key concepts here are
density, clustering, intensity (of interactions) and degree of *multiplexity* which
define the parameters that control the processes of language or lect formation. Ross's chapter should be read in conjunction with his second, detailed
case study of Papuan Tip languages in Volume II.

It is important to emphasize that the modelling of relations between
languages is not a purely linguistic problem; exactly similar problems relate
to the genesis of communities and their inventory of material culture. Some
studies in Oceania attempt to correlate the two; the chapters by Tryon and
Dutton in Volume III deal with this problem for Vanuatu and the Mailu area
on the south coast of Papua. Ross cites other studies; their results have been
ambiguous partly because they are working with over-simplified models of

community networks. As the modelling of the spread of innovation and language change in the present becomes more sophisticated, it allows for richer presentation of models for prehistory. The more we can model the processes of interaction between differing ethnolinguistic groups the more precise will be our understanding of change in material culture inventories.

Attempts to relate languages using mathematical formulae are not as common as during the high-point of faith in lexicostatistics. However, the chapter by Raman and Patrick which discusses the concept of Minimum Message Length in determining natural language relatedness is a fresh attempt to explore the notion of quantifying the relationship between languages. They apply their developed technique to comparing Frisian, Old High German and Later North-west Germanic and presenting mathematical formulae to determine numerical results. In view of the increased sociologizing of our understanding of the complexity of language relations this approach is likely to remain a minority interest.

ORAL TRADITION

This introduction has so far focused principally on aspects of historical linguistics. However, another theme in relating archaeology to language is the use of oral tradition. Oral traditions have had a tergiversatory history in the academic imagination; the recording of texts and traditions played a major role in early twentieth-century anthropology, especially in America. Despite this, the American anthropologist Robert Lowie remarked as early as 1915, 'I cannot attach to oral traditions any historical value whatsoever under any conditions whatsoever' (Lowie 1915: 598). Where they have been uncritically accepted as history a backlash has inevitably been excited; the errors and omissions they incorporate for reasons familiar to anthropologists made them open to criticism from historians with high standards of evidence. The assumption that the detection of errors made them without value could lead a distinguished figure such as G.P. Murdock (1959: 43) to say 'native historical traditions, the one type of historical information that is virtually valueless'.

Such a blanket condemnation today would be unlikely. Indeed the 1960s saw a major explosion in the collection of oral traditions, especially in Africa, and the 'Oxford Library of African Literature' and the French 'Classiques Africaines' and LACITO series made major contributions to the publication of extended texts[3] from all regions of the world. These are inevitably rather tempting to the archaeologist; settlement mounds may have traditions attached and it is tantalising to see the excavation apparently confirm these. Anthropologists such as MacGaffey who continue to sound warnings may be seen as simply curmudgeonly;

> The modern willingness to employ indigenous texts and concepts
> for historiographic purposes is not enough unless the cosmologies

that generate them can first be understood. Real history . . . cannot be inferred from tradition in any simple way. To accept as historical even such portions of tradition as look real to the foreign eye is to submit unawares to the authority of the indigenous community as much as though one had also accepted the magical portions as historically real.

(MacGaffey 1974)

In view of some of the remarkable examples reported in this section it may be tempting to over-emphasize the value of historical tradition. But the tone of such material is almost inevitably positive; where oral tradition has *no* correlation with linguistic and archaeological data it may be exemplary for students of method but makes for a poor narrative.

Lidia Ashikhmina discusses the interpretation of ancient migrations in the northern sub-Urals of Siberia. Her chapter is a fascinating demonstration of the rich mixture of Soviet ethnography; archaeology, historical linguistics, the study of ancient texts and oral traditions are all combined to tell a complex story. From the archaeological point of view, Ashikhmina is attempting to link some well-described cultures largely defined by pottery styles with much broader stories of the conflict between the Uralic and Indo-European peoples in Western Siberia. The use of folklore material, especially the conflict of Pera the giant with the wheeled people, appears to be a remarkable record of battles against people with chariots. In the meantime, Ashikhmina also proposes an interpretation of some of Herodotus' observations on this region. Even more surprisingly for western scholars, she takes on an ancient theory about the 'Arctic home' apparently described in the Vedas. This is usually regarded in a humorous light by Indo-Europeanists, but her argument at least suggests that there are elements of the account that need to be reconsidered. More generally, the type of co-operation between disciplines evident from the approach of many Russian scholars deserves to be emulated more widely.

Benin city in south-western Nigeria is one of the rare places in Africa with long dynastic traditions; the association with a remarkable network of linear walls makes for an attractive site to correlate archaeology and oral traditions. However, Benin is a living city with a still-powerful ruling house, and every incentive remains to continue to manipulate oral tradition to dovetail with current political agendas. In addition, recent years have seen a substantial body of academic work on the Edoid languages: the group of languages related to Bini. This has created an awareness of linguistic unity among the disparate speakers that did not previously exist and has been incorporated into current politics – for example in demands for the creation of new administrative units. The chapter by Joseph Eboreime discussing oral traditions of the Ẹdọ-speaking peoples gives some examples of this type of manipulation at work and takes on the broader theme of competing oral traditions. It is common in Nigeria for parallel oral traditions to exist: one reflecting a kingship system, the other, usually more diffuse, either recounting a mythical origin or a history of migration that owes little to a centralized authority. An additional problem for assessing the dynastic histories is that reliable dating for the linear walls does not exist.

The research framework common in France, whereby different disciplines are divided into *laboratoires*, under the CNRS and in Regional Centres through ORSTOM, has an important role in stimulating interdisciplinary research, especially in the collection of oral tradition. The impressive series of monographs on the Austronesian languages of the Francophone areas of the Pacific has been complemented with excavation of sites, some still identified with known historical figures. The seemingly most clear-cut case described by Garanger is in Vanuatu, where a major change in the archaeological profile is associated with a named historical figure, Roy Mata, the details of whose burial are still recalled some seven centuries later. By contrast, in the chapter by Frimigacci on Uvea, the correspondences are less clear-cut, but it is still possible to combine interpretations of the oral texts with the archaeological record. In both cases, early missionary records of the well-maintained traditions in this region of the Pacific can be set against recent versions to illustrate the stability of the texts over time. This suggests that oral traditions can be of considerable interpretative value if used with care, and that the scepticism of Lowie and Murdock was misplaced (cf. Kirch and Yen 1982 for Tikopia).

Oral traditions usually do not subsist for more than a few centuries, rarely as much as a millennium in the case of established kingship structures (see discussion in Vansina 1985). Yet Sharpe and Tunbridge present some examples from aboriginal Australia suggesting that memories of geological and zoological phenomena can persist for thousands of years. The cases of apparently remembered volcanic eruptions and dispositions of land covered by the sea more than 10,000 years ago have been confirmed by recent geological work to which the bearers of the traditions could not have had access. This seems to be without parallel elsewhere, even among other hunter-gatherers such as the southern African Khoisan.

The greater part of their chapter, however, is devoted to evidence that Aboriginal traditions retain striking images of now-vanished land mammals; some that have become extinct within the last few centuries, some apparently considerably earlier. With animals there is always the possibility that the creatures mentioned in traditions are constructs based on finds of bones; some of the comparative evidence suggests that if so, such constructs are themselves of considerable antiquity. The case of Australia is an argument for taking texts of this type very seriously and for not assuming that time-depths of oral traditions are of necessity shallow.

The chapter by Jerry Taki and Darrell Tryon concerns the island of Erromango, one of the southern islands of Vanuatu, which has been the subject of quite extensive archaeological survey. Early records suggest that there were once more languages on the island than are spoken today, and the authors consider the methods that can be used to recover information about the 'lost' languages of Erromango. It also presents an intriguing example of language fusion: the establishment of a single large Christian settlement forced speakers to develop a common idiom. The principal author, an indigenous Erromanagan, is engaged in a project to recover more of the traditions and speech of the vanished languages.

Compared with the other cases discussed here, published material on the Saami reindeer herders of Finland and northern Sweden is extremely rich; traditions and epic poems have been written down since the early eighteenth century. Inger Zachrisson presents an overview of the literature on the debate over the origin of the Saami and compares it to recent archaeological and genetic evidence for their origin.

Oral traditions remain a rich source of data for the archaeologist, where it is possible to 'read' them in conjunction with ethnographic material on the region or culture in question. The pessimism of Lowie and Murdock derived from analysing oral history according to the standards of written history and concluding that it fell well short of the standards of evidence they required. Oral traditions *can* be used but only when the social context in which they were created is fully understood.

NOTES

1 This is controversial, of course. Most of us can recall encounters with people who *appear* to be speaking such an intermediate pre-language.
2 Wave models of glottogenesis appear in older textbooks of Indo-European but have not much influenced the present generation of historical linguists.
3 It is worth observing that of these, only the LACITO series still continues – now under the aegis of the Belgian publisher Peeters. LACITO was the only one to publish oral literature on a worldwide basis.

REFERENCES

Chomsky, N. 1988. *Language and Problems of Knowledge. The Managua Lectures.* Cambridge, Mass: MIT Press.

Griaule, M. and G. Dieterlen. 1951. *Signes graphiques soudanaises.* Paris: Les Cahiers de l'Homme, Herman.

Kirch, P.V. and D. Yen. 1982. *Tikopia: the prehistory and ecology of a Polynesian outlier.* Honolulu: Bishop Museum Press (Bernice P. Bishop Museum Bulletin 238).

Lowie, R.H. 1915. Oral tradition and history. *American Anthropologist* 17, 597–9.

MacGaffey, W. 1974. Oral tradition in Central Africa. *International Journal of African Historical Studies* 7(3), 417–26.

Murdock, G.P. 1959. *Africa, Its Peoples and their Culture History.* New York: McGraw-Hill.

Nichols, J. 1992. *Linguistic Diversity in Space and Time.* Chicago: University of Chicago Press.

Pinker, S. 1994. *The Language Instinct: the new science of language and mind.* London: Allen Lane.

Pinker, S. and P. Bloom. 1990. Natural language and natural selection. *Behavioral and Brain Sciences* 13, 707–84.

Postgate, N., Tao Wang and T. Wilkinson. 1995. The evidence for early writing: utilitarian or ceremonial? *Antiquity* 69(264), 459–80.
Renfrew, C. 1992. Archaeology, genetic and linguistic diversity. *Man* 27(3), 445–78.
Vansina, J. 1985. *Oral Tradition as History*. Madison: University of Wisconsin Press.

Part I

PREHISTORY OF LANGUAGE

1 Evolution and the biological correlates of linguistic features

BERNARD H. BICHAKJIAN

INTRODUCTION

Though basic intelligence and average insight applied to readily observed data would be enough to make logical deductions, stimulate research, and seek ever-deeper understanding of underlying processes, the human mind, instead, has much too often taken perverse pleasure in referring to higher motives to deny what is obvious and impair the search for valid explanations (cf. Gross and Levitt 1994: 24 *passim*). That the study of evolution and the scholars who have conducted it have suffered – metaphorically and literally – from such an attitude hardly needs to be stated. But, however sad they may have been, those sufferings have been consigned to history, and today evolution is accepted by all serious thinkers.

What is generally accepted, however, is the evolution of species. The evolution of behaviour is certainly finding a growing number of new advocates, who deserve credit for having succeeded in reopening the nature–nurture debate. Future data and debate in the neurosciences will tell whether their conception of nature is the right one. In mainstream linguistics, evolution is simply taboo – species evolve, behaviour has perhaps an evolutionary background, but it is adamantly maintained, no doubt for 'higher motives', that languages do not evolve (Bichakjian 1993). The situation is comparable with the one denounced by Richard M. Restak, who reminds his reader that

> even as recently as the late 1960s . . . psychiatry – certainly American psychiatry – was heavily committed to the idea that mental illness resulted from psychological causes. Those few psychiatrists and psychiatric trainees who suggested that much mental illness might have physical causes . . . were invited to pursue other specialty interests.
>
> (Restak 1994: 73)

Superficially, Chomsky's innate model seems to conform with the alternative approach that Restak is advocating, but in fact the MIT model is strongly relativist. It remains so in Pinker and Bloom's (1990) recent variant, where it is argued that the alleged DNA correlates of the would-be Universal Grammar have developed according to Darwinian principles (Paul Bloom, however, is not opposed to the idea of language evolution, while Steven Pinker remains adamantly relativist [pers. comm.]).

The application of evolutionary principles to linguistics is a welcome step, but it remains to be seen whether the newly proposed scenario can be supported with empirical data and methodological arguments. This chapter will point out that such support is lacking and that the MIT model is totally untenable. Instead, it will be argued:

1   that the history of languages displays important unidirectional changes;
2   that the study of the neurological interface of outgoing and incoming linguistic features reveals an optimization process; and
3   that this optimization process is produced by the biological mechanisms that are also responsible for the physical and ethological evolution of our species.

THE UNTENABLE SCENARIO

While Chomsky had always maintained that the genetic correlates of his innate grammar had no specific phylogenetic history, Pinker and Bloom (1990) argued that the alleged DNA material had developed in interaction with grammar-related selection pressures. Though it is legitimate for Pinker and Bloom to oppose their scenario to Chomsky's, on close scrutiny their claim amounts to no more than the tautological explanation of an assumption. If syntactic structures are indeed coded in our genes, then, given the importance of language for humans, it is tautological to say that they have developed through the interplay of genetic variations and selection pressures since the Synthetic Theory has long taught us that that is how permanent features are acquired. The essential question is whether our genome does indeed code for linguistic structures, and the only objective answer is that no empirical evidence has been found to substantiate such an assumption.

From their vantage point, linguists would have been in a strong position if they could have shown that some syntactic structures are universal. Though the gap between universality and genetic coding would still remain to be bridged, the pan-linguistic occurrence of certain structural patterns would have consolidated the claim. Unfortunately, after an intensive search by an unprecedented number of linguists over nearly four decades, universality remains frustratingly elusive. Not only do some languages have structures branching out to the right while others pattern in the opposite direction, not only do some use tense while others make aspectual distinctions, but the basic structure of a sentence is not universal: languages using nominative syntax have developed subject and object functions and make sentences that are statements about the subject, while the ergative languages, where the grammatical functions have remained close to their cognitive ancestry, are structured in terms of agents and patients and produce sentences that are statements about the patient, since the latter, and not the agent, is the unmarked item.

Of course, one could always conceive abstract structures of which the existing linguistic sequences would be presumed to be the concrete implementations, just as one could imagine a universal limb underlying fins, wings, and arms, but these are mental constructs. The universal limb does not exist, and no species has such a universal code in its genes. If they have limbs, species have an evolutionary variant of the primitive model. Likewise, universal structures do not exist, languages have supplanted the ancestral model with evermore developed alternatives.

If linguistic structures were coded in our genes, the corresponding DNA sequences would trigger the formation of a neural network and thus provide humans with language areas of the brain that would be partially prewired. Since there are no universal grammatical structures, nor even universal grammatical constraints (cf. Bichakjian 1989), the linguistic data do not suggest such a hypothesis; indeed they plead against it. Even a would-be supporter of the innateness theory feels 'a mismatch between the broad exciting aims of U[niversal] G[rammar] and the triviality of some of the details'; he denounces 'the theory['s being] . . . obsessively concerned with [only] certain areas of [syntax]' and the use of 'potentially misleading' 'sentences and constructions [that] self-perpetuate themselves in the literature' (Cook 1988: 167; see also p. 79).

But linguists are not alone in their rejection of the prewired model. The evidence is also lacking at the neurological side of the interface. That the human vocal tract has been adapted to speech and that humans have developed neurons which together are capable of producing and processing linguistic messages is of course true, but this cerebral material is a genetically coded form with a functional potential, within biological constraints (speed of articulation, range of auditory perception, memory span, etc.), not a form with linguistic functions outlined within innate grammatical constraints. Such a model with prewired linguistic instructions is emphatically rejected by Merlin Donald, who, speaking of Bickerton, asks rhetorically: 'Does he still believe in innate categories and some form of genetically determined, built-in set of grammatical rules?' (1993: 780; see also Donald 1991: 60 for a rejection of Chomsky's model). Instead, Donald suggests in humans the existence and the attendant phylogenetic development of what he calls a 'linguistic controller'. On the model of Umberto Eco's quip that literature is a picnic where the author brings the words and the reader the interpretations, one could represent Donald's account of speech as a picnic where the genes bring the operating device and the (language-specific) words the operating instructions (1991: 259–60). Since syntax can never be derived from words – for instance, what would be the lexical trigger of an ergative sentence pattern? – a picnic where

genes supply the operating device, and languages (not words) bring the operating instructions would best represent the linguistic and neurological realities
of speech.

Not only do the diversity of linguistic structures and the present understanding of neurological processes plead against the existence of a genetically
coded Universal Grammar but the hypothesis of an emergence without further
development is itself in complete contradiction to the principles of evolution. The advocates of the innate model claim that when our species appeared,
or when it began to speak, the blueprint of the alleged Universal Grammar
became part of our DNA and has remained static to this day. Actual implementations of the alleged innate model vary in space, and they have varied
in time, but such differences are not given any significance because it is
assumed that the changes are not oriented and that alternative implementation models are equally gratuitous.

If speech is the important asset that we know it is for our species, how
could the linguistic implements that are needed for mental operations and
communicative expression not have been subject to selection pressures? While
selection pressures have produced our geographic adaptations, have driven
technology from stone artefacts to space engines, and fostered our less-than-
perfect, but also less-than-negligible civilizations, why would the techniques
of mental representation and oral (and written) communication be immune
to similar evolutionary forces? In one of the commentaries that accompanied
Pinker and Bloom's 1990 paper, Bates and MacWhinney (p. 728) captured
with biting humour the inadequacy of a scenario where selection pressures
suddenly stop after the initial development by comparing them to anti-abor-
tionists, who, in the words of Mario Cuomo, 'believe that life begins at
conception and stops at birth'.

Would it not be more logical to expect that in the above described picnic
genes would continue to supply the operating device, while natural selection
would pressure languages into bringing instructions that are evermore functional and evermore efficient? It would also be logical to wonder whether
selection pressures would not have driven the genes into producing an evermore powerful operating device, but such a query cannot be answered since
we will never be able to study the molecular composition of the brains of
our ancestors 50–100,000 years ago and compare it to ours.

Pinker and Bloom's abortive scenario must therefore be at variance with
the principles of Darwinian evolution, and since neither linguistics nor the
neurosciences provide any empirical support for it, the hypothesis of a universal
grammar being coded in our genes remains for the time being a gratuitous
assumption. Having reached the conclusion that the innate grammar hypothesis is neither empirically founded nor theoretically tenable, this chapter will
now present evidence showing that the historical record clearly displays a
continuous optimization of linguistic features and argue that selection pressures, working through the recognized biological channels, have produced
the evolution of languages by fostering this process.

THE HISTORICAL RECORD

When one looks at the empirical data with an open mind, the changes that are essentially unidirectional are easy to observe. I shall use examples from the Indo-European family because it provides the most representative data-bank for the study of language evolution. It has one of the longest histories; the reconstruction of its proto-language, though always hypothetical, is based on the broadest and most intensive scholarly effort; its history is the most richly documented; and it has expanded to more geographic areas and to more populations than any other language family. This is not to say of course that other language families do not provide equally interesting or even older illustrations, but the Indo-European languages have the distinct advantage of providing the most competitively analysed and best known set of data. I shall nevertheless return to non-Indo-European languages later in this chapter.

The presentation of changes that are essentially unidirectional can be organized under the headings of the three major linguistic components: phonology, morphology, and syntax. The lexicon and the attendant field of semantics will be left out, not because they do not manifest the processes observed in the other branches of linguistics but because lexicological and semantic data are less amenable to systematic studies.

In phonology two major changes can be observed. On the vowel side, the laryngeal *h*-like sonorants were eliminated very early and replaced with newer vowels such as *a* and *o*, and a set of long vowels. In turn the systematic use of the long/short distinction receded and even disappeared altogether with newer vowels such as the French *y*, the English *u* (of *but*), or the Russian *i* coming in their stead. The shift from the Latin to the French set of vowels provides a clear illustration of the second evolutionary step. On the consonantal side, and omitting the sonorants, the shift has been away from a set essentially made of stops with secondary and tertiary articulations to a set made of simple stops and the corresponding fricatives, with the voicing feature used to double the inventory of stops and often that of fricatives. The shift becomes clearly visible when one compares the Indo-European and French obstruents (or true consonants) – see Table 1.1.

In morphology, the Indo-European languages have known three distinct devices for forming grammatical variants. Vowel alternation, as seen in the English *sing/sang/sung*, was common in the proto-language, used along with suffixation, which became increasingly dominant before yielding the way to

Table 1.1 Comparison of Indo-European and French obstruents

Indo-European				Modern French		
$p^{\text{?}}$	$t^{\text{?}}$	$k^{\text{?}}$	$k^{\text{w?}}$	p	t	k
p^{h}	t^{h}	k^{h}	k^{wh}	b	d	g
b^{h}	d^{h}	g^{h}	g^{wh}	f	s	š
	s			v	z	z

independent particles. This is how prepositions, personal pronouns, articles, and modal and temporal auxiliaries emerged. Not only the marking strategy but also the nature of the grammatical distinctions within paradigms are subject to change. A significant one took place in the verbal paradigm, where the ancestral modo-aspectual system was reorganized into a set of distinctions where tense plays the major role (cf. Meillet 1952: xii, 29ff.). The history of the Indo-European languages also displays the development of a passive voice, which gradually replaced the earlier middle (Benveniste 1966: 168). It is worth observing here that if the passive voice and the passive transformation are commonly used in English and many other modern languages, neither the verbal voice nor the corresponding transformation are a universal feature of human languages. Some have developed such a distinction and the attendant syntactic potential, others have not come so far in this particular area (cf. for example, Brettschneider 1979: 381).

In syntax, a major change had taken place in the ancestral days of the proto-language, when the ergative sentence structure had been replaced with the nominative model used today by the overwhelming majority of human languages. Afterwards, and probably after the proto-language had lost its unity, the technique of embedding one sentence into another was developed, first by correlating the two elements together (as in the English *As you sow, so will you reap*) and later by subordinating one to the other (cf. Meillet 1964: 373). The other major changes consisted of reordering the constituents of syntactic units. Modern linguistics has shown that each syntactic unit is made of two parts of which one governs the other. In the most frequently used terminology the governing item is called the *head*, the governee is called the *modifier*. Though a full consensus is still lacking on what is the head and what is the modifier, everyone will agree that verbs and prepositions are heads and their objects are modifiers. Likewise temporal and modal auxiliaries are heads and the nominal or adjectival forms of the verb are modifiers. It goes without saying that nouns are heads and the attendant adjectives are modifiers. In the ancestral language, the dominant order was modifier first, head last. Over the years, this order was reversed and the prevailing one today is head first.

The evolution of word order provides a good opportunity to introduce an important qualification. The changes described above apply to all the Indo-European languages in general. But it should be borne in mind that the rates vary from one language to another: some on the whole have proceeded faster than others, and within a language the rate varies from one feature to another. Languages may be more innovative in one area and more conservative in the other. The elimination of the subjunctive mood, a remnant of the ancestral verbal system, is completed in English and in Dutch but not in French and the other romance languages – but the latter make a more extensive use of head-first structures than English and even more so than Dutch. It is therefore important not to lose sight of the woods behind the trees. The rates vary from language to language and from feature to feature, but the changes proceed in the same direction. Under normal circumstances, i.e. when free of interferences from bilingual speakers and archaizing grammarians, languages and linguistic features proceed in the directions outlined above, not in the reverse one.

DEFINING THE DIRECTION

If linguists were not able to explain the unidirectional changes discussed above, it is partially because they saw nothing in common between, say, the shift from vowel quantity to more qualitative distinctions, from an aspectual to a temporal organization of verbal systems, and from head-last to head-first structures. The casual observer may also fail to see what could be common to the developments of constant body temperature, placental reproduction, and cerebral cortex. For the evolutionary biologist, the affinity is clear, they all have a selective advantage over their respective antecedents. Could it be then that the modern linguistic features are more advantageous than the ancestral ones?

Selective advantage in linguistics

Advantage is not a commonly used criterion in linguistics. It is one of Chomsky's merits to have expanded and formalized the notion of markedness, which enables the ranking of phonological items on a complexity scale. Within such a system, the vowels of English *but* and French *beurre* 'butter' would be more marked than the vowels of English *bet* and *bought* because of their less-natural feature combination – for the English vowel, the tongue root is retracted without the expected lip rounding, and for the French vowel the lips are rounded although the tongue root is not retracted. Unfortunately, this complexity scale, resting on what Chomsky himself admits to be 'conventions' (Chomsky and Halle 1968: 409), does not have a sufficiently solid empirical basis to provide a yardstick for assessing linguistic advantages. Moreover, it applies only to phonological items.

A more reliable gauge for comparing the advantages of linguistic features can be constructed with the evidence from language acquisition. If, other things being equal, a linguistic feature is mastered before an alternative one by children learning their native languages under normal circumstances, the earlier-acquired item must be concluded to be more advantageous than the later-acquired one. The reasons for concluding that an earlier-acquired feature is more advantageous are manifold:

1   If a feature is acquired at the beginning of the plasticity period, the neural pathways that sustain it are both simpler and stronger (cf. *mutatis mutandis* LeVay et al. 1980). The simplicity of the network will ensure a more economical use of energy and a more parsimonious absorption of cerebral potential, while the greater solidity of the network will make it less vulnerable to fatigue, psychological insecurity, and degenerative decay.

2   The earlier acquisition of linguistic features is also important for the
    socialization process. If a language is made of early-acquired features,
    the children who are acquiring it as their native language can achieve
    linguistic proficiency at a younger age and by so doing expand and
    accelerate their acquisition of social skills. When the linguistically
    supported socialization process is started early, the corresponding skills
    reach a fuller development and rest on a more solid neural underpin-
    ning.
3   And last, but certainly not least, early-acquired linguistic proficiency
    helps children accelerate and expand their mental development. If, as
    Harry Jerison (1990: 15–16) points out, the 'basic role [of language is]
    in the construction of reality' and 'if one defines intelligence as the
    capacity to construct perceptual worlds in which sensory information
    . . . is integrated as information about objects in space and time', the
    sooner children are proficient in language, the sooner their intelligence
    is stimulated, whereby their mental abilities become more developed
    and endowed with better neurological support.

It is pertinent to observe that early linguistic proficiency ties in with a
remarkable feature of human gestation. The period is considerably shorter
than what the mammalian norm would predict (Gould 1977: 369). The accel-
erated birth presents a major advantage for the development of mental skills,
because the sooner neonates leave the uterine confine the sooner they can
begin with their exploration of the world. Then language becomes important because the sooner they have mastered the use of language the sooner
they can organize and process the acquired information. Thus, the earlier
acquisition of linguistic skills complements the advantages of the earlier birth.

The foregoing discussion of early-acquired linguistic features clearly suggests
that the advantage criterion has an important role to play in linguistics, and
that language acquisition, with both its linguistic and biological interfaces,
provides the best indications for comparing the advantages of alternative
linguistic features.

Shifting to more advantageous features

When the input and the output of the normally unidirectional changes are
compared, the psycholinguistic record makes it abundantly clear that the
ancestral features were acquired later – sometimes considerably later – than
the alternatives that have replaced them. The acquisition of vowel quality takes
place before the mastery of a set of long and short vowels; simple fricatives
become part of the child's repertoire before complex stops; tense is acquired
before aspect and mood; particles are used correctly before inflectional paradigms are committed to memory; subordinate clauses are properly embedded
before participial constructions are used; and head-first structures, especially
when longer, are more accessible than head-last ones (for the psycholinguistic
data, and a discussion of their interpretation, cf. Bichakjian 1988).

The psycholinguistic data and the evidence they yield now take on a heuristic significance. They provide the key observation that defines the common direction of all normally unidirectional changes, and the arguments that explain it. The normally unidirectional changes can now be defined as a shift from late to earlier acquired features, and the advantages of a linguistic head-start explain why languages have consistently moved in this direction. Language evolution is therefore an optimization process, clearly defined, and in complete agreement with evolutionary principles.

When the overall process is seen in its evolutionary perspective, it becomes clear why normally the unidirectional changes are indeed unidirectional and why they are oriented the way they are. Since the reverse process would introduce disadvantageous features, it is hardly surprising that under normal circumstances languages would not pursue such a course of action. One can admittedly prescribe a different word order, impose extended inflectional systems, or compel the use of archaic features to suit the whims and wishes of learned grammarians just as one can bind the feet of little girls, stretch cervical vertebrae and elongate skulls to meet culturally set aesthetic ideals. These, however, are outside interventions, and, as soon as the pressure to meet these dubious standards is relaxed, nature resumes its normal course. So, in spite of Luther's orderly design of having the SVO order in the main clause and the SOV order in subordinate clauses, German pursues its slow but steady course towards head-first structures (see also Bichakjian 1986 for a discussion of the aborted attempt to reintroduce vowel quantity in sixteenth-century French).

The shift to earlier-acquired features and the attendant explanation are also important for the understanding of the evolution of non-Indo-European languages. Without this evolutionary paradigm, the overall unity of the Indo-European unidirectional changes was already difficult to see, but the problems were compounded when changes from other linguistic families were added to the discussion. The disarray was then total, and the anti-evolutionists could easily carry the day with the argument that the set of changes occurring in one language family do not necessarily occur in another.

That argument is now void. The changes may indeed not be identical: the vernaculars of Africa, America and Australia, and the standardized languages of Europe and Asia, may all have travelled somewhat different paths, though in fact many of the shifts are shared (cf. Bichakjian 1991a; and Solberg 1979) and the remaining differences are often consistent with the prevailing evolutionary phases (Bichakjian 1991b), but everywhere the trend has been towards earlier-acquired features. The situation is the same in biology where the changes from reptilians to mammals are not identical with the changes from fishes to amphibians, but both sets are governed by the same principle. So, whatever their exact courses and the explanation of their differential behaviour, all human languages under normal circumstances have evolved in the direction of earlier-acquired features, and they have done so because that is the path to greater advantages.

In the foregoing discussion, it was argued that all things being equal early-acquired features are more advantageous. This is so, but all things do not have to be equal. In fact, the incoming features are often more functional than the outgoing ones. Simple fricatives, for instance, have a broader distributional range than complex stops; the passive voice offers the active greater interaction than the middle (Kuryłowicz 1964: 76), and subordinate clauses can express more modalities than participial phrases. There is, however, no single yardstick, to my knowledge, that could measure the greater functionality of fricatives, passive voice, and subordinate clauses. That is why the emphasis has been on the early acquisition advantages, because there the evidence is provided by well-established quantitative data, though in fact languages have evolved both towards earlier acquisition and greater functionality.

LANGUAGE EVOLUTION AND THE EVOLUTION OF HUMANS

The evidence supporting the existence of selective advantages in linguistics has provided the criteria and the arguments that define language evolution and explain it as an optimization process. This process complies with the principles of the prevailing theory of evolution and is consistent with both the evolution of culture and the evolution of humans – morphological and ethological.

The evolution of culture may seem difficult to define, but Leslie White has argued convincingly that its 'basic law' can be formulated, using 'the technological factor' which, according to him, is '*the* determinant of a cultural system as a whole'. That basic law is this: 'Other factors remaining constant, *culture evolves as the amount of energy harnessed . . . is increased, or as the efficiency of the instrumental means of putting the energy to work is increased*' (1969: 366, 368–9; original emphasis). The efficient use of energy seems to be deeply rooted in humans and other living organisms. 'Animals adopt a strategy that allows them to get the most food with as little energy as possible', and a recent study has revealed 'that people do the same in selecting the best strategy for making money' (Naylor 1994: 285). The optimization process observed in linguistics is therefore in harmony with the environmental strategies of human and other animals, and, as such, is an integral part of the evolution of culture.

The consistency with our biological evolution is even greater because it concerns the general direction and, probably, also the genetic mechanisms that have produced it. The structural features that are important for the success of our species have increased their potential through a neotenous process, whereby juvenile features were preserved into adulthood, while their antecedents were gradually pushed out of the individuals' lifespan (Gould 1977: 365ff.). The overall gracilization of our species could provide a visual illustration of neoteny, but the best example comes no doubt from our retention of cerebral plasticity until the onset of senility (Montagu 1989: 57ff.). The correlation between extended plasticity and increased mental potential is important for understanding the evolution of human behaviour. By acting on the biological correlates of ethological features, neoteny has also shaped the evolution of human behaviour (Lorenz 1971: 180; Montagu 1989: 61). We remain creatively active throughout our adult lives because we have been able to preserve the playfulness of our youthful years.

These close biological parallels suggest that the evolution of languages could also be the result of a neotenous process, whereby a retiming of the biochemical events that underpin the acquisition of linguistic features would produce the observed changes. This hypothesis does not advocate the existence of an innate grammar. Indeed it categorically rejects the idea of linguistic structures having genetic coding (see also Donald 1991: 60, and, more emphatically, 1993: 780). It is argued instead that language acquisition is a process of laying out neural networks. The synaptic splicing is triggered by external stimuli provided by the linguistic sources, but it is made possible by biochemical events. These events are genetically regulated and that regulation can be modified through evolutionary processes, and as the language acquisition process is modified so is the language of the future adult. A similar hypothesis is also put forward by Russell Gardner, a medical doctor working on congenital language defects (1991).

HOMOLOGOUS OPTIMIZATION PROCESSES

The evidence and arguments presented above have revealed that language evolution exists, and that its course can be defined and explained. Language moves in the direction of features that are more functional and that are acquired earlier by native children. Since an increasingly early acquisition has manifold selective advantages, language evolution emerges as an optimization process, probably produced by the same genetic mechanisms that explain the neotenous evolution of human morphology and ethology. If this probability is confirmed, the evolution of language and the evolution of humankind would become homologous processes.

REFERENCES

Benveniste, É. 1966. Actif et moyen dans le verbe. In *Problèmes de Linguistique générale*, 1, 168–75. Paris: Gallimard (first published in *Journal de Psychologie* 1950).
Bichakjian, B.H. 1986. When do lengthened vowels become long? Evidence from Latin and French, and a paedomorphic explanation. In *Studies in Compensatory Lengthening*, W.L. Wetzels and E. Sezer (eds), 11–36. Dordrecht, Holland: Foris.
Bichakjian, B.H. 1988. *Evolution in Language*. Ann Arbor, Mich.: Karoma.

Bichakjian, B.H. 1989. Language innateness and speech pathology. In *Studies in Language Origins, I*, J. Wind, E.G. Pulleyblank, Éric de Grolier and B.H. Bichakjian (eds), 209–32. Amsterdam: Benjamins.

Bichakjian, B.H. 1991a. Evolutionary patterns in linguistics. In *Studies in Language Origins, II*, W. von Raffler-Engel and J. Wind (eds), 187–224. Amsterdam: Benjamins.

Bichakjian, B.H. 1991b. From family tree to phylogeny. In *Proceedings of the Fourteenth International Conference of Linguists. Berlin 1987*, W. Bahner, J. Schildt and D. Viehweger (eds), 2446–52. Berlin: Akademie Verlag.

Bichakjian, B.H. 1993. Language evolution: one evolution that is still taboo. In *The nineteenth LACUS Forum 1992*, P.A. Reich (ed.), 425–35. Lake Bluff, Ill.: LACUS.

Brettschneider, G. 1979. Typological characteristics of Basque. In *Ergativity. Towards a Theory of Grammatical Relations*, Frans Plank (ed.), 371–84. London: Academic Press.

Chomsky, N. and M. Halle. 1968. *The Sound Pattern of English*. New York: Harper & Row.

Cook, V.J. 1988. *Chomsky's Universal Grammar. An Introduction*. Oxford: Blackwell.

Donald, M. 1991. *Origins of the Modern Mind. Three stages in the evolution of culture and cognition*. Cambridge, Mass.: Harvard University Press.

Donald, M. 1993. Précis of *Origins of the Modern Mind. Three stages in the evolution of culture and cognition*. *Behavioral and Brain Sciences* 16, 737–91.

Gardner, R. Jr. 1991. Are there language-regulating genes on chromosome 15? Paper presented at Seventh Annual meeting of the Language Origins Society, DeKalb, Illinois.

Gould, S.J. 1977. *Ontogeny and Phylogeny*. Cambridge, Mass.: The Belknap Press of Harvard University Press.

Gross, P.R. and N. Levitt. 1994. *Higher Superstition. The academic left and its quarrels with science*. Baltimore, Md: The Johns Hopkins University Press.

Jerison, H.J. 1990. Paleoneurology and the evolution of mind. In *The Workings of the Brain. Development, Memory, and Perception*, Rodolfo R. Llinás (ed.), 3–16. New York: W.H. Freeman (first published in *Scientific American*, January 1976).

Kuryłowicz, J. 1964. *The Inflectional Categories of Indo-European*. Heidelberg: Winter.

LeVay, S., T.N. Wiesel and D.H. Hubel. 1980. The development of ocular dominance columns in normal and visually deprived monkeys. *The Journal of Comparative Neurology* 191, 1–51.

Lorenz, K. 1971. *Studies in Animal and Human Behaviour*, Vol. 2. Translation by Robert Martin. London: Methuen.

Meillet, A. 1952. *Esquisse d'une histoire de la langue latine*, 6th edn. Paris: Hachette (reprint of the 3rd edn 1933).

Meillet, A. 1964. *Introduction à l'étude comparative des langues indo-européennes*. Alabama: University of Alabama Press (reprint of the 8th edn Paris: Hachette 1937).

Montagu, A. 1989. *Growing Young*, 2nd edn. Granby, Mass.: Bergin & Garvey.

Naylor, L.I. 1994. Anthropology. In *Yearbook of Science and the Future*. Chicago: Encyclopaedia Britannica.

Pinker, S. and P. Bloom. 1990. Natural language and natural selection. *Behavioral and Brain Sciences* 13, 707–84.

Restak, R.M. 1994. *Receptors*. New York: Bantam Books.

Solberg, M.E. 1979. Ontogenesis and language change. *LLBA* 13(2) Supplement 3, 132.

White, L.A. 1969. *The Science of Culture: a study of man and civilization*. New York: Farrar, Straus & Giroux.

2 Cognitive archaeology: a look at evolution outside and inside language

GÁBOR GYÖRI

INTRODUCTION

The term 'cognitive archaeology' is taken from Medin and Wattenmaker (1987), who define it as the search for biological-cognitive constraints that may become embodied in organisms as a result of their interaction with the environment during evolution. This chapter discusses how such constraints influence language evolution. If language indeed emerged in humans as a cognitive adaptation (e.g. Jerison 1988), then cognitive archaeology can have explanatory value in a theory of language evolution because these constraints must be reflected in language.

Evolution can primarily be understood as a process of change. Language can be said to evolve at two different levels. On the one hand, evolution takes place inside language when language as a system changes over time, and, on the other, we can speak of language evolving externally when language as a cognitive faculty emerges in the evolution of humans. However, the Darwinian concept of evolution also implies a process in which organisms adapt to their environment. If such an approach is valid for language, recognized by many as a complex adaptive trait (Jerison 1988; Donald 1991; Plotkin 1994), then language must reflect the interaction of humans with their environment both as a faculty and as a system. In this case 'cognitive archaeology' can be applied to both levels and should shed light on what the constraints are that become embodied in linguistic organisms (that is, humans), and how these constraints are manifest in language. The constraints should depend on the role language plays in this interaction. The chapter does not aim to point out the constraints, but focuses on the importance of language (as a cognitive device for modelling the environment) in this interaction to show that such constraints can and should be looked for.

DIGGING FOR CONSTRAINTS: THE COGNITIVE ARCHAE-OLOGY OF LANGUAGE AS A FACULTY

Any change is inherently characterized by the constraints put on it by the nature of its material and the environment it takes place in. In the case of language we can speak of change from two aspects. One is the emergence of the cognitive faculty for language. I conceive of this development as evolution outside language because the changes primarily concern the organism that develops this faculty. The other aspect, evolution inside language, is the process of change in any given linguistic system without changes to the organism itself. Indeed, similar functional constraints must be at work in both forms of language evolution.

There is much debate about the evolution of language as a cognitive faculty. Here I would like to deal with only what I consider the two main issues. One of these is the question if emergence happened by gradual accretion or abrupt appearance of skills; the other is if language has any adaptive value. Chomsky (1988), for example, tries to explain the origin of the Language Acquisition Device by some macromutation that caused the abrupt emergence of the human capacity to deal with 'discrete infinity', on which our linguistic abilities rest. Theoretically such a development is of course possible. However, not only the traditional Darwinian idea of evolution but also the hypothesis of punctuated equilibria (Gould 1980) requires that such a mutation confers some selective advantage to be able to spread in a population. The issue does not concern the possibility of macromutations but that of adaptive ones. In the case of language the idea of the abrupt appearance of skills should lead to a paradox, which stems from the fact that language is not just a faculty but also a system of signs and rules. Whereas language as a biological faculty can in theory emerge suddenly as a result of mutations, this can hardly be said about language as a system, which in reality is always one particular code of communication, however primordial, that has to be learnt. It must be clear that the language faculty in itself could not have conferred any selective advantage on its possessor(s) without the knowledge of an acquired symbol system. A further, and probably even more serious problem is that language (at least as a system of signs and rules) is a social phenomenon, which means that in order for the language faculty to carry selective advantage several individuals had to have it, coupled with a shared knowledge of a system of signs and rules. But an abrupt appearance of skills does not leave any room for the evolution of a symbol system.

Though there are attempts among generativists to show the adaptive advantage of the language faculty (Hurford 1991) and to explain generativity as the adaptive feature of the human brain that has been selected in evolution (Corballis 1991), the radical generativist approach is that language could not have evolved through natural selection because its autonomous and arbitrary grammatical structure could not have been adaptive (Piattelli-Palmarini 1989). The main argument is based on a fundamental dogma of generative grammar, which says that no biological or logical necessity accounts for the form grammatical structure takes in human language (Chomsky 1988), and thus there is no reason to believe that we use language for some function (Chomsky 1979). It has to be noted here that the autonomy and arbitrariness of grammatical structure is not generally accepted among linguists (e.g. Haiman 1985).

The idea that language did not emerge through natural selection makes some of the above problems disappear, but leaves the emergence of a code that has to be learned unexplained. Bierwisch (1992) also assumes that a full-blown language faculty had to precede the use of any symbol system and claims the functions of language to be irrelevant to its evolution. However, it has to be realized that at the basis of the debate about adaptive value of and natural selection for language lies the 'ideological' controversy between structuralism and functionalism. I do not think that function and structure can be rightfully separated for other than methodological reasons. If we look at structure in itself and refuse to take function into account (or even deny the existence of function), it is no wonder that the issue of adaptiveness cannot even be raised. Though the question of adaptation is about function, it should not be overlooked that it is always some kind of structure that carries some kind of function. In fact it is the function that a structure has that is of adaptive value, and never the structure in itself, since evolution can create different structures for the same function. In other words, a structure can be adaptive only to the extent of the function it carries. (The real issue is of course the existence of functionless structure, to which I will come back later.) For example, although the capacity for vision evolved in structurally totally different ways in insects and mammals and thus it may seem that the structures of the insect and mammalian eyes are arbitrary formations, we cannot say that they have no function and thus no adaptive value. A further example is locomotion, which is clearly an adaptive capacity but which has many structural realizations among animals. I do not want to claim that structure can never be the result of chance, and in this sense even arbitrary, as long as we realize that it must always conform to the structural possibilities inherent in evolution. Because of this I do not think that the selective advantage of language has to be or even can be accounted for by the adaptive value of its structure alone, as Pinker and Bloom (1990) have tried. It is impossible to have a selectionist approach to language evolution built on a purely structuralist basis and to disregard any possible functions of language in an explanation. This is why generative grammar is so much at odds with any sound evolutionary biological explanation of language.

The argumentation in the previous paragraph tried to show that it is odd to separate structure and function completely. Of course there can be structure that defies any functional explanation, but this does not mean (as exemplified above by the cases of vision and locomotion) that a structural explanation can account for everything. A structuralist preconception is also the reason why the generative grammatical tradition insists on language being an autonomous cognitive faculty totally independent of any other human cognitive capacities.

A rejection of any kind of functional explanation of language thus naturally leads to the rejection of its emergence through natural selection, because any selective advantages of language can work only through some kind of function. There is also a prejudice against functional approaches because function is often equated with purpose and thus any functional explanation is considered teleological (Bierwisch 1992). Hence also the idea of structures without any function. However, function in an evolutionary sense is nothing more than the use to which a certain structure is or can be put, or simply the position a structure occupies in a superstructure, without any implication of purposefulness in its emergence (Plotkin 1994). It is only in this sense that we can speak of language as having communicative and cognitive functions, and it is indeed mistaken to say that language evolved for some purpose. Though Bierwisch recognizes the social advantage of language as a symbol system, he rules out the possibility of the simultaneous emergence of the faculty and the symbol system side of language because he is convinced of the abrupt emergence of the language faculty as an 'essential totality'. Sebeok (1987) also denies the social advantage of language in the period of its emergence, though he recognizes the cognitive-modelling function of language as having a primary selective advantage compared to its social-communicative function. Sebeok correctly realizes that language is qualitatively different from animal communication systems because of its being a cognitive-modelling system. However, there seems to be a contradiction between Sebeok's claim that the modelling function in itself could have conferred selective advantage and his assumption that a very high degree of subjectivity and individuality was at work in the emergence of language. It has to be stressed here again that the cognitive modelling function of language also has to be based on a specific system of socially learned signs and rules (even if the language faculty is equipped with an innate universal grammar). Thus, the communicative function of language could not have been secondary and have appeared long after its cognitive-modelling function (cf. Sebeok 1981, 1987).

We have to see clearly that humans were not the first organisms in which the ability of cognitively modelling the environment appeared. Herrnstein (1984) attributes such an important selective advantage to the ability of categorizing which he considers characteristic of all living organisms. But with the emergence of language mental modelling could be done in a much more efficient way than ever before. Language enhanced and qualitatively changed the faculty of the human brain for modelling the environment. The function of the brain of any animal (including humans) is to construct and operate such models for the sake of adaptation to, and survival in, the environment. But for the construction of this model non-human animals have to rely on their individual experiences, because no animal's communication is powerful enough to be able to exchange parts of their models to any significant degree (cf. Csányi 1992). Though the cognitive-modelling ability in organisms existed already prior to language, the appearance of language can be explained by its vast social advantage, which in terms of group selection also meant a selective advantage.

Language did not only enable humans to construct much more precise and detailed mental models of their environment, but according to Csányi (1989, 1992) it also made the parallel connection of the modelling brains possible, which resulted in the construction of a supermodel of the environment that was not based on the experience of a single individual any more but was synthesized from the mental models of a group of individuals. This is the real social advantage of language compared to the role of information transfer that communication plays in animals. Via this supermodel members of a population could share each other's individual experience to a degree unmatched in other animals. Such a supermodel means that all members of a speech community can benefit from the knowledge of others, even from that of previous generations, without direct experience. This unique capacity can be described as *symbolic cognition* (Győri, in press a). Symbols of language carry information about reality and can substitute direct experience. It is quite evident that the larger part of our knowledge that we possess in a linguistic form is not of empirical character, and many symbolic structures do not even qualify as representing something that can be physically experienced.

Linguistic communication made it possible for the individuals of a group to have similar knowledge of their environment without physically sharing all the experience. It also enabled the group to construct more and more adequate models of reality, since it secured the control of the adequacy of these models by making the comparison and correction of individual models possible. The evolutionary role of linguistic communication was thus the diminishing of the subjectivity of individual models, which vastly increased the possibility of effective co-operation. Neither the increased communicative potential nor the increased modelling capacity in themselves can account for the emergence of language. Without being linked to symbols that bear a cognitive-representative function in the mind, communication can increase in volume and scope but not in efficiency. The same goes for cognition. Its efficiency cannot be changed qualitatively unless it is freed from being locked up in the mind of the individual. That is why language could only have emerged as the ability to manipulate *cognitive symbols* that can be used both externally in communication and internally in cognitive representation simultaneously. Thus, if language evolved with the function of making the co-operative interaction of humans with their environment more effective, then there have to be corresponding biological and cognitive constraints embodied in the faculty of language.

COGNITIVE ARCHAEOLOGY OF LANGUAGE AS A SYSTEM

Only recently, with the weakening of the generative enterprise, have some approaches to language claimed that the system of language reflects our bodily interaction with our environment (Johnson 1987; Langacker 1987). That this must indeed be so should come as no surprise after the above account. This section looks at how this correlation can be observed in the evolution of the category system of a language.

At every historical stage in the development of a language its lexicon defines a cultural system of categories, i.e. a certain common repertoire of categories is stored in the minds of the individuals of a speech community. The formation of these categories can be traced in semantic change via the etymology of words (Györi, in press b). The meanings of words denoting categories are most of the time products of historical categorization processes, i.e. they are fossilized conceptualizations of previous generations. They have outlived the speakers of the times of their emergence, and later on they impose a given categorization of the world on the coming generations. But just as these linguistically coded categories are results of previous conceptualizations on the level of a whole culture, they also provide an ever-ready source for the operation of similar cognitive processes in the future.

The basic cognitive function of human language is that it serves to operate our mental model of the environment because its building blocks, grammatical rules and linguistic signs are the 'material' out of which we create this model. The importance of this is that the individual can rely on a super-model shared with others in building and operating his or her own cognitive model of the world. In a study on naming, Carroll (1985) has shown that almost all naming in human communities happens in a descriptive categorizing manner. This is actually inherent in how linguistic signs operate: they refer to phenomena by describing them and categorizing them. Csányi's (1992) supermodel is not a model that is shared by everyone on the basis of the same genetic endowment and the same experiences, as in the case of animals sharing the same cognitive structures and being able to communicate about them. Quite the contrary: this supermodel is language based, which makes it possible that totally new concepts can be planted in the minds of other individuals, because a concept or some cognitive structure constructed actively and subjectively by one individual on the basis of experience can substitute experience in other individuals. It is the symbolic representation of concepts in words that makes it possible for humans to store concepts that are not based on experience with the help of reference to their symbols.

Language, as an instrument for the cognizance of the environment, always has to suit our cognitive needs. Any changes in the environment that are relevant at the level of a speech community call for an adaptation of language to these changes. In the interaction of humans with their environment, special mechanisms of semantic change construct new meanings to fill in the gaps arising in the semantic structure of a language. New conceptualizations of cultural relevance require new linguistic expressions (i.e. names) in order to achieve cultural validity. In this process, already established meanings are adapted in various ways for filling in the semantic gaps (Hopper 1990).

The process of cultural category formation is functional in nature since it is based on a speech community's adaptation to its environment. Etymologies reveal a great deal about this process as they show how reality can be construed in alternative ways to facilitate this adaptation. The environment in which human conceptual categories emerge is always a given culture, and the attributes of phenomena considered important for categorization reflect the characteristics of this particular culture. As cognitive analyses of historical semantic data show, a huge part of our symbol system is metaphorical in nature (Dirven 1985; Lipka 1990). This is a consequence of the analogical character of human mental processing: we make sense of the world by way of metaphorical projections of perceptual input to the nervous system.

This may sound paradoxical since this would mean that it is a figurative and thus seemingly subjective interpretation of reality that facilitates our orientation in the environment. The solution to this problem lies in the adaptive role of cognition. While reality is in fact objective, adaptation to it depends on the nature and the biology of the given organism; which means that adaptation must be understood as a subjective process. In other words, an organism can adapt itself only to what is given, but this adaptation can happen in different ways. The difference in adaptation is a result of the different biology of different organisms. Cognition is not simply knowing reality, but knowing reality in a way that it facilitates an organism's optimal adaptation to it. Because of this, parts of reality are perceived according to the role that they play in this adaptation, but the role they can play and do in fact play depends on the biology of a type of organism or the particular situation of a population. Since adaptation means a selection at the group level in the long run, certain biological–cognitive constraints become embodied in organisms (Medin and Wattenmaker 1987).

A functional view of categorization claims that the formation of categories is part of an organism's adaptive behaviour for organizing and controlling its environment (Herrnstein 1984; Rosch 1978; Zimmerman 1979). In the process of categorization the organism arranges different phenomena or stimuli into one group or class as long as their differences can be considered irrelevant to the behavioural purposes at hand (Rosch 1978: 29). Thus, the perceived similarity of stimuli is relative to the role that they play in an organism's behaviour. Behaviour in this context means any kind of interaction between an organism and its environment. This kind of similarity is called analogy, because, as Holyoak (1984: 204) puts it, 'analogy . . . is structured similarity with functional import'. The recognition of such an analogy is at the basis of the formation of human conceptual categories as well, but for the human mind analogy is not wholly based on perceptual attributes and function is rarely a matter of physical properties. As Medin and Wattenmaker (1987) have pointed out, the notion of similarity based on a set of common attributes cannot account for category cohesiveness. But similarity defined in functional rather than structural terms seems to eliminate the problems they mention.

Functional similarity is a much vaguer and broader term than perceptual similarity (based on structural correspondence). Not only it does imply similar usage, in the strict sense of physical manipulation of objects, it also embraces

the coincidence of all those attributes of entities that exhibit the same relevance for a particular type of behaviour of an organism. Thus, most of the
time functional similarity overrides mere perceptual similarity. The reason for
this is that perception is always selective since it is determined by anticipa-
tory schemata that are never independent of the organism's adaptation to its
environment (Neisser 1976). Similarity does not reside objectively in the entities themselves, but emerges in their subjective cognizing by an organism.

It is in this sense that we can speak of cognition as a subjective process.
The correspondence between objective reality and its subjective cognition is
regulated by the adaptive value of the organism's 'view' of reality. This means
that the subjectivity of the reality model that an organism operates cannot
go so far as to endanger the organism's survival. In the ideal case subjectivity
goes just so far that the facilities of reality are utilized in terms of the organism's
biology to an optimal degree. For different organisms, but also for the same
organisms under different environmental conditions (which not only include
the physical but also social, cultural, etc. aspects), different construals of phenomena may gain validity according to their adaptive value. A functional
approach should not exclude subjectivity, but view it as the basis for adaptive behaviour. Of course subjectivity must be held within certain limits, and
it is just its adaptive value that will regulate these limits. In other words,
there has to be a feedback between adaptive value and subjectivity. A construal
of reality that hinders optimal adaptation to the environment rather than facilitates it is not likely to gain validity because it would jeopardize the organism's
survival. In the case of humans the problem is of course much more complex;
adaptation and survival are by no means to be understood in the strict biological but rather in a socio-cultural sense.

Analogical thinking, which gains expression in figurative language, has
exactly this kind of adaptive role for humans. An appropriate orientation in
a given socio-cultural environment often requires different construals of
the same phenomenon. Different peoples and cultures often construe the
same phenomena of reality in different ways, because their different
environments demand different ways of adaptation to them. This kind of
cognitive flexibility is greatly enhanced by the analogical character of human
thinking. It is characteristic of human thought that all new phenomena are
mentally grasped via an analogy to already familiar cognitive structures (Lakoff
1990). Even in the case of phenomena that we can experience in a direct
physical way, we often look for functional similarities with other already well-
understood phenomena in order to have a better understanding of them
(Holyoak 1984). On the one hand, language is used to represent established
knowledge by making propositions about reality, to which we refer as objective knowledge. On the other hand, language is also the medium that makes
figurative thinking available for us, which enables us to construe our environment in new and adaptively optimal ways. Thus, figurative and
propositional modes of cognition are equally important and necessary for an
adequate cognizing of reality. This speaks for language as an adaptation in

order to facilitate a more flexible cognitive activity for the sake of an even more effective adaptation to the environment.

REFERENCES

Bierwisch, M. 1992. Probleme der biologischen Erklärung natürlicher Sprache. In *Biologische und soziale Grundlagen der Sprache*, P. Suchsland (ed.), 7–45. Linguistische Arbeiten 280. Tübingen: Max Niemeyer.

Carroll, J. 1985. *What's in a Name? An essay in the psychology of reference*. New York: Freeman.

Chomsky, N. 1979. Human language and other semiotic systems. *Semiotica* 25, 31–44.

Chomsky, N. 1988. *Language and Problems of Knowledge. The Managua lectures*, Cambridge, Mass.: MIT Press.

Corballis, M.C. 1991. *The Lopsided Ape. Evolution of the generative mind*. New York and Oxford: Oxford University Press.

Csányi, V. 1989. *Evolutionary Systems and Society. A general theory*. Durham, N.C.: Duke University Press,

Csányi, V. 1992. The brain's models and communication. In *The Semantic Web*, T.A. Sebeok and J. Umiker-Sebeok (eds), 27–43. Berlin: Mouton de Gruyter.

Dirven, R. 1985. Metaphor as a basic means for extending the lexicon. In *The Ubiquity of Metaphor*, W. Paprott and R. Dirven (eds), 85–119. Amsterdam: John Benjamins.

Donald, M. 1991. *Origins of the Modern Mind. Three stages in the evolution of culture and cognition*. Cambridge, Mass.: Harvard University Press.

Gould, S.J. 1980. Is a new and general theory of evolution emerging? *Paleobiology* 6, 119–30.

Györi, G. in press a. Symbolic cognition: its evolution and adaptive impact. In *Proceedings of the 9th Annual Meeting of the Language Origins Society*, A. Kendon and T. Chernigovskaya (eds), Silver Spring, Md: Linstok Press.

Györi, G. in press b. Historical aspects of categorization. In *Cognitive Linguistics in the Redwoods*, E.H. Casad (ed.), Berlin: Mouton de Gruyter.

Haiman, J. (ed.) 1985. *Iconicity in Syntax*. Amsterdam: John Benjamins.

Herrnstein, R.J. 1984. Objects, categories, and discriminative stimuli. In *Animal Cognition*, H.C. Roitblat, T.G. Bever and H.S. Terrace. (eds), 129–44. Hillsdale, N.J.: Lawrence Erlbaum Associates.

Holyoak, K.J. 1984. Analogical thinking and human intelligence. In *Advances in the Psychology of Human Intelligence. Vol. 2*, R.J. Sternberg (ed.), 199–230. Hillsdale, N.J.: Lawrence Erlbaum Associates.

Hopper, P.J. 1990. Where do words come from? In *Studies in Typology and Diachrony*, W. Croft, K. Denning and S. Kemmer (eds), 151–60. Amsterdam and Philadelphia: John Benjamins.

Hurford, J.R. 1991. The evolution of the critical period for language acquisition. *Cognition* 40, 159–203.

Jerison, H.J. 1988. Evolutionary neurobiology and the origin of language as a cognitive adaptation. In *The Genesis of Language. A different judgement of evidence*, M.E. Landsberg (ed.), 3–9. Berlin: Mouton de Gruyter.

Johnson, M. 1987. *The Body in the Mind: the bodily basis of meaning, reason and imagination*. Chicago: University of Chicago Press.

Lakoff, G. 1990. The Invariance Hypothesis: is abstract reason based on image-schemas? *Cognitive Linguistics* 1, 39–74.

Langacker, R.W. 1987. *Foundations of Cognitive Grammar. Volume 1: Theoretical Prerequisites*. Stanford, Calif.: Stanford University Press.

Lipka, L. 1990. Metaphor and metonymy as productive processes on the level of the lexicon. In *Proceedings of the XIVth International Congress of Linguists. Vol. II*, W. Bahner, J. Schildt and D. Viehweger (eds), 1207–10. Berlin: Akademie Verlag.

Medin, D.L. and W.D. Wattenmaker. 1987. Category cohesiveness, theories, and cognitive archeology. In *Concepts and Conceptual Development: ecological and intellectual factors in categorization*, U. Neisser (ed.), 25–62. Cambridge: Cambridge University Press.

Neisser, U. 1976. *Cognition and Reality. Principles and Implications of Cognitive Psychology*. San Francisco: Freeman.

Piattelli-Palmarini, M. 1989. Evolution, selection and cognition: From 'learning' to parameter setting in biology and the study of language. *Cognition* 31, 1–44.

Pinker, S. and P. Bloom. 1990. Natural language and natural selection. *Behavioral and Brain Sciences* 13, 707–84.

Plotkin, H. 1994. *Darwin Machines and the Nature of Knowledge*. Cambridge, Mass.; Harvard University Press.

Rosch, E. 1978. Principles of categorization. In *Cognition and Categorization*, E. Rosch and B.B. Lloyd (eds), 27–48. Hillsdale, N.J.: Lawrence Erlbaum Associates.

Sebeok, T.A. 1981. On hard facts and misleading data. *Reviews in Anthropology* 8, 9–15.

Sebeok, T.A. 1987. In what sense is language a 'primary modeling system'? In *Semiotics* J. Deeley (ed.), 15–27. Lanham, Md.: University Press of America.

Zimmerman, B.J. 1979. Concepts and classification. In *The Functions of Language and Cognition*, G.J. Whitehurst and B.J. Zimmerman (eds), 57–81. New York: Academic Press.

3 New epistemological perspectives for the archaeology of writing

PAUL A. BOUISSAC

The global search for the earliest forms of writing – and thus for the most ancient documented languages – should be distinguished from the ideological, or utopian quest for an 'Edenic' or 'Adamic', 'pre-Babel' language. Whereas the latter endeavour can be justifiably discredited because of its mythical and ethnocentric nature, the former appears to constitute a legitimate scientific inquiry – both in view of a history of successful decipherments which have consistently pushed back in time the earliest scriptural evidence, and with respect to the convergence of a set of arguments, tending to establish the plausibility of much earlier beginnings than currently accepted.

Moreover, the paradigm shift which is presently occurring in linguistics produces heuristic models and addresses fundamental issues which give relevance to the sort of questions that the search for palaeographic systems necessarily raises. The theoretical approach first propounded by Chomsky in the 1960s – and which reigned supreme, under various revised forms, until the 1980s in many influential linguistic circles – provided a particularly unfriendly environment for investigating writing systems and their early forms, if only because such projects cannot avoid tackling more or less directly the problem of the origin of language and its pre- and proto-historic forms. The restrictive assumptions which characterized mainstream linguistics for about three decades are now being increasingly challenged and are even discarded by some of their earlier proponents (Harris 1993). The renewed interest in the evolutionary approach to language is typically illustrated by linguists who, like Bickerton (1990), Pinker and Bloom (1990) or Hawkins and Gell-Mann (1992), recast the problems of the origins of human language abilities in terms of neo-Darwinian theories. From this vantage point it now makes sense to ask what kind of variations and selections, in which ecological contexts, could account for the emergence of the range of capabilities known as language, both in spoken and written forms.

Another significant paradigm shift can be observed in the renewed interest of some theoretical linguists for the hypothetical reconstruction of ancestral linguistic systems based on comparative methods (e.g. for Indo-European:

Polomé and Winter 1992; for attempts to reconstruct broader linguistic families whose branching out can be assumed to have occurred in prehistoric times: Shevoroshkin 1989, 1990, 1992). Indeed, advances in automatic computation and in statistics make it possible to replicate, on a much larger scale and with more inclusive power, the earlier theoretical reconstruction of Indo-European for instance, or of other ancestral linguistic systems from which a variety of languages have evolved. The recent development of collaborative, albeit controversial, efforts between linguists and statisticians to explore possible counter-intuitive derivative relationships between families of languages previously considered unrelated, indicates that a new horizon of research could shatter the currently accepted views mostly based on ahistorical approaches. See for instance Ringe (1992, 1993) and Greenberg (1993) for a debate concerning this issue and its review by Diamond (1993), as well as the recent results of the largest comparison of grammatical structures ever made which indicates that the common ancestor of modern world languages appears to be at least 100,000 years old (Nichols 1992, 1993). The search for evidence of a common ancestry for language macrophyla such as Indo-European, Afroasiatic, Uralic and Dravidian goes well beyond the concerns of linguists proper since 'such relationships would have major implications in anthropology, history, and human genetics' (Diamond 1993: 19), and, naturally, in archaeology and prehistory. These problems are indeed directly related to two of the most pressing topics in human evolution; namely, on the one hand, the 'out of Africa' vs 'multi-regional' hypothesis for the evolution of *Homo sapiens sapiens* (Gibbons 1994) and, on the other hand, whether the evolving of language capabilities is a relatively recent phenomenon or goes back to *Homo erectus* (Falk 1987; Tobias 1988; Koch 1991).

Finally, there is an emerging consensus that the history of writing is in need of being rewritten. The above epistemological context now provides favourable conditions for the exploration of new hypotheses. The standard reference work on the archaeology of writing goes back some forty years (Gelb 1952). Since then, there have been many discoveries and decipherments which have kept pushing back in time the apparition of early scripts or scriptoids (e.g. Schmandt-Besserat 1992), or which have shown that more recent, apparently purely figurative archaeological data were in fact written texts (e.g. Coe 1992; Justeson and Kaufman 1993). The hypothesis that palaeolithic signs, both non-figurative and figurative, might indeed be instances of writing systems is being seriously taken into consideration by some rock-art specialists, even though most are still reluctant to stray away from the early pronouncements of the pioneers of the discipline. The object of this chapter is to present a range of methodological approaches which can be used to test such hypotheses in view of the available data, and to determine some conditions for the productive gathering of new data, since those who made most of the recordings now available as 'rock art' took for granted that the data were not of a linguistic nature. In fact, most early recordings such as Breuil's (1952), whatever their artistic merits may be, are now considered to be so selective that they have little scientific validity. Even more recent, supposedly more rigorous, descriptions and photographic records have been found to be so wanting in terms of systematicity and exhaustivity that they are now in the process of being remade on more rigorous methodological bases (Lorblanchet 1995: 88).

Previous attempts to construe at least some 'rock art' as graphic systems remained suggestive and speculative, based more on impressionistic comparisons than methodical investigations. For instance Petrie (1912), Raphael (1947), and Forbes and Crowder (1979), try to draw general conclusions from sporadic morphological similarities between signs found among more or less realistic representations in cave paintings as well as mobiliary art, and signs belonging to known ancient writing systems, or by calling attention to the potential or probable systematicity of the combinations of items in prehistoric visual displays as they are observable today. But nobody seems to have seriously undertaken to demonstrate such a systematicity and to test its compatibility with the structures of known archaic writing systems or reconstructed proto-languages. A notable exception is Bornefeld (1994) whose idiosyncratic but suggestive decipherments of segments of palaeolithic scripts would deserve more critical attention on the part of rock-art specialists.

Testing the hypothesis that 'rock art', even in its more figurative examples, may actually form a corpus of palaeographic writing systems – as Bornefeld claims – is a legitimate and urgent task (e.g. Bouissac 1991, 1993, 1994a). However, the difficulties cannot be underestimated, and the task must first be divided into a number of sub-tasks. Establishing the systematicity of the organization and combination of signs within the boundaries of a given set, and characterizing such systematicity, constitutes a daunting enterprise whose prerequisites (that is, evidence of the preservation of the original data and completeness of their recording) are not readily afforded by the state of 'rock-art' research (Bednarik 1993, 1994a, 1994b). Demonstrating the probability that the combinatorial systematicity thus established is homologous to the kind of systematicity that is observed in one or several of the known writing systems documented to date is a step which must not be confused with trying to devise strategies for breaking the virtual code that such a systematicity would suggest. It is therefore important to define carefully the tasks involved in each of these stages: (1) establish the reliability of a corpus; (2) establish the systematicity of the organization of the data it contains; (3) establish the compatibility of this systematicity with known linguistic systematicities; (4) decipher the writing code by relating it to a virtual (archaic) language. For this latter stage, the reconstruction, albeit tentative, of proto-languages and macro-families might provide useful constraints for the elaboration of hypotheses.

Let us now tentatively illustrate this heuristic strategy, and the problems it implies, with some examples selected among the abundant descriptive literature in which serious attempts are made at exhaustively recording palaeographic data with a view to preserving in the records the mutual relationships of individual items within a bounded space. The first example is taken from a monograph of the *British Archaeological Reports: Palaeolithic Art in the Grotte de Gargas* (Barrière 1976). This monograph is a careful account of the topography of the cave and the works painted on its walls. These works include a remarkably small number of painted animals (four), but a large number of hands (at least 250) which 'are silhouetted in black or red paint, much more rarely in ochre, and even more rarely in white. They are mainly distributed throughout the first half of the lower cave and are grouped together in various panels' (fourteen). There are also carvings in the lateral galleries and in the second half of the lower cave, which are mostly comprised of animals and 'macaroni' drawings. We shall not deal with these here, but instead focus on the hands which appear to form a synchronic whole. The spacing and state of conservation of the hands seem to indicate that they were painted as an intended set. A great number of them are well preserved, but some are blurred by calcite deposits, or have been watered down or otherwise damaged to the point of being impossible to describe beyond the mere fact that a hand had been painted at this particular spot. The hands which can be described in detail show a clear morphological variety through 'digital' variations; that is, absence or presence of fingers, or parts of fingers, according to the natural division of the human hand into fourteen joints which can be missing because they have been cut, or because they are bent while the hands are being stencilled. Other sources of variations include lateralization (right or left), orientation (horizontal, vertical or oblique) and colour (red or black). Barrière identifies other variations such as the endings of the 'amputated' fingers (plateau, spatulate or pointed), the narrowing of the fingers in their middle (bridge) or the relative dimensions of the hands.

For our present purpose we will temporarily ignore this second set of morphological variations, and focus on the 'digital' variation which offers a clear principle of distinction based on the presence or absence of joints, and does not require qualitative appreciations of continuous forms (i.e. 'plateau', 'bridge', 'spatula'). For an interpretation of these variations, both 'digital' and 'continuous', Barrière relies on the doctoral thesis of Ali Sahly (1969), an earlier investigator of the cave of Gargas. Assuming that all the painted hands reflect the actual morphology of the individual hands which were used for the stencilling, and somewhat arbitrarily excluding ritual mutilation, Sahly proposes no less than twenty-four possible causes of accidental and pathological loss of joints (e.g. frostbite, leprosy, Raynaud's disease). The painted hands can then be considered as individual markings or mere by-products of a hypothetical ritual consisting of painting one's own hand while it rests on the rock.

An alternative hypothesis would be to consider that the morphological variation is intended and systematic rather than accidental or pathological. It is indeed noticeable that these 'hands' are arranged in sequences or clusters on the irregular surface of the cave's 'walls', and that all those which can be clearly identified can be classified according to types. These types are deter-

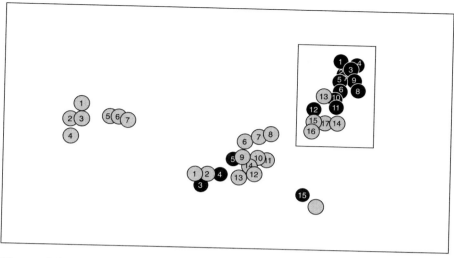

Figure 3.1 Distribution of black and red hands on a wall section of the Gargas cave. The upper-right cluster includes seventeen hands (twelve black, five red). *Source:* Barrière 1976.

mined by the combination of the possibilities of presence or absence of movable elements (whole fingers and phalanges – see Figure 3.1). Obviously, there are some anatomical and physiological constraints upon the range of possible combinations, at least as long as it is assumed that the marks are made by using real live hands rather than artefacts. The two basic matrices formed by human hands can be visualized as follows:

$$
\begin{matrix}
1 & 1 & 1 & 1 & \\
1 & 1 & 1 & 1 & 1 \\
1 & 1 & 1 & 1 & 1
\end{matrix}
\qquad
\begin{matrix}
1 & 1 & 1 & 1 \\
1 & 1 & 1 & 1 & 1 \\
1 & 1 & 1 & 1 & 1
\end{matrix}
$$

The relative proportions of the fingers are irrelevant here since it is the mere presence or absence of some elements which determine the types. Actually, a single matrix would suffice using '0' in order to indicate 'right' or 'left', and '–' or '+' for the absence or presence of an element:

$$
\begin{matrix}
+ & + & + & + & 0 \\
+ & + & + & + & + \\
+ & + & + & + & +
\end{matrix}
\qquad
\begin{matrix}
0 & + & + & + & + \\
+ & + & + & + & + \\
+ & + & + & + & +
\end{matrix}
$$

Among the various hands described by Barrière we find for instance:

$$
\begin{matrix}
- & - & - & + & 0 \\
- & - & - & + & + \\
+ & + & + & + & +
\end{matrix}
\qquad
\begin{matrix}
0 & - & - & - & - \\
+ & - & - & - & - \\
+ & - & - & - & -
\end{matrix}
$$

From this basis, it is possible to calculate the combinatorial power of the matrix, taking into account the constraints mentioned above, and to generate the types which are possible. By assigning a type to each instance of hands in the corpus formed by the Grotte de Gargas, we can determine the number of types used and identify patterns of recurrence along the sequences or in the clusters. If it can be shown that the combinations of types are not random, and that some particular groupings occur repeatedly, it would seem likely that we are in the presence of a code devised for calculations or for providing graphic renderings of articulate sounds – let them be words, syllables or phonemes. From this stage on, we could rely on epigraphic methods to restore the 'message' in its integrity by determining the most likely candidates for the hands which have been blurred or are otherwise indecipherable because of calcite deposits and other natural accidents. The antiquity of the data makes it quite improbable that a credible linguistic deciphering could be achieved. However, showing that the formal properties of these strings of signs are compatible with what we know of linguistic patterns would drastically modify our perception of early humans, and, more importantly, would undoubtedly enhance the sensitivity of those who are engaged in investigating and recording their graphic traces.

Meticulous recordings like Barrière's, in which each single instance of a hand is described, are an absolute prerequisite for such an inquiry, even if they have been undertaken with different assumptions. In the present case, the anatomical and pathological biases of the investigators served well the precision and exactness of the recordings in view of the sort of testing which is suggested in this chapter. It is interesting to note that Barrière (1981: 83) indicates in a summary titled 'Forms of mutilation' that '16 fundamental forms can be observed', and that 'the number of hands gives a false impression: one can see quite clearly that some hands, often those most severely mutilated, are repeated over and over again'.

The second example is drawn from Malmer's *A Chorological Study of North European Rock Art* (1981). This study bears upon the distribution of some 40,000 petroglyphic items over a vast area comprising Scandinavia and some portions of northern Europe. It uses as primary data a corpus of rock-art records published between 1881 and 1976. These include Hallstrom's well-known documenting of the rock carving of northern Norway and Sweden. Malmer is interested in what he calls 'motifs', i.e. categories of identifiable items such as boats, animals, foot designs and so on. Treating each item as an independent unit definable by its type or sub-type, he attempts to show statistically how the relative concentration of some types makes it possible to determine the boundaries of areas characterized by the predominance of some motifs or combinations of motifs. He is also concerned by the chronological problem of the patterns of diffusion or spreading of these motifs. Although this sort of inquiry is somewhat alien to the thrust of the hypothesis which is explored in this chapter, his method of investigation yields interesting data which are highly relevant to this hypothesis. Malmer distinguishes, indeed,

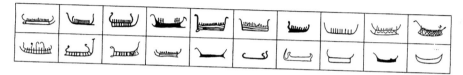

Figure 3.2 Sample of 'ship' designs in Scandinavian rock engravings.
Source: Malmer 1981.

within each type, those differences which appear to be mere accidental variations in the execution of the design, from those which are the results of the combining of design features whose list he tries to establish. Some of his findings would appear to be analogous to the distribution patterns of several contiguous writing systems.

One of the types Malmer analyses in detail is what he calls 'ships' (see Figure 3.2). Images of ships carved in the rock in clusters or in rows are distinguished from one another by a limited number of design features which can be present or absent in each instance of the type. For example: gunwale, keel, prow (on either sides or on both sides), 'ribs' (i.e. partition lines on the ship's hull), 'crew' (i.e. vertical strokes above the gunwale). And so on. Interestingly, Malmer notes that 'theoretically this system has a capacity of 135 mutually exclusive types'; but, because some characteristics are incompatible, the real capacity is ninety-nine types according to Malmer (14). However, his main concern is to correlate types and proportion of types to geographic areas, rather than study the patterns of their groupings and sequences and their combinations with other types.

Tilley (1991) examined a portion of the same corpus; namely, the records made by Hallstrom at Namforsen, in which two categories of motifs (in Malmer's sense) dominate: ships and elks. Like Malmer, but with a different interpretative goal, Tilley focuses on the combination of features which generates a number of types and sub-types approximately equal for both motifs. Tilley (1991: 104) notes that on individual carving surfaces 'on which only elks and boats are depicted a systematic relation of dispersion occurs involving:

(i) Linearity: Elks and boats may be aligned in rows either horizontally or vertically.
(ii) Superpositioning: Elks and boats may be superimposed.
(iii) Opposition: Elks and boats may be systematically structured in relation to each other.'

If this characterization of Namforsen is compared to Malmer's conclusions regarding the distribution of both motifs over the whole geographic area (e.g. two-thirds of ship designs occur in a zone of central Scandinavia), a tentative hypothesis could be that ship types and elk types in combination with other designs form two different graphic codes used to write either two different languages or the same language in two different graphic systems.

The two examples above – Barrière's and Malmer's inventories – have been chosen because they provide exhaustive and systematic descriptions of a range of consistent types on the background of theoretical views which were not biased by the sort of approach which is propounded in this chapter. Other sets of recorded data could have been used as equally interesting illustrations of the fact that palaeographic 'art' can often be characterized by formal features which could satisfy the requirements of hieroglyphic, syllabic or alphabetical systems in view of the wealth of knowledge yielded by landmark decipherments such as Linear B (Chadwick 1958) or the Maya code (Coe 1992). As indicated above, linguistic research bearing upon the gestural origin of syntax (Armstrong et al. 1994) or on the reconstruction of language macro-families (Shevoroshkin 1989) provides an epistemological context conducive to such endeavours. The brain sciences, evolutionary biology and cultural archaeology lead to a notion of 'archaic language' far more ancient than previously assumed – in the order of two million years (e.g. Deacon 1992).

The current views question the notion of a sudden apparition of language, speech as well as writing, as a sort of 'big bang' or 'miracle' due to a genetic mutation, the invention of a genius, or the advent of 'civilization'. Biological, ecological and social strictures upon the evolution of communication systems make such dramatic and simplistic scenarios unlikely (Bouissac 1994b). The emerging picture is far more complex and allows for parallel developments, false starts, diverging variety and so on. As Deacon puts it:

> [two million years] is time enough for many features of language to have arisen, flourished, and perished without a trace. It is also time enough for there to have been many stages of archaic language, and for each of these to influence and be influenced by brain and vocal tract evolution.
>
> (Deacon 1992: 77)

The evidence reviewed in Deacon's state-of-the-art article yields some hint of the nature of archaic languages and, indirectly, provides the comprehensive ground which situates the quest for palaeolithic scripts within a horizon of plausibility.

However, demonstrating that within a given area a set of consistent design-types show some recurring patterns of organization and variation – a task which should be relatively easy provided that fairly large data bases of sequences and clusters (rather than individual design items) are available – does not constitute an absolute proof that we are in the presence of linguistic data. It would nevertheless provide an impetus towards more complete and systematic research, and might even influence the way in which palaeographic records are established. As long as 'art' or 'symbol' remain the pervasive concepts which set the researchers' agenda, their attention will be focused on the individual qualities of visual motifs perceived as if they were displayed in frames, and reproduced as such in rectangular photographs, often more appropriate for coffee-table books than for methodical inquiries. Fortunately, there has been a marked change over the last few decades, when hypotheses regarding the potential symbolic relevance of the distribution of figures and their mutual relations within a site (e.g. Raphael 1945; Leroi-Gourhan 1958; Lewis-Williams 1981) have motivated more comprehensive recordings. But the assumption that those humans who engraved and painted the rocks *were pre-literate as well as pre-historic* has continued to bias the records to a degree (Leroi-Gourhan quoted by Demoule 1991). A huge task lies ahead if the tentative testing of the script hypothesis is to yield some positive results. The research agenda would then include attempts to relate contiguous graphic codes to each other as well as to the most archaic reconstructed languages, thus opening new avenues to palaeography, cryptology, and the archaeology of writing.

REFERENCES

Armstrong, D.F., W.C. Stokoe and S.E. Wilcox. 1994. Signs of the origin of syntax. *Current Anthropology*, 35(4), 349–68.

Barrière, Cl. 1976 *L'art pariétal de la Grotte de Gargas* [Palaeolithic Art in the Grotte de Gargas] *[par] Cl. Barrière; avec la collaboration du Ali Sahly et des élèves de l'Institut d'art préhistorique de Toulouse*; translated from the French by W.A. Drapkin. Oxford: British Archaeological Reports, Supplementary Series 14 (i).

Bednarik, R.G. 1993. Developments in Rock Art Dating. *Acta Archaeologica* 63, 141–55.

Bednarik, R.G. 1994a. A taphonomy of palaeoart. *Antiquity* 68(258), 68–74.

Bednarik, R.G. 1994b. On the scientific study of palaeoart. *Semiotica* 100(3/4), 141–68.

Bickerton, D. 1990. *Language and Species*. Chicago: University of Chicago Press.

Bornefeld, H.W. 1994. *The Keys to the Caverns. The Ice-age inscriptions, a partial decipherment of the enigmatic signs and animal pictures in Gaul and Iberia*. Kiel: Privately published.

Bouissac, P. 1991. Describing and interpreting prehistoric pictographs and engravings. In *Valcamonica 1991. Prehistoric and Tribal Art. Old World and New World: convergences and divergences*, 63–7. Capo di Ponte (Italy): Centro Camuno di Studi Preistorici.

Bouissac, P. 1993a. Beyond style: steps towards a semiotic hypothesis. In *Rock Art Studies: the post-stylistic era*, M. Lorblanchet and P. Bahn (eds), 203–6. Oxford: Oxbow Monograph 35.

Bouissac, P. 1993b. Ecology of semiotic space: competition, exploitation and the evolution of arbitrary signs. *The American Journal of Semiotics* 10(3–4), 143–63.

Bouissac, P. 1994a. Introduction: a challenge for semiotics. *Semiotica* 100(3/4), 99–107 (Special issue on 'Prehistoric Signs', P. Bouissac (ed.)).

Bouissac, P. 1994b. Art or script? A falsifiable semiotic hypothesis. *Semiotica* 100(3/4), 349–67.

Breuil, H. 1952. *Quatre cents siècles d'art pariétal*. Montignac: Centre d'études et de documentation.

Chadwick, J. 1958. *The Decipherment of Linear B*. Cambridge: Cambridge University Press.

Coe, M.D. 1992. *Breaking the Maya Code*. New York: Thames & Hudson.

Deacon, T.W. 1992. Brain-language coevolution. In *The Evolution of Human Languages*, J.A. Hawkins and M. Gell-Mann (eds), 49–83. Redwood City: Addison-Wesley.

Demoule, J.-P. 1991. Les images sans les paroles. *Destins de l'image. Nouvelle Revue de Psychanalyse* 44, 37–56.

Diamond, J.M. 1993. Mathematics in linguistics. *Nature* 366, 19–20.

Falk, D. 1987. Hominid Paleoneurology. *Annual Review of Anthropology* 16, 13–30.

Forbes, A. Jr. and T.R. Crowder 1979. The problem of Franco-Cantabrian abstract signs: agenda for a new approach. *World Archaeology* 10(3), 350–66.

Gelb, I.J. 1952. *A Study of Writing: the foundation of grammatology*. Chicago: University of Chicago Press.

Gibbons, A. 1994. Rewriting – and redating – prehistory. *Science* 263, 1087–8.

Greenberg, J.H. 1993. Observations concerning Ringe's *Calculating the factor of chance in language comparison*. *Proceedings of the American Philosophical Society* 137, 79–90.

Harris, R.A. 1993. *The Linguistics Wars*. Oxford: Oxford University Press.

Hawkins, J.A. and M. Gell-Mann (eds) 1992. *The Evolution of Human Languages*. *Proceedings Vol. XI*. Santa Fe Institute for Studies in the Sciences of Complexity. Redwood City: Addison-Wesley Publishing Co.

Justeson, J.S. and T. Kaufman. 1993. A decipherment of epi-olmec hieroglyphic writing. *Science* 259, 1703–11.

Koch, W.A. 1991. *Language in the Upper Pleistocene*. Bochum: Brockmeyer.

Leroi-Gourhan, A. 1958. Répartition et groupement des animaux dans l'art pariétal paléolithique. *Bulletin de la Société Préhistorique Française* 55, 515–28.

Leroi-Gourhan, A. 1992. *L'art pariétal: Langage de la préhistoire*. Grenoble: Jerome Millon.

Lewis-Williams, J.D. 1981. *Believing and Seeing. Symbolic meanings in southern San rock paintings*. New York: Academic Press.

Lorblanchet, M. 1995. *Les grottes ornées de la préhistoire. Nouveaux regards*. Paris: Editions Errance.

Malmer, M.P. 1981. *A Chorological Study of North European Rock Art*. Stockholm: Almqvist & Wiksel International.

Nichols, J. 1992. *Linguistic Diversity in Space and Time*. Chicago: University of Chicago Press.

Nichols, J. 1993. Ergativity and linguistic geography. *Australian Journal of Linguistics* 13, 39–89.

Petrie, W.M.F. 1912. *The Formation of the Alphabet*. London: Macmillan.

Pinker, S. and Bloom, P. 1990. Natural language and natural selection. *Behavioral and Brain Sciences* 13(4), 707–27.

Polomé, E.C. and W. Winter (eds) 1992. *Reconstructing Languages and Cultures*. Trends in Linguistics, Studies and Monographs 58. Berlin and New York: Mouton De Gruyter.

Raphael, M. 1945. *Prehistoric Cave Paintings*. New York: Pantheon Books.

Raphael, M. 1947. *Prehistoric Pottery and Civilization in Egypt*. Bollingen Foundation. Washington, DC: Pantheon Books,

Ringe, D.A. Jr. 1992. On calculating the factor chance in language comparison. *Transactions of the American Philosophical Society* 82, 1–110.

Ringe, D.A. Jr. 1993. A reply to Professor Greenberg. *Proceedings of the American Philosophical Society* 137, 91–109.

Sahly, A. 1969. Le problème des mains mutilées dans l'art préhistorique. Thèse de Doctorat des Lettres, Université de Toulouse. Tunis et Toulouse.

Schmandt-Besserat, D. 1992. *Before Writing* (2 vols). Austin: University of Texas Press.

Shevoroshkin, V. (ed.) 1989. *Explorations in Language Macrofamilies*. Bochum: Brockmeyer.

Shevoroshkin, V. (ed.) 1990. *Proto-Languages and Proto-Cultures*. Bochum: Brockmeyer.

Shevoroshkin, V. (ed.) 1992. *Nostratic, Dene-Caucasian, Austric and Amerind*. Bochum: Brockmeyer.

Tilley, C. 1991. *Material Culture and Text. The art of ambiguity*. London: Routledge.

Tobias, P.V. 1988. The brain of *Homo habilis*: a new level of organization in cerebral evolution. *Journal of Human Evolution* 16, 741–61.

Part II

DEEP-LEVEL LINKAGES/ HYPOTHESES

4 Principles for palaeolinguistic reconstruction

IRÉN HEGEDÜS

ABBREVIATIONS

(P)AA	(Proto-)Afroasiatic		(P)K	(Proto-)Kartvelian
(P)A	(Proto-)Altaic		(P)N	(Proto-)Nostratic
(P)D	(Proto-)Dravidian		(P)U	(Proto-)Uralic
(P)IE	(Proto-)Indo-European			

INTRODUCTION

Over the past three decades historical-comparative linguistics has witnessed the transgression of what was previously considered to be the ultimate time limit in the applicability of the traditional method. The main driving force for this has been the Nostratic hypothesis which first postulated the feasibility of a macrophylum consisting of six language phyla (Indo-European, Afroasiatic, Kartvelian, Uralic, Altaic, Dravidian).[1] This major breakthrough, however, has been met with antagonism due to the misunderstanding that the Nostratic theory violates the rules and methods of traditional historical-comparative linguistics. This chapter clarifies some of the principles followed in linguistic reconstruction at 'greater-than-usual' time-depth and tries to analyse the recent ambiguities concerning the time-depth of Nostratic.

Linguistic reconstruction – as practised for a century and a half – is directed at recovering the history of languages and at deducing their common ancestral forms. As the method has emerged in the historical-comparative study of Indo-European languages, the time limit up to which the method can be applied has been associated with the age of the reconstructed ancestor of all Indo-European languages which can be dated at *c.* 6000 BC. This tacit consensus seems to be one of the main obstacles blocking progress in the field of comparing the well-established language families (i.e. their reconstructed proto-languages). Therefore one of the major points to be discussed in the paper will be a survey of diverging and contradicting ideas concerning the applicability of the traditional historical-comparative method in linguistic reconstruction at 'greater-than-usual time depth'. My own position is that there is no reason to constrain the applicability of the traditional method as long as its basic principles are observed, i.e. we need to establish regular sound correspondences and solid semantic connections in order to find lexical and morphological cognates.[2]

PROBLEMS OF CHRONOLOGY AND TAXONOMY

The other central question relates to the problems of chronology. There still seems to be a question over time-depths of reconstructions and in that of the taxonomy of the reconstructed systems. Consequently, the absence of a well-defined relative chronology of reconstructed stages has caused both a proliferation in the construction of possible (or impossible) linguistic family trees and ambiguities in the terminology applied in referring to reconstructed systems pertaining to greater time-depths. 'Preprotolinguistics' and 'palaeolinguistics' have often been used as generic terms for linguistic investigations directed at stages preceding the time-depth of traditionally reconstructed proto-languages, and the term 'palaeolinguistics' is often used also for stages in which the human language as such evolved. The ambiguous usage leads to confusion, so a clarification and a consensus is desirable. The need for developing consistent terminology is expressed – among others – by Henrik Birnbaum:

> the possibility must be considered of positing distant genetic relationships among several broader language families, such as Indo-European, Uralic, Altaic, Kartvelian, Dravidian, Semitic-Hamitic, and that these genetic groups form what may be termed 'macro-families'. [. . .] such macrofamilies would point to the existence of yet farther removed and, by the same token, much wider ranging ancestral languages which may tentatively, and *for want of a better term, be labeled 'preprotolanguages'* [emphasis added]
>
> (Birnbaum 1980: 126–7)

Ten years ago Gyula Décsy proposed a taxonomy that is basically correct in its approach, although the dates that he provided may need adjustment in the light of present-day knowledge about the emergence and subsequent divergence of articulate human language(s). Proceeding in a retrospective order (taking the most recent period first) Table 4.1 summarizes the categories established by Décsy (1983: 49) and the modifications proposed here. The taxonomy is flexible because the time limits are set in relation to each other and they can be adjusted according to new results. The underlying principle is relative chronology: the estimation of absolute time-depth for different reconstructed systems may change, but this should not necessarily alter the relation between the reconstructed systems. The temporal limits are dependent on actual diachronic research (linguistic or other) and are thus

Table 4.1   Comparison of Décsy and Hegedüs schemas

Décsy (1983: 49)	Hegedüs (this chapter)
Proto-linguistics	Protolinguistics (5,000–13,000 BC) ?[Pre-Protolinguistics:]
Pre-proto-linguistics (10,000–6,000/4,000 BC)	
Palaeo-linguistics (20,000–10,000 BC)	Palaeolinguistics (13,000–25,000 BC)
Archaeo-linguistics (30,000–20,000 BC)	Archaeolinguistics (25,000–40,000 BC)
Glottogony (c. 35,000 BC)	Glossogenetics (prior to 40,000 BC)

Notes:

1 The category of 'pre-proto-linguistics' is rather imprecise: it could refer to any period preceding the protolinguistic stage. So the term should perhaps be dispensed with or, if it is to be retained, it could be used as a cover term for palaeolinguistics and archaeolinguistics since these precede the protolinguistic stage. As a cover term for palaeolinguistics and archaeolinguistics it may lead to an undesired juxtaposition of protolinguistics on the one hand and paleo- and archaeolinguistics on the other hand.

2 Protolinguistics refers to the period for which we possess well-established and extensively reconstructed proto-languages like Proto-Indo-European, Proto-Uralic, Proto-Afroasiatic, etc. ranging between 5,000–13,000 years BC. This is the stage where the application of the traditional historical-comparative method is unanimously supported by the community of linguists. Here it should be noted, however, that the supposedly incorrect extension of the method to earlier stages of language history is based on the 'myth' that the traditional method cannot be used for reconstruction at a time-depth greater than c. 6,000 years BC – a view based on the Indo-Europeanist tradition, where the method yields a proto-language of that age. There are various dates given as the ultimate time limit for the applicability of the traditional historical-comparative method which is indicative of the probable incorrectness of the Indo-Europeanist position. Mary R. Key observed that 'there are no criteria, in comparative linguistics, to indicate how far back one can go with the comparative method' (Key 1981:18). Moreover, there are proto-languages that are safely reconstructed in accordance with the traditional method, yet the resulting reconstructions go back to at least 10–12,000 years BC (cf. Proto-Afroasiatic, Proto-Australian).

3 Palaeolinguistics refers to the period of reconstructed macrophyla like Proto-Nostratic, Proto-Sino-Caucasian, etc. that can be dated between approximately 13,000–25,000 years BC. These would constitute the ancestral systems for the established proto-languages. The best-developed reconstruction of such a macrophylum is represented by Nostratic.

4 Archaeolinguistics will designate the period of superphyla recoverable by comparison with the reconstructed systems of the palaeolinguistic stage (approx. 26,000–40,000 BC). Some attempts have already been made in this direction,[3] and there is already a good basis for knowing which macrophyla look like good candidates for comparison and would perhaps yield regular sound correspondences.

5 Glottogony, or rather glossogenetics,[4] refers to the period of the emergence of the language(s) of *Homo sapiens sapiens*; chronologically it is identifiable with the time prior to 40,000 BC, beginning with the time of the emergence of Modern Man – to whatever date it is related.[5]

6 Décsy set the temporal borders between the different stages in his taxonomy on a purely arbitrary basis (at least I cannot see any apparent reason that would justify or motivate his dates). The modifications made here are significant in two respects: the taxonomy is *motivated* and *flexible*. This modified taxonomy is motivated by recent advances made in interphyletic comparisons during the past decade or so and fulfils the expectation that different levels of reconstruction should be separated and kept apart.

flexible. Its advantage is that it can be subject to modification as far as the actual dates are concerned but the time limits are fixed as far as the reconstructed taxa are concerned. Practically this means that, for example, Proto-Nostratic will never slip over from the palaeolinguistic to the archaeolinguistic level, even if in the future it may turn out to belong to a time considerably earlier than 13,000 BC. Similarly, the onset of the archaeolinguistic period may be adjusted to an earlier date if palaeoanthropology, archaeology, etc. would point to that in the future.

Interphyletic linguistic comparison thus means a systematic investigation of similarities between language families (phyla, e.g. Indo-European, Uralic, Afroasiatic, etc.) or between macrophyla (e.g. Nostratic, Sino-Tibetan, etc.) with an aim of establishing regular sound correspondences where possible and finding structural (morphological) correspondences that conform to the already established regular sound correspondences. As a corollary we could further assume that once regular sound correspondences are established, all the lexical and morphological correspondences that are semantically feasible and at the same time show regular sound correspondences are to be considered cognates, i.e. items with semantic and phonological similarity due to genetic inheritance, until proven otherwise. The case for genetic relationship will be corroborated if the reconstructed macrophylum or superphylum also explains linguistic forms that systematically differ from the phonologically expected development. Interphyletic comparison will imply investigations on the level of the palaeolinguistic and archaeolinguistic stages. The interdependence hierarchy between the stages is obvious: palaeolinguistic reconstruction is fed by results of protolinguistics and it can be corrective of protolinguistic reconstruction; at the same time, archaeolinguistics is to build on the achievements of palaeolinguistics and may be corrective of palaeolinguistics.

SOME PRINCIPLES TO OBSERVE IN LINGUISTIC RECONSTRUCTION IN THE DIFFERENT STAGES

Protolinguistic reconstruction

(a) One or two intermediary reconstructed levels are allowed, the constituents for reconstruction are mostly extant languages; some languages may have seemingly linear descent from the proto-language, i.e. no intermediary proto-stage is reconstructed in their evolution (divergence nodes are missing) because related languages within the branch are lost (e.g. one-member branches within Indo-European like Albanian, Armenian, Greek).

(b) Each and every branch may have an intermediary proto-stage connecting them to their ancestral proto-language.

(c) The result of linguistic reconstruction on this level is a proto-language, ancestor of a linguistic phylum. Specimen proto-languages are PIE, PU, PD, etc.

(d) The extreme time-depth of protolinguistics equals the age of the oldest reconstructed proto-language whichever language family it should belong to. The flexibility of my proposed system is exemplified by the easy accommodation of the changing date of the Afroasiatic proto-language (cf. section on time-depth ambiguities, pp. 70–1).

Palaeolinguistic reconstructions

(a) Palaeolinguistic reconstruction is based on the systemic comparison of proto-languages established by protolinguistics. Evidence from extant languages cannot be directly compared unless it conforms to already established regular sound correspondences. A phenomenon considered to be peripheral in a language family and showing semantic/phonological correspondence in another language family or language families, where the same phenomenon is well-attested and therefore reconstructed as an etymon going back to the protolinguistic level, will be considered archaic in palaeolinguistic reconstruction and will be treated as a possible cognate between the language families concerned.

(b) The result of reconstruction on this level will be a protomacrolanguage, the ancestor of a linguistic macrophylum. Specimens of macrophyla are Nostratic, Sino–Caucasian, Proto-Pama-Nyungan,[6] etc.

(c) The borderline between the protolinguistic and palaeolinguistic levels is dependent on location and on which language family we have to do with; just as in archaeology, we cannot locate something in time by simply stating that it belongs to the period of Neolithic without also stating the spatial location of the thing in question, because in different geographical regions the Neolithic started with significant differences in time. The plasticity of the protolinguistic–palaeolinguistic interface is illustrated in Figure 4.1.

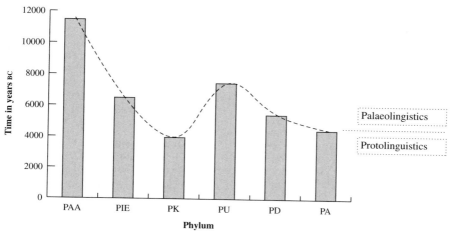

Figure 4.1 Estimated time-depths for major phyla.

Archaeolinguistic reconstruction

(a) Archaeolinguistic reconstruction will be based on the systemic comparison of macrophyla established by palaeolinguistics.

(b) Result of reconstruction on this level will yield archaeolanguages that will come close to the size of continental phyla. Several attempts have been made at comparing reconstructed macrophyla, e.g. Nostratic and Sino-Caucasian (Starostin 1989a, 1989b). American Indian languages are probably related on the archaeolinguistic level.

Basically the method applied in proto-, palaeo- and archaeolinguistics is the same, but it is most important to distinguish between the taxonomic place of the resulting reconstructions.

Glossogenetics

Contrary to the principles outlined in the previous sections, glossogenetics does (and should) not operate with linguistic reconstruction techniques. As the term itself already implies, it is not a linguistics sub-discipline. I would prefer to keep the theoretical possibility open that the results of archaeolinguistic reconstruction (if any!) could be used as input for further comparison as long as the results seem to be convergent. However, the results of archaeolinguistic research cannot form an input to glossogenetic investigation in the same obvious fashion as do those of protolinguistics to palaeolinguistics or palaeolinguistics to archaeolinguistics. Even though evolutionary continuity implies the existence of an interface between the archaeolinguistic and glottogenetic stages, this interface has to be very differently structured from the ones between the other stages. Therefore, archaeolinguistics will not tell us about the process in which human language emerged.

TIME-DEPTH AMBIGUITIES AND THE NOSTRATIC HYPOTHESIS

The Nostratic hypothesis postulates genetic relationship originally among six language phyla (PIE, PAA, PK, PU, PA, PD). Over eighty years have passed since the introduction of the Nostratic hypothesis, and some linguists still think that the Nostratic theory aims at uncovering the origin of language.[7] Nostratic theory is a development in linguistics that can have only *indirect* relevance for language origins research, which is well demonstrated by the levels of reconstruction presented above. This indirect relevance of the Nostratic theory for language origins research derives from the fact that the reconstructed Proto-Nostratic forms show similarity with those of other macrophyla, and thus Nostratic evidence is utilized in reconstructing an even deeper level of language history. Nostratic linguistics in itself has nothing to do with language origins research; it clearly belongs to the palaeolinguistic stage (see Table 4.1). At the same time, Nostratic materials can be compared with other reconstructed macrophyla, thus increasing the time-depth of linguistic reconstructions.

Time-depth ambiguities for the Nostratic macrophylum result from both internal and external factors. Internally, we have to face the problem of the increasing age of constituent proto-languages. The main dilemma is caused by the revision of the age of PAA, which turns out to be older than previous opinion. This circumstance can lead to two conclusions relevant for Proto-Nostratic:

(a) PAA is not a Nostratic sub-branch because chronologically it existed simultaneously, and is thus a sister system to Nostratic;
(b) PAA is still to be considered a sub-branch of Nostratic, but this circumstance will then force us to re-evaluate the age of the Proto-Nostratic unity.

Externally, we need to be careful with comparisons of Nostratic with other macrophyla. When trying to find an affiliation between PN and Proto-Amerind, it is crucial to observe the probable taxonomic difference between them: PN is 'only' a macrophylum, while Proto-Amerind would be the ancestor of a continental size superphylum. The taxonomy I propose here may help in solving this dilemma such as that reflected in Figure 4.2.

Amerind diverged much earlier from the same archaeolanguage, while Proto-Nostratic represents a later node in the archaeolinguistic tree.

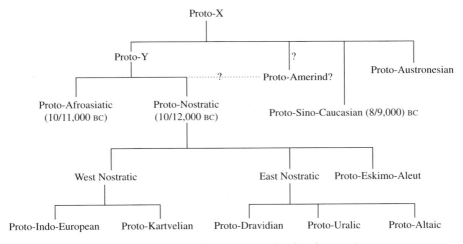

Figure 4.2 Proposed taxonomy of Nostratic and related groupings.

Source: After Aikhenvald-Angenot and Angenot 1989: 2.

ACKNOWLEDGEMENTS

The author would like to acknowledge the assistance of the Fulbright Commission, under whose auspices much of this chapter was prepared, and the Hungarian Ministry of Education and World Archaeological Congress for assistance and the opportunity to attend the WAC-III conference and present this material.

NOTES

1   The hypothesis of a Nostratic phylum was first proposed by Holger Pedersen in 1903; later the hypothesis was further developed by V.I. Illič-Svityč, A. Dolgopolsky *et al.* The opinion of some linguists involved in Nostratic research may diverge as to what languages or language families should be classified as Nostratic. However, the above-mentioned six families constitute the 'classical' notion of Nostratic and I think it can indeed be expanded in the future.

2   My opinion on this point will be convergent with that of Birnbaum (1977, 1980, 1989), Eckert (1973), Key (1981), Vovin (1994).

3   For example, Starostin's comparison of Nostratic and Sino-Caucasian (Starostin 1989a, 1989b), Austronesian additions by Pejros to Starostin's data (Pejros 1989).

4   Éric de Grolier (pers. comm. 14 July 1993) has called my attention to the fact that the term 'glottogony' is unfortunate because it has often been misused. In accordance with his proposal I decided to use the term 'glossogenetics' instead. The definition of this term has been given as the following: 'glossogenetics is the study of formation and development – ontogenetically as well as phylogenetically – of human language' (Grolier 1983: 533–4).

5   Some researchers argue that human language emerged coevally with Modern Man (*Homo sapiens sapiens*) *c.* 100,000 years BP (Cavalli-Sforza *et al.* 1988; Mellars 1989; Renfrew 1989).

6   Editors' note. This status for Pama-Nyungan is absolutely at variance with common opinion among Australianists (see Evans and McConvell, Volume II).

7   Cf. Reinhardt's idea: Die nostratische Hypothese der Sprachverwandtschaft bedeutet ohne Zweifel einen großen Schritt nach vorne unter den verschiedenen glottogonen Theorien. [The Nostratic hypothesis of language relationship undoubtedly means a big step forward for the various glottogonic theories.] (Reinhardt 1988: 288).

REFERENCES

Aikhenvald-Angenot, A.Y. and J.-P. Angenot. 1989. The Old World (Proto-Nostratic, Proto-Sino-Caucasian, Proto-Austronesian) and the South-American Proto-Je. Paper read at the 4th Encontro Nacional da Anpoll, São Paulo, Brazil (26–28 July). 10 pp.

Birnbaum, H. 1977. *Linguistic Reconstruction: its potential and limitations in new perspective* (*Journal of Indo-European Studies*, Monograph Series 2). Washington DC.

Birnbaum, H. 1980. On protolanguages, diachrony and 'pre-protolanguages' (Toward a typology of linguistic reconstruction). In *Studia Linguistica in Honorem Vladimir I. Georgiev*, 121–9. Sofia.

Birnbaum, H. 1989. Genetic and typological approaches to external comparison of languages. In *Explorations in Language Macrofamilies. Materials from the First International Interdisciplinary Symposium on Language and Prehistory, Ann Arbor, 1988*, V.V. Shevoroshkin (ed.), 10–33. Bochum: Universitätsverlag Brockmeyer (Bochum Publications in Evolutionary Cultural Semiotics Vol. 23).

Cavalli-Sforza, L.L., A. Piazza, P. Menozzi and J. Mountain. 1988. Reconstruction of human evolution: bringing together genetic, archeological and linguistic data. *Proceedings of the National Academy of Sciences* 85, 6002–6.

Décsy, Gy (ed.). 1983. *Global Linguistic Connections*. Bibliotheca Nostratica vol. 5., Bloomington, Ind.: Eurolingua.

Eckert, R. 1973. Review of V.M. Illič-Svityč 'Opyt sravnenija nostratičeskih jazykov. Vol. 1. Moscow, Nauka. 1971'. *Zeitschrift für Phonetik, Sprachwissenschaft und Kommunikationsforschung*, 26(3–4), 395–401.

Grolier, É. de. 1983. Proposal for a transdisciplinary symposium on glossogenetics. In *Glossogenetics. The origin and evolution of language*, É. de Grolier. (ed.), 533–42. Chur, London, Paris, Utrecht, New York: Harwood Academic Publishers.

Key, M.R. 1981. *Intercontinental Linguistic Connections*. Humanities Inaugural Lecture Series, 30 pp. Irvine: University of California.

Mellars, P. 1989. Major issues in the emergence of modern humans. *Current Anthropology* 30(3), 349–85.

Pedersen, H. 1903. Türkische Lautgesetze. *Zeitschrift der deutschen morgenländischen Gesellschaft* 57, 535–61.

Pejros, I.I. 1989. Dopolnenije k gipoteze S.A. Starostina o rodstve nostratičeskih i sino-kavkazskih jazykov [Supplement to S.A. Starostin's hypothesis of the relationship between Nostratic and Sino-Caucasian languages (in Russian)]. In *Lingvističeskaja rekonstrukcija i drevnejšaja istorija Vostoka* vol. 1, I.S. Bljumhen *et al.* (eds), 125–30. Moscow: Institute of Oriental Studies – USSR Academy of Sciences.

Reinhardt, J. 1988. Holzwege der nostratischen Sprachwissenschaft. In *Akten der 13. österreichischen Linguistentagung*, 275–85. Graz.

Renfrew, C. 1989. Models of change in language and archaeology. *Transactions of the Philological Society*, 87(2), 103–55.

Starostin, S.A. 1989a. Nostratic and Sino-Caucasian. In *Lingvističeskaja rekonstrukcija i drevnejšaja istorija Vostoka* vol. 1, I.S. Bljumhen *et al.* (eds), 106–24. Moscow: Institute of Oriental Studies – USSR Academy of Sciences.

Starostin, S.A. 1989b. Nostratic and Sino-Caucasian. In *Explorations in Language Macrofamilies*, V.V. Shevoroshkin (ed.), 42–66. Bochum: Universitätsverlag Brockmeyer.

Vovin, A. 1994. Long-distance relationships, reconstruction methodology, and the origins of Japanese. *Diachronica* 9(1), 95–114.

5 The diffusion of modern languages in prehistoric Eurasia

Marcel Otte

THE PRINCIPLE

Lithic industries help one retrace how fossilized concepts fit together: they thus provide an account of an evolution of thought (Leroi-Gourhan 1964). Their shapes are innovatory and repetitive plastic creations; they are the outcome of gestures, recur and become more complex over time. A lithic industry is proof of a 'minimal' capacity for mastering abstractions as well as for the function of teaching and transmitting information. Concepts and language seem to go together and depend on each other (Bühler 1990). The concepts required for technology therefore demand an equivalent degree of language, necessary both for the control of gestures and for explanation during transmission (Light and Girotto 1989). So the origin of language is a purely theoretical notion since it simply corresponds to the developmental stages of thought as reflected in behaviour. There is no precise moment of the origin of language, any more than there is one of the origins of humanity itself. For every stage of evolution there is a corresponding stage in the development of language.

This evolution is not only visible in technology but also in various more fundamental though less spectacular behavioural capacities. The location of palaeolithic sites in the landscape demonstrates a capacity for prediction with regard to the sources of raw materials that also takes into account the means of obtaining food supplies. Hunting methods bear witness to a capacity for observation and intelligence as well as a sound knowledge of the habits of prey. Inter-individual organization also displays a capacity for social co-ordination, and hence for the transmission of – and respect for – its conceptualized codification. All these elements appear in the earliest Palaeolithic, several hundred thousand years ago. Their evolution is extremely slow and virtually no breaks can be observed in this continuity.

The end of the Lower Palaeolithic in Eurasia is marked by increasingly clear regional differentiation; minor technical processes that do not affect principal functions appear repeatedly within a limited geographical area. These multiple technological innovations thus evoke recognizable distinct traditions maintained by autonomous ethnic groups. During this period, the Mousterian (between 100,000 and 50,000 years BP), technical innovations multiply, at the same time as the density of sites increases; in the same way, the appearance of funerary rites and the increase in variability lead one to suppose that the capacity for adaptation (and the concepts this implies) developed quite radically. This phase is crucial in Europe, because it directly precedes the appearance of anatomically modern man and what is called the 'Upper Palaeolithic' way of life.

Considered globally, this phenomenon cannot be seen as a typically European and isolated innovation; rather, it results from the differences in the speed of evolution of various prehistoric peoples. The technically most advanced populations progressively dominated the others, while the new technologies supplanted older traditions (though not without undergoing their influence). The inrush of Upper Palaeolithic people appears abrupt because, having come in from outside, it imposes itself on evolutionary traditions that remained at an earlier stage. In other words, evolution happened slowly and on the outside probably in the steppes of Eurasia where the environment is favourable (contrary to the curious theory of the African Eve) (Otte 1994a). The abrupt aspect of this break in Europe is thus simply due to the migratory movements of populations whose evolution, faster than that of the indigenous peoples, enabled them to adapt better; as a consequence, their demographic rate increased and led to further movements (Otte 1994b).

Hence the continuity of concepts seems well established; however, it is marked by the acceleration of a constant process. The barrier often used arbitrarily as the point of departure of human language is thus nothing but an archaeological contrivance, linked to ethnic modifications that are 'historical' in nature and not biological. The very notion of image, brought in and maintained by this new ethnic group, is merely the prolongation of the 'natural images' already used by the Neanderthals: horns, antlers, long bones, fossils, minerals. The latter are selected, and hence designated in nature; the former are created on the natural model. The conceptual leap is important, but it is only a matter of degree, not the nature of the phenomenon. It also defines a different relationship between Man and Nature when he chooses animal defences (antler spearpoints); it also recovers the 'right to the animal image' by seizing its power through imitation of its form. This mutation is peculiar to the Eurasian steppes where a lack of wood during the Pleistocene led Man to use animal materials while profoundly transforming his metaphysical relationship with wild Nature.

All these elements, coupled with the dates and geographical areas, retrace an evolution of thought and of language, its obligatory auxiliary. They display a general trend in its development, without a starting or finishing point. This is a global process, closely linked to the other behavioural capacities that are reconstructed through material traces (habitation, hunting, burial, technical co-ordination). On the other hand, this fundamental evolution is marked by internal transformations of lesser magnitude that are apparently linked to movements of peoples. To the same extent as for historical periods, the Eurasian Palaeolithic is traversed by complex phenomena that have an impact on its linguistic 'history': a traditional or regional impact, growing complexity of concepts and their arrangement, abrupt innovations through imitation (the western Châtelperronian), slow diffusion or more clear-cut phases of migration.

ARCHAEOLOGICAL INDO-EUROPEANS

Different approaches have been tried out to rediscover the key episode when the Indo-European languages (and even peoples) appeared. At first based on linguistic or mythological arguments (Dumezil 1983), they were then strongly illustrated by archaeology (Gimbutas 1973; Renfrew 1987), and finally by mixed approaches, known as 'ecumenical', that combine these different trends (Martinet 1986).

As an archaeologist, I do not seek to 'cross swords' with linguistic special-ists, but cannot resist noting that the depth of the phenomenon requires at the very least some verification, through material data, of their own hypotheses. Where archaeology is concerned, the 'short' theory linked to the Kurgan peoples, the introduction of metallurgy and the modification of the pantheon (Dumezil 1983; Gimbutas 1973) cannot long withstand criticism. First, because these populations from north of the Black Sea were in close contact with the Balkans for much longer; second, because the metallurgical modifications were an internal phenomenon there, and not the result of an invasion; and finally, the modifications in religion reflect the evolution of a society and not an abrupt change. Technical, social and religious elements are combined very naturally to strike a balance within a general evolutionary process. So one cannot say that the diffusion of a pantheon reflects that of a people (Masson 1993), but simply that of a way of life, itself expressed by religious images that correspond to it, wherever and whenever it may be. Besides, nowhere in Europe is there any break at the turning point of the Metal Ages; rather, there is a local ethnic continuity doubtless marked by the diffusion of new ideas, values and behaviours linked to the exploitation of metals.

The 'long' theory presented by Renfrew (1987) and based on the diffu-sion of agriculture is no more convincing, despite its evident charm. First, Anatolia, apparently already Indo-European (the base of this theory), diffuses to the Balkans a way of life and a population whose non-Indo-European nature has not been established. Second, the neolithic movement that subse-quently affected the rest of Europe (for example, the Danubian current) only came about after a major pause, put to good use by the local populations in adapting the economic innovations to the forest environment of the continent.

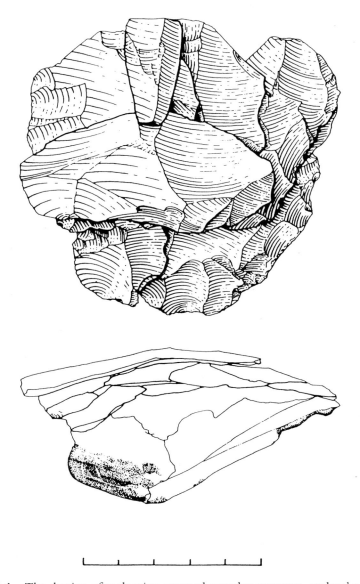

Figure 5.1   The shaping of tools using grouped complex processes, under the generic name of 'Levallois', demonstrates the capacity for predicting resources and the calculation of gestures in terms of the tool's silhouette and the final technical function (Roebroecks *et al.* 1992). This long sequence is integrated into a way of life in equilibrium with a changing natural environment. This method testifies to conceptual possibilities that are equivalent to those of modern man. So the differences lie in the products and not in the potential, in exactly the same way as any contemporary primitive people is capable of integrating our technology although it has never produced it spontaneously.

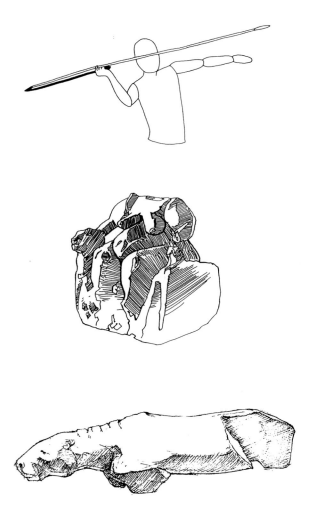

Figure 5.2 The spearthrower sets different forces into action through the complex interplay of the levers located in the arm and shaft. This palaeolithic 'machine' uses ballistic laws to master time, space and the prey's vitality. It thus implies a new insertion of man into the natural world, dominated symbolically by the image and effectively by weapons, themselves shaped from the animals' natural defences (antlers, ivory tusks). This situation of man mastering nature conferred a new metaphysical position on him that lies at the source of the mythologies of historically known predators. It also conferred on him a new destiny, in a constant state of flux entirely through his own will. From now on, his 'historical' evolution was set in motion and the phenomena of convergence appeared (agriculture, anthropomorphic divinities, metallurgy), giving the illusion of an evolution marked by the so-called 'Indo-European' invasions. Yet all these innovations are inscribed on a common ethnic base, long predating the first written sources and stretching from the Atlantic to the Caspian Sea.

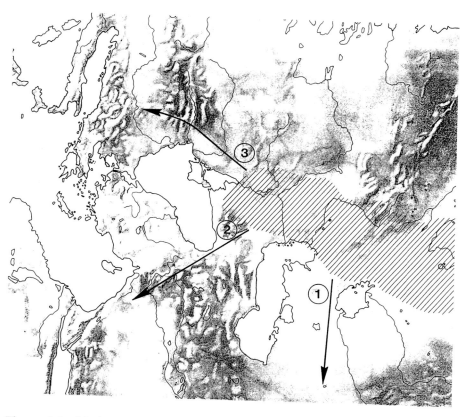

Figure 5.3   Nuclear zone of the Eurasian steppes in which the technical and symbolic modifications (with regard to animals) occurred the earliest. The transition to anatomically modern man seems to have happened here at the same time. Diffusion then occurred between 40 and 35,000 years ago, towards nothern India, the Levant (Aurignacian around 32,000) and the Balkans (Bacho Kiro around 40,000), then along the Mediterranean route (the Adriatic was then partially dry land). This radical break in the archaeological evolution is the only one that can explain a profound ethnic modification equivalent to the appearance of the Indo-European peoples.

This internal European current forms the main process of neolithization, after the eastern impulse. In the hypothesis according to which the latter was a truly determining factor – which is probable in my view – it concerned only a modification of the way of life within a population that was homogeneous and already 'Indo-European' or its linguistic equivalent for the period.

ANOTHER MODEL

Even more troubling is the situation on the 'fringes' of the European continent. When the diffusion of Neolithic peoples is accomplished to the north and west of the continent, one observes a persistence of predatory ways of life in the islands and on lake-shores: Brittany, Ireland, Scotland, Scandinavia. Art bears the imprint of the persistence of this way of life. A specific form of sedentism seems to occur here, thanks to the diversity of wild local resources (fishing, hunting, gathering). Only a few technical elements (pottery) seem to diffuse into here from the nearby neolithic farming populations. More profound modifications will only appear with the Middle and Late Neolithic (megaliths, mining) but only as the diffusion of a way of life grafted onto an unchanged indigenous population.

In other words, from the strictly archaeological point of view, the fringes of the European continent retrace a phenomenon of complete continuity between the last hunters and the most authentic Indo-European populations known from texts: Celts, Germans, Slavs. On the one hand, neolithic movements seem to occur within a homogeneous ethnic mass; on the other, the isolated areas where this continuity becomes evident reveal their purely Indo-European nature. The other innovations (religious, metallurgical, agricultural) merely accompany a fundamental evolution that is peculiar to the whole of humanity: one finds them in the New World, in sub-Saharan Africa and in the Far East.

Going backwards from the local Mesolithic to the ancestral cultures, one can harmoniously trace things back through migrations and adaptations to the Magdalenian cultures and then to the whole of the European Upper Palaeolithic. All the history of this period in Europe is now well established and forms a coherent picture in which extra-European interventions are almost non-existent (Kozłowski and Kozłowski 1979; Otte 1994b).

Finally, the only true break visible in terms of archaeology and human palaeontology (and hence of ethnic group) corresponds to the transition from the Middle Palaeolithic (Neanderthal Man) to the Upper Palaeolithic ('Modern' or 'Cro-Magnon Man'). It is from this moment onward that a history of cultures develops on this continent in an autonomous way. It is also from this moment that continuity begins and lasts until protohistory. It is also from this moment that the non-Indo-European peoples appear as a stark contrast against this communal background: Finno-Ugric speakers or Turco-Mongols. The ensemble is linked to the south of the Eurasian steppes where the population took shape both anatomically and technically (Sokal *et al.* 1992). Well adapted to this open environment located around the Caspian Sea and the north of the Black Sea, it developed new values and then diffused broadly westward as far as Gibraltar, and to the south and east through northern India and Iran, where the final palaeolithic industries present close analogies with those of Anatolia (Otte *et al.* 1994).

The complexity of the concepts peculiar to the Upper Palaeolithic (images, myths, pendants), as much as their integration into a social environment that was both supple and effective (composite tools, ballistic weapons), displays a language capacity that is equivalent to that of today. This potential was in place 40,000 years ago, and from then on permitted the later development of ideas and words without any apparent archaeological discontinuity up to present-day peoples.

REFERENCES

Bühler, K. 1990. *Theory of Language. The representational function of language.* Philadelphia, Pa.: J. Benjamins.

Dumezil, G. 1983. *La courtisane et les seigneurs colorés, Esquisses de mythologie.* Paris: Bibliothèque des Sciences Humaines.

Gimbutas, M. 1973. Old Europe c. 7,000–3,500 BC: the earliest European civilization before the infiltration of the Indo-European peoples. *Journal of Indo-European Studies* 1, 1–20.

Kozłowski J.K. and S.K. Kozłowski. 1979. *Upper Palaeolithic and Mesolithic in Europe. Taxonomy and Palaeohistory.* Wroclaw: Polska Akademia Nauk - Oddział W Krakowie. Prace Komisji Archeologicznej no. 18.

Leroi-Gourhan, A. 1964. *Le geste et la parole, Technique et langage,* Paris: Albin Michel.

Light, P. and V. Girotto. 1989. Les bases pragmatiques du raisonnement déductif chez l'enfant. *Annales de la Fondation Fyssen* 4, 39–47.

Martinet, A. 1986. *Des steppes aux océans: l'indo-européen et les 'Indo-européens'.* Paris: Payot.

Masson, E. 1993. Vallée des Merveilles, un berceau de la pensée religieuse européenne. *Les dossiers de l'Archéologie* no. 181, Dijon. 141 pp.

Otte, M. 1994a. Origine de l'homme moderne: approche comportementale. In *Comptes Rendues. Académie Scientifique, Paris* 318, série II, 267–73.

Otte, M. 1994b. Europe during the Upper Palaeolithic and Mesolithic. In *History of Humanity,* Vol. I. *Prehistory and the Beginnings of Civilizations,* 207–24. Paris: UNESCO.

Renfrew, C. 1987. *Archaeology and Language: the puzzle of Indo-European origins.* Cambridge: Cambridge University Press.

Roebroeks, W., N. Conard and T. Van Kolfschoten. 1992. Dense forests, cold steppes and the palaeolithic settlement of northern Europe. *Current Anthropology* 33(5), 551–67.

Sokal, R., O. Neal and B. Thomson 1992. Origins of the Indo-Europeans: genetic evidence. *Proceedings of the National Academy of Sciences of the United States of America* 89, 7669–73.

6 *World linguistic diversity and farming dispersals*

COLIN RENFREW

INTRODUCTION

For some time now there have been indications that a new synthesis is emerging between the disciplines of historical linguistics, prehistoric archaeology and molecular genetics (Renfrew 1991: 20). But there are many potential pitfalls in seeking to relate these disciplines, and the history of misunderstandings between linguistics and archaeology offers many cautionary tales. In particular, the notional correspondence between linguistic change and linguistic phylogeny on the one hand, and the development of genetic diversity among human populations on the other (Cavalli-Sforza *et al.* 1988, Figure 6.1) is, I think, in part an illusory one. For as I shall argue here, the correspondences arise more from a significant number of dispersal episodes in post-Pleistocene human history (in which influential demographic processes were involved, where linguistic and genetic replacement were indeed correlated) than from strictly comparable processes of linguistic and genetic evolution or equivalent rates of linguistic and genetic divergence.

These dispersal processes have radically transformed the linguistic map of the earth over the past 10,000 years. It is argued here that the demographic, economic and social processes underlying the existence of language families of very great territorial extent must be carefully elucidated if any meaningful explanation for those family distributions is to be attempted. Moreover the whole issue of *time depth* in the origin of language families has been inadequately handled. Glottochronological or lexicostatistical approaches applied to individual pairs of languages, working backwards in each case from the present time, do not necessarily offer a precise guide when we are talking about the relationships between languages and language families in a more remote past, and at a time when population densities were much less than at present, and when the written word was not available to enhance language stability. In general I believe that historical linguists have tended to underestimate the age of the family relationships which they analyse. And nowhere is any closely argued rationale offered for the proposed time-scales. Instead there is a tendency to base judgements upon conventional wisdom in one or two well-known cases, which are then generalized uncritically. (These remarks do not apply to Hymes, the original inventor of glottochronology. His formulation was a very exact one, but it has not found many followers in precisely the version in which it was formulated.)

Set in this wider context, the Indo-European problem, at least in its outlines, becomes somewhat clearer, although it is an issue of such complexity that no single principle or explanation can hope to be sufficient. But as Dolgopolsky (1987, 1993) has pointed out, the convergence between the linguistic arguments indicated by him and the archaeological approach outlined here is so close that the mutual reinforcement, of an entirely independent nature, is considerable.

THE GEOLINGUISTIC PATTERNING OF LANGUAGE FAMILIES

When the geographical distributions of the languages which comprise language families are examined upon the map, they fall into two broad classes. Some language families are of very great spatial extent – a figure of a quarter of a million square miles has been suggested by Nichols (1992: 17) – with the languages themselves quite closely related to each other (hence implying a shallow time depth). Others show a much greater concentration of linguistic diversity, and often these are in more isolated locations.

This question has been considered by Austerlitz (1980), who noted that language families and language isolates (which he termed genetic units) were more frequent – i.e. more tightly packed together – in North (and South) America than in Europe and Asia. Johanna Nichols (1992: 13–14; Ch. 8, this volume) has similarly distinguished what she terms 'spread zones' from 'residual zones', where there is much higher linguistic diversity and, in her view, greater antiquity of the indigenous language stocks.

Let us call the latter group, with high linguistic diversity, Class A, and the group of language families of greater spatial extent and less diversity, Class B. There is, I would argue, a good reason for the distinction. The language families of Class A, with their 'high genetic unit density ratio' (Austerlitz), and greater antiquity of the indigenous language stocks (Nichols) are exemplified by the North Caucasian language family, by the languages of northern Australia, and by many of the language families of the Americas. It can be argued that, in most cases, speakers of those languages have occupied very much the same geographical position since the end of the Pleistocene period, some 10,000 years ago.

On the other hand the language families of Class B, occupying what Nichols has termed 'spread zones', exemplified by the Niger-Congo, the Indo-European and the Austronesian language families, would be generally agreed to be of more recent origin. It is my proposal that the language families of Class B are indeed the result of language dispersals which have taken place since the end of the Pleistocene period. I shall argue that these dispersals were, in effect, in most cases episodes of language replacement (see Renfrew 1989), generally following the subsistence/demography model, but in a few cases the result of episodes of elite dominance.

Language families of Class A, as already indicated, would have occupied very much their present territories since before the end of the Ice Age, some 10,000 years ago. They are thus the product of processes of initial dispersal, supplemented by later divergence (and sometimes episodes of convergence). The position is summarized in Table 6.1, although inevitably the matter is over-simplified in so concise a statement.

FARMING DISPERSALS

It is argued here that by far the greater number of language families falling within Class B are the products of episodes of language replacement, and that they are best explained by processes of linguistic replacement. The most important of these has been summarized in the demographic-subsistence model. Farming dispersal is the most obvious instance, but it may not be the only one. For instance the Pama-Nyungan family of Australia, discussed by Evans and McConvell (Volume II) is likely to be the product of a dispersal process within this broad category, but not one of farming dispersal.

A few others may well be the result of élite dominance processes. Such may be the case for much of the Altaic language family distribution, and perhaps also for the Indo-Aryan branch of the Indo-European family, although that is a matter much discussed. The present distribution of each language family or language area is accounted for by one of the five processes shown in Table 6.1. It is suggested that the greater number of the language families in Class B are, however, the product of farming dispersal processes, as has been argued previously by Bellwood (1991a, 1991b) and myself (Renfrew 1992, 1994). The basic concepts for farming dispersal are summarized in Table 6.2.

A frequently quoted example of a farming dispersal model is the 'demic diffusion' or 'wave of advance' model of Ammerman and Cavalli-Sforza (1973), but other models are possible. Not all of them would lead to language replacement, and of course language replacement can indeed occur without an accompanying adoption of farming practices. But there is good genetic evidence that, at least in some cases, the farming spread did involve some demic diffusion. Language replacement is a distinct possibility in such cases.

The Austronesian dispersal is one of the best documented, and has been well discussed by Bellwood (1985, 1987, 1991a), and by Kirch (1986) and Terrell (1988). In Polynesia this was, of course, a case of initial colonization as well as of farming dispersal, The case for the Austroasiatic and Austro-Tai families is argued by Higham (Volume II), and the concept is clearly a powerful one as applied to south-east Asia.

Table 6.1   Explaining world linguistic diversity

Class A: Pleistocene

1 *Initial colonization prior to 12,000 BP*:
'Khoisan', 'Nilo-Saharan' (plus later 'aquatic' expansion), North Caucasian,
South Caucasian, 'Indo-Pacific' (plus later farming changes), North Australian
(i.e. non-Pama-Nyungan), 'Amerind'. Localized ancestral groups of 2 and 3
(below).

Class B: Post-Pleistocene

2 *Farming dispersal after 10,000 BP*:
Niger-Congo (specifically the Bantu languages), Afroasiatic, Indo-European,
Elamo-Dravidian, Early Altaic, Sino-Tibetan, Austronesian, Austroasiatic.

3 *Northern, climate-sensitive adjustments after 10,000 BP*:
Uralic-Yukaghir, Chukchi-Kamchatkan, Na-Dene, Eskimo-Aleut.

4 *Elite dominance*:
Indo-Iranian, Later Altaic, Southern Sino-Tibetan (Han).

5 *Long-distance maritime colonization since 1400 AD*:
Mainly Indo-European (English, Spanish, Portuguese, French).

Table 6.2   Farming dispersal

1 *Suitability for* transplantation into *new ecological niches* of the plants (and animals),
when sustained with the appropriate exploitative technology by the
accompanying human population, with propagation (i.e. seeding/planting
or controlled breeding), protected growth (by weeding and manuring, or
controlled feeding, e.g. by transhumance), and organized harvesting (or culling).

2 *Increased birth rate* and reduced rate of human infant mortality, and sometimes
increased post-infantile life expectancy, associated with aspects of the subsistence
regime. These accompany the *sedentary* life which farming facilitated.

3 *Greater intensity of production* as measured in terms of food (calories) per unit
area, permitted by the new economy. Agricultural economies, even of a simple
and non-intensive nature, are characteristically fifty times more productive in
this sense than mobile hunter-gatherer economies, or have the capacity to
be so.

A *nuclear area* is defined as supporting initially a specific range of wild plants
(and sometimes animals) which later proved amenable to domestication. The
farming 'package' of plants (and, where appropriate, animals), along with the
appropriate exploitative techniques, becomes an expansive one dependent
upon three factors (Table 6.2).

In favourable cases the language or languages of the nuclear area are transmitted along with the plant and animal domesticates either through *demic
diffusion* of the farming population (the 'wave of advance' model), or through

adoption by local hunter-gatherer groups of the new language along with the new agricultural economy (*acculturation*: the 'availability model'). The genetic effects of the two mechanisms are significantly different.

The mechanisms for the dispersal of the Bantu languages of Africa have been very extensively discussed (Phillipson 1977, 1985), and there seems a general consensus that this episode is associated with the dissemination of new subsistence practices. For Europe, the case has been set out in some detail (Renfrew 1987), and in a modified form has found the support of a number of archaeologists, including Zvelebil and Zvelebil (1988). The matter is still one of controversy. I have suggested that comparable arguments would lead one to suggest that the present distribution of the Afroasiatic language family is also the product of farming dispersal – in this case one initially of sheep and goat, and only later of cereal crops – taking place from the Levant with the inception of agriculture at the end of the Natufian period. Of course the matter is far from clear, and the pattern today involves the working of many subsequent processes also. But if one looks for a mechanism of dispersal underlying the undoubted elements of linguistic unity for Afroasiatic, one cannot escape the archaeological reality that domesticated sheep and goat came first to the Nile valley from the Levant and then spread further west at the time in question. Nor does it seem now to be disputed that the first domesticated cereals – emmer, einkorn, barley – came to North Africa from the same area. The processes by which farming economies were set up were very different to those in Europe, and the local African contribution was greater than the local contribution had been in central Europe, being perhaps more analogous to the situation in the west of Europe (including Iberia), where local factors had a more significant role.

I am aware, of course, that most linguists would seek to locate Proto-Afroasiatic within Africa. But no general mechanism of widespread application has been suggested which compares in its simplicity with that of farming dispersal. Above all, as Shnirelman has also indicated (1989), the archaeological evidence is clear that there was indeed a farming dispersal, first of sheep and goat, and then of cereal crops, at about the time that linguists would seek to date the dispersal on linguistic grounds.

It still seems likely, from the evidence at Mehrgarh, that cereal cultivation was initially an importation into the Indian sub-continent from the West, and the same may be true for sheep and goat also. So that if there is indeed a linguistic relationship of a family nature between Elamite and the Dravidian languages then a farming dispersal from the nuclear area in southern Iran may offer a potential explanation. Comparable arguments might be adduced to account for the very early spread of the Altaic languages, perhaps locating Proto-Altaic originally in Turkmenia where the Djeitun neolithic may be the area of origin for a significant farming dispersal process. Of course the later history, in each of these cases, is as much a part of the story as the early phases we are discussing here, and in the case of the Altaic languages there were clearly significant later episodes of elite dominance.

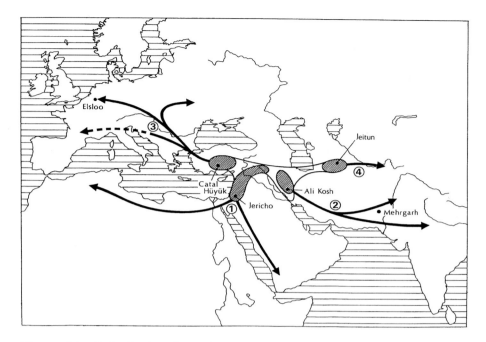

Figure 6.1   Early farming dispersals.

The position is set out in schematic way in Figure 6.1, which brings out the comparable nature of the processes at work in the different areas. The particular point of interest here is that the language families in question all serve to constitute the Nostratic family group, as defined by Illič-Svityč (1989, 1990, 1971-84) and by Dolgopolsky (1973, 1989). It is particularly interesting, therefore, that our arguments would place the respective homelands of the Proto-Indo-European, Proto-Afroasiatic, Proto-Elamo-Dravidian and Proto-Altaic languages within a relatively circumscribed Near Eastern heartland. If these languages are indeed related, then the archaeological arguments would place Proto-Nostratic as a language spoken in this area, presumably a few millennia prior to the dispersal phase around 8,000 to 6,000 BC.

TIME-DEPTH

It is only possible to set out these arguments schematically and concisely here. But it will readily be seen that a general case — which is not to say a universal one — is being argued, where the evidence from one area may be used to give general support to the interpretation in another. Fortunately the dates of the archaeological processes discussed here are not in the least hypothetical. We have good evidence, and are continually adding more, for the inception of farming in the regions discussed and in many others. The processes of domestication are becoming better understood also, as well as the mechanisms of dispersal.

What is entirely hypothetical, at present, is whether the economic and demographic processes which I have alluded to did indeed have linguistic consequences of the kind suggested here. Scepticism on that point among linguists and others is entirely legitimate. But it is important not to make the error that the archaeological datings are in some way uncertain or unsteady. On the contrary they are well-founded and improving all the time.

It does seem appropriate, therefore, to ask historical linguists whether the generally rather short time-scales which they have in the past chosen to adopt may not in fact be too conservative – just as were archaeological time-scales until the advent of radiocarbon dating thirty years ago. I have never been able to find any very coherent rationale for these short time-scales – they seem rather to be used to reinforce each other, so that the linguistic changes in area K are dated with reference to the accepted chronology in areas L and M, while the changes in area L are dated by the widely accepted dates for K and M. The argument for the measuring scale has never been made clear to me.

So I would like to ask whether a greater time depth may not indeed be acceptable among linguists. For then it would be much easier to bring into coherent coincidence the farming dispersal episodes mentioned here, and the broad linguistic changes within the distribution areas of the language families of Class B indicated at the beginning of this chapter.

THE IMPACT OF MOLECULAR GENETICS

The emerging synthesis, of which mention was made at the outset, relies to a considerable extent upon the information obtainable from molecular genetics. Already what may now be regarded as classic methods in biochemistry – the use of blood groups and immune systems – has allowed comparisons of gene frequencies among different populations to be used to some effect (Cavalli-Sforza *et al.* 1994). But more sophisticated methods, using nuclear and mitochondrial DNA, are already proving very informative (e.g. Ward *et al.* 1991)

Of course, such methods do not tell us anything about language directly: they are informative about the inheritance of genes, and hence about ancestry. But in the cases of farming dispersal discussed above, the study of gene frequencies has already shown its usefulness in confirming some of the demographic implications (Sokal *et al.* 1991). And results of analyses in the Americas show a correlation between genetic characteristics and the membership of tribal groups which are also language groups. In such a case inferences about genetic descent can hold implications for linguistic descent also. The challenge, as so often, is an interpretative one, and here there are difficulties of methodology not yet resolved (Maddison 1991; Templeton 1992). Ultimately, however, linguists, archaeologists and geneticists are all dealing with different aspects of a single reality: what happened in certain specific contexts in the past. The models and the interpretative techniques of each discipline may be different, but they will ultimately have to be at least to some extent congruent if they are to reflect this underlying reality.

REFERENCES

Ammerman, A.J. and L. Cavalli-Sforza. 1973. A population model for the diffusion of early farming in Europe. In *The Explanation of Culture Change: Models in Prehistory*, C. Renfrew (ed.), 335–58. London: Duckworth.

Austerlitz, R. 1980. Language-family density in North America and Eurasia. *Ural-Altaische Jahrbücher* 52, 1–10.

Bellwood, P. 1985. *Prehistory of the Indo-Malaysian Archipelago*. New York: Academic Press.

Bellwood, P. 1987. *The Polynesians*. (2nd edn) London: Thames & Hudson.

Bellwood, P. 1991a. The Austronesian dispersal and the origins of languages. *Scientific American* 265, 88–93.

Bellwood, P. 1991b. Prehistoric cultural explanations for widespread language families. Paper presented to the conference 'Archaeology and Linguistics: Understanding Ancient Australia'. Darwin, 8–12 July.

Cavalli-Sforza, L.L., A. Piazza, P. Menozzi and J. Mountain. 1988. Reconstruction of human evolution: bringing together genetic, archaeological and linguistic data. *Proceedings of the National Academy of Sciences of the USA* 85, 6002–6.

Cavalli-Sforza, L.L., A. Piazza and P. Menozzi. 1994. *The History and Geography of Human Genes*. Princeton: Princeton University Press.

Dolgopolsky, A.B. 1973. Boreisch – Ursprache Eurasiens? *Ideen des Exacten Wissens, Wissenschaft und Technik in der Sowietunion* 73(1), 19–30.

Dolgopolsky, A.B. 1987. The Indo-European homeland and lexical contacts of Proto-Indo-European with other languages. *Mediterranean Language Review* 3, 7–31.

Dolgopolsky, A.B. 1989. Problems of Nostratic comparative phonology. In *Reconstructing Languages and Cultures*, V. Shevoroshkin (ed.), 90–8. Bochum: Brockmeyer.

Dolgopolsky, A.B. 1993. More about the Indo-European homeland problem. *Mediterranean Language Review* 7, 230–48.

Illič-Svityč, V. 1971–84. *A Comparison of the Nostratic Languages, vols I–III*. (in Russian). Moscow: Nauka.

Illič-Svityč, V. 1989. The relationship of the Nostratic family languages: a probabilistic evaluation of the similarities in question. In *Explorations in Language Macrofamilies*, V. Shevoroshkin (ed.), 138–67. Bochum: Brockmeyer.

Illič-Svityč, V. 1990. Nostratic reconstructions (translated and arranged by M. Kaiser). In *Proto-Languages and Proto-Cultures*, V. Shevoroshkin (ed.), 138–67. Bochum: Brockmeyer.

Kirch, P.V. 1986. Rethinking East Polynesian prehistory. *Journal of the Polynesian Society* 95, 9–40.

Maddison, D.R. 1991. African origin of human mitochondrial DNA re-examined. *Systematic Zoology* 40, 355–63.

Nichols, J. 1992. *Language Diversity in Space and Time*. Chicago: Chicago University Press.

Phillipson, D.W. 1977. The spread of the Bantu languages. *Scientific American* 236(4), 106–14.

Phillipson, D.W. 1985. An archaeological reconsideration of Bantu expansion. *MUNTU* 2, 69–84.

Renfrew, C. 1987. *Archaeology and Language, the Puzzle of Indo-European Origins.* London: Jonathan Cape.

Renfrew, C. 1989. Models of change in language and archaeology. *Transactions of the Philological Society* 87(2), 103–55.

Renfrew, C. 1991. Before Babel: speculations on the origins of linguistic diversity. *Cambridge Archaeology Journal* 1(1), 3–23.

Renfrew, C. 1992. World languages and human dispersals: a minimalist view. In *Transition to Modernity, Essays on Power, Wealth and Belief,* J.A. Hall and I.C. Jarvie (eds). Cambridge: Cambridge University Press.

Renfrew, C. 1994. World linguistic diversity. *Scientific American* 270(1), 116–23.

Shnirelman, V.A. 1989. *Vozniknovenie proizvodjasoego xozjaistva* [The Emergence of a Food-Producing Economy]. Moscow: Nauka.

Sokal, R.R., N.L. Oden and C. Wison. 1991. New genetic evidence supports the origin of agriculture in Europe by demic diffusion. *Nature* 351, 143–4.

Templeton, A.R. 1992. Human origins – analysis of mitochondrial DNA sequences. *Science* 255, 737.

Terrell, J. 1988. *Prehistory in the Pacific Islands.* Cambridge: Cambridge University Press.

Ward, R.H., B.S. Frazier, K. Dew-Jager and S. Pääbo. 1991. Extensive mitochondrial diversity within a single Amerindian tribe. *Proceedings of the National Academy of Sciences of the USA* 88, 8720–4.

Zvelebil, M. and K.V. Zvelebil. 1988. Agricultural transition and Indo-European dispersals. *Antiquity* 62, 574–8.

Part III

PROBLEMS OF METHOD

7   *The homelands of the Indo-Europeans*

JAMES P. MALLORY

INTRODUCTION

After over 150 years the search for the homeland of the Indo-Europeans (IE) has still not achieved the type of solution that commands more than either partisan support or acceptance (often uninformed) by those wishing to defer to whatever 'experts' with whose works they have come into contact. That the homeland has been discovered there can be no doubt as it has been sought anywhere from the North to the South poles and from the Atlantic to the Pacific (Mallory 1973). Temporally, it has been located anywhere between 80,000 BC (Neanderthals) and *c.* 1600 BC (the expansion of chariot warfare from eastern Anatolia).

The underlying premise of the IE homeland problem is that the differentiation of Proto-Indo-European (PIE) into its various stocks (Celtic, Italic, Germanic, Baltic, Slavic, Albanian, Greek, Armenian, Anatolian, Indo-Iranian, Tocharian, etc. – Figure 7.1) was a factor of both time and space. All languages change through time, and hence differentiation between different speakers of any language can be expected to occur over time. As speakers of any particular language are increasingly dispersed, mutual interaction and communication will diminish such that the course and direction of language change will vary from one region to another. It should be emphasized that both factors themselves are liable to other constraints which will affect both the speed and the intensity of language change (Fodor 1965) – for example, economic systems, the nature of the terrain separating peoples, the existence of written standards or prestige dialects, foreign substrates/adstrates/superstrates, etc. But no matter how these may specifically influence language change, it is commonly accepted that at one time there existed a PIE language (or languages) whose dialects were far more closely related or similar than may be found among the different IE stocks known from their earliest entrance into the written record of the Late Bronze Age or Iron Age. The location of the IE-speakers before major differentiation into the various stocks is the IE homeland.

Figure 7.1 Distribution of the major stocks of the Indo-European languages.

SOME PRINCIPLES AND ASSUMPTIONS

A problem that has been so resistant to solution owes as much of its intractability to methodological matters (Dressler 1965) as it does to empirical data. Consequently, a preamble to any discussion of the homeland problem should lay down some basic principles.

Linguistic primacy

As the IE homeland problem involves a spatial definition of a prehistoric *linguistic* construct, the utility of any other discipline, such as archaeology, depends on whether a linguistic entity can be translated into something discernible in the archaeological record. In short, any solution not *purely* linguistic must involve some form of indirect inference whose own premises are usually, if not invariably, far from demonstrated.

Linguistic limitations

There is no purely linguistic method which resolves the problem of IE origins. Time does not permit a rehearsal of all the various linguistic solutions nor, probably, could the tolerance of any reader (insomniacs are directed to Mallory 1975 for a broad sample). We must deny ourselves the pleasure of marvelling at such works as that of Alexander Jóhanesson (1943) who argued that the proliferation of velars in PIE roots was imitative of the harsh cries of sea birds (hence a Baltic homeland), and, like Dr Watson's readers, the world is probably still not ready to entertain the consequences of Georg Schwidetsky's

(1932) comparison of Proto-Indo-European, Mongolian and Chimpanzee! But even after a judicious application of Pinkerton's principle – to confute absolute nonsense is surely as ridiculous as to write it – there are certain linguistic techniques that are widely recognized and these do warrant serious consideration.

CENTRE OF GRAVITY PRINCIPLE

The centre of linguistic dispersal is held to lie where there is the greatest degree of linguistic variation, while the peripheries are marked by the greatest degree of homogeneity (age–area hypothesis). This principle (beginning with Latham 1851, 1862) has been employed in locating the origin of many language families, e.g. Athabaskan (Sapir 1936: 234), Numic (Lamb 1958: 98), Salish (Jorgensen 1969: 105), etc. With respect to the IE homeland problem, it has often led to the conclusion that the centre of dispersion should be somewhere in south-eastern Europe since this region would embrace

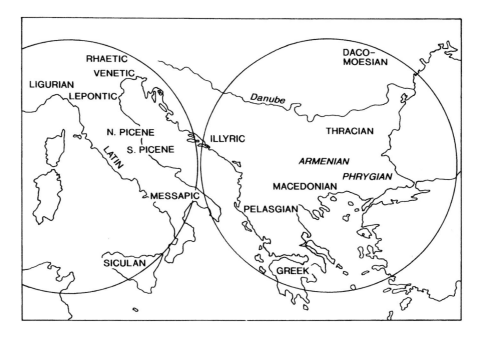

Figure 7.2 Centres of gravity. The Balkan centre of gravity proposed by Dolgo-polsky consists of one language (Greek) which is well known and a series of languages such as Pelasgian, Macedonian, Illyric, Thracian and Daco-Moesian which are mini-mally (and generally only secondarily) attested, or languages putatively derived from the Balkans (Armenian, Phrygian) from an earlier temporal horizon than the other languages. An alternative homeland might just as well be set to Italy where there are even more (minimally attested) languages. Obviously, any employment of the 'centre of gravity' principle must be based on well known languages attested from the same temporal plane.

the greatest number of IE stocks (Mallory 1989: 152–3). It is worth taking a close look at this argument by citing its recent use by Aron Dolgopolsky:

> The Balkans constitute the area of the highest genetic diversity within the entire IE field: among the 12 (or 13) known branches of Late IE, 7 (or 8) were found in (or originated from) the Balkans: Greek, Macedonian, Phrygian, Armenian (originated from the Balkans according to ancient authors and the linguistic evidence), Thracian, probably Daco-Moesian (if it is not a branch of Thracian), Illyric (or different Illyric branches?), Pelasgian (one of several branches of IE preserved in a substratal lexical layer of Greek and in the few Philistine terms in Hebrew).
>
> (Dolgopolsky 1988: 12)

But what is the actual nucleus of this centre of gravity (Figure 7.2)? In the Balkans it basically consists of one language of which we know a great deal (i.e. Greek), and a series of ethnonyms that have been served up as distinct languages when the hard evidence is almost entirely confined to personal and place-names (which need not derive from the native languages in the first place) and a series of glosses. As we cannot decline a single noun, conjugate a single verb, count or even make it to square one of a Swadesh basic word list with these 'languages', i.e. Illyrian, Thracian, Macedonian (if not simply a Greek dialect (Brixhe and Panayotou 1994a)), Daco-Moesian (if not a Thracian dialect (Brixhe and Panayotou 1994b)), Pelasgian (lexical items in Greek believed to be remnants of an earlier language), it is extraordinary that we can pretend that they have different atomic weights, all contributing to an IE nucleus. We could just as easily place the homeland in Italy (Figure 7.2) and cite Ligurian, Lepontic, Rhaetic, Venetic, north Picenian, south Picenian, Messapic, Osco-Umbrian, Latin-Faliscan and Siculan (nine – one more than the Balkans). And as for Dolgopolsky's two additional languages – Armenian and Phrygian – which seemed to have escaped the orbit of the nucleus, even if we admit that they did have a Balkan origin, it was clearly at a date long before we have any evidence for our other various Balkan languages (similarly with the 'Pelasgian' remnants). Packing one's nucleus on the basis of 'privileged information' (i.e. assigning to the nuclear area languages which derive from different temporal horizons), is methodologically unsound unless, of course, we are also to be permitted to augment the Italian homeland argued above with Greek, Albanian, Sardinian, and all the modern dialects of Italy as well.

A final reason to be suspicious of employing the centre of gravity principle to argue a Balkan homeland is the dialectal position of Tocharian. For along with the diversity expected at the centre, one also expects peripheral homogeneity which seems to be breached in Indo-European as Tocharian is so markedly different from its neighbours of the Indo-Iranian superstock and is invariably associated on morphological and lexical grounds with IE stocks far to its west (Adams 1984). Whatever the path of IE dispersions, its trajectory does not seem to be transparently reflected in the position of the IE stocks. The (Late) IE homeland may have been in the Balkans, but it will require better evidence than the centre of gravity principle to demonstrate this.

CONSERVATISM PRINCIPLE

The centre of linguistic dispersal is held to lie where there is the least linguistic change from the proto-language, as this area is most likely to have been the least affected by foreign substrates (e.g. Poesche 1878: 66; Bender 1922: 53, etc.). This principle has been employed in a variety of ways, ranging from counting cognate clusters by stock to scoring (intuitively) the retention of PIE features – stress, accent, morphological features, etc. – across the various IE stocks. It is most often invoked to support a homeland in the Baltic region on the basis of the conservatism of Lithuanian (Hirt 1895: 653; Bender 1922: 55; Pisani 1940: 278; Georgiev 1966: 351) or the retention of alleged PIE river names in the Baltic region (Schmid 1972). The principle itself (which incidentally appears to contradict the assumptions of the 'centre of gravity' principle) is suspect because:

1   it presumes that the single or main cause of linguistic change is contact with other languages;
2   it requires one to 'measure' the degree of linguistic change between different languages on a commensurate scale; e.g. one might argue that Celtic retains the PIE stops better than Germanic but Germanic retains the differences between series much better than Celtic – how are such differences to be weighted?;
3   the principle leads to egregiously false conclusions – i.e. on an intuitive basis, Icelandic might well be regarded the most conservative of the Scandinavian languages but derivation of the rest of the Scandinavian languages from Iceland is historically absurd.

EXTRAFAMILIAL CONTACTS

The homeland is held to lie adjacent to the language family that shares the greatest similarity with the Indo-European family. This has been variously argued for Semitic (Hommel 1879; Schott 1936; Levin 1971, Hodge 1981; Dolgopolsky 1993), with a presumed Anatolian/Near Eastern homeland; Kartvelian (Gamkrelidze and Ivanov 1995), with an east Anatolian homeland; North-west Caucasian (Colarusso 1994), with a north Pontic homeland; and Uralic (Anderson 1879; Uesson 1970, Napolskikh 1995), with homelands ranging from northern and central Europe to the Urals or beyond.

Distinguishing between the level of contact between these other language families and the nature of the contacts (e.g. deep genetic contact between proto-languages, contacts between stocks of one family with the proto-language of another, etc.) is, as Aron Dolgopolsky (1993: 241–4) rightly argues, critical to the construction of a valid argument concerning geographical location. But to argue that 'unlike archaeological evidence, linguistic evidence (especially that of loanwords) is not liable to conflicting historical interpretations and is therefore decisive [in demonstrating the superiority of PIE-Semitic contacts]' is a remarkable statement indeed. If this essentially linguistic problem could have been resolved in the cold logic of linguists of good will, then one might well wonder what they have been up to this past century and a half. Take, for example, a set of well-known cultural words (boar, slave, pig, bee, honey, seven, etc.) that were borrowed into Finno-Ugric from (some form of) Indo-European. According to Dolgopolsky (1993: 242) they are Indo-Iranian and 'suggest that proto-Indo-Iranian . . . was once spoken in the vicinity of Finno-Ugric'. When we turn to the writings of Thomas Gamkrelidze and Vyacheslav Ivanov (1995: 815) we read that 'these [same] Finno-Ugric words are specifically early Iranian, not Aryan [i.e. Indo-Iranian] and above all not Sanskrit'. But then a review of J. Harmatta's (1981) detailed chronological ordering of these loanwords by Satya Misra (1992: 24) 'reveals that most of the loan words and the corresponding phonological changes ascribed to Indo-Iranian or Proto-Iranian are Indo-Aryan'. Some of these very words elicited as deriving from some stage of the Indo-Iranian superstock have also been regarded as '(quasi-) Tocharian' (Napolskikh 1994). Will the 'real' linguist please stand up?

It should be obvious that linguists have as much difficulty in establishing the chronological relationships between loanwords as any other 'historical science'. That there has been a loan of some type may be indisputable, and one may also find comparative agreement concerning both the direction of the borrowing and the relative chronological period in which the loan should have taken place. But there is no criteria where one can take a number of loanwords and read off distance and direction in kilometres. Furthermore, as the homelands of the other language families putatively in contact with Proto-Indo-European are no more securely located than that of the Indo-Europeans (although often argued as if they were), dead reckoning one unknown from the position of another unknown can hardly inspire confidence.

The conclusion here is that linguistics *alone* is unable to determine the prehistoric location of the PIE language irrespective of the confidence of individual linguists to make such claims.

The IE homeland is time factored

It is impossible to determine the geographical location of a prehistoric entity unless its chronological position is also determined. For example, in tracing the spread of English across the world today, the suggestion that it spread from England *c.* AD 1100–1900 is valid, while tracing it to the bearers of the Beaker 'culture' (*c.* 2500–1800 BC) and then on to North America, Australia or India is patently absurd. Yet we find a similar range of dates among the various proposals for an IE homeland in Anatolia which begin with the Early Neolithic in the 7th millennium BC (Renfrew 1987; Safronov 1989), then range on to the 5th millennium BC (Gamkrelidze and Ivanov

1995) to finish with the 2nd millenium BC (Drews 1988). Although all look to the same general homeland, they are not identifying the same people nor tracing the same expansions, and, given the fact that the 5,000-year gap between these theories could not help but result in massive linguistic evolution, there are no grounds to assume that they are talking about the same language either. Hence, the chronological position of PIE must be (approximately) determined before one may even hope to apply some form of indirect inference and determine its geographical location by some other means such as archaeology.

Linguistic date of Proto-Indo-European

Although PIE is a linguistic construct, there are no purely linguistic methods for providing absolute dates for a prehistoric language that are *verifiable* (Mallory forthcoming a). In the history of the IE homeland problem, three purely linguistic techniques have been employed: external contact dating, glottochronology and estimation.

EXTERNAL CONTACT DATING

There have been a few attempts to place PIE in real time by anchoring its lexicon to datable texts in another language family. As only Semitic, Sumerian and Elamite texts are likely to pre-date the earliest appearance of the IE stocks, it requires that one identify loanwords in PIE whose base form is precisely dated in an early literate language. Attempts to link words such as PIE $*h_2estar$ 'star' with Akkadian *astar* (Ipsen 1923) are controversial in the first place (Diakonoff 1985; Dolgopolsky 1993) and appear to lack the chronological shading once imputed them (indeed the word itself may well derive from the PIE verbal root $*h_2eh_x$ – 'burn' – and require no Semitic explanation). As external contact dating must be anchored to datable written texts in other languages, it is unlikely that there can be any suggestion of creditable matches before the 3rd millennium BC, a time by which most scholars would assume that PIE had already begun differentiating into its various stocks. The method is, therefore, so far useless if intended to associate the IE *proto-language* with a written language.

GLOTTOCHRONOLOGY

The dating of language separations on the basis of either the theoretical premise that there is a constant decay rate in the basic vocabulary of a language or on the basis of observed language splits in the written record (Swadesh 1960; Tischler 1973) is currently disregarded by most linguists *involved in IE studies* (*pace* Ehret 1988) who find neither the premise nor its implementation valid in an IE context. Since this technique is still applied in other linguistic regions (to the astonishment of some Indo-Europeanists) and attempts are even now being made to refine the technique (V. Blažek, pers. comm.; but see also Coleman 1994), the ball is clearly in the court of those who support glottochronology to demonstrate why anyone should accept their findings.

ESTIMATION

The technique whereby linguists 'estimate' the time-depth necessary for separation between languages, especially between the earliest appearance of IE
languages in the Bronze Age (Anatolian, Greek, Indo-Iranian), generally leads
to estimates that fall somewhere between 5,000 and 2,500 BC (e.g. Milewski
1968: 39; Cowgill and Mayrhofer 1986: 69–70; Zimmer 1988; sometimes
still earlier, e.g. Dolgopolsky 1993: 238–9). This forms an extensive body of
'informed speculation', but it offers neither means of testing nor, indeed, is
the reasoning for such estimates usually made explicit. While the 'weight of
linguistic opinion' does require serious consideration, it is sobering to reflect
that prior to the invention of radiocarbon dating and its calibration, European
archaeologists grossly underestimated the antiquity of the European Neolithic.

CONCLUSION

Linguists generally date the initial separation of the IE stocks to the period
c. 5,000–2,500 BC but these dates are provided largely on the basis of estimation rather than the product of an empirically validated methodology.

Linguistic-cultural date of PIE

The application of the comparative method to reconstruct the cultural vocabulary of a proto-language (e.g. Gamkrelidze and Ivanov 1995), coupled with
archaeological evidence, may provide very broad dates for the separation of
a proto-language (Mallory 1976). Reconstructed PIE reflects a vocabulary
which unequivocally exhibits an economy based on domesticated plants (grain)
and animals (cattle, sheep, goat, pig, dog), and associated technology (grinding
stone, sickle) indicating that the separation of the IE stocks was unlikely
to have occurred anywhere before c. 7000 BC and later, depending on its
geographical location. It also contains a number of items such as plough,
yoke, wheeled vehicles, wool, possibly silver, which are not generally attested
earlier than c. 5000–3000 BC (Mallory 1989). It should be emphasized that
the time-depth of these reconstructions is valid for *all* IE languages, and
Dolgopolsky's (1993: 240–1) suggestion that Anatolian preserves an especially
archaic vocabulary, untouched by subsequent later cultural developments
reflected in the other IE languages which moved away from an IE homeland in Anatolia, is very difficult to sustain. While terms are not abundant,
Anatolian does reflect many of the latest IE technological or cultural items
and even supporters of same Anatolian homeland, e.g. Gamkrelidze and
Ivanov (1995: 623–7), employ Anatolian cognates in their reconstruction of
Proto-Indo-European words for 'yoke', 'wheel', 'harness', 'thill' and (less
convincingly) even 'ride (in a vehicle)'. To this list may also be appended
other items such as 'wool'. On lexico-cultural grounds alone, there are no
convincing reasons to separate Anatolian from the other IE languages with
respect to time-depth. On the other hand, it is necessary to emphasize that
the utility of such dates is limited by the following factors:

1   The reconstructed vocabulary (assuming that it meets all linguistic criteria) indicates only the cultural items known to IE speakers before differences between them became so great that loanwords might be marked. It does not necessarily (although it could) reflect the vocabulary within the specific borders of the 'homeland' itself.

2   Mobile items in the reconstructed vocabulary (e.g. horses, wheeled vehicles, etc.) may have entered any region later than the initial spread of PIE provided that they arrived before the IE language of the particular area had differentiated sufficiently to permit the detection of loanwords (Mallory forthcoming a).

It should be noted that the actual utility of the reconstructed lexicon is very much tied to the construction of test cases. For example, one may wish to propose that the Proto-Greeks (or Proto-Indo-Europeans whose language would eventually evolve into Greek) occupied Greece since the beginning of the Neolithic, i.e. *c.* 7000–6500 BC. If one grants to the IE lexicon a word for 'horse', a reconstruction that is attested in so many IE stocks that it can hardly be denied (Hamp 1990a) and whose cognate forms are to be found in both Mycenaean and Classical Greek (Plath 1994), then one must explain the fact that the earliest evidence for the horse in Greece only dates to the Bronze Age, *c.* 3500 years *after* its occupation by our putative Proto-Greeks. To explain this by a later loanword is not particularly convincing since it requires us to believe that the Proto-Greek language remained essentially unchanged from the beginning of the Neolithic to the Bronze Age to accommodate the borrowing of the word for 'horse' in a way undetectable from all of the otherwise inherited items of the PIE vocabulary. The same would go for later technological items such as wheeled vehicles.

CONCLUSION

Linguistic–cultural analysis suggests broad dates for PIE running from *c.* 7000–2500 BC; the most recent items suggest *termini* for the separation of the IE stocks at around 4000–3000 BC but they do not necessarily reflect the earliest date for the actual expansion of PIE.

Non-conformity of disciplines

Attempts to date PIE result in broad bands of (unquantifiable) probability that generally fall between *c.* 7000 BC, the earliest appearance of the Neolithic economy reflected in the reconstructed lexicon, and *c.* 2000 BC, the dawn of the appearance of historically attested IE stocks in Anatolia. Even the more precise dating frameworks that include both 'informed estimate' and the cultural vocabulary, i.e. *c.* 5000–2500 BC, envisage a process of IE divergence over a period of 2,500 years and may allow for its continuance over many more centuries.

A prehistoric linguistic construct must by its very nature be temporally less precise and, if the borders of a language family are dynamic, geographically

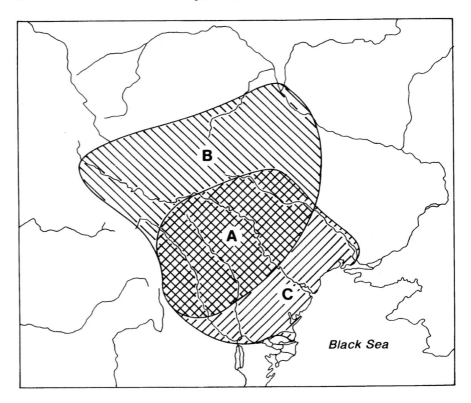

Figure 7.3 Non-conformity of disciplines: a hypothetical Indo-European homeland set to the region of the Tripolye culture. The area marked A comprises the earlier distribution which later expanded into B and finally included area C. Although temporal and spatial borders of the culture may be defined with some precision by archaeologists, there is no way that a linguist could determine at what stage the proto-language had begun to diverge; e.g. had palatalization of the velars begun in area A, or B or C or even later?, and how could one possibly know? Most solutions to the homeland problem involve even larger-scale entities with even greater imprecision.

less precise than an archaeological construct e.g. – the temporal band of a radiocarbon date at two standard deviations or the geographical distribution of archaeological culture(s). For example, even if we were somehow divinely inspired with the knowledge that the Tripolye culture of the north-west Black Sea region was '(Proto-) Indo-European', the nature of the archaeological entity does not accommodate a clear linguistic description through time (Figure 7.3). The culture existed for some 1500 years over a variety of periods and with dynamic cultural borders. There is no point in its existence (temporal or spatial) in which a linguist might confidently declare that the velars had not yet been palatalized, the feminine had been formed, or heteroclitics had ceased to be productive; i.e. there is no chronological or geographical slice of this culture which might be declared pre-IE, proto-IE, or already differentiated IE. Thus, a solution expressed in terms of archaeological cultures with narrow dates occupying well-defined territories theoretically exceeds the precision that can be given for the temporal definition of Proto-Indo-European. The quest for the IE homeland in archaeology bears an awful similarity to seeking the day, month and year of the Renaissance or Industrial Revolution.

CONCLUSION

Even ignoring the problems of translating the PIE speech community into a phenomenon reflected in the archaeological record, no solution to the homeland problem can reflect with archaeological precision either the exact temporal or geographical borders of the IE homeland.

Linguistic relationship principle

A minimum requirement of any solution to the IE homeland problem must be congruence with the most basic linguistic relationships between the various IE stocks (i.e. major isoglosses). While there may be dispute over the internal relationships between some of the stocks, there is broad linguistic agreement (e.g. Adrados 1982; Hamp 1990b; Gamkrelidze and Ivanov 1995) that envisages the following relationships:

1   A separation of Anatolian from the other IE stocks.
2   A central area involving Greek, Armenian, Indo-Iranian.
3   A north(western) area involving Germanic, Baltic and Slavic in some late linguistic relationship.
4   A western area (perhaps) involving Celtic and Italic, which was perhaps more closely linked to 3 than 2.
5   The position of Tocharian is disputed but does not include an early close relationship with the Indo-Iranian superstock.

A viable solution to the IE homeland problem must somehow accommodate these relationships or, at least, not propose vectors of expansion that would obviously transgress such relationships.

Total distribution principle

A valid solution to the IE homeland problem must explain the distribution of *all* the IE languages. The nature of any 'solution' for one region of Eurasia has implications (chronological, contact) for others that cannot be ignored. Hence, an explanation for one region, no matter how satisfying, is valueless unless it is articulated with explanations for all IE-speaking regions.

While the principle is clear enough, its violation is so frequent that it demands some additional comment, especially as it often involves largely archaeological solutions to the homeland problem. For the early nineteenth century, it was regularly claimed (and demonstrated to the satisfaction of its proponents) that the Germanic peoples/languages had been, as Tacitus observed, autochthonous in northern Europe. Any archaeologists could then trace, through retrograde reconstruction, cultural continuity from the Nordic Iron Age cultures (Jastorf, etc.) back through the Late Bronze Age to the Early Bronze Age (no essential break in continuity) to the Later Neolithic (Corded Ware/Battle-axe horizon) to the Neolithic TRB and then Ertebølle and still earlier Mesolithic cultures. If the Germans could not be explained by migrations from the outside then they must have originated in northern Europe, and if the Indo-Europeans occupied a confined homeland, and we know that the Germans hadn't moved, then it must have been the rest of the IE-speaking peoples who had left a north European homeland. This argument of archaeological continuity could probably be supported for every IE-speaking region of Eurasia where any archaeologist can effortlessly pen such statements as 'while there may be some evidence for the diffusion of ideas, there is no evidence in the archaeological record for a population movement' or 'while admitting some minor population intrusions, these hardly suffice to explain a shift in language'.

The current penchant for demanding local continuity is by no means confined to proponents of European homelands as it now also appears to be a product of certain post-colonial Indian archaeologists and linguists who assert that Indo-Aryan has always been spoken in the north-west of the sub-continent and that all other IE peoples have migrated from there (Misra 1992; Deo and Kamanth, 1993, but see also the more balanced works of others, e.g. Sharma 1993, 1995). The ramifications of such theories are seldom if ever contemplated and after decisively demonstrating (to their satisfaction) that all Indo-Europeans originated in north-west India, the remaining IE stocks are left very much to their own devices (unaided by archaeological evidence or linguistic credibility) to find their own way to their historical seats. In any event, India has not been rejected as a potential homeland of the Indo-Europeans (*pace* Misra 1992: 41) only because 'it is a nice place to live and people would not move outside it'!

Non-IE periphery

The periphery of the IE world at its earliest reflection in the written record indicates the current or previous existence of non-IE languages, i.e. Iberia–south France (Tartessian and Iberian, Basque), central Italy (Etruscan, ?etc.), Crete (?), central and eastern Anatolia (Hattic, Hurrio-Urartian), Iran (Elamite), and India (Munda, Dravidian/Brahui). It is less likely (although not entirely impossible) that the IE homeland was situated within a territory occupied by non-IE languages at the time of the earliest written records.

ASSESSMENT PRINCIPLES

In assessing the plausibility (rather than validity) of any solution to the homeland problem, there should at least be a series of consistent principles employed.

Drawn from the above discussion, the following minimum criteria should be satisfied by any potential solution.

Temporal plausibility

The homeland should be identified at a time consistent with the broad parameters of linguistic estimation of time-depth and the evidence of lexico-cultural seriation – i.e. the Neolithic through Early Bronze Age. Any date later than the Early Bronze Age (i.e. later than *c.* 2500 BC), is too late to accommodate the degree of linguistic divergence that we encounter in the Later Bronze Age when the earliest IE stocks are recorded (Anatolian, Indo-Aryan, Mycenaean Greek). Any date earlier than the Neolithic requires us to reconstruct a PIE speech community lacking most of its culturally diagnostic vocabulary. That the Proto-Indo-Europeans had linguistic predecessors is self-evident, but the term 'Proto-Indo-European' must have chronological parameters like any other linguistic entity and can no more be applied to a population of speakers who predate the reconstructed IE lexicon than we can assign a Bronze Age date to 'proto-French'.

Exclusion principle

The homeland should lie in a territory not demonstrably non-IE at a time proximate to IE expansions; i.e. those territories of Europe or the Near East with non-IE populations from the earliest historical (Bronze Age) testimony are unlikely to have been the IE homeland. Obviously, it is just possible that already by the earliest written records IE-speaking populations may have been displaced by non-IE populations. But given the fact that we are attempting to describe the dispersion of a truly enormous language family and there are no apparent directional patterns of IE dialectology that might conform to a model of an external 'push', it seems unlikely that already by the earliest written records the Indo-Europeans had been displaced from their original area of distribution.

Relationship principle

Expansions from the homeland should conform with the broad interrelationships between the IE stocks; i.e. they should not require an entirely different series of movements to explain the major morphological and lexical isoglosses between the various IE stocks. Given that the inter-stock relationships within IE are not particularly precise, there is wide room for latitude here although some theories do seem to transgress any obvious relationships.

Total distribution principle

A homeland solution must provide a plausible case for the dispersion of *all* IE languages. While it will be readily admitted that there are many areas in which it is extremely difficult to date or trace the movements of IE-speakers into a particular region, there are also cases that can be made and arguments that need to be addressed. This principle will be applied to any theory in which major sections or stocks of the IE language family have been left to their own devices to explain their existence.

Archaeological plausibility

The archaeological expression of an IE homeland and dispersions should be supported by evidence which at least *might* be argued to reflect culturally similar, related or historically associated cultures or culture groups or the vectors by which language may have spread. While it must be granted that there is no direct correlation between archaeological culture and language group, the lack of a total correlation does not mean that no correlation exists at all (Clarke 1978: 302–5). While there have been some attempts to discuss the nature of relationships between both archaeology and migration, e.g. Rouse (1986), Anthony (1990), Kristiansen (1989), and archaeology and language (Mallory 1992), none of these have yet created the sought for 'middle range theory' that might tie hard archaeological evidence to the movement of linguistic entities. Nevertheless, a solution to the IE problem that explains the dispersion of all the various IE stocks must rest on something stronger than its proponent's ability to wield a felt-tip pen. In short, there must be some supporting archaeological evidence for the arrows drawn on a map that suggest the course of IE dispersals.

INDO-EUROPEAN HOMELANDS

Although there is a wide range of solutions to the IE homeland problem, current discussion is largely confined to about four basic models, albeit with many variations (Figure 7.4). These are arranged here in chronological order. In presenting each case, an attempt has been made to indicate why such a theory is attractive, critically evaluate it according to the criteria laid down above, and, where possible, suggest modifications that might enhance the theory's credibility.

Model 1: Baltic-Pontic(-Caspian)

TIME: MESOLITHIC (e.g. Killian 1983; Häusler 1985)

This solution embraces two regions which later exhibit population movements and/or widespread cultural homogeneity that may be associated with linguistic entities ancestral to many of the IE stocks. The north European component of this solution embraces a presumed continuum that runs from the TRB Culture through the Globular Amphora and Corded Ware cultures of the Late Neolithic to the Bronze Age sequence of Unetice > Tumulus > Urnfield. This comprises a vast area of northern and central Europe which can underlie the later emergence of Celts, Germans, Balts and Slavs; possibly also Italic and Illyrians. The eastern territory of this solution also includes the steppe and forest-steppe regions of the Pontic-Caspian – i.e. the Sredni

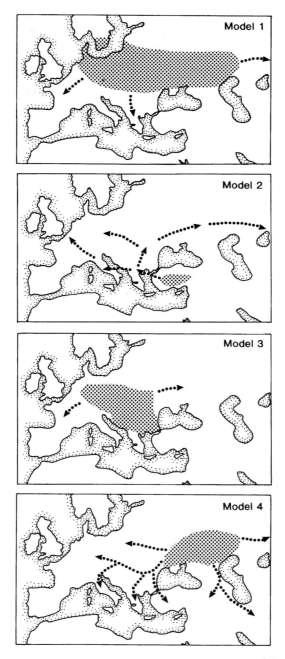

Figure 7.4 Four main models of the homeland and dispersion of the Indo-European languages.

Stog–Khvalynsk–Botai cultures with the later Yamna, Catacomb/Poltavka, and, by the Later Bronze Age, the Srubna and Andronovo cultures which would involve expansions eastwards from the European steppe through Kazakhstan and on into central Asia and beyond. Developments in this region could be seen to underlie the later Indo-Iranians, possibly the Thracians, Dacians, Tocharians, and, if Eneolithic and Early Bronze Age expansion from the steppe into SE Europe/Anatolia is allowed, then Anatolians, Phrygians, Armenians, and Greeks might be arrayed in this solution. This model provides a convenient homeland for those who argue either genetic or early contact relations between Proto-Indo-Europeans and the Uralic language family (and North Caucasian).

EVALUATION

1   The time-depth of the solution is usually taken to represent the Mesolithic and it is nearly impossible to envisage why such populations, stretching from the Baltic to the Black Sea or Caspian, might share at this time a common vocabulary for domestic plants, animals and items of late Neolithic/Early Bronze Age technology such as wheeled vehicles, or gain this vocabulary without evidence of borrowings, thousands of years after the Mesolithic period.

2   The territory was not demonstrably occupied by non-IE populations at any time although there is a considerable literature devoted to non-IE substrate lexical items from northern and central Europe (e.g. Hamp 1990b; Huld 1990; Polomé 1990).

3   Expansions from the general area indicated can be seen to accommodate most linguistic models of the dialectal relationships between the IE stocks; i.e. one may at least propose a series of movements centrifugal from this region which would not be incongruent with the major dialect groupings of the IE stocks.

4   This solution provides a convenient ancestry to the IE languages of much of Europe and those of Asia since it requires minimum movements of population from areas where IE-speaking populations are later encountered. However, its explanation of IE stocks in the Balkans, Greece and Anatolia requires it to subsume elements of the Pontic-Caspian solution (see pp. 112–13).

5   Archaeologically, the homeland area is an artificial construct and consists of at least two distinct cultural regions from the Mesolithic period onwards; i.e. there is no underlying cultural reason why one might impute the same language to Mesolithic populations from the Baltic to the Caspian as there is no reason to suggest a major interaction sphere in this region, similarity of physical type, or any other phenomena which might lead one to conclude that we are dealing with a common linguistic region.

MODIFICATION

The time-depth of this solution may be altered to the Neolithic which miti-
gates the criticism stemming from the first criterion. On the other hand, the
territories of central Europe and those of the steppe region are so culturally
distinct (and agreed so even by the supporters of this solution) that it still
seems to argue against a common linguistic basis. Indeed, a modification to
the Neolithic raises almost as many problems as it resolves. It is, for example,
difficult to separate the origins of the Neolithic in Danubian Europe from
Neolithic cultures of south-eastern Europe and, by extension, Anatolia and
western Asia, while altering the time-depth of this solution to a later period
transforms it largely into the Model 2 solution (see next section). Resistance
to moving the dates of PIE to the Neolithic are necessitated by the recognition (among supporters of this particular solution) that the steppe-region is
culturally distinct, and it is extremely difficult to build any archaeological
model that supports strong cultural links between central Europe (or the
Balkans) and the steppe region either at the initiation of or during the
Neolithic.

Model 2: Anatolia

TIME: EARLY NEOLITHIC, *c.* 7000–6000 BC (Renfrew 1987; Safronov
1989; Cavalli-Sforza *et al.* 1994)

This solution provides IE expansions with a substantial vector in demic diffusion (i.e. a 'wave of advance'), that carried speakers of IE over a vast area
of Europe from an area (Anatolia) where IE speakers are later found in the
Bronze Age. The mechanism for expansion is seen in the spread of a new
subsistence economy based on domestic plants and animals. This would have
stimulated population growth such that random budding off would have
resulted in the expansion of people from Anatolia across Europe and Asia
and provided the immigrant farmers with selective advantages whereby they
would have assimilated local populations of hunter-gatherers. The solution
also unites populations from the Balkans (and probably Danubian Europe)
and Anatolia which, in the Neolithic, are both physically and culturally related
(Schwidetsky and Rosing 1990), and which could argue for a common
linguistic area. The solution provides a convenient geographical relationship
for those who suggest extra-linguistic connections between Indo-European,
Semitic and Kartvelian.

EVALUATION

1   The solution requires IE expansions from the beginning of the Neolithic
    and postulates the existence of a series of IE-speaking cultures across
    Eurasia in areas which, *at the time postulated*, do not reflect temporally
    critical items of the reconstructed PIE vocabulary. For example, the
    same word for horse is attested in almost all IE stocks (from Ireland
    to Chinese Turkestan) and yet the animal is not known in Anatolia

until the 4th millennium BC (and *pace* Dolgopolsky 1993: 240, the Luvian and Lycian cognates of the PIE word for horse are as likely to be inherited as borrowed from an Indo-Iranian language) or Greece until the Bronze Age (and can only be explained away by presuming long-distant acquaintance with the horse). Even more serious are items such as wheeled vehicles which have no archaeological expression at such an early date yet are attested in the inherited PIE vocabulary of Anatolian. Linguistic diffusion at *c.* 7000 BC is considerably earlier than is usually accepted by linguists on their admittedly intuitive estimations of PIE time-depth.

2   With the emergence of the earliest written records an Anatolian homeland falls either within or on the immediate periphery of non-IE populations; i.e. the Hatti, whose territory the Hittites occupied, or the Hurrians of east Anatolia. Both languages are radically different from IE and provide no grounds whatsoever for suggesting that they developed together among related dialects at the beginning of the Neolithic. Anatolian scholars (e.g. Singer 1981; Steiner 1981; Puhvel 1994), on both linguistic grounds and the self-testimony of Hittite documents, regard the Hittites as intruders into their territory and not autochthons. On the other hand, linguistic records are 'mute' for prehistoric western Anatolia where one might prefer to anchor the PIE homeland.

3   The course of Neolithic expansion proposed, for example, by Colin Renfrew, violates the interrelationships of the IE languages, i.e. the proposed population movements are not always congruent with the isoglosses within the IE family and it proposes historical connections and lines of development contradicted by the linguistic evidence; e.g. close relationships between Anatolian and Greek, between Greek and Italic, etc. Other configurations involving a secondary IE homeland for the non-Anatolian stocks in south-east Europe, e.g. Dolgopolsky (1988, 1993), can be made to accommodate better the dialectal relations of the different IE stocks.

4   The theory provides a plausible archaeological vector for the Europeans but it has serious problems explaining the IE-speakers of Asia. Renfrew's Plan A, for example, derives them from the Near East at the spread of the Neolithic, against the fact that between his 'homeland' and the historical seats of the Indo-Iranians are historically attested non-IE populations (Elamites, Sumerians, Dravidians) who demonstrably or circumstantially should have preceded the movement of Indo-Europeans. His Plan B requires a demic diffusion from the Balkans across the Pontic-Caspian steppe which is regarded by many (supporters of the Model 1 and Model 4 theories) as contradicted by the archaeological evidence that suggests two very different cultural and physical worlds with no demic diffusion (or if there is, it was moving from east to west).

5   Archaeological plausibility is tied to the vector of demic diffusion which
    is certainly 'arguable' for large parts of Europe and, if acculturation be
    allowed, for most of Europe. To this have been added genetic argu-
    ments where an analysis of the first principle component involving the
    constellation of ninety-five gene frequencies of modern European popu-
    lations suggests a movement from south-west Asia towards Atlantic
    Europe (Cavalli-Sforza *et al.* 1994: 291). What is not necessarily demon-
    strated is that this represents a movement coincident with the origins
    and dispersal of agriculture rather than something else, e.g. the spread
    of modern human populations through south-west Asia from an African
    'Eve'. Moreover, it is questionable whether such genetic maps actually
    provide independent support for archaeological migrations when the
    map prepared from the second principal component would, in the
    absence of negative archaeological evidence, support a migration from
    Finland to Iberia (or the reverse)! Evaluation of the genetic map against
    the patterns of migrations and linguistic affinities proposed for this
    theory have been challenged by statistical analysis (Sokal *et al.* 1992).

MODIFICATION

The theory can be (and has been) modified (Zvelebil and Zvelebil 1988,
1990; Sherratt and Sherratt 1988) which can ameliorate some of the objections. If demic diffusion be limited to western Anatolia, the Balkans and
Danubian Europe, and this be regarded as a linguistically interactive zone
from the 7th to the 4th millennium BC, then it may be possible to envisage
the dissemination of cultural terms within this region that are reconstructed
to the proto-language. The homeland territory, if placed further west in
Anatolia (where the archaeological evidence is admittedly quite sparse), helps
obviate the need to derive the earliest attested Indo-Europeans from a region
occupied by non-IE peoples (e.g. Hatti or Hurrian territory). If the theory
avoids attempting to explain the spread of all IE stocks in the Neolithic but
allows for their spread later in the Bronze and Iron Ages, then it permits
different trajectories for the distribution of the IE stocks that may accommodate their linguistic interrelationships; e.g. Celtic and Italic could then
derive from Danubian Europe and not Greece > Italy > France. The revised
model might also include the establishment of a sphere of interaction in the
north Pontic to avoid the difficulties of deriving the Eurasian steppe
Neolithic/Eneolithic solely from (unattested) demic diffusion from the Balkans
(Sherratt and Sherratt 1988).

Model 3: Central Europe–Balkans

TIME: EARLY NEOLITHIC *c.* 5000 BC (Gornung 1964; Diakonoff 1985)

A homeland in central Europe to the Balkans is situated in a region which
would satisfy those linguists who adhere to the use of the centre of gravity
principle. It also provides a reasonably close contact zone between IE and

the Uralic or North Caucasian languages suggested by some linguistic models. From an archaeological standpoint, this is the territory of the *Linearbandkeramik* which occupied a broad area of Europe, Atlantic to the Ukraine, and shows remarkable uniformity which is suggestive (at least to some) of a common linguistic horizon, e.g. Bosch-Gimpera (1960), Devoto (1962), Makkay (1991, 1992). Later developments within the Danubian and Balkan regions see the emergence of all the later cultural elements ascribed to PIE by the 4th millennium BC.

EVALUATION

1   The time perspective of this solution can generally accommodate most temporal models of PIE.

2   The proposed homeland solution is devoid of any evidence other than IE-speakers from the earliest historical records. But, as with the Model 1 solution, arguments for non-IE substrates exist also for central Europe and the Balkans.

3   An expansion from this region can be made to conform with the dialectal relations of the IE stocks.

4   The model is critically deficient in explaining the IE stocks of Asia and in general does not satisfactorily project IE-speakers east of the Dnieper unless it adopts elements of the Model 1 solution which, consequently, then fail the test of chronology and archaeological plausibility.

5   The archaeological evidence can be pressed to service over much of northern and western Europe but it is not easy (although not impossible) to support an expansion of Danubian or Balkan cultures either into Anatolia or across the steppe into the staging areas – much less the historical seats of the Indo-Iranian and Tocharians. Inherent in this solution is also a rejection of the Model 2 solution which is problematic since it excludes that which the Anatolian solution supports most strongly, i.e. cultural (and linguistic) links between Anatolia and the Balkans. It must be admitted, however, that this model has a great many variations among which many would support the model of the *Linearbandkeramik* culture as an autochthonous development in the Neolithic, ethnically and linguistically unrelated to the neolithic cultures of south-east Europe although influenced by them with respect to subsistence agriculture and technology.

Model 4: Pontic-Caspian

TIME: ENEOLITHIC *c.* 4500–3000 BC (Gimbutas 1977, 1980, 1991; Anthony 1991)

The solution accommodates the widespread belief that the earliest IE-speakers were primarily mobile pastoralists rather than settled agriculturalists, and the location satisfies those who believe that the closest extrafamilial links with

PIE are to be found in Uralic and North Caucasian. The Pontic-Caspian steppe and forest steppe region produces a number of broad cultural entities which may be seen as interaction spheres within a single language family, and there is archaeological evidence of expansion from this region both westwards into the Balkans and eastwards into Kazakhstan. The vector for the initial expansion is seen in a highly mobile economic strategy with a social organization capable of absorbing and dominating various different ethnolinguistic groups.

EVALUATION

1   The time-depth for a PIE homeland in the Eneolithic (i.e. 5th and 4th millennia BC), has no difficulties in satisfying the general expectations of linguists for PIE time-depth nor for accounting for the lexico-cultural elements ascribed to PIE – e.g. wheeled vehicles, horse (riding), secondary products, etc.

2   The area, only attested in historical records since the Iron Age, has never been shown to be demonstrably non-IE in the prehistoric period, although it has seen more recent intrusions from Turkic-speaking peoples.

3   Centrifugal expansion of IE from a Pontic-Caspian centre can accommodate the basic interrelationships of the IE stocks and has been accepted by a number of linguists (e.g. Adrados 1982).

4   The model proposes to explain the later historical position of all IE languages, both those in Europe and Asia, i.e. this solution 'bridges' the cultural (Dniester–Dnieper) gap envisaged in the Model 1 and Model 3 solutions and not convincingly resolved in Model 2 (see pp. 106–12).

5   There is solid archaeological evidence for population movements from the steppe region but only as far west as the Tisza river and the Balkans. All further expansions, either to the west or the north (i.e. the presumed staging areas for Celtic, Germanic, Baltic and perhaps Slavic), are founded on evidence which is frequently dismissed as too generic to compel belief (e.g. spread of domestic horse, wheeled vehicles, defensive architecture, tumulus burial, battle-axes, animal burial, etc.). The evidence for expansions southwards into Anatolia is similarly questionable. While a good case can be made for an expansion of Pontic-Caspian pastoralists onto the Asiatic steppe, and perhaps also into the belt of central Asian urban centres (Parpola 1988), it is still difficult to demonstrate movements from the steppe into the historical seats of the Indo-Aryans and the Iranians of Iran itself (Mallory forthcoming b).

CONCLUSIONS

The temptation to conclude with the last solution as the most probable must be resisted and, in the limitations of this chapter, it is perhaps advantageous to set aside all non-archaeological aspects of the problem as peripheral and focus on one of the key archaeological elements of any solution. The various archaeological models proposed here must each confront a common problem which Harold Peake and Herbert Fleure, perhaps simplistically but still neatly, described as the difference between the 'steppe and the sown'. This dichotomy is probably overdrawn (Mallory forthcoming c) but there is, nevertheless, widespread recognition that the cultural trajectories of the European Neolithic and Copper Age cultures and those of the Pontic-Caspian region would appear to be extremely different. Yet by the end of the Neolithic or during the Bronze Age, both regions must be accommodated within a single covering model that explains why they should both belong to the same language family and be ancestral to most of the known IE stocks. A cultural trip line or watershed is then proposed, somewhere between the Dniester and the Dnieper rivers (cf. Kosko 1991), which must somehow be bridged (Figure 7.5). Two

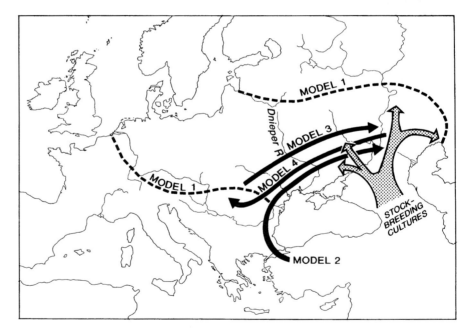

Figure 7.5 The Dnieper 'border'. Model 1 embraces both sides of the Dnieper border, while Models 2 and 3 require population movements in a west–east direction associated with the spread of agriculture from Anatolia through the Balkans; Model 4 suggests that the movement went from east to west and finds a more convenient source of the neolithic economy in the Caucasus.

of the solutions, the Anatolian (Model 2) and Central European/Balkan (Model 3) attempt to bridge from the west; the Pontic-Caspian (Model 4) attempts to bridge from the east, and supporters of the Baltic–Pontic solution (Model 1), finding the pitch already too cluttered with opposed cultural trajectories in the Neolithic, move the goal posts back to the Mesolithic. None of these solutions is entirely convincing, and I would emphasize that I do not personally think that the Pontic-Caspian solution is the best solution but merely the 'least bad' solution. But preferences aside, I would like to conclude with a look at some of the critical problems involved.

If we examine the various theories in reverse chronological order, then the Pontic-Caspian solution marks the most recent 'breach' of the Dniester–Dnieper barrier. This 'breach' occurs by *c.* 4000 BC (Manzura *et al.* 1995), and it should be emphasized that the days when one envisaged purely a movement of Yamna tribes to the west – i.e. a phenomenon of the 3rd or late 2nd millennium BC (e.g. Alekshin 1994) – are long since passed. That there was population movement into the Balkans seems difficult to fault unless one wishes to deny all evidence of migration in the archaeological record; i.e. it comes fairly close to the same type of evidence we would employ to identify Anglo-Saxon burials in Britain. But such evidence is only solid as far as the Tisza river (Ecsedy 1979), and beyond that the entire construct of 'Kurgan invasions' is far more problematic and insecure (Mallory 1989: 243–57). What is most disturbing perhaps is that the evidence of the steppe-type burials occurs generally in those environments similar to that encountered on the steppe and, consequently, suggests that there were ecological limits to such intrusions. Moreover, the movement of steppe populations into the rest of Europe is also historically attested, most visibly in the migrations and settlement of Sarmatian tribes during the Iron Age, but these most certainly did not lead to the permanent extension of the Iranian language into areas beyond the Pontic steppe – much less an Iranian domination of eastern Europe.

If Anthony (1990) is correct in seeing the adaptation of horse-riding not only as a stimulus to expansion but also one that may have definite environmental limitations, then we can see all too clearly that the so-called Kurgan solution does not do enough to resolve the problem of origins for most of the IE stocks beyond the Balkans. But this weakness applies only if one presumes that the Pontic-Caspian solution relies entirely on a mobile horse-riding model. The origins of cultures such as the Globular Amphora, initially derived directly from the steppe in the early writings of Marija Gimbutas, are now sought elsewhere. Polish archaeologists are increasingly coming to accept a local (Lengyel) origin for the Globular Amphora (e.g. Cofta-Broniewska 1991). Now such a model is not incongruent with the latter writings of the late Marija Gimbutas who argued for a much more diffuse spread of 'Kurgan traits' among a variety of east and central European Late Neolithic cultures. Her most recent models (e.g. Gimbutas 1991) had moved considerably from the simple concept of a wave of horse-riding warriors, a fact that her critics often appear to forget. But her models moved into an area of more subtle cultural interrelationships, a 'cumulative kurganization' to steal a phrase from Christopher Hawkes, which will require both far greater evidence and argument to be properly discussed or dismissed.

Two of the other theories attempt to bridge the Dniester–Dnieper gap from the west. Of the two, it is most difficult to credit the *Linearbandkeramik* solution since the number of attempts to propose cultural movements during the Middle or Later Neolithic from the west on to the steppe are few indeed (e.g. Klein (1963) and Shevchenko (1986)), and little regarded. Even if we should see the Cucuteni-Tripolye culture as an eastern extension of the *Linearbandkeramik* under the influence of Balkan cultures, we can track its settlements spatially only as far as the Middle Dnieper and, worse, tempo- rally only as *synchronous with* rather than *ancestral to* the Pontic-Caspian cultures that emerged many hundreds of kilometres to its east. If the Tisza marks the western border of Pontic-Caspian incursions, so the Dnieper marks the eastern border of central European or Balkan movements.

Can the Dniester–Dnieper gap be bridged during the inception of the Neolithic? This has been presumed on occasion, but in reality the case for demic expansion ends with the Tripolye culture, and it is exceedingly diffi- cult to make a solid case for a population movement at the beginning of the Neolithic crossing the Pontic-Caspian region and then moving into Kazakhstan by the 4th or 3rd millennium BC. Even the origin of domestic livestock and plants in the Pontic-Caspian region appears to have had staging areas different from south-east Europe, and both central Asia (Merpert 1974; Matyushin 1986) and (more plausibly), the Caucasus (Shnirelman 1992) have been proposed. Given that mixed agriculture in the Caucasus was as early as that in the Balkans, and more proximate to the earliest neolithic sites in the lower Don region, it would provide a source for a strain of domestic sheep most similar to that of the Pontic-Caspian, and is thus clearly the preferred hypothesis.

If a case for linguistic expansion from the Balkans across the steppe and forest-steppe is to be sustained, it is more likely to hang on some form of elite dominance. In considering the possible evidence, one could point to the circulation of Tripolye wares and figurines in Sredny Stog burials (Telegin 1973) or, more extensively, the movement of copper and copper artefacts of Balkan provenance across the steppe as far as the Volga (Chernykh 1992: 42–8). But even here it is difficult to warrant these as a mechanism for pres- tige social relationships between Balkan traders(?) and local Pontic-Caspian populations. The very mechanism of these contacts has been credited to the highly mobile steppe populations who themselves produced this interaction sphere by pushing into the territory of the west (Chernykh 1992: 44). Moreover, there is at least some evidence that the steppe and forest-steppe populations worked the imported copper themselves and founded their own metallurgical tradition. The other possible prestige metal – silver – also circu- lated through this interaction sphere in the 4th and 3rd millennia (Mallory and Huld 1984; Jovanovic 1994), but here again we are hardly talking about the expansion of a prestige Balkan dialect across the steppe. The most obvious Near Eastern impact on the Pontic-Caspian region is evident in the Maykop culture and, given the location of the Maykop remains, we might better expect the expansion of north-west Caucasian than Indo-European into the steppe region. In short, putative IE homelands set to the west of the Dniester–Dnieper border are even less likely to produce a model of cultural much less linguistic transgression across this border than those who place the homeland on the steppe and forest-steppe.

The attraction of somehow combining at least two-thirds of the disparate geographical elements of the homeland puzzle in the Baltic-Pontic solution (Model 1) are obvious since such a homeland pre-empts any necessity for devising demic or elite movements crossing the Dniester–Dnieper border, as this region sits in the middle of the homeland territory. But other than by an act of cartographic fiat, what is there to justify drawing a circle around the various cultures from the Baltic to the Pontic or Caspian and declaring them all to be Indo-European? Not only is there no common Mesolithic tradition or techno-complex underlying this entire area but even appeals to similarities in physical anthropology, the so-called robust proto-Europoids, have been dismissed with reference to the Dnieper–Donets region (Jacobs 1993). The reconstructed cultural vocabulary of PIE makes it clear that if this solution is to be validated it must show how central and northern Europe, as well as the Pontic-Caspian, shared the same inception of the Neolithic economy and subsequent technological developments. As this is the very stumbling block of the other solutions, it can hardly be applied here.

In sum then, we have different sub-regions of an early IE world, scattered in space from the Baltic to Anatolia and east across the European steppe, and set in time somewhere between what we would recognize as PIE unity and the emergence of the major IE stocks. To unite these disparate geographical elements together into a single 'unified field theory' seems to be as distant to those seeking such a goal in Indo-European studies as it is for physicists.

REFERENCES

Adams, D.Q. 1984. The position of Tocharian among the other Indo-European languages. *Journal of the American Oriental Society* 104, 395–402.

Adrados, F. 1982. *Die räumliche und zeitliche Differenzierung des Indoeuropäischen im Lichte der Vor und Frühgeschichte.* Innsbrucker Beiträge zur Sprachwissenschaft 27.

Alekshin, V.A. 1994. On the location of the Indo-European homeland. Unpublished precirculated paper for Theme 3: Language, Anthropology and Archaeology. World Archaeological Congress 3.

Anderson, N. 1879. *Studien zur Vergleichung der indogermanischen und finnisch-ugrischen Sprachen.* Shnakenburg: Dorpat.

Anthony, D. 1990. Migration in archeology: the baby and the bathwater. *American Anthropologist* 92, 895–914.

Anthony, D. 1991. The archaeology of Indo-European origins. *Journal of Indo-European Studies* 19, 193–222.

Bender, H. 1922. *The Home of the Indo-Europeans*. Princeton, N.J.: Princeton University Press.

Bosch-Gimpera, P. 1960. *El Problema Indoeuropeo*. Mexico: Universita Nacional Autónoma de Mexico.

Brandenstein, W. 1936. *Die erste 'indogermanische' Wanderung*. Vienna: Gerold.

Brixhe, C. and A. Panayotou 1994a. Le Macédonien. In *Langues Indo-Européennes*, F. Bader (ed.), 205–20. Paris: CNRS.

Brixhe, C. and A. Panayotou. 1994b. Le Thrace. In *Langues Indo-Européennes*, F. Bader (ed.), 179–203. Paris: CNRS.

Cavalli-Sforza, L.L., P. Menozzi and A. Piazza. 1994. *The History and Geography of Human Genes*. Princeton, N.J.: Princeton University Press,.

Chernykh, E.N. 1992. *Ancient Metallurgy in the USSR*. Cambridge: Cambridge University Press.

Clarke, D.L. 1978. *Analytical Archaeology* (2nd edn). London: Methuen.

Cofta-Broniewska, A. 1991. *New Tendencies in Studies of Globular Amphorae Culture*. Warsaw, Cracow, Poznan: Jagiellonian University.

Colarusso, J. 1994. Phyletic links between Proto-Indo-European and Proto-Northwest Caucasian. *Mother Tongue* 21, 8–20.

Coleman, R. 1994. The lexical relationships of Latin in Indo-European. In *Linguistic Studies on Latin*, J. Herman (ed.), 359–77. Amsterdam: Benjamins.

Cowgill, W. and M. Mayrhofer 1986. *Indogermanische Grammatik, Band I*. Heidelberg: Carl Winter.

Deo, S.B. and S. Kamanth. 1993. *The Aryan Problem*. Pune: Bharatiya Itihasa Sankalana Samiti.

Devoto, G. 1962. *Origini Indeuropee*. Firenze: Sansoni.

Diakonoff, I. 1985. On the original home of the speakers of Indo-European. *Journal of Indo-European Studies* 13, 92–174.

Dolgopolsky, A. 1988. The Indo-European homeland and lexical contacts of Proto-Indo-European with other languages. *Mediterranean Language Review* 3, 7–31.

Dolgopolsky, A. 1993. More about the Indo-European homeland problem. *Mediterranean Language Review* 6–7, 230–48.

Dressler, W. 1965. Methodische Vorfragen bei der Bestimmung der 'Urheimat'. *Die Sprache* 11, 25–60.

Drews, R. 1988. *The Coming of the Greeks*. Princeton, N.J.: Princeton University Press.

Ecsedy, I. 1979. *The People of the Pit-grave Kurgans in Eastern Hungary*. Budapest: Akemiai Kiado.

Ehret, C. 1988. Language change and the material correlates of language and ethnic shift. *Antiquity* 62, 564–74.

Fodor, I. 1965. *The Rate of Linguistic Change*. The Hague: Janua Linguarum 43.

Gamkrelidze, T. and I. Ivanov. 1995. *Indo-European and the Indo-Europeans*. Berlin and New York: Mouton.

Georgiev, V. 1966. *Introduzione alla Storia delle Lingue Indeuropee*. Rome: Edizioni dell'Ateneo.

Gimbutas, M. 1977. The first wave of Eurasian steppe pastoralists into Copper Age Europe. *Journal of Indo-European Studies* 5, 277–338.

Gimbutas, M. 1980. The Kurgan wave #2 (c. 3400–3200 B.C.) into Europe and the following transformation of culture. *Journal of Indo-European Studies* 8, 273–315.

Gimbutas, M. 1991. *Civilization of the Goddess*. San Francisco: Harper.

Gornung, B. 1964. *K Voprosu ob Obrazovaniy Indoevropeyskoy Yazykovoy Obshchnosti*. Moscow: Nauka.

Hamp, E.P. 1990a. The Indo-European horse. In *When Worlds Collide*, T.L. Markey and J.A.C. Greppin (eds), 211–26. Ann Arbor, Mich.: Karoma.

Hamp, E.P. 1990b. The Pre-Indo-European language of northern (central) Europe. In *When Worlds Collide*, T.L. Markey and J.A.C. Greppin (eds), 293–309. Ann

Arbor, Mich.: Karoma.

Harmatta, J. 1981. Proto-Iranians and Proto-Indians in Central Asia in the 2nd millennium B.C. (linguistic evidence). In *Ethnic Problems of the History of Central Asia in the Early Period*, 75–83. Moscow: Nauka.

Häusler, A. 1985. Kulturebezeihungen zwischen Ost- und Mitteleuropa im Neolithikum? *Jahresschrift für mitteldeutsche Vorgeschichte* 68, 21–74.

Hirt, H. 1895. Die Urheimat und die Wanderungen der Indogermanen. *A. Hettners Geographische Zeitschrift* 1, 649–65.

Hodge, C.T. 1981 Indo-Europeans in the Near East. *Anthropological Linguistics* 23, 227–44.

Hommel, F. 1879. Arier und Semiten. *Korrespondenzblatt der deutschen Gesellschaft für Anthropologie, Ethnologie und Urgeschichte* 1879, 52–6, 59–61.

Huld, M.E. 1990. The linguistic typology of the Old European substrate in north Central Europe. *Journal of Indo-European Studies* 18, 389–423.

Ipsen, G. 1923. Sumerisch-akkadische Lehnwörter im Indogermanischen. *Indogermanische Forschungen* 41, 174–83.

Jacobs, K. 1993. Human postcranial variation in the Ukrainian mesolithic-neolithic. *Current Anthropology* 34, 311–24.

Jóhanesson, A. 1943. *Um Frumtungu Indógermana og Frumheimkynni*. Reykjavík: Árbók Háskóla Íslands.

Jorgensen, J.G. 1969. *Salish Language and Culture: a statistical analysis of internal relationships, history and evolution*. Language Science Monographs 3. The Hague.

Jovanovic, B. 1994. Silver in the Yamna (pit-grave) culture in the Balkans. *Journal of Indo-European Studies* 21, 207–14.

Killian, L. 1983. *Zum Ursprung der Indogermanen*. Bonn: Habelt.

Klein, L.S. 1963. A brief validation of the migration hypothesis with respect to the origin of the Catacomb culture. *Soviet Anthropology and Archaeology* 1(4), 27–37.

Kosko, A. 1991. The Vistula–Oder basins and the north Pontic region. *Journal of Indo-European Studies* 19, 235–57.

Kristiansen, K. 1989. Prehistoric migrations – the case of the Single Grave and Corded Ware cultures. *Journal of Danish Archaeology* 8, 211–25.

Lamb, S. 1958. Linguistic prehistory in the Great Basin. *International Journal of American Linguistics* 24, 95–100.

Latham, R.G. 1851. *The Germania of Tacitus, with ethnological dissertations and notes*. London: Taylor, Walton & Maberly.

Latham, R.G. 1862. *Elements of Comparative Philology*. London: Walton & Maberly.

Levin, S. 1971. *The Indo-European and Semitic Languages*. Albany, N.Y.: State University of New York Press.

Makkay, J. 1991. *Az Indoeurópai Népek [um]Ostöorténete*. Budapest: Gondolat.

Makkay, J. 1992. A neolithic model of Indo-European prehistory. *Journal of Indo-European Studies* 20, 193–238.

Mallory, J.P. 1973. A short history of the Indo-European problem. *Journal of Indo-European Studies* 1, 21–65.

Mallory, J.P. 1975. The Indo-European homeland problem: the logic of the inquiry. Ph.D. dissertation, UCLA, Xerox Microfilms, Ann Arbor, Michigan.

Mallory, J.P. 1976. Time perspective and Proto-Indo-European culture. *World Archaeology* 8, 44–56.

Mallory, J.P. 1989. *In Search of the Indo-Europeans*. London: Thames & Hudson.

Mallory, J.P. 1992. Migration and language change. In *Peregrinatio Gothica III*, E. Straume and E. Skar (eds), 145–53. Oslo: Universitets Oldsaksamling.

Mallory, J.P. forthcoming a.The Indo-European homeland problem: a matter of time. *Journal of Indo-European Studies*.

Mallory, J.P. forthcoming b. The Indo-European homeland: an Asian perspective. *Bulletin of the Deccan College Post-Graduate and Research Institute*.

Mallory, J.P. forthcoming c. Aspects of Indo-European agriculture. *Festschrift for Jaan Puhvel.*

Mallory, J.P. and M.E. Huld 1984. Proto-Indo-European 'silver'. *Zeitschrift für vergleichende Sprachforschung* 97, 1–12.

Manzura, I., E. Savva and L. Bogataya. 1995. East–West interactions in the Eneolithic and Bronze Age cultures of the north-west Pontic region. *Journal of Indo-European Studies* 23, 1–51.

Matyushin, G. 1986. The Mesolithic and Neolithic in the southern Urals. In *Hunters in Transition,* M. Zvelebil (ed.), 133–150. Cambridge: Cambridge University Press.

Merpert, N.Ya. 1974. *Drevneishie Skotovody Volzhsko-Uralskogo Mezdurechya.* Moscow: Akademiya Nauk.

Milewski, T. 1968. Die Differenzierung der indoeuropäischen Sprachen. *Lingua Posnaniensis* 12–13, 37–54.

Misra, S.S. 1992. *The Aryan Problem: a linguistic approach.* New Delhi: Munshiram Manoharlal.

Napolskikh, V. 1994. Uralic and Tocharian: linguistic evidence and archaeological data. *Language, Anthropology and Archaeology,* World Archaeological Congress 3, New Delhi, Precirculated papers.

Napolskikh, V. 1995. *Uralic Original Home: History of Studies. A Preliminary Review.* Izhevsk: Udmurt Institute for History, Languages and Literature.

Parpola, A. 1988. The coming of the Aryans to Iran and India and the cultural and ethnic identity of the Dasas. *Studia Orientalia* 64, 195–302.

Pisani, V. 1940. Geolinguistica e Indeuropeo. *Atti della Reale Acadenia Nazionale dei Lincei,* ser. VII, vol. ix, fasc. 2.

Plath, R. 1994. Pferd und Wagen im Mykenischen und bei Homer. In *Die Indogermanen und das Pferd,* B. Hänsel and S. Zimmer (eds), 103–14. Budapest: Archaeolingua.

Poesche, T. 1878. *Die Arier. Ein Beitrag zur historischen Anthropologie.* Jena: Costenoble.

Polomé, E. C. 1990. The indo-europeanization of northern Europe: the linguistic evidence. *Journal of Indo-European Studies* 18, 331–8.

Puhvel, J. 1994. Anatolian: autochthon or interloper? *Journal of Indo-European Studies* 22, 251–63.

Renfrew, C. 1987. *Archaeology and Language: the puzzle of Indo-European origins.* London: Jonathan Cape.

Rouse, I. 1986. *Migrations in Prehistory, inferring population movement from cultural remains.* New Haven (Conn.), London: Yale University Press.

Safronov, V.A. 1989. *Indoevropeyskie Prarodiny* [Indo-European homelands]. Gorky: Volgo-Vyatskoe knizhnoe izdatel'stvo.

Sapir, E. 1936. Internal evidence suggestive of the northern origins of the Navaho. *American Anthropologist* 38, 224–35.

Schott, A. 1936. Indogermanisch-Semitisch-Sumerisch. In *Germanen und Indogermanen: Volkstum, Sprache, Heimat, Kultur; Festschrift für Herman Hirt,* H. Arntz (ed.), Vol. 2, 45–95. Heidelberg.

Schmid, W. 1972. Baltische Wässernamen und das vorgeschichtliche Europa. *Indogermanische Forschungen* 77, 1–18.

Schwidetsky, G. 1932. *Schimpanisch – Urmonglisch – Indogermanisch.* Leipzig: Deutscher Verlag.

Schwidetsky, I. and F.W. Rosing. 1990. Vergleichend-statistische Untersuchungen zur Anthropologie von Neolithikum und Bronzezeit. *Homo* 35, 4–45.

Sharma, R.S. 1993. The Aryan problem and the horse. *Social Scientist* 21, 3–16.

Sharma, R.S. 1995. *Looking for the Aryans.* Hyderabad: Orient Longman.

Sherratt, A. and S. Sherratt. 1988. The archaeology of Indo-European: an alternative view. *Antiquity* 62, 584–95.

Shevchenko, 1986. Antropolgiya naseleniya yuzhno-russkikh stepey v epokhu bronzy. In *Antropologiya Sovremennogo i Drevnego Naseleniya Yevropeyskoy Chasti SSSR*, 121–215. Leningrad.

Shnirelman, V. 1992. The emergence of a food-producing economy in the steppe and forest-steppe zones of Eastern Europe. *Journal of Indo-European Studies* 20, 123–43.

Singer, I. 1981. Hittites and Hattians in Anatolia at the begining of the second millennium BC. *Journal of Indo-European Studies* 9, 119–34.

Sokal, R.R., N.L. Oden and B.A. Thomson. 1992. Origins of the Indo-Europeans: genetic evidence. *Proceedings of the National Academy of Sciences of the USA* 89: 7669–73.

Steiner, G. 1981. The role of the Hittites in ancient Anatolia. *Journal of Indo-European Studies* 9, 150–73.

Swadesh, M. 1960. Unas correlaciones de arqueologia y lingüistica. In *El problema indoeuropeo*, P. Bosch-Gimpera, 343–52. Mexico: Universita Nacional Autónoma de Mexico.

Telegin, D.Ya. 1973. *Seredno-stohivska Kultura Epokhy Midi*. Kiev: Naukova Dumka.

Tischler, J. 1973. *Glottochronologie und Lexikostatistik*. Innsbruck: Institut für Sprachwissenschaft der Universität Innsbruck.

Uesson, A.-M. 1970. *On Linguistic Affinity: the Indo-Uralic problem*. Malmö: Fårlags AB Eesti Post.

Zimmer, S. 1988. On dating Proto-Indo-European: a call for honesty. *Journal of Indo-European Studies* 16, 371–5.

Zvelebil, M. and K. Zvelebil. 1988. Agricultural transition and Indo-European dispersals. *Antiquity* 62, 574–83.

Zvelebil, M. and K. Zvelebil. 1990. Agricultural transition, Indo-European origins and the spread of farming. In *When Worlds Collide*, T.L. Markey and J.A.C. Greppin (eds), 237–66. Ann Arbor Mich.: Karoma.

8   The epicentre of the Indo-European linguistic spread

JOHANNA NICHOLS

INTRODUCTION

The vast interior of Eurasia is a linguistic spread zone – a genetic and typo-logical bottleneck where many genetic lines go extinct, structural types tend to converge, a single language or language family spreads out over a broad territorial range, and one language family replaces another over a large range every few millennia.[1] The linguistic geography of the central and western grasslands, from at least the Neolithic until early modern times, has consisted of an overall westward trajectory of language spreads and three more specific trajectories leading through the forest from the middle Volga to the Baltic Sea coast, across the steppe to the Danube plain, and across the desert south of the Caspian Sea to the Near East and Anatolia. Meanwhile, loanwords and cultural influence moved far out in all directions from the urban centres, beginning with ancient Mesopotamia, and these loanword trajectories are independent of language spread trajectories and sometimes move in the oppo-site direction. The wide linguistic ranges, westward trajectories of languages, and mechanisms of language spread in central Eurasia – as well as the nature of spread zones in general – are described in Volume II.

Detailed reconstruction of language family histories in a spread zone presents a theoretical conundrum: the range of a protolanguage like Proto-Indo-European (PIE) was great, yet reconstructed etyma and sound changes show that borrowings into the protolanguage and innovations within it could and did spread to all or most of the daughter branches. This chapter uses the theoretical notion of LOCUS to solve this dilemma and to clarify in other ways the dynamic and source of the early Indo-European (IE) spread. The locus is a smallish part of the range which functions in the same way as a dialect-geographical centre: an epicentre of sorts from which innovations spread to other regions and dialects, and a catchpoint at which cultural borrow-ings and linguistic loanwords entered from prestigious or economically important foreign societies to spread (along with native linguistic innovations) to the distant dialects. If an innovation arose in the vicinity of the locus, or a loanword entered, it spread to all or most of the family; otherwise, it remained a regionalism. Diversification of daughter dialects in a spread zone takes place far from the locus at the periphery, giving the family tree a distinctive shape with many major early branches, and creating a distinctive dialect map where genetic diversity piles up at the periphery. These principles make it possible to pinpoint the locus in space more or less accurately even for a language family as old as IE. Here it will be shown that the locus accounting for the distribution of loanwords, internal innovations, and genetic diversity within IE could only have lain well to the east of the Caspian Sea.

POSITION OF THE LOCUS ALONG LOANWORD TRAJECTORIES

The initial development of agriculture and stockbreeding must have entailed that terms for the new domesticates spread outward from the centre of innovation as agriculture spread over Europe and western Asia. Whether farming spread by human migration, cultural diffusion, or some combination of the two, a terminology must have accompanied its spread. For several millennia after the initial innovation, Mesopotamia and the Fertile Crescent remained important cultural and economic centres, and loan vocabulary must have continued to diffuse outward, following the same trajectories as the initial spread of agriculture: to central Europe via the Bosporus and the Balkans, to the western steppe via the Caucasus (the importance of this route has recently been argued by Shnirelman 1992), and eastward via Iran to western central Asia (see Volume II for these loanword trajectories).

The movement of loan vocabulary in cases of diffusion is notoriously chaotic: borrowings go in various directions, each borrowing language rephonemicizes or reanalyses or more generally garbles its borrowed words, and each language contributes some of its own native stock to others as well as passing on some borrowed words. Still, whenever the diffusion emanates from a cultural centre there must be a predominance of outward movement along trajectories such that languages closer to the centre contribute more loans (their own native stock or transmitted loans) to more distant languages than vice versa. Six to ten millennia later, we can hardly hope to unravel the entire complex history of loan vocabulary in western Eurasia, but two important general assumptions can be made: first, some ancient *Wanderwörter* can be discerned among reconstructed words in protolanguages that had any cultural connection to the ancient Near East, and second, protolanguages that were then located along the same loanword trajectory will share several protovocables in their cultural vocabulary while protolanguages that were on different trajectories will have few or no such sharings. Figure 8.1 shows some hypothetical configurations schematically. In this schema, lexical resemblances in cultural vocabulary are to be expected between A and B, between C and D, and between E and F.

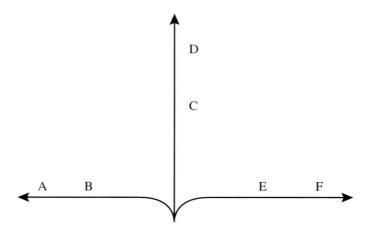

Figure 8.1 Hypothetical arrangement of some protolanguages along loanword trajectories.

A–F: languages (today's protolanguages). Arrows: loanword trajectories. A and B are in Anatolia, C and D in the Caucasus, and E and F in Iran or western Central Asia. The pairs A–B, C–D, and E–F will show lexical resemblances in cultural vocabulary, while other pairs (A–C, D–E, etc.) will have few or no such resemblances. A's loan vocabulary will be predominantly derived from B, D's from C, and F's from E.

This arrangement makes it possible to confirm and falsify hypotheses about the relative locations of ancient protolanguages, specifically about whether they were on the same trajectory or not. More precisely, it gives evidence for locating the PIE locus along one or another trajectory. The various PIE homelands proposed in recent years cover all three trajectories: the Pontic steppe homeland described by Mallory (1989) and Anthony (1991, 1995) is along the Caucasian loanword trajectory; the northern Mesopotamian or Transcaucasian homeland posited by Gamkrelidze and Ivanov (1984, 1994) is also along the Caucasian loanword trajectory, but closer to the centre; a pre-PIE origin in the eastern Pontic steppe (Gimbutas 1977, Anthony 1995) puts the locus in the central Asian trajectory; Diakonoff's Balkan–Carpathian homeland (1985) is in the Balkan trajectory, as is Dolgopolsky's (1987, 1993) two-stage sequence of an earlier Anatolian homeland and a secondary Balkan homeland.

The first step in specifying a locus for the IE homeland is to narrow it down to one of these three trajectories, and that can be done by comparing areal *Wanderwörter* in the IE cultural vocabulary to those of other language families that can be located relative to one or another trajectory in ancient times. There are four ancient languages whose location in the fourth and third millennia is more or less clear from their early attestation: Proto-Semitic, which extended from southern Mesopotamia to the south-eastern Mediterranean; Sumerian (a language isolate) and Elamite (probably an isolate) in Mesopotamia; and Hattic (an isolate) in northern Anatolia, predecessor to Hittite. Nakh-Daghestanian (see Figure 8.3, p.129) is an old family, evidently indigenous to the Caucasus and with an arguable identity to archeological cultures in the eastern Caucasus going back to before the Bronze Age (Markovin 1969, Gadžiev 1991), so it too can be given approximately its present location in the fourth or third millennium. The locations of the following are less secure: Hurrian-Urartean (attested fairly early in northern Mesopotamia and the Transcaucasus), Abkhaz-Circassian (or North-west Caucasian) (now located in the western Caucasus and along the eastern Black Sea coast; no ancient attestation), Kartvelian or South Caucasian (presently in the South Caucasus; attested only from the fifth century AD). Of these last three, Hurrian-Urartean and Kartvelian are well within the desert language trajectory of language spreads and could therefore be recent entrants. (This is particularly likely for Kartvelian, as argued on pp. 127–8.) Abkhaz-Circassian is distant from the mainstream of either the steppe or desert trajectory, and has been well established at least since early medieval times both north and south of the main Caucasus range and along a sizable stretch of the eastern Black Sea coast, a range unlike that of any recent entrant to the Caucasus; it is therefore quite likely to be ancient in its present territory. To summarize, I will assume that in the fourth millennium Semitic, Elamite, and Sumerian (or their ancestors) were in or near southern Mesopotamia, Hattic was in northern Anatolia, Abkhaz-Circassian along the Black Sea coast, and Nakh-Daghestanian in the eastern Caucasian foothills and Caspian coastal plain. (Of these, Semitic and Nakh-Daghestanian are comparable to IE in age; Kartvelian is somewhat younger, about 4,500 years; Abkhaz-Circassian is difficult to date, but evidently younger than IE and older than Romance.) The locations of PIE, Kartvelian, and Hurrian-Urartean in the fourth millennium are unknown. The task is now to compare possibly borrowed cultural vocabulary in IE to that of the proto-languages and ancient languages whose location is fairly firm. Of these I will consider Semitic, Sumerian, Abkhaz-Circassian, Nakh-Daghestanian, and Kartvelian in comparison to IE. Hattic, Hurrian-Urartean, and Elamite are less accessible to me and are left out here. Tables 8.1–8.6 (see pp. 142–5) show selected lexemes from the six language families.[2]

There have been many studies drawing lexical comparisons among some or all of these groups, with the purpose of tracing either genetic or areal links among them. My impression is that most of these seek positive evidence supporting one or another hypothesis and do not document or interpret negative evidence, and that none of them has a firm standard for what is admissible as a resemblance or sharing. I have defined a small semantic sample in advance and have attempted to survey it identically in all six families covered, interpreting non-sharings as well as sharings. A resemblance (of lexemes between protolanguages or a protolanguage and an ancient language) requires identity (or large overlap) in meaning and substantial phonological resemblance between at least two segments which must occur in the same order in a root or stem of similar overall skeletal shape. (Phonological resemblance takes into account the known distribution and behaviour of protosegments. For details see Tables 8.1–8.6.) Thus PIE *woino-, Kartvelian *ɣwino-, and Semitic *wajn, all 'wine', count as comparanda, since they have three segments *w, *i or *j, and *n in common as well as their meaning. (Dolgopolsky (1987: 20) regards the Kartvelian form as a borrowing specifically from pre-Armenian.) Of the various words for 'gold', PIE *Haus- and Sumerian guškin count as comparanda because of the segments -us-, similar shape C(a)us-, and identical meaning; Akkadian ḫurāṣu is suggestive but not a strict resemblance because of its different syllabic shape; Abkhaz-Circassian *dèša and Nakh-Daghestanian *mis- (Daghestanian branch), *D=aš- (Nakh) are not strictly resemblant because they contain only anterior fricatives but no -u- element (the Daghestanian form, with its labial nasal, comes close, but I judge *u and *m to be very different).

A comparison that is suggestive but formally and distributionally weak is the Nakh-Daghestanian words for 'horse' (Table 8.2). These have been compared to PIE *eḱwos (Gamkrelidze and Ivanov 1984: 919; Starostin 1985: 89; Dolgopolsky 1987: 19), but the Nakh-Daghestanian daughter languages offer not only forms like Andic ičwa (which resembles the PIE form in its general shape) but also forms like Dargi urci (where the labial element precedes the palatal), Avar and Lak ču (where there is no initial vowel), and Xinalug pši (where the labial element surfaces as an obstruent). The Proto-Daghestanian form can be represented as *W či, with *W representing a labial prosody which has no specific segmental position and cannot either satisfy or violate my requirement that the two compared segments have the same order. (Correspondences of this type are frequent in Nakh-Daghestanian. The labial prosody may have something to do with the prefixal *b of the gender class associated with large animates in several daughter languages. In various daughter languages the labial prosody is spelled out as an initial segment, consonant labialization, and rounded vowels.) There is no Nakh cognate and hence no grounds for attributing the Daghestanian form to Proto-Nakh-Daghestanian. Thus this resemblance to PIE is borderline.

There are some resemblances that are formally good but semantically and/or distributionally weak, e.g. PIE *gwou- 'cow' beside Nakh (but not Proto-Nakh-Daghestanian) govr 'horse' and Kabardian (but not Proto-Abkhaz-Circassian) gwaw 'bull', or PIE *eḱuwos 'horse' beside Georgian aču (interjection for urging horses on, fraught with the same comparability problems as English giddy-up or lateral click) and nursery word ačua 'horse'. In totalling up resemblances I count the firm ones as one point each, cases with either semantic or distributional problems as half a point, and cases with both semantic and distributional problems as one-quarter point. The results are shown in Table 8.6. The degree of resemblance of a language family to IE is shown in the number of these lexical sharings.

It is difficult to know what to make, in terms of language history or sociolinguistics, of the very general resemblance in words for 'five' in Abkhaz-Circassian, Nakh-Daghestanian, Kartvelian and IE, but each of them contributes its half point to the total degree of resemblance to IE. The significance of the resemblance of the Kartvelian and IE words for 'seven' to that of Semitic is easier to interpret: seven was a culturally salient number in the ancient Near East, used to measure seven-day weeks whose cycle had religious significance, and it must have been a good candidate for borrowing. On Tables 8.2 and 8.6 this probable explanation is not given separate weight, but rather the words for 'seven' simply make their one-point contributions to their languages' degrees of resemblance to IE.

By far the largest number of resemblances is found between IE and Kartvelian. IE also has sharings with Nakh-Daghestanian, Semitic, and Sumerian. IE and Kartvelian, and no other languages, share numerals with Semitic. Kartvelian has as many sharings with Semitic as IE does, and there are two IE–Kartvelian–Semitic sharings. There are two exclusive IE–Kartvelian sharings: '4' and '6'.[3] The sharings with Nakh-Daghestanian are less clear and less strongly cultural. There are almost no resemblances between Kartvelian and either Nakh-Daghestanian or Abkhaz-Circassian. Abkhaz-Circassian has almost no resemblances with IE (or for that matter with Nakh-Daghestanian).

These distributions point to the following linguistic geography for these language families in the fourth millennium. Culturally laden loan vocabulary emanated from ancient Mesopotamia, much of it originating in Sumerian and Semitic. Abkhaz-Circassian was not directly along a loanword trajectory, and had neither direct nor indirect interaction with either Nakh-Daghestanian or Kartvelian. Nakh-Daghestanian was closer to a trajectory and closer to IE and Kartvelian, but not in direct interaction with either of them; nor does Mesopotamian vocabulary appear to have been filtered through either IE or Kartvelian on its way to Nakh-Daghestanian. None of the Nakh-Daghestanian–IE resemblances involve words of clearly native IE origin; this indicates that PIE was not in a location or economic position to exert cultural influence on Nakh-Daghestanian, which probably means that PIE did not lie between Nakh-Daghestanian and Mesopotamia. IE and Kartvelian were in the main current of a loanword trajectory which was also connected to Semitic and Sumerian. IE and Kartvelian were close to each other, but the phonology of their sharings is not so close that the two protolanguages must be assumed to have been adjacent to each other; the PIE–Kartvelian sharings seem not to have been direct borrowings.[4] The Semiticisms are likewise not direct borrowings from Semitic, and neither the IE nor the Kartvelian Semiticisms are obviously derived from the other. The connection between Mesopotamia, IE, and Kartvelian was thus close but not direct. There was at least one intermediary involved. Figure 8.2 represents these relationships graphically. Abkhaz-Circassian and Nakh-Daghestanian are in approximately their modern locations, and Kartvelian and IE are to the east.

These presumed borrowings between protolanguages pinpoint homeland locations to one or another loanword trajectory, and they show whether pairs or groups of protolanguages were along the same or different loanword trajectories. When a loanword is well attested in all the branches of a borrowing lan-

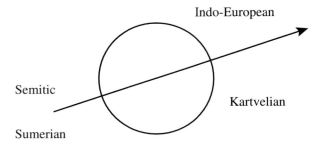

Figure 8.2 Schematic rendition of the locations of Semitic, Sumerian, Abkhaz-Circassian, Nakh-Daghestanian, IE, and Kartvelian in the fourth millennium. Arrow: loanword trajectory. Circle: intermediary (or intermediaries).

Spatial distance reflects linguistic distance. Spatial direction represents compass directions, based not on loanword data but on other factors.

guage it can be assumed to have entered in the vicinity of the locus, while a dialectal attestation indicates entry at the far periphery of the range. Thus loanwords can shed some light on the position of the locus in relation to the loanword trajectory. The words considered here reconstruct as PIE, and this indicates that the PIE locus was in the sphere of cultural influence of Mesopotamia, but not close to central Mesopotamia; not particularly close to the Caucasus, and certainly not south of it; and in the same general area as Kartvelian, though not immediately adjacent to it. Kartvelian seems to have moved to the southern Caucasus sometime after the IE dispersal, by which time the westward trajectory of languages had certainly begun to operate. Kartvelian is therefore likely to have emanated from somewhere to the south-east of the Caspian, where it was in a position to be pulled into the desert trajectory of language spreads, thus to spread westward to its present location. The locus of PIE was farther east and farther north, so that it spread to the steppe as well.

If resemblant proto-forms can help pinpoint the PIE locus, later and dialect forms can shed light on the chronology and direction of language spread along the language trajectories. This is a matter for separate studies, but as an example consider English *buck* and its cognates. The word is found in Germanic and Celtic in the sense 'male goat, buck'. The other IE cognates are Iranian and Armenian, and they point to a palatovelar as the second consonant: e.g. Avestan *būza* (for the full set, see Gamkrelidze and Ivanov 1984: 586 = 1994: 501). A clear resemblant to the European forms in Nakh-Daghestanian is Nakh *bʕok'* 'male goat', not found in Daghestanian. If the Nakh form is a borrowing from

IE it comes from a *centum* dialect (and need not be ancient), and this suggests interaction between IE dialects and Nakh-Daghestanian languages where the steppe trajectory passes north of the Caucasus.[5]

There is another resemblant form with a similar distribution in Nakh-Daghestanian and IE: a Nakh and western Daghestanian word, Nakh *ga:za* 'goat', Lak and Dargi *gada* 'kid', recalls the dialectal IE **ghayd-* that is reflected in Germanic (English *goat*) and Italic (Lat. *haedus*) and also Semitic **gadj-* (for this comparison and Semitic reflexes see Gamkrelidze and Ivanov 1984: 872 = 1994: 769). (Nakh *z* renders IE *d* in some evident early loans, e.g. Nakh **pa:z-* in 'sock' and other words referring to feet and footwear, but it does not correspond to Lak and Dargi *d*.) As this word for 'goat' is dialectal in both Nakh-Daghestanian and IE, its ultimate source may well lie in Semitic, but its occurrence far from the Near East in the north Caucasus and Europe may again point to an interaction of western IE dialects and northern Nakh-Daghestanian dialects somewhere on the western steppe after the IE spread was well underway.

THE ROOT OF THE INDO-EUROPEAN FAMILY TREE

It is a basic tenet of migration and homeland theory that the geographical location of a language family's proto-homeland is to be sought in the vicinity of the root of the family tree (i.e. in the region where the deepest branches come together on a map); or, more generally, that the homeland is to be sought in

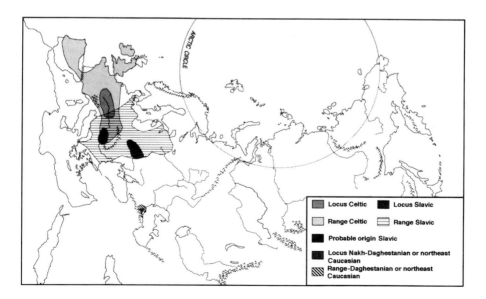

Figure 8.3 Example of locus and range of particular language spreads.

the region of present greatest genetic diversity of the family (Sapir [1916] 1949; Dyen 1956). This principle works well whenever languages from the family in question continue to be spoken in or near the proto-homeland. It works well, for example, for Austronesian, which is presumed to have spread from the vicinity of Taiwan, where its deepest branching is now found (Blust 1984/5); for the Benue-Congo family, which spread from the vicinity of southern Nigeria where representatives of all of its daughter branches can be found (Williamson 1989: 270); for Uralic, whose deepest two branches meet east of the Urals, whence its Finno-Ugric branch moved progressively westward; and for many others. But for language families that have their origins in spread zones this principle is unlikely to be straightforwardly applicable, and for those of central Eurasia it is demonstrably false. The central Eurasian spread zone (Figure 8.4), as described in Volume II, was part of a standing pattern whereby languages were drawn into the spread zone, spread westward, and were eventually succeeded by the next spreading family. The dispersal for each entering family occurred after entry into the spread zone. The point of dispersal for each family is the locus of its proto-homeland, and this locus eventually is engulfed by the next entering language. Hence in a spread zone the locus cannot, by definition, be the point of present greatest diversity (except possibly for the most recent family to enter the spread zone). On the contrary, the locus is one of the earliest points to be overtaken by the next spread.

For each family that dispersed from the central Eurasian spread zone, an area of greatest genetic diversity can be defined somewhere along the perimeter of the range, or at the far end of the trajectory of language spread. For IE, great diversity is attested from very early at the western edges of both the steppe and desert trajectories. The southern trajectory led south of the Caspian, and west of there even in very early times the genetic diversity of IE was great: in order from east to west, known ancient branches there are Indo-Iranian (in the form of Mitannian Aryan, and later Old Persian; a *satem* branch); ancestral Armenian (*satem*); Anatolian (*centum*, with some positional palatalization of velars); Phrygian (if that was not ancestral Armenian, and if it was not a recent entry from the north via the Balkans; for a discussion of Phrygian see Diakonoff 1980; in any event Phrygian has a mixture of *centum* and *satem* reflexes); and Greek (*centum*). These branches not only span the entire range from *centum* to *satem*, but also exhibit a great variety of reflexes of the three IE stop series, and Anatolian is distinctive enough, phonologically and grammatically, to be a candidate for a sister rather than a daughter of IE, or for the earliest daughter branch to split off (Warnow *et al.* in press, find Anatolian to be the first split, but see, for example, Weitenberg (1987) and Garrett (1990) for recent demonstrations of the fundamental Indo-European-ness of Hittite gender and declension, features long thought to be evidence for an early split). Gamkrelidze and Ivanov (1984, 1994), Diakonoff (1985), and Dolgopolsky (1987) invoke the great diversity of the IE languages in this region as support for their proposed homelands (trans-Caucasian, Balkan-Carpathian and Anatolian-Balkan respectively).

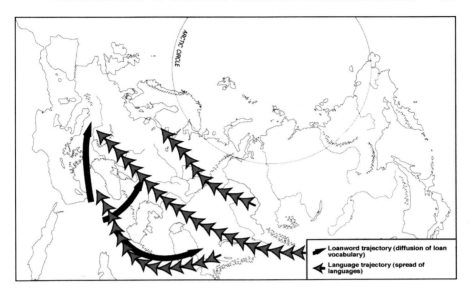

Figure 8.4   The central Eurasian spread zone.

The IE diversity at the western end of the steppe and northern trajectories where they converged in Europe is also considerable: Italic, Celtic, Germanic (all *centum*), Balto-Slavic (*satem* with frequent and perhaps systematic *centum* reflexes, especially in Slavic; see Gamkrelidze and Ivanov 1984: 112 = 1994: 96; Kortlandt 1978; Shevelov 1965: 141ff.), and less well-attested languages such as Venetic and Thracian. Furthermore, unlike the southern route, Europe has a definable small area where several branches meet: central Europe, where Celtic, Germanic, Balto-Slavic, and Thracian were probably all to be found in late La Tène to Roman times.

The Iranian family (Figure 8.5), which was next to sweep across the steppe and deserts, finds its region of greatest diversity in the central Asian mountains (Èdel'man 1980), and its ancestral Indo-Iranian family finds its own greatest diversity in the mountain region from central Asia to northern India (i.e. Bactria-Sogdiana and parts just south). Èdel'man emphasizes explicitly that the central Asian mountains cannot have been the actual point of origin for Iranian, but would be taken as such if the principle of greatest genetic diversity were mechanically applied. Another region of great diversity for Iranian is the southern Caucasus, where Ossetic (of the north-eastern branch of Iranian), Talysh and Kurdish (north-western) and Persian (south-western) are all to be found. The Caucasus might be another serious contender for the Proto-Iranian homeland, were it not for historical evidence to the contrary and the implausibility of an Iranian homeland so distant from that of Indic and the Nuristan languages.

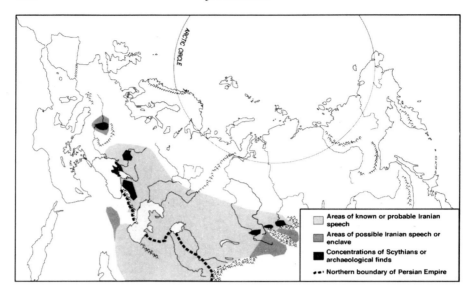

Figure 8.5   The Iranian language family, early first millennium BC.

The Turkic family (Figure 8.6), underwent an initial split into two branches, one of them represented now only by Chuvash of the middle Volga (and formerly also by Bulgar north of the Black Sea). Thus the point of greatest diversity for Turkic today is the Volga, where Chuvash lies close to Tatar, a representative of the other branch, Common Turkic. In the seventh century AD another point of comparable Turkic diversity was north of the Black Sea where Bulgar met westernmost Common Turkic. The Volga is well to the west along the steppe route, and the Black Sea is at the far west. Thus, if the principle of least moves is followed mechanically, the Turkic proto-homeland must be located in the western steppe. The chief reason that the principle is not applied mechanically to determine the Turkic homeland is that historical records – Chinese, central Asian, and then Byzantine sources – testify to the Turkic spread from the vicinity of Mongolia, and ancient Turkic itself is directly attested in seventh-century inscriptions from western Siberia and central Asia. The Common Turkic branch finds its point of greatest present genetic diversity in the vicinity of the mountains to the west and north-west of Mongolia.

Mongolian is a family so shallow that it is difficult to assess its diversity except by counting individual languages. Most of them are spoken in or near Mongolia (Figure 8.6).

In summary, for the language spreads from central Asia regions of great, and sometimes even greatest, genetic diversity are historically attested at the western periphery of the trajectory: for IE, greater Anatolia and central Europe are the diverse points, for Iranian the Caucasus, and for Turkic the western

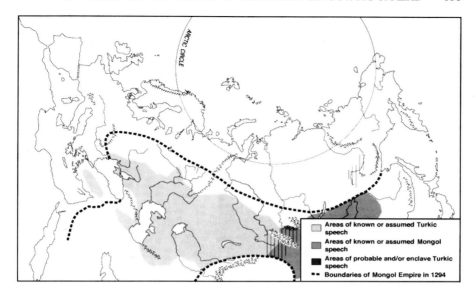

Figure 8.6   The Turkic and Mongolian language families, end of thirteenth century
AD.

steppe. For Iranian and Turkic, other points of great diversity are to be found
in western central Asia, and on the strength of historical evidence these are
usually taken to be near, but not identical, to the proto-homelands. Only
for Mongolian, the most recent spreading family, is there no westward point
of great diversity; but that is because the Mongol expansion was stopped on
its western fronts in the late Middle Ages.

For Turkic and Iranian, the westward regions of diversity are clearly the result
of secondary accumulation rather than primary differentiation. In the case of
Iranian, the approach of Kurdish and Persian to the Caucasus is a relatively
recent phase in their westward expansions, and Ossetic is known to have
entered the Caucasus during Scytho-Sarmatian times. In the case of Turkic, the
meeting of Bulgar and Kipchak north of the Black Sea was an ephemeral first
stage in the spread of Turkic. Common Turkic, advancing westward in the
form of Kipchak, overtook Bulgar and eventually absorbed most of its speakers (and those who moved westward in front of the Kipchak advance to settle
in Bulgaria eventually became Slavicized). For both Iranian and Turkic, diversity survives in refuge areas: the Caucasus, a well-known reservoir of linguistic diversity; the middle to upper Volga, where two branches of Finno-Ugric
and two branches of Turkic have persisted through Turkic, Mongol, and
Russian control of the steppes; and the central Asian mountains, where south-
eastern Iranian languages and the Nuristan branch of Indo-Iranian survive, as
well as the isolate Burushaski. Since all the attested survivals of deep diversity

are secondary accumulations, there is no reason to see the great ancient IE diversity of the Transcaucasus and Anatolia as anything other than an early secondary accumulation. This early diversity testifies to the range of PIE and the direction of its trajectories, but not to its locus of spread.

Only for the PIE spread do we lack historical evidence that would help us pinpoint the locus of spread and/or the region from which it entered the spread zone. The Iranian, Turkic, and Mongol spreads have by now obliterated any IE branches that survived for any time in the mountains of western central Asia. But Tocharian, which survived until the early centuries AD in the desert oases of what is now Xinjiang, well to the east of the eastern range of Iranian, suggests strongly that there was structural diversity of IE in western central Asia prior to the Turkic spread. Tocharian is a *centum* branch, while Iranian is *satem*; thus both *centum* and *satem* languages were found in central Asia before the Turkic spread, and therefore the early central Asian languages spanned the entire range of dialectal differences in disintegrating PIE.

Thus the structure of the IE family tree, the distribution of IE genetic diversity over the map, and what can be inferred of the geographical distribution of dialectal diversity in early IE all point to a locus in western central Asia (Figure 8.6), Let us now consider how this fits linguistic migration theory.

As defined by Dyen (1956), a homeland is a continuous area and a migration is any movement causing that area to become non-continuous (while a movement that simply changes its shape or area is an expansion or expansive intrusion). The linguistic population of the homeland is a set of intermediate protolanguages, the first-order daughters of the original protolanguage (in Dyen's terms, a chain of co-ordinate languages). The homeland is the same as (or overlaps) the area of the largest chain of such co-ordinates; i.e. the area where the greatest number of highest-level branches occur. Homelands are to be reconstructed in such a way as to minimize the number of migrations, and the number of migrating daughter branches, required to get from them to attested distributions (Dyen 1956: 613).

No migrations are required to derive the attested IE distribution from a reconstructed homeland consisting of a locus in western central Asia and a range over the steppe and desert. Sometime in the fourth to early third millennium, PIE spread along the steppe and southern trajectories to occupy the entire reconstructed range: the steppe, the desert of western central Asia, part of the adjacent mountains, and perhaps some of south-west Asia. At this time its distribution was continuous, and that distribution had been achieved not by migration but by expansion. Later, by the end of the third millennium or the beginning of the second, Proto-Thracian, Proto-Italic, Proto-Venetic (unless that was part of Italic), Proto-Celtic, and perhaps Proto-Germanic were somewhere in the vicinity of central Europe, and Proto-Greek, Proto-Illyrian, Proto-Phrygian (unless that was part of Proto-Thracian), Proto-Anatolian, and Proto-Armenian stretched from north-western Mesopotamia to the southern Balkans. I assume that the central European languages formed

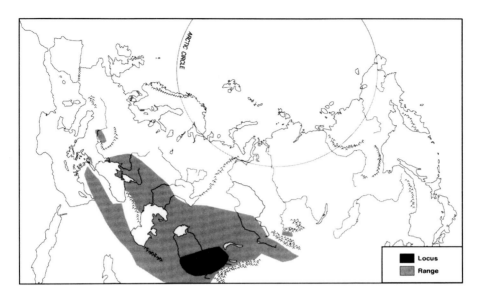

Figure 8.7   The locus and range of Proto-Indo-European.

a continuous chain in Dyen's sense and the languages of greater Anatolia
formed another. (Though some non-IE languages were also found in both
areas, I assume both chains were continuous in the technical sense.) Proto-
Indo-Iranian had already begun its spread over the former PIE range,
and ancestral Proto-Indo-Aryan was spreading into northern India. Proto-
Tocharian remained close to the original locus, east of Iranian.

At this stage there were two chains of co-ordinate languages (in Dyen's
sense): one in central Europe and one in greater Anatolia. Iranian was not
co-ordinate to any of these; it was a daughter of the co-ordinate Proto-
Indo-Iranian. Its spread along the two trajectories was not a migration but
an expansion, and the consequence was a greatly expanded but still continuous distribution for Indo-Iranian. The Iranian expansion had, however,
split the first-order IE daughters into two non-contiguous co-ordinate
chains (one in central Europe and one in greater Anatolia) and Proto-
Tocharian, a separate in Dyen's terms. It did this by spreading over the
steppe and desert and thereby separating the dialects at the western peripheries of those trajectories from the eastern part of the range and from
Tocharian. A language map of this time, taken at face value, would suggest
eastern Europe as the IE homeland: there were two chains of co-ordinate
first-order IE daughters there, and to the east only the Indo-Iranian branch
and the separate Tocharian.

This is precisely the interpretation summarized succinctly by Burrow:

At an ancient period we find enormous stretches of Asia in the occupation of Indo-Iranian, a single member of the family, and as yet little differentiated; in Europe on the other hand a concentration of many languages occupying comparatively restricted areas, and already markedly different from each other. It follows of necessity that the presence of Indo-European in the Indo-Iranian area is the result of late colonial expansion on a vast scale, while in Europe the existence of such great diversity at the earliest recorded period indicates the presence there of Indo-European from remote antiquity.

Burrow (1959: 9)

In fact, however, the European diversity is a matter of secondary accumulation at the periphery, and the Indo-Iranian distribution is the result of a later, post-PIE spread.

By sometime in the first millennium BC the central European branch had expanded well into Europe, and the two chains had joined in the northern Balkans: between the Danube plain and western Anatolia ran a continuous IE chain comprised of Dacian, Thracian, Illyrian, Greek and Phrygian (unless the latter was part of Thracian), and the other branches extended from both ends of this chain. At this point, eastern Europe would be the clear choice for the IE homeland based on a mechanical argument from diversity. Meanwhile, ancestral Italic and Venetic had spread from central Europe, and ancestral Celtic had begun a spread to the south-west, west, and north-west that would eventually cover more than half of western and central Europe. About a millennium later would come a Germanic expansion and the Gothic state, and a few centuries later ancestral Slavic would begin a rapid spread that would cover central and eastern Europe from the Baltic to the Adriatic and from the Elbe to east of the Dniepr in the course of one century. In the same time-frame Latin would spread over the continental Celtic range. None of these European language spreads involved migrations; all were expansions. To the east, Tocharian continued to occupy its territory along the eastward trade routes, becoming separated from the rest of IE only in the early centuries AD when Turkic began to spread eventually to succeed Iranian over almost all of its range.

Thus no major migrations are required to explain the distribution of IE languages at any stage in their history up to the colonial period of the last few centuries. All movements of languages (or more precisely all viable movements – that is, all movements that produced natural speech communities that lasted for generations and branched into dialects) were expansions, and all geographically isolated languages (e.g. Tocharian, Ossetic in the Caucasus, ancestral Armenian, perhaps ancestral Anatolian) appear to be remnants of formerly continuous distributions. They were stranded by subsequent expansions of other language families, chiefly Turkic in historical times.

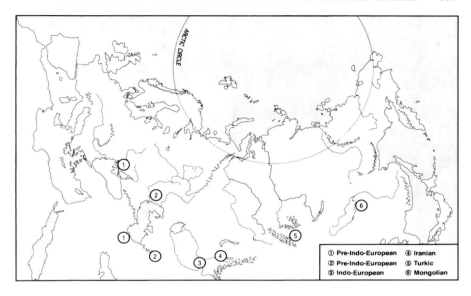

Figure 8.8   The trajectory of loci for language spreads in central Eurasia. Numbers indicate relative chronology and approximate locations (firm only for 4–6). The two points 1 and the two points 2 are synchronous but unconnected loci for distinct spreads of unrelated languages.

FURTHER IMPLICATIONS

Several kinds of evidence for the PIE locus have been presented here. Ancient loanwords point to a locus along the desert trajectory, not particularly close to Mesopotamia and probably far out in the eastern hinterlands. The structure of the family tree, the accumulation of genetic diversity at the western periphery of the range, the location of Tocharian and its implications for early dialect geography, the early attestation of Anatolian in Asia Minor, and the geography of the *centum–satem* split all point in the same direction: a locus in western central Asia. Evidence presented in Volume II supports the same conclusion: the long-standing westward trajectories of languages point to an eastward locus, and the spread of IE along all three trajectories points to a locus well to the east of the Caspian Sea. The *satem* shift also spread from a locus to the south-east of the Caspian, with *satem* languages showing up as later entrants along all three trajectory terminals. (The *satem* shift is a post-PIE but very early IE development.) The locus of the IE spread was therefore somewhere in the vicinity of ancient Bactria-Sogdiana. This locus resembles those of the three known post-IE spreads: those of Indo-Iranian (from a locus close to that of PIE), Turkic (from a locus near north-western Mongolia), and Mongolian (from north-eastern Mongolia) as shown in Figure 8.8. Thus in regard to its locus, as in other respects, the PIE spread was no singularity but was absolutely ordinary for its geography and its time-frame.

To summarize the important points of dialect geography in the Eurasian spread zone, the hallmark of a language family that enters a spread zone as an undifferentiated single language and diversifies while spreading is a multiple branching from the root. This is the structure of the IE tree, which has the greatest number of primary branches of any known genetic grouping of comparable age. The hallmark of developments that arise in or near the locus is that they appear along more than one trajectory. This is the distribution of the *centum/satem* division in IE, and in the later Indo-Iranian spread it is the distribution of the Indo-Aryan/Iranian split (as argued in Nichols, Volume II). The reason that dialect divisions arising in the locus show up along more than one trajectory is that the Caspian Sea divides westward spreads into steppe versus desert trajectories quite close to the locus and hence quite early in the spread. In contrast, developments that occurred farther west, as the split of Slavic from Baltic in the middle Volga may have, continue to spread along only one trajectory. This is why the Pontic steppe is an unlikely locus for the PIE spread.

The locus proposed here is unlike any other proposed homeland, though the range and trajectory of PIE include all proposed homelands. Of the proposals in the literature, the PIE homeland of Gamkrelidze and Ivanov (1984, 1994) is most like the locus described here. Their homeland is south of the Caucasus, near ancient Mesopotamia, and near Proto-Kartvelian. My locus is not south of the Caucasus, but it is along the southern trajectory; it is not near to Mesopotamia, but in its sphere of influence and near a trajectory mainstream; it is not far from Proto-Kartvelian, but not adjacent to it. A major difference is that I do not assume Kartvelian has been in its present location for six millennia. Kartvelian, like IE, was absolutely ordinary for its geography and its time-frame, and like Anatolian, Persian, and Turkish it spread along the desert trajectory from central Asia and took root near the periphery of the spread zone.

CHRONOLOGY AND ORIGINS

Central Eurasia is a linguistic bottleneck, spread zone, and extinction chamber, but its languages had to come from somewhere. The locus of the IE spread is a theoretical point representing a linguistic epicentre, not a literal place of ethnic or linguistic origin, so the ultimate origin of PIE need not be in the same place as the locus. There are several linguistically plausible possibilities for the origin of Pre-PIE. It could have spread eastward from the Black Sea steppe (as proposed by Mallory 1989 and by Anthony 1991, 1995), so that the locus formed only after this spread but still very early in the history of disintegrating PIE. This large eastward spread would be a departure from the general westward trajectory of spreads in central Eurasia, occasioned by the epoch-making domestication of the horse and development of wheeled transport. Pre-PIE could have been a central Asian language long before its rapid spread; if so it had a large range before its expansion, and the dispersal began with the development of the locus in a pre-existent range. It could have come into the spread zone from the east as Mongolian, Turkic, and probably Indo-Iranian did. Or it could have been a language of the early urban oases of southern central Asia. These cities were outposts of Near Eastern culture: for instance, Jeitun, to the west of Bactria in southern Turkmenistan, derived its agriculture and livestock from the Near East, and both it and its Eneolithic successor culture took in occasional infusions of Near Eastern pottery styles and the like which may indicate migrations and certainly indicate cultural influence (Masson and Sarianidi 1972: 45 *passim*; Harris *et al.* 1993).

Whatever the ultimate origin of pre-PIE, it seems likely that the development of the PIE locus was connected with interaction between nomads of the central Asian grasslands and the settled farmers of the oasis towns. An origin history of this sort is attractive because it makes it possible to retain what is valuable in the speculations of Trubetzkoy (1939) while dismissing the wildly implausible parts. Trubetzkoy observed that earliest reconstructable pre-PIE had typological affinities to south-western Eurasia but IE dialects gradually acquired an eastern typological cast over time. His interpretation – that the IE range is the result of convergence rather than spread – is based on a very primitive understanding of typology, grammatical change, and language contact, and is untenable. But the core observation that pre-PIE had a western structural cast is intuitively perceptive and probably worth salvaging. Perhaps pre-PIE, prior to the formation of its locus of spread, belonged to a language area marked by typological affinities to ancient Mesopotamia and Asia Minor.

The chronological framework of the central Eurasian spread zone is critical to the question of where IE ultimately came from. If the spread zone already existed well before the IE breakup, then PIE is likely to have entered the spread zone from 'upstream' and unlikely to have entered it from 'downstream'. If, on the other hand, the spread zone first took shape with the IE spread, then we have fewer directions of origin to rule out in advance.

It was shown in Nichols, Volume II, that the linguistic geography of the IE spread demands an IE breakup and dispersal around 3700 BC to 3300 BC, as is generally consistent with the results of comparative-historical work. Gimbutas's first wave of steppe nomadic influence on Europe began nearly a millennium earlier, around 4400–4300 (Gimbutas 1977, 1991), and this is too early to have been IE. All three of Gimbutas's waves spread from the steppe to central Europe and from there in various directions across Europe, and this means that at least the pattern of spreads to and then from central Europe, which marks the western terminus of the steppe trajectory, was functioning as of 4400 BC. The usual interpretation seems to be that this first wave originated in the western steppe (Gimbutas 1991: 353ff. and maps on pp. 358–9; Mallory 1989: 186ff.), where from the early fifth millennium on there is evidence of a group of related cultures with features recalling those of early IE culture. (These are the Srednyj Stog culture, of which Srednyj Stog and Dereivka are well-known sites, and the Novodanilovka culture, with Mariupol a well-known site. All are just north of the Black Sea.) If (as both Gimbutas and Mallory assume) the first steppe wave into Europe was IE, then the western steppe is the logical arena for differentiation of the IE daughter branches. But, as we have seen, a fifth-millennium differentiation of the IE daughter branches is too early. The western steppe cultures of 5000 BC can tell us only that the same process of differentiation on the western steppe that accounts for the European daughter branches of IE was also taking place earlier. Thus the mechanism that drove the central European spreads at the western terminus of the steppe trajectory may have been in place by 5000 BC, but PIE was not there yet.

Roughly contemporaneous to these cultures, in the central or north Caspian steppe, is the possibly related Samara culture (major sites are Khvalynsk and Šezžee), and its general similarity to the western steppe cultures at least suggests that the central steppe was in the spread zone at this time. The successor culture in the western and central steppe is what is variously called Yamnaya[6] and Pit-Grave, which has kurgan burials and other features reminiscent of early IE culture. With this culture we have even clearer evidence of continuity over a large portion of the steppe, in the right time-frame for the IE dispersal (3600–2200 BC: Mallory 1989: 211). The cultural continuity indicates that at this time the entire steppe was in the spread zone.

The archaeological sources on which this summary is based (Danilenko 1974; Merpert 1974a and b; Vasil'ev 1981; Vasil'ev and Sinjuk 1985; Jablonskij 1986; Dergachev 1989; Anthony 1991, and others) most often describe the westward cultures as derived from, or extensions from, the eastern ones. Mallory (1989) and Anthony (1991, 1995) interpret the directionality of cultural derivation as west to east. It is the east-to-west directionality of cultural derivation that would be consistent with the east-to-west linguistic trajectory, since spread of a whole culture is likely to involve language spread (and vice versa). A predominantly east-to-west directionality of cultural derivation and descent for the Eneolithic steppe would be a strong indication that the spread zone with its westward trajectories had taken shape. This is a purely archaeological question, but it is important to dating the rise of the linguistic spread zone.

The prehistory of the Uralic language family supports the view that the IE spread was not the first steppe spread. Proto-Uralic broke up around the fourth millennium or earlier, during what was still the Mesolithic in its homeland, which is usually placed in the central Urals or western Siberia (Gulya 1974; Hajdú 1975; Harms 1987). The modern Uralic distribution, extending from Siberia to Estonia and Finland, follows a trajectory north of and parallel to the steppe trajectory. Throughout its history, Uralic has interacted linguistically with the spreading steppe languages, most notably when Proto-Finno-Ugric took on a number of early Iranian or Indo-Iranian loans (see Nichols, Volume II) and when ancestral Hungarian joined a Turkic confederation on the steppe. But there has been no such interaction between Proto-Uralic and PIE.[7] IE loans intersect an already differentiated Uralic: there are Proto-Iranian (or Proto-Indo-Iranian) loans into Proto-Finno-Ugric but not into Proto-Uralic. If, as seems likely, the Uralic spread was somehow correlated with spreading on the steppe, then the relevant influential linguistic spread on the steppe was not IE and must therefore have been pre-PIE. We may never be able to recover lexical evidence of this spread: unless we find a survivor of the pre-PIE language somewhere, we will never be able to distinguish its loans from native Uralic vocabulary. But linguistic geography and the dates of Uralic–IE intersection suggest strongly that a pre-PIE, non-IE spread was a reality. If, as is sometimes assumed, Uralic is a sister of Yukagir, an east Siberian language, then the Uralic spread probably began even earlier and even farther east, making an early northern trajectory a virtual certainty.

The Eurasian spread zone had a beginning somewhere in time, and it had an end. The end took place in historical times and is relatively well understood. Just before the end, in the Middle Ages, the locus shifted to eastern Mongolia and the Mongolian spread began, resulting in the Mongol conquests and domination around most of the steppe periphery, as well as the beginning of what would by now have become a spread of Mongolian language over the entire area. In the early to mid-thirteenth century the Mongols conquered Kiev and other cities of the western steppe periphery and ruled what is now eastern Ukraine and southern Russia for 200 years. At that point Russia began winning victories against the Mongols. By the sixteenth century Mongol power was pushed back to the Volga, and by the end of that century Russia had taken Astrakhan on the lower Volga and other key posts and began its rapid and ethnically devastating conquest of the steppe, Siberia, central Asia, and the Caucasus. (For the conquest of Siberia, see Forsyth 1992. For the first westward expansion on the steppe, the conquest of Bashkiria, see Donnelly 1968.)

This reversal and the eastward Russian spread reflected the eastern front of a process of European expansion that began much earlier, around the seventh century, in western Europe. The following summary is based on White (1962) and Duby (1974). In the seventh century, somewhere in central Europe, the mouldboard plough was invented. At the cost of higher requirements of draught power – a team of eight oxen was required, instead of the one or two required for the simple plough – the mouldboard plough could turn prairie soil and heavy lowland soils, thereby making possible agricultural exploitation of newer, and richer, soils. The result was consolidation of small fields into larger ones more easily ploughed by a large team, and larger fields lent themselves well to improved crop rotation schemes which improved soil productivity while also increasing the protein in the human diet by favouring the raising of more legumes. Population growth followed at each step, resulting in massive clearing of forests, increased arable, and more population growth. Two horses can pull the plough that requires eight oxen, and two horses require less feed than eight oxen, so the mouldboard plough eventually led to the replacement of oxen by horses as draught animals, and routine maintenance of horses on farms increased the number and genetic variety of horses available to European cavalries. The result of population growth and larger, better-equipped cavalry was military superiority. These changes spread from north-western Europe, drove the German eastward expansion (at the expense of the western Slavs), and reached Russia in the late Middle Ages. Meanwhile, firearms were developed and cities could be defended against nomadic invaders with cannons. This eastward trajectory of population growth and military strength destroyed mounted nomadism and brought an end to the ancient central Eurasian spread zone. It also led to the eventual destruction of the environment, native economies, and native cultures across northern Eurasia. The Black Sea steppe is now mostly fenced and ploughed, and formerly nomadic peoples are settled and sometimes also marginalized and/or Russified. A new locus of language spread formed in the west, and in just over half a millennium the new spread overran the range, trajectory, and locus that had dominated the linguistic geography of Eurasia for many millennia.

APPENDIX

Table 8.1   Words for numerals in selected proto-languages

	Indo-European	Kartvelian	Nakh-Daghestani	Abkhaz-Circ.[†]	Semitic[‡]
1	*sem-; *oino-	*ert-	*ca	*za	
2	*dwō-	*jor-	?	*Tq'wa	
3	*trei-	*sam-	*ƛVb	*š: 'a	
4	*kwetwer-	*o(š)tx(w)-[§]	*-q'- ?	*Pɫ'a	arba?
5	*penkwe	*xu(š)t-	*Wƛƛi	*Txwa	
6	*sweḱs-	*ekšw-	*VRƛƛ	*xa	
7	*septm̥-	šwid-	*VRƛ	*Pla	*sabʕ(-at)
8	*oḱtō-	*arwa-	*bVRƛ	*ya	
9	*newen-	*čxra-	?	*Pɣw	tis?
10	*deḱm̥-	*a(š)t-	*-c'-//*-cc'- ?	*Pš'a	ašr

Notes:
Capital letters are generic: V, vowel; R, resonant; for Abkhaz-Circassian, T and P have neutralized manner of articulation in clusters. *š, č = abstract reconstruction for Kartvelian (reflexes: Georgian s, others š), but an alveo-palatal series for Abkhaz-Circassian. Nakh-Daghestanian *W = labial prosody. Italic forms are resemblant (within rows).

[†] For all the Abkhaz-Circassian numerals the vowel is what Kuipers reconstructs as *(a), i.e. a vowel giving both a and ə reflexes. I write *a for simplicity.

[‡] Unasterisked forms are Arabic. The parenthesized element in '7' is the feminine suffix.

[§] Kartvelian '4' resembles PIE '8', which is morphologically a dual (Gamkrelidze and Ivanov 1984: 849–50), and Kartvelian '8' resembles Semitic '4'.

Table 8.2   Words for cattle and 'horse' in selected proto-languages

	'Bull'	'Cow'	'Horse'
PIE	*tawro-s ('wild bull'?)	*gwow–	*eḱwo-s
	*stewro-s		
Kartvelian	*qan–	*pur–	–†
Nakh-Dagh.	*W stu- or *stw–	*žVW‡	*W či (Dagh.)
			govr, din (Nakh)
Abkhaz-Circ.	*č:wə	*č ':aməš	*čʰə
Semitic	*ṯawr–		
Sumerian		Ñu(d)	
Basis	stw- or twr	Gu	-k'w-, -čw-

Italic forms are resemblant (within columns). The 'basis' row shows the segments shared by all the resemblant forms. There must be at least two, and they must occur in the given order (with some leniency where labialization is a prosody, as in Proto-Nakh-Daghestanian, or a coarticulation feature as in Abkhaz-Circassian). Phonetic similarities can be fairly broad within the bounds of plausible diachronic change: T subsumes dental and alveolar stops and affricates ([t, c]), and K′ and G′ subsume palatals of various kinds ([č] and PIE palatovelars).

† Cf. aču 'interjection for urging horses on', ačua 'horse' (nursery word).
‡ Cf. Chechen-Ingush govr 'horse' (*gaBr).
§ Cf. Kabardian gwaw 'bull'.

Table 8.3   Words for selected metals in selected proto-languages

	'Gold'	'Silver'	'Copper'
PIE	*Haus–	*Harĝ–	*reudh–
Kartvelian	*okro–	*werčxl–	–
Nakh-Daghestani	*mis- (Dagh.)	*arci (Dagh.)	–
	*D=aš- (Nakh)	*D=at-, *t'at- (Nakh)	
Abkhaz-Circassian	*dəśa	[*t:əž 'ə]	
Semitic	Akkad. ḫurāṣu		
Sumerian	guškin		urudu
Basis	-us-	-rK'-, -rc-	-rud-

Nakh D= indicates gender prefix (variously b-, d-, v-, j-). Other conventions as in Table 8.2.

Table 8.4   Words for 'wine' and 'honey' or 'sweet' in selected proto-languages

	'Wine'	'Honey'
PIE	*woin–	*meli(t)–; *medhu–
Kartvelian	*ɣwino–	*tapl–
Nakh-Daghestani	–	*(V)mVcc'– (Dagh.)
		*moc' (Nakh)
Abkhaz-Circassian	–	*śwawə
Semitic	*wajn–	*mVtḳ 'sweet' (?)
Basis	wjn, wVjn	mVT

Table 8.5 Words for 'yoke' in selected proto-languages

	'Yoke'
PIE	*γug-om
Kartvelian	*uχ-el-
Nakh-Daghestani	*r=u$\lambda\lambda$' (Daghestani)
	*r=uλ' (Nakh)
Abkhaz-Circassian	*Pž 'ə
Semitic	
Basis	-uG

Conventions as in Table 8.2.

Table 8.6 Summary of Tables 8.1–8.5: Proto-forms or ancient forms resemblant to PIE

Gloss	Abkhaz-Circassian	Nakh-Daghestani	Kartvelian	Semitic	Sumerian
1	no	no	no		
2	no	no	no		
3	no	no	no		
4	no	no	yes		
5	maybe[†]	maybe	maybe		
6	no	no	yes		
7	no	no	yes #	yes #	
8	no	no	#	#	
9	no	no	no (#?)	no (#?)	
10	no	no	#	#	
Bull	no	yes	no	yes	
Cow	maybe	maybe N[‡]	no		yes
Horse	no	maybe D[‡]	–[§]		
Gold	no	no	no		yes
Silver	no	maybe D	yes		
Copper	no	–	–		yes
Wine	–	–	yes	yes	
Honey (sweet)	no	yes	no	yes	
Yoke	no	yes	yes		
Totals	0.5	3.75	6.75	4	3

Totals: each 'yes' = 1, 'maybe' = 0.5, partial 'maybe' = 0.25, 'no' or no entry = 0. # = Kartvelian-Semitic resemblance lacking in IE. – = no proto-form with this meaning reconstructs for the family.

[†] The 'maybe' entries share a vaguely similar shape: initial stop-like element, medial voiceless posterior obstruent, labial element. To PIE *penkwe and Abkhaz-Circassian *Txwa compare daughter Nakh-Daghestanian reflexes Xinalug (Daghestanian) pxu, Chechen-Ingush (Nakh) pxi-, and possibly even Kartvelian (Georgian) xut-.

[‡] 'Maybe N' = maybe, and the possible candidate is only Nakh; 'maybe D' = maybe, and the possible candidate is only Daghestanian.

[§] Possible resemblant forms in interjection and nursery word in one daughter language only; counted as 0.25.

Sources for proto-forms in Tables 8.2–8.5:

PIE: Gamkrelidze and Ivanov (1984, 1994), Pokorny (1959).
Kartvelian: Klimov (1964).
Nakh-Daghestanian: My reconstructions, based on Daghestanian correspondences from Gigineišvili (1977), Proto-Nakh from Imnaišvili (1979) and my own work, and modern Daghestanian words (entailing some corrections in Gigineišvili's correspondences) from Kibrik and Kodzasov (1988, 1990).
Abkhaz-Circassian: Proto-Circassian from Kuipers 1975; corroboration and some further forms from Šagirov (1977).
Semitic: Gamkrelidze and Ivanov (1984, 1994).

NOTES

1   Some of the research on Nakh-Daghestanian livestock terminology reported here was done in Moscow and Groznyj in 1989 as a participant in the ACLS-Academy Exchange of Senior Scholars sponsored by the International Research and Exchanges Board. Research defining the structural type of Indo-European has been supported in part by grant no. DBS 9222294 from the National Science Foundation to the University of California, Berkeley. An earlier version of this chapter was read at the Second Annual UCLA Indo-European Conference, 24 May 1990.
2   Forms and proto-forms come from standard sources (see Table 8.5). The Nakh-Daghestanian reconstructions are mine, based on an ongoing comparison of the Nakh languages (which I know) to Daghestanian (for which the basic phonological correspondences are identified in Gigineišvili 1977), using Kibrik and Kodzasov (1988, 1990) as the main source of phonological and grammatical information. Very different Nakh-Daghestanian reconstructions are offered by Starostin (1985), Diakonoff and Starostin (1986), and Nikolayev and Starostin (1994) (unavailable to me until just before this chapter was submitted), sources which use very different cognate sets. Starostin and his coauthors all assume Nakh-Daghestanian and Abkhaz-Circassian are related and assemble cognate sets accordingly, evidently picking Nakh-Daghestanian words first for their phonological resemblance to Abkhaz-Circassian words. The result is that with some frequency a cognate set assembled for Nakh-Daghestanian finds its members dispersed among two or more putative Abkhaz-Circassian–Nakh-Daghestanian sets. Consequently not only the cognate sets but the correspondences, putative sound changes, and reconstructions differ. The Nakh-Daghestanian sets and correspondences in the present chapter are strictly what is demanded by Nakh-Daghestanian.
3   The '4' sharing is between Kartvelian '4' and IE '8', the latter formally a dual; but there is also an attested IE reflex, Avestan ašti 'width of four fingers' (*oḱt-) supporting the meaning '4'. This analysis is taken from Gamkrelidze and Ivanov (1984: 850 = 1994: 747).
4   This is more generally true of proposed IE–Kartvelian sharings. The following are two of the sharings described here and three more proposed by Gamkrelidze and Ivanov (1984: 877ff. = 1994: 774ff.), in both standard reconstruction and that of Gamkrelidze and Ivanov (G&I). For neither reconstruction are the obstruent manners of articulation identical, though (as Gamkrelidze and Ivanov argue in detail) the consonant inventories of Proto-Kartvelian and PIE are likely to have been quite similar. Likewise, PIE and Proto-Kartvelian forms are not identical to their Semitic comparanda. I suspect that direct borrowings among PIE, Proto-Kartvelian, and/or early Semitic would have produced much closer resemblances.

Gloss	PIE	PIE (G&I)	Proto-Kartvelian
yoke	yugom	yuk'om	*uɣ-(el-)
seven	septm̥	septʰm̥	šwid-
goat	digh-	t'igʰ	dqa-
harvest	kerp	k̂erpʰ	k'rep-
heart, chest	k̂erd-	k̂ert'-	m̥-k'erd-

5   A brief disquisition on *centum* and *satem* languages may be in order for non-linguists. These are two non-genealogical groupings of IE daughter branches. Centum languages (named for the Latin reflex of PIE '100') have velar consonants (*k*, *g*, etc.) corresponding to sibilant reflexes (*s*, *z*, etc.) in the *satem* languages (named for the Avestan reflex of the same word). The consonant series that yields these reflexes is named palatovelar. Its exact phonetics is unknown, but it must have been some kind of velar stop series since its reflexes merge with the PIE velars *k*, *g*, etc. in the *centum* languages, and it must have been palatalized since its reflexes have undergone assibilation, affrication, and the like in the *satem* languages.

6   This should simply be Yama Culture in English or, better Pit Culture. Russian *Jamnaja-kul'tura* contains the common noun *Jama* 'pit' made into an adjective and agreeing in gender, number, and case with *kul'tura* 'culture' as required by the rules of Russian grammar. The whole noun phrase is a proper noun, but neither of its components is.

7   There are a few Proto-Uralic-PIE lexical sharings such as PU *wete* 'water' : PIE *wed* ± *r/n* 'water'. These are probably indicative of some historical connection, but they do not reflect the kind of interaction with steppe languages that is at issue here, which produce more loans and involve only branches such as Iranian and Finno-Ugric. They are sharings of roots, while only sharings of stems would be diagnostic of borrowing from a particular source. Campbell (1990) gives a large number of resemblances between PIE and PU tree names, which again clearly indicate some kind of historical connection but do not indicate just what kind of connection.

REFERENCES

Anthony, D. 1991. The archeology of Indo-European origins. *Journal of Indo-European Studies* 19(3/4), 193–222.

Anthony, D. 1995. Horse, wagon, and chariot: Indo-European languages and archaeology. *Antiquity* 69, 554–65.

Blust, R. 1984/5. The Austronesian homeland: a linguistic perspective. *Asian Perspectives* 26, 45–67.

Burrow, T. 1959. *The Sanskrit Language*. London: Faber & Faber.

Campbell, L. 1990. Indo-European and Uralic tree names. *Diachronica* 7(2), 149–80.

Danilenko, V.N. 1974. *Èneolit Ukrainy*. Kiev: Naukova Dumka.

Dergachev, V. 1989. Neolithic and Bronze Age cultural communities of the steppe zone of the USSR. *Antiquity* 63, 793–802.

Diakonoff, I.M. 1980. Frigijskij jazyk. In *Drevnie jazyki Maloj Azii*, I.M. Diakonoff and V.V. Ivanov (eds), 357–77. Moscow: Progress.

Diakonoff, I.M. 1985. On the original home of the speakers of Indo-European. *Journal of Indo-European Studies* 13, 92–174.

Diakonoff, I.M. and S.A. Starostin. 1986. *Hurro-Urartean as an Eastern Caucasian Language*. Münchener Studien zur Sprachwissenschaft, Beiheft 12, Neue Folge. München: Kitzinger.

Dolgopolsky, A. 1987. The Indo-European homeland and lexical contacts of Proto-Indo-European with other languages. *Mediterranean Language Review* 3, 7–31.

Dolgopolsky, A. 1993. More about the Indo-European homeland problem. *Mediterranean Language Review* 6–7, 230–48.

Donnelly, A.S. 1968. *The Russian Conquest of Bashkiria, 1552–1740: a case study in imperialism.* Yale Russian and East European Studies, 7. New Haven, Conn.: Yale University Press.

Duby, G. 1974. *The Early Growth of the European Economy: warriors and peasants from the seventh to the twelfth century* (translated by H.B. Clarke) Ithaca, N.Y.: Cornell University Press.

Dyen, I. 1956. Language distribution and migration theory. *Language* 32, 611–26.

Èdel'man, D.I. 1980. K substratnomu naslediju central'noaziatskogo jazykovogo sojuza. *Voprosy Jazykoznanija* 5, 21–32.

Forsyth, J. 1992. *A History of the Peoples of Siberia: Russia's north Asian colony, 1581–1990.* Cambridge: Cambridge University Press.

Gadžiev, M.G. 1991. *Rannezemledel'českaja kul'tura Severo-vostočnogo kavkaza.* Moscow: Nauka.

Gamkrelidze, T.V. and V.V. Ivanov. 1984. *Indoevropejskij jazyk i indoevropejcy.* Tbilisi: Tbilisi University Press and Georgian Academy of Sciences.

Gamkrelidze, T.V. and V.V. Ivanov. 1994. *Indo-European and the Indo-Europeans.* Berlin: Mouton de Gruyter.

Garrett, A. 1990. The origin of NP split ergativity. *Language* 66(2), 261–96.

Gigineišvili, B.K. 1977. *Sravnitel'naja fonetika dagestanskix jazykov.* Tbilisi: Tbilisi University.

Gimbutas, M. 1977. The first wave of Eurasian steppe pastoralists into Copper Age Europe. *Journal of Indo-European Studies* 5, 277–338.

Gimbutas, Marija. 1991. *The Civilization of the Goddess: the world of old Europe.* San Francisco: Harper San Francisco.

Gulya, J. 1974. Prarodina finno-ugrov i razdelenie finno-ugorskoj ètničeskoj obščnosti. In *Osnovy finno-ugorskogo jazykoznanija: Voprosy proisxoždenija i razvitija finno-ugorskix jazykov*, V.I. Lytkin, K.E. Majtinskaja and K. Rédei (eds). Moscow: Nauka.

Hajdú, P. 1975. *Finno-Ugric Languages and Peoples.* (Translated and adapted by G.F. Cushing.) London: Andre Deutsch.

Harms, R.T. 1987. Uralic languages. *Encyclopedia Britannica, Macropedia* 22, 701–11.

Harris, D.R., V.M. Masson, Y.E. Berezkin, M.P. Charles, C. Gosden, G.C. Hillman, A.K. Kasparov, G.F. Korobkova, K. Kurbansakhatov, A.J. Legge,and S. Limbrey. 1993. Investigating early agriculture in Central Asia: New research at Jeitun, Turkmenistan. *Antiquity* 67, 324–38.

Imnajshvila, D.s> 1977. *Istoriko-svavnitel'nyj analiz fonetikt naxskix jazykov.* Tbilisi: Mecniereba.

Jablonskij, L.T. 1986. Antropologija ranne-èneolitičeskogo naselenija Prikaspii. In *Drevnejšie skotovody Volžsko-Ural'skogo meždureč'ja*, N.J. Merpert (ed.), 94–108. Moscow: Nauka.

Kibrik, A.E. and S.V. Kodzasov. 1988. *Sopostavitel'noe izučenie dagestanskix jazykov: Glagol.* Moscow: Moscow University.

Kibrik, A.E. and S.V. Kodzasov. 1990. *Sopostavitel'noe izučenie dagestanskix jazykov: Imja. Fonetika.* Moscow: Moscow University.

Klimov, G.A. 1964. *Ètimologičeskij slovar' kartvel'skix jazykov.* Moscow: AN.

Kortlandt, F. 1978. I.-E. palatovelars before resonants in Balto-Slavic. In *Recent Developments in Historical Phonology*, J. Fisiak (ed.), 237–43. The Hague: Mouton.

Kuipers, A.H. 1975. *A Dictionary of Proto-Circassian Roots.* Lisse: Peter de Ridder Press.

Mallory, J.P. 1989. *In Search of the Indo-Europeans: language, archaeology, and myth.* London: Thames & Hudson.

Markovin, V.I. 1969. *Dagestan i gornaja Èečnja v drevnosti*. Moscow: Nauka.

Masson, V.M. and V.I. Sarianidi. 1972. *Central Asia: Turkmenia before the Achaemenids* (translated and edited by R. Tringham). London: Thames & Hudson.

Merpert, N.J. 1974a. *Drevnejšie skotovody Volžsko-Ural'skogo meždurečja*. Moscow: Nauka.

Merpert, N.J. (ed.) 1974b. *Drevnie kul'tury Severnogo Prikaspija*. Kujbyšev: Kujbyševskij gos. ped. institut.

Nikolayev, S.L. and S.A. Starostin 1994. *A North Caucasian Etymological Dictionary*. Moscow: Asterisk Publishers.

Pokorny, J. 1959. *Indogeramisches etymologisches Worterbuch*. Bern-Muenchen: Francke.

Sapir, E. [1916] 1949. Time perspective in aboriginal American culture: a study in method. In *Selected Writings of Edward Sapir in Language, Culture, and Personality*. D.G. Mandelbaum (ed.), 389–462. Berkeley–Los Angeles: University of California Press.

Šagirov, A.K. 1977. *Ètimologičeskij slovar' adygskix (čerkesskix) jazykov* (2 vols). Moscow: Nauka.

Shevelov, G.Y. 1965. *A Prehistory of Slavic: the historical phonology of common Slavic*. New York: Columbia University Press.

Snirelman, V.A. 1992. The emergence of a food-producing economy in the steppe and forest-steppe zones of Eastern Europe. *Journal of Indo-European Studies* 20 (1/2), 123–43.

Starostin, S.A. 1985. Kul'turnaja leksika v obščeseverokavkazskom slovarnom fonde. In *Drevnjaja Anatolija*, B.B. Piotrovskij, V.V. Ivanov and V.G. Ardzinba (eds), 74–94. Moscow: Nauka.

Trubetzkoy, N.S. 1939. Gedanken über das Indogermanenproblem. *Acta Linguistica* 1, 81-9.

Vasil'ev, I.B. 1981. *Èneolit Povolž'ja (Step' i lesostep')*. Kujbyšev: KGPI.

Vasil'ev, I.B. and A.T. Sinjuk. 1985. *Èneolit Vostočno-evropejskoj lesostepi*. Kujbyšev: KGPI.

Warnow, T., A. Taylor and D. Ringe. In press. *Reconstructing the Cladistic Tree of Indo-European: a character-based computational approach*.

Weitenberg, J.J.S. 1987. Proto-Indo-European nominal classification and Old Hittite. *Münchener Studien zur Sprachwissenschaft* 48, 213–30.

White, L.D., Jr. 1962. *Medieval Technology and Social Change*. Oxford: Clarendon.

Williamson, K. 1989. Benue-Congo overview. In *The Niger-Congo Languages*, J. Bendor-Samuel (ed.), 247–74. Lanham: University Press of America.

Are correlations between archaeological and linguistic reconstructions possible?

ILIA PEJROS

PROTO-LANGUAGES

The essential aim of comparative linguistics is to investigate language families and to reconstruct a proto-language (a common ancestor) for each family. Reconstructions of the phonological, grammatical and lexical systems of a proto-language are based on the comparison of its daughter languages. The study of prehistory based purely on lexical reconstruction traditionally occupies only a marginal place within comparative linguistics.

A proto-language – one which gave rise to all the languages of a particular family – should possess the typical features of any human language. In particular it must be linked to a specific community whose members used this language in their everyday life. Sometimes a community's linguistic repertoire can be rather complex, displaying regional dialects, multilingualism, different language codes or other features. Such features are rarely reconstructed and this may constrain our knowledge of a proto-language without denying its reality.

Any language adequately maintains communication among its community members. Everything known to the speakers can be represented by means of their language. To enable this representation speakers simply put together particular units of meaning according to the grammatical, semantic and other rules of their language. Since these units of meaning also belong to the language structure, the language itself is a repository of information about the world (culture, environment, social relationships) of its speakers. Changes in this world always affect changes in language; new ideas are absorbed into the speakers' culture along with their language representations. Losses in knowledge are followed by the disappearance of the corresponding language representations.

This leads us to the major postulate of the discussion: the world of a community can be investigated through the study of the language spoken by its members. This postulate has never been thoroughly investigated in any case study, and is based solely on conclusions drawn from theory. It seems however to be quite reasonable, and also to be applicable to the study of modern spoken languages as well as to proto-languages.

Information about a speaker's world is kept mostly in the language's lexicon. We can distinguish two major types of lexicon which co-exist in a language: the morpheme lexicon and the world lexicon. The morpheme lexicon includes roots (lexical morphemes) and affixes (grammatical or derivational morphemes). Usually each word of a language has at least one root, and may have no, one or several affixes, depending on its grammatical structure. The world lexicon includes:

1   simple lexemes formed by one root and if necessary by grammatical affixes: golov-a = head-Ø;
2   complex words which can be of two different types:
    (a)   derivatives, formed by one root accompanied by derivational and grammatical affixes: bez-golov-yj = head-less-Ø;
    (b)   compounds formed by two or more roots and grammatical affixes: sky-scrape-(e)r-Ø;
3   fixed phrases (sometimes called *idioms*) formed by two or more simple or complex words. A fixed phrase has its own meaning, which is not just a sum of the meanings of its parts but rather defines the whole phrase as a total entity: whooping cough and potter's wheel are examples of fixed phrases, since knowing only the meanings of their constituents ('whoop' plus 'cough' or 'potter' plus 'wheel') we cannot understand either of these phrases.

The ratios between these three groups as represented in a world lexicon depend on the particular language, but simple words often form the largest group and fixed expressions usually the smallest. The number of roots in any language is always smaller than the number of words, although it may be slightly larger than the number of simple words, as some roots are found only in complex words and not in simple ones.

We can assume that simple basic meanings are generally associated with roots and simple words, albeit that this assumption is not supported by any case study. Other meanings tend to be represented by complex words and even by fixed expressions. The idea of 'potter's wheel' is, for example, represented by fixed expressions in most of the languages where it is found.

We do not yet know to what extent the lexical morphemes of a particular language represent the world of its speakers. It is clear that such a representation would be narrower than that based on words, but work with languages of Siberia, south-east Asia and Australia suggests that this form of representation has some validity. Detailed case studies and typological comparison are needed to clarify this point.

The details of the lexicon of a proto-language can never be fully known, and instead we must work with lists of morphemes rather than with lists of words. Technical problems inherent in lexical reconstructions mean that complex words and fixed expressions (which were definitely used in proto-languages) are usually invisible. Occasionally we can reconstruct the rules of word formation, but cannot verify that a certain derivation was used in the proto-language. On account of this and because of numerous semantic changes which take place in the daughter languages, a significant portion of the proto-language lexicon is inevitably lost without trace. If there is sufficient data from daughter languages it is possible, however, to reconstruct fairly representative lists of roots and words which can be used in cultural studies. Roots are usually more stable than words, and consequently they play an important role in such studies.

Since the lexicon reflects the world of language speakers it is theoretically possible:

(a) to analyse this world using lexical data;
(b) to work out a description of this world based purely on evidence from a particular language.

No dictionary can represent the complete lexicon of any language. Even a very large dictionary includes only words which seem to be important to the compiler and/or the speakers of the language. Members of the community often know many words which are absent from any dictionary of their language. However, dictionaries usually represent words in everyday use quite well, and we can expect the most important features of a community's life to be captured in the available dictionaries of its language. The gap between a language's lexicon as opposed to a collection of its words (its dictionary) adds more uncertainty to cultural reconstructions.

Proto-language roots and forms are reconstructed though the comparison of data included in dictionaries of recorded languages, which means that those dictionaries are the only source of information for a particular proto-lexicon. The reliability of reconstructed lists is dependent on the accuracy and comprehensiveness of the primary sources, and the publication of a new dictionary can sometimes alter a cultural reconstruction entirely.

LINGUISTIC ACCOUNTS OF PREHISTORY

An analysis of the lexicon can locate the language community in different dimensions: ecological, ethnic and cultural. This is the lexicon of a language in contradistinction to its dictionary. Real cultural studies based on dictionaries are always reliant on the amount of data included in a dictionary. Information about the ecological dimension can be found in the following three groups of words:

(a) words for different wild plants specific to a particular zone like Siberian cedar, mangrove or *mulga* trees.
(b) words for different wild animals, like crocodile, polar bear, kangaroo, and many others found in limited regions;

(c) words for specific natural phenomena such as monsoon, northern lights or earthquake known in one area but not familiar in others.

Information from group (a) is quite area-specific, while words from group (c) are associated with a more diffuse area.

An analysis of all these groups can provide us with detailed information about the ecozone where a proto-language would have been spoken, although one cannot expect simply to find the corresponding area on a map. Most of the reconstructed features of such a territory are subject to drastic changes which may have occurred since the period of the proto-language disintegration. This means that a purely linguistic localization based on this data is not an absolute, but a relative, one. It is only with the help of extralinguistic data such as that obtained from palaeoclimatology and palaeobotany that it becomes possible to connect this ecological dimension with a specific region on the map for a given period.

The method of *geographical pin-pointing* of the proto-language homeland involves interpreting the geographical distribution of daughter languages. A region in which several genetically diverse languages are represented (assuming that the languages did not arrive there in a single wave of migration) is more likely to be the homeland of the proto-language than a linguistically homogeneous region. Other things being equal, and ignoring such hypotheses as language refuge zones, it is easier to accept that remotely related languages developed separately within the same region rather than that several unconnected waves of migration to that same region brought remotely related languages with them. The genetic classification of the language family is crucial to this method as it is only such a classification that can provide us with information about genetic relationships within a language family. An area of older settlement is marked also by a greater diffusion of features throughout its dialects or languages, some isoglosses even crossing dialectal borders (Dolgopolsky, pers. comm.). This gives additional evidence for the pin-pointing of the homeland on a map. As this method is practically independent of the procedure for ecological localization, a correlation between their respective results makes the identification of the original territory more reliable.

Loans in the proto-language (PL) and borrowings from it in other (proto-) languages provide linguists with information about contacts between different communities and help them to localize the proto-language in an ethnic dimension. Here again we cannot map this information to find out which languages were spoken north from the PL. We can only show that two languages were spoken not far from each other, but usually it is impractical to work out a more detailed description. The ethnic dimension need not necessarily correlate with the ecological dimension reconstructed through other data. In some cases, however, borrowings reflect an ecological knowledge and they can then be considered to indicate that migrations have taken place.

A localization in the cultural dimension is based on analyses of other types of words, in particular words associated with:

(a) the economic activity of the speakers;
(b) the social structure of the community;
(c) the beliefs and rituals prevalent in the community.

The first group of words is usually the largest, so it often becomes the source of most detailed information.

Lexical comparison of two languages is problematic when speakers practise totally different economic activities, such as cultivation and hunting. In the language of the farming community we would find quite numerous terms for crops and agricultural techniques which would be absent from the language of the other group. But what are some of the other distinctive features embedded in the languages of different cultures?

Dictionaries of three languages were compared – Bruu (a Mon-Khmer language spoken by farmers of northern Thailand), and two languages of hunters and gatherers of Australia: Yir-Yoront (Cape York) and Warlpiri (central Australia). The three dictionaries are reasonably large, with more than 1,200 roots for Yir Yoront (Alpher 1991), 3,000 roots for Bruu (Theaphan Thongkum and See Puengpa 1980), and even more for Warlpiri (Swartz n.d.). The single difference between the dictionaries which is worth mentioning is the fact that the dictionaries of the two Australian languages contain significantly more names for plants and animals than can be found in Bruu. A possible explanation of this would be that such words are simply missing from this particular Bruu dictionary (though not from the lexicon of Bruu), and that further research would discover them and add them to the list. But why then are these words missing not only in the Bruu dictionary but in most dictionaries of south-east Asian languages? This observation perhaps reflects the fact that the words corresponding to such objects do not play any significant role in the life of these speakers and for that reason they are not represented in dictionaries. It is fairly clear that such words are known to some groups of speakers, but the tendency not to include them in dictionaries indicates that their role in everyday life is perhaps different from the role of plant or animal names in Australian Aboriginal communities. The absence of plant names from a dictionary definitely affects the cultural reconstructions which are based on the information in the dictionary. This is why we are not able to say much about localization of Proto-Tai, as names of wild plants are not included in most dictionaries of Tai languages.

The only reliable cultural reconstructions are based on comparisons of languages whose speakers are associated exclusively with food-producing economies. Languages of hunter-gatherers have never been investigated for the purpose of cultural reconstructions. This results in all our theoretical reconstructions being rather one-sided.

In a dictionary we can find names for various objects ('bow', 'millet', 'dugout', etc.) and activities ('to plough', 'to bake', etc.) associated with the economy of the speakers' community. These names do not provide us with precise information about the corresponding facts of the real world. They simply refer to a certain class of objects or actions whose members are classified as being identical and so are labelled with the same word. Each class includes objects whose functions and forms are identical from the language's point of view. Thus all objects which can be called 'axes' have a similar function and a more or less similar form. Their function and forms are quite different from those of 'knives'. 'Daggers' can be differentiated from 'knives' mainly because of their function; their difference from 'swords' lies mostly in their function, which is reflected in their forms. In any case one has to know how to classify and label an object (what is 'knife' and what is 'dagger'?). The criteria for those processes are often specific across languages and cultures.

Objects which share the same name can still be quite different from each other. Two knives may be of different size, may have different forms or patterns on their handles, but both would still be labelled with the same word. All the differences between these two objects can be represented through language, but that would have to be achieved by the free combination of words; for instance, 'knife with horse head on its handle'. Naturally, this type of combination would never be represented in a dictionary. The situation just outlined leads us to the conclusion that even if we know a word, we cannot say much about the physical appearance of the corresponding object. The word 'loom' does not describe a real object, while the word 'to weave' says nothing about the actual activity. What we can do is simply recognize that the speakers wove cloth using looms, but if we had several different looms in front of us there would be no way of connecting a particular loom with a word that we know. Also we can only speculate as to the nature of the action of 'weaving'. For these reasons an analysis of reconstructed words will tell us more about the functions of corresponding objects than about their appearances. In this sense, when we use linguistic data we can manage only a functional reconstruction of culture. Such a reconstruction provides a list of the cultural achievements of a particular community and places them within a typology of cultures. It does not, however, refer to real objects and cannot therefore be directly linked to any set of objects discovered by archaeologists.

Dating remains a serious problem in cultural reconstructions. There are two major ways to obtain absolute dating within comparative linguistics. One method is rather subjective and is based on the following logic: suppose there are two related languages A and B which are quite different from each other in their grammar and lexicon. We know that they separated, say, 2,000 years ago. This means that all the differences between them have only accumulated within this period of time. So if we have two related proto-languages and the differences between them are more or less the same as those between A and B, we can assume that the time elapsed since their disintegration would be similar to that in the case of A and B. But as the rates of change for different languages and even for different subsystems of the same language are not a constant factor, dating based on this logic is usually extremely approximate.

Glottochronology is another method of absolute dating used by some comparative linguists. It has been demonstrated that the original glotto-chronological method and its results are not reliable, making this procedure a rather infamous one in linguistics. The revised procedure and glotto-chronological formulae suggested by Starostin (1989) give acceptable results in the cases where independent verification is possible. This leads us to believe that in other cases the results would also be acceptable. Yet glottochronology remains a hypothesis which cannot be proved correct for every case. As contradictory cases using Starostin's approach are not known the dating obtained through this method can be used. Each glottochronological date, if accepted, is a date which can be considered as no better than probable from a statistical viewpoint. The actual event in question could have occurred much earlier or later than the time suggested by glottochronology.

A combination of all linguistic findings can be summarized in a so-called 'linguistic account' of a prehistoric community. This account pertains to the life of a prehistoric community as it is represented in the language (actually the proto-language) spoken by its members. Linguistic data is crucial for such an account while data from other disciplines such as geography, palaeobotany or archaeology is used only as a secondary source to clarify some points.

CORRELATION BETWEEN LINGUISTIC AND ARCHAEOLOGICAL ACCOUNTS

A linguistic account describes a community from a particular perspective with the limited framework provided by lexical reconstructions. Archaeology studies the same community from a different perspective based on the analysis of real objects and their remains collected during excavations. An interpretation of the findings leads to a reconstruction of the material culture of the com-munity which in its turn provides data for other types of reconstructions dealing with such phenomena as social structures, beliefs or contacts. The results of the reconstructions can be summarized in an 'archaeological account' of the prehistoric community. The question then becomes: is it possible to correlate the linguistic and archaeological accounts? This chapter argues that a direct correlation between the two accounts is theoretically impossible and that the sole link between them is the community itself.

Various characteristics of any community can be detected by direct obser-vation. These include language, various elements of material culture or rituals, behaviour of community members and many others. Sometimes a certain combination of these characteristics is quite specific and thus is sufficient to identify a particular community. In other cases several communities can share some or even most characteristics, while remaining absolutely distinct. The characteristics are often quite independent of each other and can be adopted by a community from totally disparate sources. Members of two communities can speak the same language(s) yet have totally different material cultures, or having similar material cultures they can speak absolutely different languages. Change in one characteristic does not necessarily imply changes in others.

Those detectable characteristics are not enough to distinguish two communities. The identity of a community is based on the 'inner image' shared by all its members. This includes, among other things, ideas about what is normal and accepted in a community, how its members should act and even how they should think in any standard situation. It also prescribes 'proper' appearance of objects used in the community: what colour of clothing is appropriate for a young girl, what forms and patterns should be used for pottery, what the structure for a normal dwelling is, and so on. Members of a community should be able to identify any object, no matter how insignificant, as normal and acceptable for the community, and 'inner image' enables them to do this. Another function of 'inner image' is to maintain the identity and integrity of the community by governing the behaviour and thoughts of individuals. That is why a major condition of being a member of a particular community is the acceptance of its 'inner image' and in turn the necessity to be accepted by it.

In traditional communities each element of material culture is produced according to the patterns approved by the 'inner image' of the community. As a result most elements have some kind of 'tint' or 'colouring' associated with the community. Because of this an object can often have a quite distinctive appearance and be somewhat different from functionally similar objects of neighbouring communities. The objects might be used for the same purpose, but their forms, sizes and colours can be totally different. So we can describe two different representations of the community's material culture: 'deep' and 'surface'. The surface representation includes real objects and the way they are used in the community. The deep representation deals with objects and actions free of the specific 'tint', though in this case all of them tend to be functions rather than objects.

In a comparison of two communities we may find that the surface representations of their cultures (real objects and actions) are quite different, while their deep representations (functions) are identical. It seems that in any particular area we can find many communities which share the same deep representation of their material cultures, yet are totally different in their surface representations.

It seems reasonable to assume that it is not the surface but the deep representation of material culture which is reflected in language. A word is a label for a group of objects with the same function and more or less similar forms. Identification of forms is less important than of functions and thus the outward appearance of two objects can be quite different, but this fact would not prevent them from sharing the same name. If this is so, it means that we are not able to connect any proto-language with a particular archaeological culture. Migrations which bring communities with their own languages and cultures to territories occupied by totally different groups are a separate case. The only justifiable step we can take is to connect a proto-language with a territory, which according to archaeologists reveals the same deep representation of material culture as is found in our linguistic cultural reconstruction. In so doing we cannot talk about communities at all. What we can demonstrate is that the language was spoken in this area, but there is no way to show that it was the only language, nor that one single community occupied the territory. Investigation of those problems remains beyond the discussed procedures and I am not aware of any attempts to address them to date.

REFERENCES

Alpher, B. 1991. *Yir-Yoront Lexicon: sketch and dictionary of an Australian language*. Berlin and New York: Mouton de Gruyter.

Starostin, S. 1989. Comparative-historical linguistics and lexicostatistics (in Russian). In *Lingvisticheskaja rekonstrukcija i drevnejshaja istorija Vostoka*, I. Pejros *et al.* (eds), 1–39. Moscow: Nauka.

Swartz, S. n.d. *Warlpiri–English Dictionary*. Aboriginal Studies Electronic Data Archive. Canberra: Australian Institute of Aboriginal and Torres Strait Islander Studies.

Thongkum, T.L. and S. Puengpa. 1980. *A Bruu–Thai–English Dictionary*. Bangkok: Chulalongkorn University.

10 Linguoarchaeology: goals, advances and limits

Victor Shnirelman

INTRODUCTION

Russia is famous for its long tradition of ethnogenetic studies — i.e. investigations of the origins of particular peoples: how, when, under what conditions different peoples came into being.[1] This tradition is deeply rooted in the Age of Nationalism when various European peoples occupied themselves with the search for their ancestors and past cultures. A peculiar feature of the Russian approach was the idea that there were no pure peoples or cultures. This idea, already forged by the mid-nineteenth century (Khomiakov 1871), stressed that different components with their own histories and cultures played an important role in each particular ethnogenesis. One had to reveal these components and to study their particular histories. Since the processes in question took place in the very remote past, when written sources were scarce or non-existent, the researcher had to rely on the indirect evidence of material and skeletal remains or linguistic data.

Thus, archaeology, palaeoanthropology and historical linguistics were treated as the main disciplines capable of solving ethnogenetic problems. Until very recently they struggled with one another for priority in ethnogenetic studies. However, a consensus has been established during recent decades when scholars agreed that ethnogenetic studies should be based on a multi-disciplinary methodology.

Thus, co-ordinating data from different disciplines became a very important task, since more often than not these data did not agree with each other. If they did not correlate, what could be the basis for interdisciplinary co-operation and how could one obtain a non-contradictory result? Several Soviet scholars and academic teams (Diakonoff 1981; Gamkrelidze and Ivanov 1984; Bongard-Levin and Gurov 1985) tried to develop a more sophisticated methodology in the 1970s and 1980s. Linguoarchaeology started in the 1980s, developed by the author in co-operation with the linguists Alexander Militarev and Ilia Pejros (Militarev and Shnirelman 1984, 1988; Militarev et al. 1988; Pejros and Shnirelman 1989a, 1989b, 1992; Shnirelman 1989b, 1992, 1994).

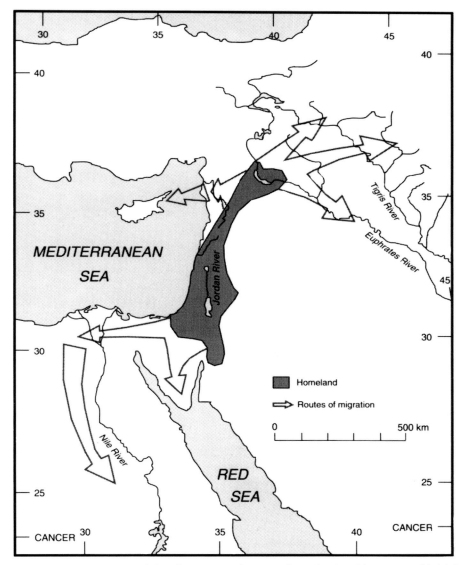

Figure 10.1 A proposal for the Proto-Afroasiatic homeland, with routes of initial migration.

Its main goal was to improve methodological procedures in co-ordinating archaeological and linguistic data.

Working out a more sophisticated methodology is an urgent task – especially now when a renewed emphasis on ethnicity results in claims for lands, power and cultural legitimacy based on ethnogenetic arguments. Indeed, the modern efflorescence of ethnogenetic mythology plays a major role in the development and maintenance of the ideology of inter-ethnic tensions and confrontations (Shnirelman 1993, 1995).

Unfortunately, sometimes even respected scholars localize ancient linguistic entities in space and time without rigorous arguments, thereby providing conflicting versions of ethnogenesis. For instance, Arutiunov (1982: 74–5) identifies the earliest Near Eastern farmers with proto-Nostratic speakers while Dolukhanov (1989) treats them as proto-Indo-European speakers. His approach forces proto-Semites deep into the Arabian desert, and leaves no place for proto-Elamo-Dravidians. On the other hand, Khalikov (1993) considers that the earliest Near Eastern farmers were proto-Elamo-Dravidian speakers. All these ideas were put forward without analysing the substantial body of both archaeological and linguistic evidence.

In many cases Soviet and non-Soviet archaeologists identified the same archaeological culture with speakers of different languages. Thus, it became important to explore the limits of academic studies, the results scholars can or cannot reach, the reliability of ethnogenetic constructs, and how their reliability can be improved. This was the purpose in developing the linguo-archaeological approach.

Until recently such studies were often one-sided in that they were made primarily by either archaeologists or linguists divorced from one another. To be more productive and to obtain more reliable results a team must incorporate both archaeologists and linguists. This strategy was exploited by our team to reconstruct aspects of proto-Afroasiatic (together with proto-Semitic) and Dravidian prehistory, and to study the cultural context of the rice domestication and spread in east and south-east Asia (Volume II).

To obtain more precise results independent approaches were used to test them against each other. The approaches included:

1 chronologies based on both calibrated radiocarbon dates and glottochronological calculations;
2 a study of the selected reconstructed lexicon (ecological and subsistence-technological terms) relevant to given archaeological patterns;
3 an investigation of external cultural contacts in both archaeological and linguistic terms;
4 a discussion of the problem of the disintegrations of prehistoric linguo-cultural entities revealed through modern linguistic, archaeological and linguo-geographical data (Militarev et al. 1988).

This strategy helped us control the results at various stages of our studies. The goals of linguoarchaeological reconstructions are:

1 to localize a homeland of a given linguistic entity in time and space;
2 to describe various cultural aspects as fully as possible (including technologies, social and political structure, warfare, ideology etc.);
3 to study external cultural relations (which helps to localize adjacent linguistic entities);

4   to discuss the problem of such entities' disintegration (cause and effect, time and space, migration routes, etc.).

An important prerequisite for the linguoarchaeological approach is the ability of linguists and archaeologists to explore the same processes using their own methods independently.

The approach can be exploited most productively in dealing with basic transformations in culture and society, explicitly reflected both in material culture and language. The worldwide importance of the transition to a food-producing economy is an appropriate object of study (Shnirelman 1989a) together with an analysis of subsistence intensification (Shnirelman 1980: 218ff. and 1988: 15–48, 51–5; Sherratt 1981, 1983, 1988). Limitless optimism is not in order; more often than not archaeological and linguistic data characterize various aspects of culture quite differently. An archaeologist who intends to use a reconstructed lexicon must be aware of the realities that it can clarify. The existence of a reconstructed term for a particular type of stone cannot be used to infer an obsidian trade.

There are, moreover, chronological divergences between the patterns revealed by linguistic and archaeological data. For instance, a 'proto-farming' lexicon can emerge before a true farming, and traces of farming in the archaeological record are usually dated to a somewhat later period than the emergence of true farming. Although the Aborigines of the Eastern Cape York Peninsula, Australia, depended on the wild yam as a staple and replanted numerous plant species, they would not thereby be classified as cultivators. Nevertheless, the Aborigines themselves define yam stands as 'gardens for yam' in modern Creole. While revisiting former home sites after a long period the Aborigines complained 'Poor old country come wild now. No-one to look after him' (Hynes and Chase 1982: 40–1). It is possible to imagine this situation on the eve of agriculture. Since the first cultivated plants and herded animals did not differ morphologically from their wild relatives, it is not easy to judge whether incipient farming or specialized food-collecting is in use, in terms of technology.

Such examples have been extensively discussed elsewhere (Shnirelman 1994), and it can be assumed that a linguistic reconstruction may reflect a situation prior to the emergence of true farming while archaeological data reflects a later state of affairs. The proto-Afroasiatic reconstruction of Militarev and Shnirelman (1984, 1988) illustrates this pattern.

Ecological terms are commonly used to localize the homeland of a proto-language. It is usually assumed that it is not difficult to reconstruct the ecological setting of that homeland, although in practical terms this is by no means simple. Linguists usually reconstruct generic rather than specific terms, which can seriously limit interdisciplinary research since both floral and faunal generic realms are often too broad to be very useful. Indeed, animals are more restricted in their habitats in contrast to plants, and the floral realms implied by a given proto-lexicon usually point to a more extensive region than the restricted areas occupied by proto-language speakers. For instance, an analysis of the proto-Central-Southern Dravidian lexicon revealed a vast area which coincided with a dry tropical deciduous forest zone inhabited by all the daughter languages since their dispersal (Pejros and Shnirelman 1989a, 1992). Initially the homeland occupied a more restricted territory; this could only be inferred with a more sophisticated methodology.

It is more difficult to localize a homeland where the daughter languages have diffused beyond the original ecology. Semantic shift is very common and it is difficult to reconstruct the original meanings of terms. A proto-Afroasiatic reconstruction can serve as an example in this respect (Militarev and Shnirelman 1984, 1988). The meanings of the faunal terms are unproblematic since the animal species in question inhabit the areas where the daughter languages are still situated. However, the meanings of some floral terms are obscure since plants have more restricted habitats than animals. The same situation is represented by a proto-Indo-European reconstruction; the same term means 'oak' in some languages and 'pine' in others, hence the well-known 'beech' controversy (Gamkrelidze and Ivanov 1984, vol. 2: 612–14, 621–2).

The referents of terms for domestic species are more conservative since they were brought by people to new habitats in the course of their migrations. On the other hand, terms for domesticates are easily borrowed between languages. Data from proto-lexicons are especially welcome when there is detailed and reliable information on the centres of origins of various domesticated species and on the routes of their dispersal (Shnirelman 1989a).

This methodology works as follows. It is well established now that by the late 3rd millennium BC agriculture in some areas of western India (southeastern Rajasthan, eastern Gujarat, western Madhya-Pradesh) was based on three different components originating from different areas:

(a) a Middle-Eastern wheat–barley complex introduced to the Indus valley long before and recognizable already in the proto-Dravidian lexicon;
(b) an African component (sorghum, or *jowar*, and possibly some millet species);
(c) an Eastern component (primarily rice).

The two latter components were introduced into the area in question during the late 3rd millennium BC according to archaeological data. These conclusions coincide with the linguistic data on the disintegration of proto-Central-Southern Dravidian (CSD) by 2000 BC just after sorghum, millet and rice appeared in the area (Pejros and Shnirelman 1989a, 1992).

Another example demonstrates the robustness of the methodology in question. A term for a eggplant was reconstructed in the CSD lexicon. Initially we did not expect to have its archaeological traces since they easily decay. However, Dr Kajale (pers. comm.) tells us that eggplant remains were discovered in the Chalcolithic layers of Inamgaon. No traces of contacts with Indo-Europeans were present in proto-Dravidian and CSD lexicons. The

Indo-Aryans were thus still absent from the Indus Valley prior to the 2nd millennium BC. On the other hand, CSD-speakers borrowed a term for rice from Sino-Tibetan speakers, i.e. they were in contact with each other in the late 3rd millennium BC (Pejros and Shnirelman 1989b: 186).

A reconstructed lexicon gives generic ecological terms, or terms which we inevitably treat as generic. If there are different reconstructed terms for the same plant, say rice, in proto-Sino-Tibetan (ST) and proto-Austro-Asiatic, their precise meaning is difficult to establish. Are they plants of various maturity?, tended differently or under different conditions?, or sub-species? In such cases, hypotheses must take various additional evidence into consideration. From the different origins and dispersal routes of Indian (*Oryza indica*) and Japanese (*Oryza japonica*) rice sub-species one can assume that, first, there were several independent centres of rice domestication in east and south-east Asia; and, second, a dispersal of the Japanese sub-species along the Yangtze River Valley and beyond in late 4th–3rd millennium BC was connected with migrations of Sino-Tibetan groups (Pejros and Shnirelman 1989b). The proto-Austronesians (AN) and some Austroasiatic groups borrowed ST terms for rice which initially denoted just *Oryza japonica*. This data in question can also suggest the spatial-temporal localization of Sino-Tibetan, Austroasiatic and Austronesian groups at that period.

A limit of the methodology is that cultivation of particular plant species was geographically restricted where there was rudimentary farming technology. To move to a new ecological area one had either to select new cultivated sub-species and to improve the farming techniques (to introduce irrigation, for instance) or to domesticate local plants better preadapted to the new ecological setting. Changes in the lexicon followed: either an original term was extended to a new plant, thereby changing its meaning, or a new lexeme coined. Where Afroasiatic and Dravidian groups migrated from the winter rain zone, with wheat and barley as staples, to summer rain ecologies, millet and sorghum displaced them. As a result, specific original terms for cultivated cereals cannot be reconstructed with great accuracy; we are compelled to use imprecise generics such as 'grain', 'cereal species', and the like. This may also have been true for the early Indo-Europeans. This often leads researchers to conclude that farming was a less important occupation than pastoralism among the groups in question. Thus, only a detailed investigation can interpret a prehistoric subsistence pattern correctly.

Finally, it helps to be aware of the kind of entity reconstructed using the linguoarchaeological methodology. I suggest that it is not a people or an ethnic group; indeed I believe that we should reject labels like 'people', '*ethnos*', 'ethnicity', since they give the illusion of a continuous evolution from particular prehistoric groups to modern peoples. Although these conjectures may be naive and erroneous, potentially they can result in modern inter-ethnic tensions and clashes. The only linguo-cultural entities we can reconstruct with plausibility are autonomous bands or communities. Though sharing a common language and culture the latter never identified themselves with one another, and never perceived themselves as a common body, at least in operational terms. Their composition was fluid and played a variety of roles in the formation of later peoples.

NOTE

1 The present chapter was sent by e-mail and has thus been formatted and extensively rewritten in places by Roger Blench. For any distortions in the meaning that have entered into the text the editor apologizes.

REFERENCES

Arutiunov, S.A. 1982. Etnicheskije obshchnosti doklassovoj epokhi. In *Etnos v doklassovom i ranneklassovom obshchestve*, Y.V. Bromlej (ed.), 55–82. Moscow: Nauka.

Bongard-Levin, G.M. and N.V. Gurov. 1985. Genezis dravidijskoj kul'tury. *Vestnik Akademii Nauk SSSR* 10, 68–81.

Diakonoff, I.M. 1981. Early Semites in Asia. *Altorientalische Forschungen Berlin* 8, 23–74.

Dolukhanov, P.M. 1989. Cultural and ethnic processes in prehistory as seen through the evidence of archaeology and related disciplines. In *Archaeological Approaches to Cultural Identity*, S. Shennan (ed.), 267–77. London: Unwin Hyman.

Gamkrelidze, T. and V.V. Ivanov. 1984. *Indojevropejskij yazyk i indijevropejtsy* (2 vols). Tbilisi: Tbilisi University.

Hynes, R.A. and A.K. Chase. 1982. Plants, sites and domiculture: Aboriginal influence upon plant communities in Cape York Peninsula. *Archaeology in Oceania* 17(1), 38–50.

Khalikov, A. K. 1993. Ural'tsy i dravidijtsy na severe tsentral'noj chasti Yevrazii. In *Arkheologicheskije kul'tury i kul'turno-istoricheskije obshchnosti bol'shogo Urala*, I.B. Vasilijev *et al.* (eds), 208–13. Yekaterinburg: Institute of History and Archaeology.

Khomiakov, A.S. 1871. *Zapiski o vsemirnoy istorii. Polnoje sobranije sochinenij*. Moscow: Bekhmetev.

Militarev, A.Y., I.I. Pejros and V.A. Shnirelman. 1988. Metodicheskije problemy linguoarkheologicheskikh rekonstruktsij etnogeneza [Methodological problems of the ethnogenetic linguoarchaeological reconstructions.] *Sovijetskaja Etnografija* 4, 24–38.

Militarev, A.Y. and V.A. Shnirelman. 1984. K probleme lokalizatsii drevnejshikh afrazijtsev: opyt linguoarkheologicheskoj rekonstruktsii [On the problem of the most ancient proto-Afrasian home localization: an experiment in linguoarchaeological reconstruction]. In *Lingvisticheskaja rekonstruktsija i drevnejshaja istorija Vostoka*, Part 2, I.F.Vardul' (ed.), 35–53. Moscow: Nauka.

Militarev, A.Y. and V.A. Shnirelman. 1988. The problem of proto-Afrasian home and culture (an essay in linguoarchaeological reconstruction). Paper presented at the 12th International Congress of Anthropological and Ethnological Sciences, Zagreb.

Pejros, I.I. and V.A. Shnirelman. 1989a. Towards an understanding of proto-Dravidian prehistory. In *Reconstructing Languages and Cultures*, V. Shevoroshkin (ed.), 70–1. Bochum: Brockmeyer.

Pejros, I.I. and V.A. Shnirelman. 1989b. Vozniknovenije risovodstva po dannym mezhdistsiplinarnykh issledovanij [The emergence of rice cultivation according to interdisciplinary researches]. In *Lingvisticheskaja rekonstruktsija i drevnejshaja istorija*

Vostoka, Part 1, Materialy k diskussijam na mezhdunarodnoj konferentsii (Moscow, 29 May–2 June 1989), I.I. Pejros *et al.* (eds), 179–195. Moscow: Nauka.

Pejros, I.I. and V.A. Shnirelman. 1992. V poiskakh prarodiny dravidov [In search of the Dravidian homeland]. *Vestnik Drevnej Istorii* 1, 135–48.

Sherratt, A. 1981. Plough and pastoralism: aspects of the secondary products revolution. In *Pattern of the Past. Studies in honour of David Clarke*, I. Hodder, N. Hammond and G. Isaac (eds), 261–305. Cambridge: Cambridge University Press.

Sherratt, A. 1983. The secondary exploitation of animals in the Old World. *World Archaeology* 15(1), 90–104.

Sherratt, A. 1988. Review of C. Renfrew, *Archaeology and language*. *Current Anthropology* 29(3), 458–63.

Shnirelman, V.A. 1980. *Proiskhozhdenije skotovodstva* [Origins of animal husbandry]. Moscow: Nauka.

Shnirelman, V.A. 1988. Proizvodstvennije predposylki razlozhenija pervobytnogo obshchestva [Productive prerequisites of the primeval society decline]. In *Istorija pervobytnogo obshchestva. Epokha klassoobrazovanija*, Y.V. Bromlej (ed.), 5–139. Moscow: Nauka.

Shnirelman, V.A. 1989a. *Vozniknovenije proizvodijashchego khoziajstva* [The emergence of a food-producing economy]. Moscow: Nauka.

Shnirelman, V.A. 1989b. Historical linguistics through the eyes of non-linguist. In *Reconstructing languages and cultures*, V. Shevoroshkin (ed.), 84–7. Bochum: Brockmeyer.

Shnirelman, V.A. 1992. Etnokul'turnyje kontakty i linguisticheskije protsessy v Severnoj Amerike [Ethnocultural contacts and linguistic processes in Northern America]. In *Amerika posle Kolumba: vzaimodejstvije dvukh mirov*, V.A. Tishkov (ed.), 17–30. Moscow: Nauka.

Shnirelman, V.A. 1993. Nauka ob etnogeneze i etnopolitika. In *Istoricheskoje poznanije: traditsii i novatsii*, V.V. Ivanov and V.V. Puzanov (eds), 3–6. Izhevsk: Udmurt State University.

Shnirelman, V.A. 1994. Sravnitel'no-istoricheskoje jazykoznanije i arkheologija: problemy korreliatsii [Historical linguistics and archaeology: problems of correlations]. Unpublished ms.

Shnirelman, V.A. 1995. From internationalism to nationalism: forgotten pages of Soviet archaeology in the 1930s and 1940s. In *Nationalism, Politics, and the Practice of Archaeology*, P.L. Kohl and C. Fawcett (eds), 120–38. Cambridge: Cambridge University Press.

11 Crabs, turtles and frogs: linguistic keys to early African subsistence systems

ROGER BLENCH

What Song the *Syrens* sang, or what name *Achilles* assumed when he hid among the women, although puzzling Questions are not beyond all conjecture. What time the persons of these Ossuaries entered the famous Nations of the dead, and slept with Princes and Counsellors, might admit a wide solution. But who were the proprietaries of these bones, or what bodies these ashes made up, were a question above Antiquarism.

Thomas Browne, *Hydriotaphia*, Cap. V

Nomina debent naturae rerum congruere.

Thomas Aquinas

ABBREVIATIONS

*	Reconstruction established from complete analysis of sound-change
#	'Pseudo-reconstruction' established from quick inspection of cognates. In some extra-African cases I have generated this from cognate sets proposed without a reconstruction
AA	Afroasiatic
BC	Benue–Congo
C	Consonant
CB	Common Bantu
KS	Khoisan
NC	Niger–Congo
NS	Nilo-Saharan
PB	Proto-Bantu
PBC	Proto-Benue-Congo
PC	Proto-Cushitic
PWN	Proto-Western Nigritic
PWS	Proto-West Sudanic
V	Vowel

African language data is extracted from standard sources on the languages cited. Where no source is given for non-African data, terms have been extracted from standard dictionaries.

INTRODUCTION

One of the standard techniques of cultural and linguistic reconstructions of prehistory is the reconstruction of lexical items associated with subsistence. The assumption is that the presence of a plausible proto-form indicates that speakers of the proto-language were familiar with the object or practice in question. If, for example, 'dog' can be reconstructed for Proto-Indo European (PIE), the assumption is that speakers of *PIE were familiar with dogs.

Objections have been raised to this type of argument, focusing particularly on semantic change. If a root can switch the species of tree or fish to which it is applied during the evolution of a language phylum then it may be an unreliable guide to the ecology experienced by speakers of proto-languages (see Shnirelman, Ch. 10, this volume). A related problem is that if no secure date can be attached to the dispersal of a phylum then reconstructions cannot be reliably matched with a known climatic record and, by implication, a specific faunal or vegetational environment.

This chapter[1] focuses on a problem that is rarely raised in relation to reconstruction: the presence of apparently related lexemes across presumably unrelated language phyla. It starts from the observation that remarkable similarities exist between words applied to 'crab', 'turtle' and 'frog' in Africa's four language phyla[2] as shown in the Appendix tables (see pp. 177–80). This is presumably neither accidental, nor are the relevant terms loanwords in the usual sense; nor would this usually be taken as constituting evidence of genetic affiliation. The base forms of these lexemes are all apparently quite similar to one another, with the formula $kVrV$. Strikingly, no similar comparisons can be made for what should be more 'marked' categories, such as megafauna.

The chapter explores the role of these creatures in prehistoric subsistence strategies in the context of theories of aquatic adaptation. It then summarizes briefly the zoological literature for Africa and comments on the linguistic evidence compiled in the Appendix tables. Evidence that these terms are also attested outside Africa is compiled in additional sub-tables. It is argued that the existence of transphylic roots that are apparently not borrowings is best explained by phonaesthetic association. The conclusion speculates on a possible coming together of aquatic adaptations with sound symbolism and explores the implications both for our notions of prehistory and for genetic linguistics.

CRABS, TURTLES AND FROGS

Turtles and tortoises

The freshwater turtles of Africa are described in Durand and Levêque (1981) and the tortoises in Villiers (1958), while Ernst and Barbour (1989) provide a worldwide overview. In African languages a common name is often applied to both, although individual species, especially of turtles, may also have specific names. Tortoiseshell can be recovered in the archaeological record, but the soft-shelled turtles are less easy to recognize. Turtles and tortoises are relatively easy to capture as the defence represented by their carapace is no match for humans armed with tools, and they are eaten all over the continent.

Appendix Table A.1 presents a sample of turtle and tortoise names in all Africa's major language phyla (see also Blench, Volume III). A form of the root #-*kuru* is present in all four language phyla. Most riverine peoples recognize various species of river-turtle, but there is usually a generic to refer to the whole set, which is the term presented here. Turtles and tortoises are given the same name in many languages, or simply qualified 'of the river' and 'of the land'.

Crabs

African crabs are highly speciated but can be divided into three categories;

(a) marine crabs;
(b) freshwater crabs;
(c) land crabs.

Atlantic marine crabs are treated in some detail in Schneider (1990), and Fischer (1990) provides a useful survey of Indian Ocean crabs. Freshwater crabs are studied in Durand and Levêque (1981). Material on land crabs is not easily available, but they are widespread throughout the continent and are frequently culturally important because of the role they play in divination systems. Crab divination is reviewed briefly in Blench and Zeitlyn (1989/90) who argue that the words for spider and crab are etymologically interconnected in the Bantu borderland because of their comparable role in divination systems.

Appendix Table A.2 presents a sample of crab names in all Africa's major language phyla. The evidence here is weaker than for turtles and frogs, largely because words for crab are much more rarely cited. Many of the sources used for the other two tables simply lack the lexeme 'crab'. However, as noted in the commentary, 'crab' in particular seems to have extra-African associations, especially in Indo-European and the Pacific.

Frogs and toads

The ranide fauna of Africa is complex in the extreme, and it is unlikely that there is anywhere a description as complete as exists for Papua New Guinea or some Amerindian regions (see Bulmer and Tyler 1968 and Berlin 1992).

Reid *et al.* (1990) list the frogs and toads of south-east Nigeria and include a valuable bibliography of descriptive literature for West Africa. Generic terms for 'toad' and 'frog' are often the same, although this is not the case in Benue-Congo languages. Most languages have a series of names for partic-ular species that fall under the generic term.

Frogs are commonly eaten throughout Africa, although they are a taboo food for some peoples and frog-eating is often the topic of inter-ethnic abuse. Toads, on the other hand, do not seem to be eaten, and indeed are usually considered poisonous due to the exudate from glands on their backs. Toads are extremely salient, since they appear in large numbers every dry season even in quite urbanized regions and are visible by lamplight catching flying insects.

Appendix Table A.3 shows a sample of names for frog and toad in the major African language phyla. In the case of toads and frogs, onomatopoeic origins for some of the names are more likely than for turtles and crabs. Aristophanes' famous *brekekek koax, koax* is presumably related to the Greek *batrachos*. Talmudic Hebrew *qūrqūr*, the 'croaking of frogs', must connect to Arabic *qurra*, 'frog'. None the less, there is a surprising uniformity across language phyla boundaries, although the evidence for Khoisan remains patchy.

Other riverine fauna

Other faunal species fall into the category of aquatic subsistence, most notably shrimps and prawns, snails and shellfish. Remains of snails and molluscs are often extremely abundant in pre-Iron Age sites in Africa (Volam 1978). Unfortunately, lexical data on these rather more obscure items is much harder to come by, since they are hard to elicit and harder still to match vernac-ular and scientific names, due to the lack of easily available reference volumes. Hard-shelled freshwater gastropods can be expected to survive in the archae-ological record, in contrast to shrimps and prawns.

PHONAESTHEMES, RETENTION AND SALIENCE

The data

The Appendix tables show that the lexemes applied to the main species discussed above have undergone remarkably little change despite being spread across much of Africa. Although affixes have clearly been added in many languages, the same roots occur across phylum boundaries and also in isolates such as Hadza and Laal. The usual interpretation of such a situation would be recent loanwords, although this is evidently impossible. Unfortunately it is easier to remark this than to provide a convincing explanation. These lexical items run counter to usual hypotheses of genetic affiliation and create problems for the classic version of the comparative method. Other types of explanation must therefore be considered.

Ideophones and phonaesthemes

African languages are rich in ideophones, words expressive of sounds, states and visual images. These are frequently lexicalized – i.e. a term for 'cat' or 'cock' that starts as an imitation of its cry is assimilated to a morphological system and gains affixes unrelated to its original imitative nature (e.g. Kunene 1978; Childs 1994). This concept grades into what has been termed a 'phonaestheme' (Bolinger 1968). Phonaesthemes associate an experience or state with specific phonetic elements, but need not have any onomatopoeic component. An example from English is initial *gl-*, occurring in gleam, glitter, glow, gold, glamour, etc. These are not affixes or morphemes in the usual sense, but deep semantic associations that cause convergence of forms in etymologically unrelated words. For example, initial *fVl-* for meanings such as 'fly, flow, flutter' have been argued as a universal of language (Swadesh 1970). For this reason, phonaesthemes are usually ruled out as indicators of genetic connection (Campbell 1973). Little is known about how they arise in language, and to what extent they are properties of particular phyla rather than universal.

Sapir (1929) may have been the first to test experimentally Aquinas's principle, cited at the beginning of the chapter, by showing that subjects can often interpret words that are invented or unknown to them by phonetic structure alone. Swadesh (1970) argued for this in some detail and proposed phonaesthetic associations for particular vowels and consonants. What mechanisms are at work remains to be explained, but Berlin (1992), for example, reports on experiments showing that the association of word-shapes and qualities is better than chance. Berlin (1994) proposes phonetic commonalities that define zoological classes, such as fish and birds in Amerindian languages.

Most of this work is language-internal, i.e. it tends to illustrate that specific languages obey sound-symbolic rules. As Diffloth (1994) has pointed out, it can be problematic to generalize about vowel sounds on the basis of a small sample of similar languages. There is, however, a difference, since the phenomenon of names for aquatic fauna is more than simply a case of sound-symbolism relating to size. It can be argued that a *general* association such as phonetic shape and size may be prewired, part of the genetic underlay of language. But the relation of classes of specific fauna to consonantal frames widespread in languages in a wide geographical area must be cultural since the very existence of such creatures is arbitrary.

Clues to the processes at work in African languages can be gained by comparison with Indo-European associations of words for 'crab'. Indo-European has a root #kar- meaning 'hard' which has a complex association with words for 'crab'.[3] Latin *cancer* and Greek *karkinos* are both derived from reduplications of the original root, the image apparently being the hardness of the crab's shell (Watkins 1982). A similar association also exists in Niger-Congo; Westermann (1927: 240) reconstructs #kual- for 'to be hard' in Proto-Mande-Congo, and #-kal- for 'crab'. These forms are very similar, and yet Niger-Congo and Indo-European are not generally considered to be related except by advocates of monogenesis.

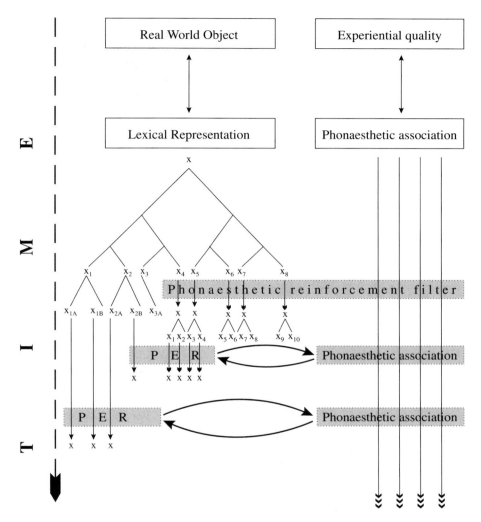

Figure 11.1 Operation of phonaesthetic feedback loops.

These are either remarkable coincidences or similar processes are at work in very dissimilar language phyla. Once a root describing a quality becomes established in a language phylum an association can be forged between that quality and a concrete external object, so that 'hardness' is persistently associated with crabs. Such an association must exist at a level of abstractness greater than language itself. If a link is culturally maintained over long periods of language diversification, then feedback loops can come into play; in other words, once an association is forged, speakers re-analyse existing forms. Word-structures that have tended to diverge according to the standard historical changes in a given language are reformatted to bring them back to the arche-typical structure. Figure 11.1 graphically represents this process, which is parallel to the process of folk etymology. The English words 'bell' and 'belfry' were originally etymologically distinct but have become convergent through this type of reanalysis.

These phonaesthetic associations suggest that similar relations between expe-riential qualities and consonant–vowel–consonant (CVC) structures may arise over wide language areas. Whether these are worldwide or merely areal remains to be tested; however, they do not apparently arise because of genetic links between language phyla. If these processes do occur, the question remains, why crabs, turtles and frogs? Why are these items of fauna burned into African languages in a way far more significant than large land mammals? The answer is that they appear to reflect an ancient cultural salience.

RIVERINE SUBSISTENCE IN AFRICAN PREHISTORY

One of the more well-known theories exploring riverine adaptations in Africa and their relationship with language phyla is the 'Aqualithic' of Sutton (1974, 1977). Sutton argued that a techno-complex combining harpoons, wavy line pottery and other implements was extremely widespread in a region encom-passing most of the Sahara and that this could be associated with the dispersal of Nilo-Saharan languages. The notion that there was an important phase of 'aquatic' adaptation in African prehistory is now quite widely accepted (see Haaland 1992). This has been reviewed by Muzzolini (1993), who concludes that despite changed emphases on diversity in technology, the concept remains broadly valid. However, aquatic adaptation should be placed much further back than Sutton was willing to propose. Studies by Stewart (1989) in the Nile Valley have recently placed what Haaland (1992) calls 'hunting and gath-ering with simple fishing technology' at 40,000–25,000 BP. Similar dates have been given for southern Africa by Volman (1978). In Central Africa, the lakeshore adaptations evidenced at the site of Ishango in eastern Zaïre contain substantial evidence of lithic technology and bone harpoons, suggesting a subsistence strategy based on fishing, shellfish gathering and some hunting (Brooks and Smith 1987). The dates originally ascribed to these sites (21,000 BP) have recently been set substantially further back, as far as 90,000 BP (Brooks et al. 1995; Yellen et al. 1995). If these dates are ultimately accepted then aquatic adaptations in Africa have by far the longest history of any so far recorded anywhere.

Living by rivers does not necessarily mean fishing. Wetterstrom's (1993) review of the lead-up to agricultural economies in Egypt points out that the technology of catching fish did not develop all at once. Although catching fish with only very simple technology may seem obvious when you live by rivers, creatures that move more slowly or are more available will constitute a major part of the diet.[4] In the case of Egypt, to judge by the bone remains, a major item of diet appears to have been the catfish, *Clarias* spp., which spawns in great numbers and can be caught without specialized fishing gear. Other items that would have been easily exploited include crabs, frogs, turtles and tortoises, molluscs and snails. Unfortunately, the archaeological visibility of these is very variable, although molluscs and snails are often conserved and are sometimes found in great numbers.

Wadi Kubbaniya in Egypt, which goes back to 18,000 BP, also has imbalances in the faunal remains (Wendorf and Schild 1989). Fish bones are dominant, with relatively small quantities of large fauna, suggesting that the technology to hunt down fast-moving plains animals (i.e. bows and arrows and poison) was lacking at this period. Subsistence was from easily gathered items, such as plants and riverside creatures. Crabs, frogs, turtles and tortoises, molluscs and snails would have played a crucial part in diet for a long stretch of human prehistory, certainly in Africa and possibly throughout the world.

Even today, crabs, turtles and frogs represent significant elements in the diets of riverine peoples in Africa, although they are generally outweighed by fish in abundance. In the Late Pleistocene and Holocene, when most of the common types of fishing technology in Africa were still to be introduced, these easily caught riverine species would have played an important role in the diet. If so, they may have been much more central to the cultures of these people and had a role in verbal and imaginative life which seems improbable today.[5]

This type of salience operates elsewhere in the world. A commentator on the rural blues once observed that critics were fond of proposing metaphorical explanations for the prominence of bullfrogs in song lyrics. However, a few nights in the American South and it becomes evident that no ulterior explanation is necessary, so far does their croaking dominate the soundscape.

If crabs, turtles and frogs became extremely culturally salient, then associations between phonaesthemes suggesting hardness and salient fauna would have been created. These would have become deeply culturally embedded at a time when the language phyla of Africa were beginning to diversify. In terms of resulting lexemes, this would be a weak type of determination, as surface forms could be over-ridden by cultural imperatives (such as the need to distinguish a large variety of sub-types).[6] None the less, the cultural embedding and the constant reference back to a conservative phonaesthetic would have meant that the relevant lexemes did not ramify and diversify in the same way as more normal lexical items. These faunal names are a special type of phonaestheme, associated imaginatively with creatures that were once the basis of subsistence.

Such a situation has also been hypothesized elsewhere in the world. Berlin (1992) attempts to demonstrate that words for 'frog' have a specific phonological element, notably -r- in C_2 position. His examples are almost entirely from Amerindian languages, so this is hardly a generalization, although, as Appendix table 11.3 shows, some African languages support this. However, the fifty-three terms applied by the Karam of New Guinea to species of frog show no examples of the word-structure he proposes (Bulmer and Tyler 1968).

The Tables A.1b, A.2b and A.3b represent a preliminary attempt to compile some resemblants of the African lexemes from language phyla outside Africa. This is most successful in the case of 'crab' where the #kar- root seems to have a near-global distribution. It has been argued for both Austroasiatic (Stampe, pers. comm.) and Austronesian (Mahdi, pers. comm.) that ka/qa- represents a prefix for (small) living creatures. If it turns out that this association is not limited to these two phyla then it may underlie many of the occurrences of the #kar- root worldwide.

OTHER TRANSPHYLIC SOUND-ASSOCIATIONS

This chapter has taken the example of riverine fauna because they form an exceptional category in relation to other native African animals and plants and are not explicable by more common onomatopoeic processes. There is at least one other example of an animal species, the domestic dog. Proto-Omotic (the primary branch of Afroasiatic) *kon is apparently close to Proto-Indo-European *kuon. It has long been observed that a similar root is also reflected in Chinese, and Sasse (1993) has argued that it is worldwide. Rosenthal (1985) has discussed the common roots for dog in Amerindian languages. It is just possible these are very early loans, as the domestic dog was first recorded some 10,000 years BP and probably spread rapidly across Eurasia and across the Bering Strait. Even so, terms for 'dog' have strikingly failed to diversify in the pattern common to individual phyla in the same way as crabs, turtles and frogs. This suggests that these processes are common and may occur with salient fauna.

However, the basic structure of the root is also important; the kVR- root also appears in other transphylic contexts. For example #kur- 'skin' has a pan-African distribution (Table 11.1). A similar word for 'knee' is found within Africa (Table 11.2). This strongly suggests that the associations are not random; that kVr- structures appear to be particularly persistent.

Table 11.1   #kulu 'skin, hide'

Phylum	Family	Language	Witness
KS	Central	Naro	khó-ba
NS	Songhay	Songhay	kúurú
NS	Saharan	Teda	koro-ta
NS	ES	Nuer	kul
NC	Mande	Bozo	korõ
NC	Atlantic	Gola	koro
AA	Chadic	Tala	kuur

Table 11.2 #kulu 'knee'

Phylum	Family	Language	Witness	Gloss
KS	Southern	!Xóõ	g‖xúũ	
KS	Kxoe	/Anda	kúrù	
KS	Northern	Ju|'hoan	g!xòà	
NS?	Shabo	Shabo	hutu/kutti	
NS	Maba	Mesalit	kàdíɲó	
NS	Fur	Fur	kùrù	
NS	ES	Kenzi	kur(ti)	
NS	CS	Aja	kuku	
NS	Saharan	Zaghawa	kurru	
NS	Kadugli	Katcha	-kuge (nu-)	
NC		#PWN	-kwudi-	
NC	Ubangian	Gbaya	gulu	
NC	Kwa	Ewe	kòlí	
NC	Bantu	*PB	-gudu	'leg'
AA	Cushitic	Proto-Cushitic	*gulb-/*gwilb-	

One author who has attacked this problem on a worldwide basis is Ciccotosto (1991), used a test sample of sixteen lexical items of 'core vocabulary . . . routinely used by linguists to trace genetic relationship among language phyla' sampled across 'virtually all known language phyla' to challenge the 'Saussurean assumption' that the phonetic structure of morphemes is generally arbitrary.[7] He found 'striking similarities' across apparently unrelated phyla and also drew the conclusion that the usual explanatory structures of historical linguistics cannot be marshalled to account for this situation. This is clearly similar to the faunal vocabulary and, moreover, the roots also have a similar form. Two principal explanations are offered to account for this: monogenesis and 'resistant phonemes'.

Monogenetic explanations

One explanation repeatedly proffered for this type of widespread root is monogenesis; in other words, these forms were part of the original lexical stock of 'Proto-World' or 'Proto-Human' (e.g. Ruhlen 1994: Ch. 5). This is virtually untestable, in part because the existence of such a hypothetical proto-language is doubted by many linguists. Even if it were true that all languages have 'sprung from a common source', we are presently far from demonstrating this. However, this would still not account for the phenomenon of transphylic roots; if they are so very ancient we would expect them to have undergone considerable diversification over such a long period. Indeed the presence of transphylic roots may well be an argument against Proto-World, since it suggests that cross-language similarities may not reflect ancient genetic affiliation.

Resistant phonemes

Another explanation is that these patterns are 'more resistant' to change than other, less-favoured phonemes. At one level, this is empirically true, as the additional examples given above suggest. However this does not constitute an explanation, since both /k/ and /r/ seem readily susceptible to phonological change in other lexical items. The fact that these resistant structures apply only to particular lexemes seems to be a strong argument against a purely phonetic explanation in favour of cultural salience.

CONCLUSION

The comparative method assumes that sound-change is regular once loanwords, false etymologies and other confusing factors have been eliminated. However, if phonaesthetic considerations can operate on concrete nouns to an as yet unknown extent, this introduces into historical linguistics yet another element of uncertainty.

If these arguments are accepted, some conclusions can be drawn for historical linguistics that are also relevant for reconstructions of prehistory. These are:

(a) Certain lexemes do not reconstruct normally, and seem to be not only borrowed between phyla but not to undergo regular phonological changes.

(b) The basis for this is apparently phonaesthetic in its broadest sense. There are deep-level links between types of quality or states expressed by particular sequences of vowels and consonants that in turn reinforce the surface forms of concrete lexical items. Although there is, except in the case of frogs, no evidence for an onomatopoeic component, a deep association between sequences of consonants and particular lexical items apparently develops.

(c) The reasons for this focus on particular lexical items remain open to speculation, but in the case of aquatic fauna they may at some time have played a major role in subsistence or in relations with the environment.

(d) The extent of such phonaesthetic associations is unknown but is surely much wider than is presently realized. It is far from clear whether certain associations have their roots in universal human psychology or simply in the diffusion of human culture.

(e) This in turn may have significant implications for claims concerning genetic relations between languages. Without answers to these rather fundamental questions, the nature and definition of genetic affiliation, especially between phyla, must remain in doubt.[8]

This is a cautionary tale without a clear moral except that its conclusions will not sit easily with proponents either of macrophyla or of the comparative method as it is usually applied. At another level, this type of compilation may give us access to some fragments of the earliest forms of speech and perhaps the mental world of the Palaeolithic. Despite the pessimistic prognostication of Sir Thomas Browne, perhaps these are not 'questions above Antiquarism'.

APPENDIX

Beneath the Appendix tables are additional tables noting possible parallels for African language terms outside Africa. This is much more speculative, and remains to be fully investigated. However, this type of phonaesthetic association is probably applicable to an area much broader than just Africa. Data sources used to complete the tables not specifically referenced in the text are listed in the References section.

The arrangement of the lexical data is intended to indicate a tentative morphological analysis of the individual terms, with corresponding syllables arranged in vertical columns.

Table A.1a   #*kuru* (tortoise, turtle)

Phylum	Family	Language		Witness			Gloss
–	Sandawe	Sandawe		kʰú	rú		tortoise
–	Hadza	Hadza		k'ò	ló		tortoise
–	Hadza	Hadza		k'ú:	tá-		turtle
–	Laal	Laal		kú	nán		'petite tortue'
KS	Northern	Auen		!gu	ru		tortoise-shell
KS	Khoe	Naro		ʁιgo	e		tortoise
KS	Khoe	Mohissa		cu	ru		tortoise
NS	Komuz	Kwama		k'	u	kiʃ	turtle
NS	Songhay	Songhay	n	ku	ra		small tortoise
NS	Saharan	Kanuri		kó	ro	wú	tortoise
NS	Maba	Aiki		ká(bú)rù		dà	tortoise
NS	Maba	Maba	fa	k	ruu	n	tortoise
NS	Surmic	Didinga	bo-	ko	l		tortoise
NS	ES	Dinka	le-	ku	r		tortoise
NS	CS	Bongo		ká	ndá		small turtle
NS	CS	Ma'di	o	kù			tortoise
NS	Kadugli	Krongo		-kó	ò	ŋ (ní-)	tortoise
NC	Kordofanian	Masakin		(k)ə	rə		tortoise
NC	Mande	Yaure		kú	lú		tortoise
NC	?	Pre		k	ru	wɛ	tortoise
NC	Atlantic-Congo	*PWN		-kwú	lu		tortoise
NC	Gur	Dagbane		ku	-r		tortoise
NC	Kwa	Lyele		ku	l	sebwa	tortoise
NC	WBC	Igbo	é-	kpù	ru		tortoise
NC	Plateau	Doka	a-	ku	l		tortoise
NC	Bantu	*CB		-ku	lu		tortoise
AA	Cushitic	Burji		ko	c'a		tortoise, turtle
AA	Cushitic	Dullay	kon-	ko	lo		tortoise
AA	Beja	Beja	se	ku	ur		tortoise
AA	W. Chadic	Hausa	kùŋ	ku	ruu		tortoise
AA	W. Chadic	Mwaghavul		kú	r		tortoise
AA	C. Chadic	Huba	kwà	kú	rù	m	tortoise
AA	Masa	Lame		gu	re	i	tortoise sp.
AA	E. Chadic	Toram	kùn	gù	rù		turtle
AA	Berber	Kabyle	tafe	k	ru	rt	tortoise

The diversity of the forms attested may reflect the fact that different species may have compound names (see the Kanuri and Aiki forms). Greenberg (1966) cites parallels from Kordofanian and also Keiga, now classified as NS. Mukarovsky (1976–7: I, 225) reconstructed a form for Atlantic-Congo. Hoffmann (1970: 15–16) points out that this word was also borrowed into Chadic from Benue-Congo, occurring throughout West Chadic and sporadically in Central Chadic. Ironically, he concluded that this might be evidence that these attestations were unconnected.

Evidence for this form outside Africa is distinctly weak compared with other roots (Table A.1b).

Table A.1b Sample names for turtle/tortoise outside Africa

Phylum	Family	Language	Witness	Gloss	Source
Austroasiatic	Munda	Sora	kolla	tortoise, turtle	Stampe (p.c.)
Dravidian		Tamil	kuruḷai	tortoise	

Table A.2a #kala- (crab)

Phylum	Family	Language	Witness	Comment
–	Hadza	Hadza	goma:	Probably unrelated
NS	C. Sudanic	Mbay	kə́-bàr	
NC	Mande-Congo	PWS	–ka(l)–	
NC	Mande	Mende	kaku	
NC	Unclassified	Pre	kamu	
NC	Atlantic	Temne	a–kara	
NC	Ijoid	Nembe	à-kàngà	
NC	Gur	More	gará̰-ga	
NC	Kwa	Ewe	à-gálà̰	
NC	WBC	Nupe	kara	
NC	Mambiloid	Mambila	kaab[21]	
AA	W. Chadic	Hausa	ƙaagwaa	
AA	C. Chadic	Mafa	tsakaɓam	
AA	Berber	Beni-Snus	kúrzma	

Westermann (1927: 230) considered 'crab' to be Proto-West Sudanic and proposes a root of the form –ka(l)–. Mukarovsky (1976–7: I, 144) adds further Niger-Congo cognates. The Niger-Congo roots are discussed in Williamson and Shimizu (1968: 92). Although the crab is less well represented within Africa by comparison with other fauna it appears to have striking associations beyond Africa (Table A.2b).

Table A.2b Sample names for crab outside Africa

Phylum	Language	Witness	Source
Japonic	Modern Japanese	kani	
Altaic	Modern Korean	ke	

Table A.2b – *cont.*

Phylum	Language	Witness	Source
Austroasiatic	Proto-Mon-Khmer	★kə (n)taam	Diffloth (1994)
	Proto-North Bahnaric	★katam	Smith (1972)**Table**
Austronesian	Proto-Austronesian	★kaRang	Mahdi (pers. comm.)
	Proto-Nuclear Micronesian	★karika	Marck (pers. comm.)
Andamanese	Aka Biada	kátta-da	Portman (1887:22)
	Onge	tekandue	Dasgupta and Sharma (1982)
Sino-Tibetan	Proto-Tibeto-Burman	★d-ka·y	Benedict (1972: 25)
Dravidian	Proto-Dravidian	kup(p)i	Burrow and Emeneau (1984: 158)
Indo-European	Greek	karkinos	
Basque	Basque	karramorro	Trask (pers. comm.)

Table A.3a   #kad- (frog, toad)

Phylum	Family	Language	Witness	Gloss
–	Hadza	Hadza	bililiyako	frog★
–	Sandawe	Sandawe	ǂʔoroŋ'	frog
KS	Central	Hiecware	kwee	bullfrog
KS	Khoe	‖Ani	ǂqòbé	frog
NS	Kuliak	Ik	k'waátᵃ	frog
NS	Songhai	Gao	nkorokoro	toad
NS	Saharan	Kanuri	kókó	toad
NS	Fur	Fur	gɔrɔŋ	frog
NS	Maba	Masalit	ámbɔ-kɔlà	frog
NS	Tama	Tama	bɔr-kʷɔid	frog
NS	Surmic	Didinga	lo-kido-dók	frog
NS	E. Sudanic	Temein	kwúḍó'	frog
NS	C. Sudanic	Bagirmi	káró	frog
NS	C. Sudanic	Mbay	kùrkùtə	frog
NS	Kordofanian	Koalib	kw-urɔ́	frog
NC	Kordofanian	Heiban	gwudo	frog
NC	Mande	Bobo	kwia	frog
NC	Atlantic	Balanta	ko̲de	frog
NC	Ijoid	I̲zo̲n	àkpálò̲	frog
NC	Kwa	Baule	klo̲	frog
NC	Benue-Congo	Yoruba	kere	frog
NC		Ibibio	ikwot	toad
NC	Bantu	Common Bantu	-kédè	frog sp.
AA	N. Omotic	Koyra	ḍo-qaree	frog
AA	N. Omotic	Koyra	koppe	toad
AA	Agaw	Bilin	qware'	frog, toad
AA	Cushitic E.	Burji	koopi	toad
AA	Cushitic E.	Arbore	koraankorač	frog
AA	Chadic (W.)	Hausa	kwaɗo	frog, toad
AA	Chadic (C.)	Mafa	kudaf	frog
AA	Chadic (E.)	Migama	kál-tám	frog

Table A.3a — *cont.*

Phylum	Family	Language	Witness	Gloss
AA	Egyptian	New Kingdom	q-r-r	frog, toad
AA	Semitic	Amharic	inqurarit	frog, toad
AA	Semitic	Arabic	qurra	frog
AA	Berber	Kabyle	amqerqur	frog, toad

* Without more information about Hadza morphology it is difficult to know whether the -ko is a significant element.

The two Koyra citations in Table A.3a are given to demonstrate that these roots have split, at least in Omotic. South Omotic, incidentally, appears not to share any of these forms. None the less, there appears to be such frequent semantic joining and splitting that the hypothesis of a common origin is not excluded. One proposal for an Indo-European reconstruction of frog/toad is $\star g^web^h$-, which would certainly link with the Khoisan and East Cushitic forms. Sasse (1979) proposes $\star$kub- for Proto-East Cushitic.

Table A.3b gives some examples of apparently similar forms outside Africa:

Table A.3b   Sample names for frog/toad outside Africa

Phylum	Language	Witness	Gloss	Source
Miao-Yao	Proto-Miao-Yao	qɛŋ	frog	Purnell (1970: 81)
Miao-Yao	Miao	⋆kai	toad	Purnell (1970: 213)
Daic	proto-Thai	#kop	frog	Benedict (1972: 297)
Austroasiatic	Cham	kap	small frog	Benedict (1972: 297)
Austronesian	Formosan: Paiwan	#qub	frog	Benedict (1972: 297)
Dravidian	Proto-Dravidian	#kappe	frog	Burrow and Emeneau (1984:114)

NOTES

1   I would like to thank Philip Allsworth-Jones and Kevin MacDonald for assisting me with the relevant archaeological literature, and Václav Blazek, Kay Williamson and Bruce Connell for carefully reading a first draft of the chapter and giving me numerous useful comments. Rainer Voßen and Klaus Keuthmann kindly gave me additional Khoisan lexical data and Dick Hayward supplied some Omotic material. In New Delhi, I benefited from the comments of other researchers, notably Nick Evans. I hope this revised version adequately addresses their concerns. Subsequently I was able to seek comments on extra-African occurrences of some of the terms discussed from the listserver Arcling. I am grateful to all those who replied, especially Waruno Mahdi and Jeff Marck.
2   Khoisan languages are less well represented – partly for lack of adequate lexical data, partly because these items of fauna are excluded in much of the desert habitat of the Khoisan.
3   I am grateful to Václav Blazek for this observation.
4   There is a curious parallel here with the Tasmanians, who seem to have developed a taboo on fish-eating well after they settled the island and seem to have subsisted largely on shellfish.
5   Although perhaps the widespread assignment of rather improbable roles to the tortoise in folk-tales is a relic of this.
6   This type of discrimination is apparently culturally determined. There is no evidence for any African language distinguishing such a large number of species, although the biotic variety is just as great in some regions.
7   Victor Golla (on the Linguist List) drew my attention to this interesting thesis.
8   The fact that they cross phylum boundaries so freely, *as if* they were loanwords, is a less controversial reason for ruling them out.

REFERENCES

Benedict, P.K. 1972. *Sino-Tibetan: a conspectus*. Cambridge: Cambridge University Press.
Berlin, B. 1992. *Ethnobiological Classification: principles of categorization of plants and animals in traditional societies*. Princeton N.J.: Princeton University Press.
Berlin, B. 1994. Evidence for pervasive synesthetic sound symbolism in ethnozoological nomenclature. In *Sound Symbolism*, L. Hinton, J. Nichols and J.J. Ohala (eds), 76–93. Cambridge: Cambridge University Press.
Bleek, D.F. 1956. *A Bushman Dictionary*. New Haven, Conn.: American Oriental Society.
Blench, R.M. 1993. Recent developments in African language classification and their implications for prehistory. In *The Archaeology of Africa. Food, metals and towns*, T. Shaw, P. Sinclair, B. Andah and A. Okpoko (eds), 126–38. London: Routledge.
Blench, R.M. and D. Zeitlyn. 1989/90. A web of words. *Sprache und Geschichte in Afrika*, 10/11, 171–86.
Bolinger, D. 1968. *Aspects of Language*. New York.
Brooks, A.S. and C.C. Smith. 1987. Ishango revisited: new age determinations and cultural interpretations. *African Archaeological Review* 5, 65–78.
Brooks, A.S. *et al.* 1995. Dating and context of three Middle Stone Age sites with bone points in the Upper Semliki Valley, Zaïre. *Science* 268, 548–53.
Bulmer, R.N.H. and M.J. Tyler. 1968. Karam classification of frogs. *Journal of the Polynesian Society* 77, 333–85.
Burrow, T. and M.B. Emeneau. 1984. *A Dravidian Etymological Dictionary* (2nd edn). Oxford: Clarendon Press.

Campbell, L. 1973. Distant genetic relationship and the Maya–Chipaya hypothesis. *Anthropological Linguistics* 15(3), 113–35.

Childs, G.T. 1994. African ideophones. In *Sound Symbolism*, L. Hinton, J. Nichols and J.J. Ohala (eds), 178–204. Cambridge: Cambridge University Press.

Ciccotosto, N. 1991. *Sound symbolism in natural languages*. Ph.D. in Linguistics, University of Florida.

Diffloth, G. 1994. The lexical evidence for Austric, so far. *Oceanic Linguistics* 33(2), 309–21.

Durand, J.-R. and C. Levêque. 1981. *Flore et fauna aquatiques de l'Afrique sahélo-soudanienne. Tome II*. Paris: ORSTOM.

Ernst, C.H. and R.W. Barbour. 1989. *Turtles of the World*. Washington, DC: Smithsonian Institution Press.

Fischer, W. *et al.* 1990. *Guia de Campo das espécies comerciais marinhas e de águas salobras de Moçambique*. Rome: FAO.

Greenberg, J.H. 1966. *The Languages of Africa*. The Hague: Mouton (published for Indiana University).

Haaland, R. 1992. Fish, pots, and grain: early and mid-Holocene adaptations in the Central Sudan. *African Archaeological Review* 10, 43–64.

Hoffmann, C. 1970. Ancient Benue-Congo loans in Chadic. *Africana Marburgensia* 3(2), 3–23.

Kagaya, R. 1993. *A Classified Vocabulary of the Sandawe Language*. Tokyo: Institute for the Study of Languages and Cultures of Asia and Africa.

Kunene, D.P. 1978. *The Ideophone in Southern Sotho*. Berlin: Dietrich Reimer.

Mukarovsky, H. 1976–7. *A Study of Western Nigritic* (2 vols). Wien: Institut für Ägyptologie und Afrikanistik, Universität Wien.

Muzzolini, A. 1993. The emergence of a food-producing economy in the Sahara. In *The Archaeology of Africa. Food, metals and towns*, T. Shaw, P. Sinclair, B. Andah and A. Okpoko (eds), 227–39. London: Routledge.

Purnell, H. 1970. Towards a reconstruction of proto-Miao-Yao. Ph.D. Cornell University, Ithaca, New York.

Reid, J.C., A. Owens and R. Laney. 1990. Records of frogs and toads from Akwa Ibom State. *Nigerian Field* 55, 113–28.

Rosenthal, J.M. 1985. Dogs, pets, horses, and demons: some American Indian words and concepts. *International Journal of American Linguistics* 51(4), 563–6.

Ruhlen, M. 1994. *The Origin of Language*. New York: John Wiley & Sons.

Sapir, E. 1929. A study in phonetic symbolism. *Journal of Experimental Psychology* 12, 225–39.

Sasse, H.-J. 1979. The consonant phonemes of Proto-East-Cushitic: a first approximation. *Afroasiatic Linguistics* 7(1), 1–66.

Sasse, H.-J. 1993. Ein weltweites Hundewort. In *Sprachen und Schriften des antiken Mittelmeerraums. Festschrift fuer Juergen Untermann zum 65. Geburtstag*, F. Heidermanns, H. Rix and E. Seebold (eds), 349–66. Innsbrucker Beiträge zur Sprachwissenschaft, 78. Innsbruck Institut für Sprachwissenschaft.

Schneider, W. 1990. *Field Guide to the Commercial Marine Resources of the Gulf of Guinea*. Rome: FAO.

Smith, K.D. 1972. *A Phonological Reconstruction of Proto-North-Bahnaric*. Asian-Pacific Series, No. 2. Santa Ana, Calif.: Summer Institute of Linguistics.

Sutton, J. 1974. The aquatic civilization of Middle Africa. *Journal of African History* 15(4), 527–46.

Sutton, J. 1977. The African aqualithic. *Antiquity* 51, 25–34.

Stewart, K.M. 1989. *Fishing Sites of North and East Africa in the Late Pleistocene and Holocene*. Cambridge Monographs in African Archaeology, 34. Oxford: BAR.

Swadesh, M. 1970. *The Origin and Diversification of Language*. Chicago: Aldine & Co.

Villiers, A. 1958. *Tortues et crocodiles de l'Afrique Noire*. Initiations Africains, 15. Dakar: Institut Fondamental de l'Afrique Noire.

Volam, T.P. 1978. Early archaeological evidence for shellfish collecting. *Science* 201, 911–13.

De Voogt, A.J. 1992. Some phonetic aspects of Hadza and Sandawe clicks. Doctorandus scripsie for Afrikaanse Taalkunde, Leiden.

Watkins, C. 1982. *Indo-European Roots Dictionary*. Appendix to the Houghton Mifflin Canadian Dictionary of the English language. Boston: Houghton Mifflin.

Wendorf, F. and R. Schild. 1989. *The Prehistory of Wadi Kubbaniya*. Dallas: Southern Methodist University.

Westermann, D. 1927. *Die Westlichen Sudansprachen und ihre Beziehungen zum Bantu*. Berlin: de Gruyter.

Wetterstrom, W. 1993. Foraging to farming in Egypt: the transition from hunting and gathering to horticulture in the Nile Valley. In *The Archaeology of Africa. Food, metals and towns*, T. Shaw, P. Sinclair, B. Andah and A. Okpoko (eds), 165–226. London: Routledge.

Williamson, K. and Kiyoshi Shimizu. 1968. *Benue-Congo Comparative Wordlist, Vol. 1*. Ibadan: West African Linguistic Society.

Yellen, J. *et al*. 1995. A middle Stone Age worked bone industry from Katanda, Upper Semliki Valley, Zaïre. *Science* 268, 553–6.

12 Linguistic archaeology: tracking down the Tasaday language

LAWRENCE A. REID

ABBREVIATIONS

Language abbreviations		Other abbreviations	
Bon	Bontok	k.o.	kind of
Ilk	Ilokano	loc.	location
ItgB	Binongan Itneg	var.	variant
Klm	Kulaman		
MboBkd	Binukid Manobo		
MboSrn	Sarangani Manobo		
PMP	Proto-Malayo-Polynesian		
SblBt	Botolan Sambal		
Sml	Samal		
SubS	Sindangan Subanun		
Tag	Tagalog		
Tbl	Tboli		

All transcriptions are phonemic. The phonological inventory of Tasaday is identical to Blit and Kulaman Valley Manobo, with fifteen consonants and five vowels, alphabetized as follows: ʔ, a, b, d, ə, e, g, h, i, k, l, m, n, ŋ, o, p [f], s, t, u, w, y. All Tasaday and Blit data are cited from my field notes, and Kulaman Valley data are cited from Errington and Errington (1981), but in phonemic transcription. Other languages such as Botolan Sambal, Binukid, Sarangani Manobo, Bontok, Ilokano, etc. are cited from either Reid (1971, 1976) or from field notes.

INTRODUCTION

In July 1971 a report by Manuel Elizalde Jr.,[1] then Presidential Assistant on National Minorities in the Philippines (Elizalde and Fox 1971) to the Smithsonian Institution's Center for Short-Lived Phenomena from Southern

Cotabato, Mindanao in the Philippines, informed the world of a small, isolated group of hunter-gatherers supposedly living in caves in the rain forests of southern Mindanao in the Philippines. The group of six families numbered approximately twenty-seven individuals, ranging in age from infancy to old-age, including a retarded male albino child with severe skin lesions and an elderly couple both of whom were said to be deaf-mutes. The group had a few metal tools, used stone tools, and were claimed to have no knowledge of agriculture or domesticated plants, including rice. They wore loin cloths, made either of old cotton fabric, bark cloth or the leaves of a ground orchid. They were said to have had no knowledge of tobacco or alcoholic drinks, but were familiar with betel nuts and chewed them with lime and a variety of leaves and bark from plants in their environment.

Initial reports claimed that prior to June 1971, when they were first contacted by members of PANAMIN at Mutu'lung, a clearing at the edge of the rain forest, the Tasaday had been in contact with only one outsider, a hunter named Dafal, although they knew of two other forest groups, called respectively Sanduka and Tasafeng, with whom they intermarried. The contacts with Dafal occurred during his various hunting trips into the mountains where the Tasaday lived. Dafal was born in the nearest agricultural community to the Tasaday area: a place called Blit. The Blit community was the furthest expansion east from the Kulaman Valley of a group of Manobo whose language is referred to in the literature as South Cotabato Manobo. One other language – Tboli – is commonly spoken in the area, and most people in Blit are conversant with both languages. A full record of the events surrounding the 'discovery' of the Tasaday, and of the controversy that has accompanied these events, is found in Nance (1988).

The Tasaday, when first contacted by the PANAMIN group, supposedly spoke a language considerably different from either the Manobo or Tboli dialects spoken in Blit and the surrounding areas, although comparison of word lists taken by linguists and anthropologists soon revealed that the language spoken by the Tasaday was far more similar to the Manobo spoken in Blit than it was to Tboli.

Initial reports stated that apart from their contact with the hunter Dafal, they had had no 'recurring' contacts with other people, although they had seen the houses and fields of peoples who lived at lower elevations than themselves, presumably the Blit community which was at that time only about a three- to four-hour hike away from the caves to the west. A number of Blit individuals were involved with the initial contact arrangements when Elizalde first flew in, and have remained in close contact with them since. These include the leader of the Blit community, Datu' Dudim, and several members of his large family. Datu' Dudim's son by the second of his seven wives (Luan), a young man named Mafalu, learned to operate communications equipment for Elizalde's organization, PANAMIN, and assisted in other ways. It was Datu' Dudim's oldest daughter Sindi (by his first wife, Kelaya) who was persuaded to become the wife of the Tasaday Belayem, who, probably in his early twenties, had not been able to acquire a wife for himself from the traditional sources of Tasaday spouses. It was also Datu' Dudim's daughter Soléh (by his fifth wife, Filey) who became Belayem's second wife in the early 1980s, after Sindi had failed to bear children. Datu' Dudim told me that he had seen the Tasaday in the forest during hunting trips in his youth, but that they had always run away from him.

THE HOAX CLAIMS

After the initial flurry of news reports, documentaries, and some preliminary investigative work by various scientists, including linguists, anthropologists, a botanist, a sociologist, etc., and the establishment by the Marcos government of a 19,000-hectare reservation in 1972 to protect the rain forest surrounding the Tasaday caves from the incursions of several logging companies, the Tasaday were left to resume their chosen way of life. In 1974, visitors were prohibited from entering the reservation without special permit, and for the next twelve years nothing more was heard of the Tasaday.

In 1986, news of the Tasaday reappeared in the media. A Swiss journalist, Oswald Iten, claimed to have visited the Tasaday in the aftermath of the overthrow of Marcos, in the company of a number of local individuals who told him that the Tasaday were not what they had been claimed to be, but were a mixed group of Manobos and Tbolis motivated by promises of land and money to act the part of cave-dwelling, stone-tool-using primitives whenever Elizalde required them to do so. Various other individuals had questioned the authenticity of the Tasaday prior to this, most notably the Filipino anthropologist Zeus Salazar (1971, 1973). However, it was Iten's report which spawned the virulent controversy that was first officially debated at a conference (the International Conference on the Tasaday and Other Urgent Anthropological Issues) at the University of the Philippines in 1986. At this conference, University of the Philippines anthropologist Zeus Salazar presented a series of genealogical charts which he claimed was evidence that the Tasaday were blood relatives (some of them college-educated) of various individuals living in communities outside of the rain forest. The genealogies however were not collected in the usual manner by interviewing the individuals concerned, but were reported to him on the eve of the conference by George Tanedo, a well-known son of an Ilokano settler in Maitum, part of the Tboli area. The real names of the individuals who supposedly participated in the scheme were given, with their corresponding Tasaday aliases.

A second symposium was held as part of a conference in Zagreb in 1988 (The International Congress on Anthropological and Ethnological Studies), and in 1989 a third conference (a special Invited Session of the 88th Annual Meeting of the American Anthropological Association) to discuss the Tasaday controversy was held in Washington, DC. A number of papers, both pro and con (e.g. Berreman 1992), which were presented at the last conference were published in a volume (Headland 1992), and probably did little to change anyone's opinion on the status of the Tasaday. Headland's summary attempted to claim the middle ground between two diametrically opposed points of view, the one being that prior to Elizalde's involvement in the events there were no Tasaday people as such, they were a group of disparate individuals brought together from various communities who were instructed to rush to the caves, dress like primitives, and told how to act and what to say (and not to say) whenever they were required to be shown off to gullible journalists, prominent personalities (and scientists). The polar opposite of this point of view was that the Tasaday were remnants of some paleolithic population who had survived in isolation in the rain forest for perhaps thousands of years, or at least five to seven hundred years, based on one published glottochronological estimate (Llamzon 1989: 61), without contact with peoples outside the rain forest.

At the Washington conference in 1989, a carefully prepared set of genealogies by Rogel-Rara and Nabayra (1992) which included each of the Tasaday as well as each of what were called the Tasaday poseurs, seemed to show conclusively that the Salazar genealogies were false. This, as well as the linguistic evidence presented in several papers (Molony 1992; Elkins 1992; Johnston 1992; Reid 1992), was suggestive that the Tasaday were in fact a separate ethnolinguistic group, distinct from either Blit Manobo or Tboli. Headland however claimed that it would have been impossible for the Tasaday to have lived in total rain-forest isolation without regular access to cultivated foods, especially the rice which was grown in the clearings around the Blit community.

THE RESEARCH STRATEGY

I had been present at the 1988 conference in Zagreb, and was intrigued by the claims that were being made by those who said that the Tasaday were a hoax, and that all but two of the participants in the supposed charade were really Tbolis who could speak Manobo. I was puzzled as to why the supposed orchestrators of the hoax had required the whole group (including children) to speak Manobo, the language of the two-member minority, rather than Tboli, supposedly the language of the majority. However, be that as it may, if it were true that they were mainly Tboli speakers, evidence should be forthcoming from the data that was first gathered by linguists and anthropologists in 1971 and 1972, to support it. There should be clear evidence of borrowing from Tboli.

After examining all of the early lists collected in 1971, I presented a paper at the Washington conference to show that I could find no evidence at all of Tboli influence, and that the types of responses given by the Tasaday to the field workers' questions about their language suggested a degree of naïveté that would not have been present if the respondents had been other than what they claimed to be.

At the Washington conference, results of a three-day visit to the Tasaday by a Filipino husband and wife linguist team, Cesar and Araceli Hidalgo, were presented. They claimed that they had collected data from the Tasaday which were considerably different from that which was collected by the linguist Carol Molony twenty years earlier. They further claimed that their data represented an older form of the language, one which was spoken prior to the considerable language changes that had resulted from their contact with the Blit Manobos following the initial contacts with them in 1971. The Hidalgos believed that by 1972 the Tasaday were speaking a pidginized form of Manobo and that the evidence suggested a very long period of independent development from other Manobo languages.

In 1989, I had the opportunity to also collect data from some of the Tasaday during a ten-day visit to the Tboli area (Reid 1993). Although my data did not completely coincide with that presented by the Hidalgos there was sufficient overlap with their data, in forms which were supposedly old terms not recorded in the 1970s, that I decided to spend an extended research period with the group. My plan was to try to find out as much as possible about the language that they currently speak, and as much as could be discovered about the Tasaday language as they claimed to have spoken it twenty-five years ago. I would compare these forms of speech with that spoken by the nearest agricultural community to Tasaday, the Manobo dialect of Blit, for which almost no data was at that time available, and with the Manobo dialect of Kulaman Valley (Klm), often referred to in the literature as Southern Cotabato Manobo, for which I had available an unpublished dictionary of about 3,500 entries (Errington and Errington 1981), as well as a number of published articles on phonology, morphology and syntax written by the Erringtons and other members of the Summer Institute of Linguistics who had lived in the Kulaman Valley area. I hoped furthermore to be able ultimately to try to identify etymological sources for those terms that were said to be old Tasaday and for which no obvious cognates existed in the surrounding languages.

The project was planned to take place over a period of three years. The first fieldwork stage consisted of three periods of residence with the Tasaday totalling approximately two and a half months between February and July 1994.[2] A second period of fieldwork was conducted during the summer of 1995,[3] and a third trip in the summer of 1996. This chapter is in effect a report of the results of the analysis that I have been able to do of the data collected during the first half of 1994.

THE FIELDWORK

The first month of fieldwork, from mid-February to mid-March 1994, was conducted at the site where the majority of Tasaday now live. This is a small cleared valley about twenty minutes' walk from the caves which they still claim as their home. The place is called *magtu iliŋan*, literally 'New Learning', and sometimes by a term, obviously adapted from English, *nu bəliginiŋ* 'New Beginning', and is about a two-day hike north-west from Lake Sebu.

I was taken directly to the thatch-roofed, split palm and bamboo home of Udelen and his wife Dul and their family. In 1971, this couple had only two small sons. Dul had delivered her first daughter, Okon, the following year. When I arrived, Dul was nursing her tenth child, and Okon, now married, was also in the home, mourning the loss of her first child, stillborn only days prior to my arrival. Their oldest son, Sius, lived in an adjacent house with his wife and child; Maman, the second son, who had married a young Tboli woman, was living away from the group with his wife's family. He periodically visited during the time that I was there. His first child was born a couple of months after my arrival. The other children of the family, Diha', Sungo, Talihin, Dihut, Klohonon, and Fakal also lived in the house, except during periods when the older children accompanied their father on trips to gather palm pith, or to another area of the forest that they were cutting back to form a new *kaingin*.

Also living with the family during the period of my stay there was a Belgian, Pascal Lays, a member of the London-based organization Survival International. He had been living on a fairly regular basis with the Tasaday for more than two years, studying their language and culture, and making extensive collections of botanical and zoological specimens from the rain forest. He was able to communicate quite well with the Tasaday in the language that they are presently using to outsiders as well as among themselves. Lays told me that it was the language of the Blit Manobos, from whence most of the outside wives of Tasaday men have come since 1972. He agreed to assist me as interpreter during the early stages of my research in that community.

Since my primary object was to discover as much as possible about the language spoken prior to 1971, I decided to work with Belayem, now a man probably in his late forties or early fifties. He had the reputation of being the most articulate of the Tasaday even when the group was first studied. He was fully aware of the controversy that surrounds the group, and readily consented to be my main Tasaday language assistant, although Dul, and often other younger Tasaday, were also present at most of the language gathering sessions. Bilengan, one of the older Tasaday men who also lived in Magtu Ilingan and is now becoming deaf, periodically sat in although he did not actively participate in the data gathering.

Datu' Dudim's son Mafalu was invited to come from Blit and was requested to assist by providing Blit Manobo equivalents for the Tasaday terms that Belayem would give me. Mafalu was one of the few available Manobo-speaking Blit villagers who could communicate also in Tagalog. He was, in addition, the brother-in-law (twice over) of Belayem, and had been in contact with the group for at least the last twenty-three years.

I conducted fairly short morning and afternoon sessions for approximately one month with Belayem and Mafalu, gathering supposedly old Tasaday forms

and their Blit Manobo equivalents and recording several Tasaday and Blit
texts. A second period of research lasting about about one month (April 1994)
was held in Mutu'lung, close to the site of the first contact between the
group and Elizalde. Belayem and his two Blit wives had decided to begin a
new settlement there because of its associations and because they would be
closer to their two older children now attending grade school about a kilo-
metre away in Blit. When I arrived, clearing had begun on a small ridge
above a creek, and a bamboo platform had been erected with palm leaf walls
and temporary roof for protection from the constant rains. Over the next
three weeks groups of relatives and friends came from Blit on an almost daily
basis to complete the building of the house, while with Belayem and Mafalu
I continued investigations into the similarities and differences between their
two languages. A third period of research lasting about two weeks (July 1994)
was conducted in Blit.

THE DATA

From the outset, the data received from Belayem seemed to confirm the
claim that prior to their contact with outsiders they were indeed using a very
different form of speech than that used by the Blit. For almost every Blit
word that a Tasaday equivalent was requested, a Tasaday translation was given,
and Mafalu would often claim that the term provided was not known to
him, or that it had a different meaning in Blit.

Before long, however, I began to become suspicious of the data that
Belayem was giving. I noted that he was making a conscious effort to distinguish the forms he gave me from those of Mafalu. Sometimes he would do
this by simply switching the affixation on a verb, or by using a different
pronominal ending. At other times, it seemed that the forms that he was
giving me were deliberate phonological distortions of Blit forms. Data sets
1–56 (see Appendix, pp. 196-9) are examples of some of these items. However,
systematic comparison of the data with Kulaman Valley Manobo showed that
at least some of the forms (e.g., sets 57–60) corresponded exactly to their
Kulaman Valley cognates, and it was the Blit form that was phonologically
different. This kind of evidence suggested that the irregular forms were not
entirely the result of conscious distortion, but rather that at least some of the
cases were the result of unconscious, sporadic phonological change.
Nevertheless, by the end of the second period of residence in the area
I was convinced that some of Belayem's forms, which were completely
different phonologically from their Blit equivalents, were indeed fabricated
by him.

Between the second and third periods of residence with the Tasaday, the
task of systematically entering the data into a database[4] was begun, so that
the material could be compared with the Manobo spoken in the Kulaman
Valley. At the end of this period, I had a list of about 750 lexical items

supposedly used by Tasaday prior to 1971 that were unknown to Mafalu. An additional list of 1,200–1,500 items formed a second lexical set that were known to both Belayem and Mafalu, and constituted the Blit Manobo corpus.

At this point the Manobo dictionary was searched for possible cognates of the 'unique' old Tasaday data; i.e., those forms that Mafalu had claimed were unknown to him. To my considerable surprise I found that a large number (approximately 300) of the items that had seemed to be completely new coinages by Belayem had similar forms in the Kulaman Valley dictionary. A small set of these is given in the Appendix (61–6). However, there remained a large number of forms that had no equivalents in any of the lexical sources then available to me, forms that are potentially evidence of fabrication; but on the other hand such forms may be genuinely unique, old Tasaday terms. A short list of these items is given in datasets 67–86.

A comparison with other Philippine languages of a number of the Tasaday forms that have no Blit or Kulaman Manobo equivalents, revealed that there are a number that do have possible cognates in other Manobo languages (sets 88, 90, 92, 93), and some that have cognates with languages outside the Manobo group (sets 89, 91, 94, 95, 96), but not with Manobo languages. Such forms are potentially of great value in establishing the relative length of time that the Tasaday language may have been developing independently from other Manobo languages; that is, they are possibly retentions of forms that have been lost in other Manobo languages but which are still retained in Tasaday. At this point, however, the possibility of their being borrowings, or alternatively that cognates will turn up in other Manobo languages, must still be considered.

Of the forms that were known to both Belayem and Mafalu, a considerable number showed some kind of semantic change. Usually a Tasaday form was claimed to have a wider reference than its Blit equivalent (see datasets 97–116). A few sets show a narrower reference (117–18), while others show a clear semantic shift (119–29).

One of the features of Tasaday that has been mentioned a number of times in the literature to support the claim of an extended period of isolation from other groups is the lack of borrowed terms from Spanish or other languages for concepts (such as 'war'), or for post-western contact cultural items that are a ubiquitous part of Blit and other surrounding languages but which were supposedly unknown to the Tasaday prior to 1971. Typically in the Philippines, terms for such items are adapted from a donor language, either Spanish or more recently English. Tasaday is unusual among Philippine languages in that not only are such forms absent, but that even today there is a clear avoidance of them. Belayem consistently used either paraphrastic expressions or metaphorical extensions of 'native' Tasaday terms for items that are claimed to have been introduced to the Tasaday since 1971. Data sets 130–53 are examples of some of these. The data provided by Belayem are unusual in other respects. Data sets 154–73 are paraphrastic expressions for terms that are not introduced concepts, but are items that languages typically have single lexical items for, although at least the term for 'river' (154) is in many languages simply the term otherwise translated as 'water'. This data is suspect and may have been constructed by Belayem to further distinguish his dialect from that of Blit. His choice of one of the terms of certain synonym sets (such as those in 174–5) found in both Blit and Kulaman, while denying the use of the other, was also a practice admitted by Dul to Pascal Lays while I was there as a means of distinguishing the two dialects. Although now only the first member of such sets is used by Belayem, the other member was commonly recorded by earlier researchers, such as Molony (1976), and it still appears in certain fixed expressions such as 133, 143.

The absence of Spanish borrowings has never seriously been challenged, but there are a couple of forms that probably show them. Early word lists, such as that by Molony (1976: 85), give the word *laŋit* for 'sky', a term which has cognates in Blit, Kulaman and many other Philippine languages. Presently Belayem uses the term *lugabuan* ('sky'). This is almost certainly a paraphrastic expression meaning 'place of the moon' combined from a Spanish term widely distributed throughout the Philippines, *lugar* ('place') with regular loss of a final *l* (from *r*) plus what appears to be the Tagalog form *buwan* ('moon'). It is no doubt a term of recent provenance. The other form *epe?* has an older provenance in the group, in that it appears in Molony (1976: 78). It is transcribed there as *'efe'* (meaning 'spirit'), with *'efe' ilib* (meaning 'owner of the cave, the white-haired spirit'). This is probably the Spanish form also widely distributed in Philippine languages, *jepe* ('chief, leader'), there being no other Philippine terms meaning 'spirit' or 'owner' with which it could reasonably be associated.

There also appears to be some Tboli influence on some of the lexicon and also the morphology of some of the verb forms that Belayem uses. In Tboli the regular development of an earlier *a vowel is Tboli *o*. For example, Tboli *hulo?* < *pula?* ('red'), Tboli *sobow* < *sabaw* ('soup'), Tboli *?owoŋ* < *?abaŋ* ('boat'), Tboli *kulon* < *kudan* ('rain'), Tboli *holol* < *palad* ('palm of the hand'), etc. Although there is no clear evidence of borrowing of lexical items from Tboli into Tasaday, several forms which are probably new developments by Belayem show *o* for expected *a*, and are possibly the result of phonological influence from Tboli (e.g. 176–7). The first of this pair is a metaphorical extension of the cognate term in Kulaman, but has an unexpected *o* vowel in the final syllable. The second, *pondol*, is apparently a reduced paraphrastic expression, consisting of the first three segments of each of the words in the phrase **panaw dalan**, literally 'walk path', but with the vowels altered as indicated above. It should be noted however that the words themselves are not Tboli.

Tboli influence on verbal morphology is seen in Belayem's use of the *-in-* affix. In Tboli the affix does not mark completive aspect as it does in Kulaman and other Philippine languages. It is simply the marker of what is commonly called an 'object focus' verb, and can therefore appear on verbs that have future time reference, and even on imperative forms. This use of the infix is not unique to Belayem. It is commonly heard also in Blit.

CONCLUSIONS

The data discussed above appear to be of two very different kinds and lead to two quite different conclusions. A person who is sceptical of the authenticity of the Tasaday would focus on one set and surely jump to the conclusion that here is the evidence that is needed to settle the case: distorted forms, borrowings from Spanish, influence from Tboli, apparent coinages, and a host of paraphrases apparently developed by Belayem to make his language different from that of his Blit neighbours. Such a conclusion would have to disregard the other set; namely, the considerable body of data that apparently does not have Blit equivalents (at least not according to Mafalu), but for which corresponding forms can be found in either Kulaman Valley – an area which Belayem has never visited – or most importantly, in neither Blit nor Kulaman but in other Manobo languages or even in more distant Philippine languages.

What then is the explanation for the first set? There is no doubt that much of the data that Belayem gave me were indeed made up for the occasion, or are part of a 'new Tasaday' that he has produced not only for me but also for the Hidalgos in their research. Although Belayem has an excellent memory for such forms, many that he had given me in the earlier periods of my fieldwork were rejected by him as being not Tasaday when I rechecked them at later stages of the project.

At the root of this apparent obfuscation is the obviously deep-rooted sense of identity that the Tasaday (not only Belayem) have of themselves. In the twenty-three years since their first publicized meeting with outsiders, not a single member of the original Tasaday group has 'recanted', even though the supposed motivation for their formation as a group, the all-powerful influence of their mentor, Elizalde, has long since faded. The group lives in poverty, and has no reason to continue the charade, if indeed there was one. Time and again, Belayem and other members of the group expressed frustration and anger over the questions that have been raised about their authenticity. The English term 'fake' is now a part of the Tasaday vocabulary.

Belayem realized from the beginning of the fieldwork that my object was to examine the relationship between his earlier language and that of Blit. He did not know whether I was looking for evidence to further cast doubt on their authenticity, but probably suspected it. He never, for example, allowed me to visit the actual cave site, less than twenty minutes' hiking from the Magtu Ilingan settlement, since he knew that others who had been there had left after seeing the caves and published negative reports about the group.

I consider that the efforts Belayem went to in order to create differences between his Tasaday language and that of Blit were directly the result of his knowledge of the hoax controversy and were for the purpose of attempting to validate himself and the other members of the group as a distinct ethnolinguistic group.

A number of interesting parallels can be drawn between the Tasaday in south-east Asia and another ethnolinguistic group that has recently been

described – the Minor Mlabri, an 'evasive' and 'extremely shy' group of
hunter-gatherers (only eleven surviving members), living in the border area
between North Thailand and Laos (Rischel 1995). In many parts of the
description of this group one could replace the name Minor Mlabri
with Tasaday without doing violence to the facts. Rischel describes them as
follows:

> They have in the past lived on food they could find by moving
> about in the dense forests of the high mountains without settling
> for more than a few days in any particular place. Until recently
> their shyness and ability to hide in the forest has prevented their
> culture and language from being exposed to outsiders except for
> a few encounters with expeditions.
>
> (Rischel 1995: 23)

He cites Boeles's (1963: 150) description of them as 'a group of people who
have not known a stone age and thus have no pottery, who do not make
their own clothing, who do not practice agriculture, who do not build houses,
and who do not wear ornaments'. He suggests that, 'their culture may even
reflect *regressions* from more developed stages to a survival culture' (Rischel
1995: 22).

There is another, larger group of Mlabri (the 'β-Mlabri'), previously studied
by Rischel, hence the term Minor Mlabri (or 'α-Mlabri') for the smaller
group that he describes. The larger group have given up a hunter-gatherer
lifestyle. Rischel says that they are

> rapidly adjusting to peasant life since it is becoming impossible to
> sustain life on the things they can gather in the forest. The α-
> Mlabri on the other hand, still prefer to stay in the forest as much
> as possible in an attempt to survive as part-time hunter-gatherers.
>
> (Rischel 1995: 36).

The relationship between the two Mlabri groups parallels in several respects
the relationship between the Tasaday and the Blit groups. Rischel states:

> The relationship between the two varieties of Mlabri is enigmatic.
> On my first encounter with speakers of Minor Mlabri, I was
> intrigued by the paradoxical situation that a large proportion of
> the words they used in everyday communication were totally
> unknown to me although they clearly spoke the very language I
> had been studying for several years together with my colleagues.
> I was further intrigued by finding that there was virtually no differ-
> ence in segmental phonology between the two varieties of Mlabri
> although they differed strikingly in prosody (rhythm and intona-
> tion) as well as lexicon . . .
>
> Structurally, the two kinds of Mlabri are so extremely close that
> one may speak of sub-dialects of one dialect. **The two varieties**

have almost the same phonology and morphology, and to the extent that lexical material is shared, it occurs in largely the same phonological shape . . . There are *segmental* differences between α-Mlabri and β-Mlabri in the pronunciation of several words, but there is also idiolectal variation . . . The lexical differences may have at least three different causes. They may in some cases reflect the existence of synonymous (or near-synonymous) word pairs in Old Mlabri. Synonymy was then lost as one variety retained only one word, and the other variety retained only the other synonym: . . . there are several instances where one variety of Mlabri has an ordinary Mon-Khmer etymon whereas the other variety has a word exhibiting peculiar features, **suggesting that it is a deliberate innovation** . . . Often a word used in one variety is known but considered obsolete or stigmatized by speakers of the other variety. In several instances **speakers even deny any knowledge of a word used by the other group**. The linguistics attitudes toward lexical materials is a complex issue . . . . **The differences in lexicon are so great that one would not expect easy intercommunication between the two groups** . . . This lexical divergence, as contrasted with the structural similarity of the two varieties of Mlabri, must be recent but is so strong **that it suggests an effort to mark the distinction between the α- and β-Mlabri**.

(Rischel 1995: 16, 26–7; bold emphasis added)

The linguistic characteristics noted by Rischel which distinguish the two Mlabri dialects are precisely those that are found between Blit and Tasaday; namely, almost identical phonology and morphology; lexicon which is very divergent between the two groups suggesting, at least in some cases, (relatively) recent deliberate innovation in order to mark the difference between the two groups. The two situations are, however, not completely parallel. The two Mlabri groups continue to avoid one another and to maintain their linguistic distinctiveness, whereas the Blit and the Tasaday now intermarry, and are merging as a single group, with the children of Tasaday families studying in school in Blit, and speaking Blit Manobo in the home rather than the using the Tasaday forms of their parents, just as the children of mixed Tasaday-Blit families do.

So what was the language of the Tasaday like in 1971? Was the conclusion of early researchers correct that Tasaday at that time was simply a close variant of Blit Manobo, or of Kulaman Valley Manobo, which was the conclusion that must be drawn from the Molony study? Or was there really a body of lexical differences that were never reported at that time simply because by the time Molony got there in 1972 they had already adapted to the Blit language and her data reflects the language that they had begun to use in place of the older forms that others didn't understand?

Some tapes that were secretly made in the caves during Elizalde's first and subsequent visits to the Tasaday caves have been made available to me. Rough English translations of parts of these tapes were published in Nance (1988), but no transcriptions were made of the actual language used. Recent research during which these tapes were transcribed and translated (Reid 1996) shows that although at that time there were a number of distinctive lexical forms that were commonly being used by the Tasaday, many of the forms that Belayem commonly uses today and which he claims to be 'real' Tasaday are probably recent innovations and serve the purpose of distinguishing his dialect from that of his Blit neighbours. Nevertheless, the evidence of clearly unique innovations in Tasaday which predate the initial contacts, and the retention of older forms in Tasaday which have apparently been lost in neighbouring Manobo languages, indubitably establish the Tasaday as a distinct ethnolinguistic group.

APPENDIX: TASADAY DATA

Possible phonologically distorted Tasaday forms

1 Tasaday beʔeʔ 'grandparent, grandchild'.
    Blit bebeʔ 'grandparent, grandchild'.
2 Tasaday bəliʔəgaŋ[5] 'molar'.
    Blit biʔəgaŋ, Klm biʔigaŋ 'molar'.
3 Tasaday bikət (var. dikət)[6] 'sticky'.
    Blit, Klm liməkət 'sticky'.
4 Tasaday bulas 'semen'.
    Blit, Klm bulos 'semen'.
5 Tasaday bulat 'flower'.
    Blit, Klm bulok 'flower'.
6 Tasaday butəd (var. libutəd) 'k.o. edible wood grub living in sago palms'.
    Blit gutəd basag 'k.o. edible wood grub living in sago palms'.
7 Tasaday datək 'k.o. leech'.
    Blit limatək 'k.o. leech'.
8 Tasaday dəpəŋ 'to be next to one another'.
    Blit lətəŋ 'to be next to one another'.
9 Tasaday əlam (əg-) 'feel sick', (nək-) 'menstruate'.
    Tasaday əlaʔ 'pain, injury'; Klm əlaʔ 'crack'.
10 Tasaday gədub (var. kedub) 'hot' (weather); 'fever'.
    Blit, Klm ədup 'hot' (weather); 'fever'.
11 Tasaday gipis (var. nigpis, lugpipiʔ) 'thin'.
    Blit nipis 'thin'.
12 Tasaday hayaʔhayaʔ (var. kayaʔkayaʔ) 'knee'.
    Klm kayaʔkayaʔ 'knee'.

13 Tasaday iyub 'back of a person'.
    Blit, Klm iyug 'back of a person'.
14 Tasaday kayampeŋ 'hawk'.
    Blit kayamba 'hawk'.
15 Tasaday kəbugat 'k.o. bird'.
    Blit bugat 'k.o. bird'.
16 Tasaday kəlawawan (var. lawawan) 'body'.
    Blit lawa 'body'.
17 Tasaday kuməlukesan 'old man, old woman'.
    Blit lukəs 'old man, married man'; Klm lukəs 'old man, old
        woman'.
18 Tasaday lakipəs 'k.o. civet cat'.
    Blit kipəs 'k.o. civet cat'.
19 Tasaday lambuyug 'k.o. bumblebee'.
    Blit təbuləg 'k.o. bumblebee'.
20 Tasaday ləbaw 'to swell, of an injured limb or a flooded river'.
    Blit, Klm ləbag 'to swell, of an injured limb or a flooded river'.
21 Tasaday ləgəmeʔ 'noise of tearing'.
    Blit ləgisiʔ 'noise of tearing'.
22 Tasaday ləgkaʔ 'to depart; to leave'.
    Blit, Klm ləgkaŋ 'to depart; to leave'.
23 Tasaday ləha 'testicle'.
    Blit, Klm laha 'testicle'.
24 Tasaday ləkotok 'to boil, bubble'.
    Blit, Klm lukotok 'to boil, bubble'.
25 Tasaday ləkud (var. səkud) 'flesh, muscle'.
    Blit, Klm əkud 'flesh, muscle'.
26 Tasaday ləmol 'rattan fruit'.
    Blit limulan 'rattan fruit'.
27 Tasaday ləpaʔ 'arm span, space between the tips of one's outstretched
        arms'.
    Blit lipo 'arm span, space between the tips of one's outstretched
        arms'.
28 Tasaday libəl 'to throw away, throw out'.
    Blit diwəl 'to throw away, throw out'.
29 Tasaday linabuʔ[7] 'to fall'.
    Blit, Klm nabuʔ 'to fall'.
30 Tasaday lugaŋan 'parent-in-law; co-parent-in-law'.
    Blit, Klm nugaŋan 'parent-in-law; co-parent-in-law'.
31 Tasaday lugkip 'to have a piece cut out'.
    Blit lugkab 'to have a piece cut out'.
32 Tasaday lugkug 'hunched, stooped'.
    Blit logkog 'hunched, stooped'.
33 Tasaday lugpayas 'nice, bright, clear, good weather, smooth, light,
        beautiful'.

Blit lugkayat 'nice, bright, clear, good weather, smooth, light, beautiful'.

34 Tasaday lumitan 'k.o. moss'.
    Blit lumut 'k.o. moss'.

35 Tasaday məʔambəm 'man'.
    Blit, Klm məʔama 'man'.

36 Tasaday məʔitas 'crow'.
    Blit məʔitəs 'crow, dark feathered domesticated chicken'.
    Blit, Klm uwak 'crow'.

37 Tasaday nadəg 'odour; smell, good or bad'.
    Blit, Klm ŋadəg 'odour; smell, good or bad'.

38 Tasaday pulut 'to tie, as a string, the top of a skirt'.
    Blit, Klm sigpalut 'to tie, as a string, the top of a skirt'.

39 Tasaday pundaŋ 'buttocks'.
    Blit, Klm punuk 'buttocks'.

40 Tasaday saluŋan 'shadow'.
    Blit, Klm aluŋ 'shadow'.

41 Tasaday saluwaga 'k.o. snake'.
    Blit suwaga 'k.o. snake'.

42 Tasaday səluʔuŋ 'hat'.
    Blit səlaʔuŋ 'hat'.

43 Tasaday sinəm 'mole on one's body'.
    Blit, Klm sonəm 'mole on one's body'.

44 Tasaday susuʔ 'breast'.
    Blit susu 'breast'.

45 Tasaday takəwəs 'stomach'.
    Blit təkuwan, təkuwis, Klm təkuwəs 'stomach'.

46 Tasaday taŋəg 'to nod one's head'.
    Blit taŋuʔ, Klm taŋu 'to nod one's head'.
    Klm taŋəd 'to shake uncontrollably, of one's head or hands'.

47 Tasaday tawawan 'person'.
    Blit, Klm ətaw 'person'.

48 Tasaday təkəmuʔ 'to grab'.
    Blit kəmuʔ 'to grab'.

49 Tasaday tələgkəb 'to lie on one's stomach'.
    Blit, Klm lagkəb 'to lie on one's stomach'.

50 Tasaday təligəsa 'other'.
    Blit tigəsa 'other'.

51 Tasaday tələub 'belch'.
    Blit tələʔiyub 'belch'.

52 Tasaday tigduduʔ (var. tignuduʔ) 'index finger'.
    Blit tigtuduʔ, Klm katuduʔ 'index finger'.

53 Tasaday tokoʔ 'short'.
    Blit, Klm pokoʔ 'short'.

54 Tasaday tugʔinəp 'dream'.

Blit tigʔinəp, Klm təgəʔinəp 'dream'.
55   Tasaday tulu 'fingernail, toenail'.
      Blit, Klm sulu 'fingernail, toenail'.
56   Tasaday tuŋal (var. təŋal)[8] 'nape of neck'.
      Blit, Klm təŋəl 'nape of neck'.

Phonological change in Blit but not in Tasaday

57   Tasaday kumabus 'rib cage'; Klm kumabus 'lower ribs'.
      Blit kəmabus 'lower ribs'.
58   Tasaday, Klm səgələt 'sound of creaking, grinding'.
      Blit sələgək 'sound of creaking, grinding'.
59   Tasaday, Klm bahaʔən 'to sneeze'.
      Blit baʔən 'to sneeze'.
60   Tasaday, Klm lipədəŋ 'to close one's eyes'.
      Blit pemideŋ 'to close one's eyes'.

Tasaday forms shared with Kulaman, but not with Blit

61   Tasaday, Klm ələd (-um-) 'sink in water, set (of the sun)'.
      Blit sandəp agdaw 'sunset'.
62   Tasaday, Klm hibat 'lie down on one's back'.
      Blit dəgaʔ 'lie down on one's back'.
63   Tasaday lagas 'female genitals'; Klm lagas 'seed, fruit; female
         genitals (euph)'.
      Blit, Klm bətiʔ 'female genitals'.
64   Tasaday, Klm pəŋiyab 'yawn'.
      Blit kəluyab 'yawn'.
65   Tasaday, Klm ələt 'space between two objects'.
      Blit tiwadaʔ 'space between two objects'.
66   Tasaday, Klm səgodoy 'drag; pull something'.
      Blit hənat 'drag; pull something'.

Possible Tasaday unique forms

67   Tasaday aŋgel 'angry'.
      Blit, Klm bulit 'angry'.
68   Tasaday bələŋus 'nose'.
      Blit, Klm iduŋ 'nose'.
69   Tasaday bəliboy 'child, young'.
      Blit, Klm anak; bataʔ 'child, young'.
70   Tasaday bətikənan 'lower leg, ankle area'.
      Blit sokil, pəniŋtiŋ 'lower leg, ankle area'.
71   Tasaday bugəl 'base (as of a tree)'.
      Blit, Klm pəsu 'base (as of a tree)'.
72   Tasaday dawdaw 'be near'.
      Blit, Klm dapag 'be near'.
73   Tasaday dontot 'drink'.

Blit, Klm inəm 'drink'.

74 Tasaday kuməmil 'touch'.
    Blit, Klm kuməbit 'touch'.

75 Tasaday kundom 'eat'.
    Blit, Klm kaʔən 'eat'.

76 Tasaday lagiŋsiŋan (var. lagisiŋan) 'curly, of hair'.
    Blit kulət 'curly, of hair'.

77 Tasaday ləgədol 'chin'.
    Blit bəhaʔ, Klm bahaʔ 'chin'.

78 Tasaday lətəkok (var. ligtəkok) 'to vomit'.
    Blit suwa, Klm suwah 'to vomit'.

79 Tasaday palihan 'wind'.
    Blit, Klm kəlamag 'wind'.

80 Tasaday lubad 'liver'.
    Blit, Klm atay 'liver'.

81 Tasaday tələwon 'orphan'.
    Blit, Klm nəʔilu 'orphan'.

82 Tasaday pəgloʔon 'sun'.
    Blit, Klm agdaw 'sun'.

83 Tasaday sagdigan[9] 'hear, listen'.
    Blit, Klm dinəgan 'hear, listen'.

84 Tasaday subəŋan[10] 'answer'.
    Blit, Klm sagbiʔ 'answer'.

85 Tasaday tənək 'thorn'.
    Blit, Klm dugi 'thorn'.

86 Tasaday tupasan 'soil, earth, ground'.
    Blit, Klm tanaʔ 'soil, earth, ground'.

Tasaday forms not shared with Blit or Klm, but found in other languages

87 Tasaday bəliwəs; Bon balliwəs[11] 'dance'.
    Blit adal 'dance'; Klm sayaw, dəlayaw 'dance'.

88 Tasaday dələman; MboSrn dələm; MboBkd daləman 'night'.
    Blit, Klm sigəp 'night'.

89 Tasaday duda; Tag duraʔ; SubS, SblBt dulaʔ 'spit'.
    Blit, Klm iləb 'spit'.

90 Tasaday huməs; MnbSrn aməs; MboBkd haməs 'wet'; Bon ʔəməs
    'take a bath'.
    Blit, Klm pələʔ 'wet'.

91 Tasaday kuʔkuʔ;[12] Bon ʔukʔuk; SblBt 'kukuʔ 'cough'.
    Blit, Klm buhaʔ 'cough'.

92 Tasaday lipot;[13] Tboli lipot; MboBkd, Ilk lipat 'forget'.
    Blit, Klm lipəŋ 'forget'.

93 Tasaday lisahaʔ 'head louse';[14] MboSrn lisehaʔ (< PMP *liseSeq)
    'nit, louse egg'.
    Blit, Klm kutu 'head louse'.

94 Tasaday liyaŋ 'a natural hole in the ground'; Bon liyang 'cave'.
    Blit kokob 'a natural hole in the ground'; Klm tosoŋ 'hole'.
95 Tasaday məlum 'afternoon'; NB: PMP *elem 'shade, darkness'.
    Blit mapun, Klm məhapun 'afternoon'.
96 Tasaday sakat[15] 'leg and hoof of an animal'; Tag, ItgB saka 'leg'.
    Blit səki, Klm kələmagiŋ 'hoof of an animal'.

Tasaday forms showing semantic extension

97 Tasaday balu't baŋag 'head hair, eyebrow'.
    Blit, Klm balu't ulu 'head hair'.
98 Tasaday baŋag 'head, skull'.
    Blit baŋag 'skull'; Blit, Klm ulu 'head'.
99 Tasaday ləgləg 'fire'.
    Blit, Klm ləgləg 'flame'; Blit, Klm apuy 'fire'.
100 Tasaday dita? 'blood, sap, resin'.
    Blit, Klm dita? 'sap, resin'; Blit nəpanug, Klm dəpanug 'blood'.
101 Tasaday əpuy 'snake' (general term).
    Blit əpuy 'snake species'; Blit uləd 'snake' (general term).
102 Tasaday mətimbulu 'male genitals'.
    Blit, Klm bulu 'rounded, bulging'; Blit, Klm lasu? 'penis'.
103 Tasaday bitbit 'to bring, to carry'.
    Blit, Klm bitbit 'to hold in one's free swinging hand';
        Blit, Klm uwit 'carry'.
104 Tasaday əlam (əg-) 'feel sick', (nək-) 'menstruate'.
    Blit pa?an (mə-) 'happen, be sick, menstruate';
        Blit ha?a (nəkə-) 'menstruate'; Klm bulan (-ən) 'menstruate'.
105 Tasaday ha?a (-um-) 'see, know, be acquainted with';
        peha?a 'eye'.
    Blit, Klm ha?a (-um-) 'see'; Blit, Klm mata 'eye';
        Blit, Klm kilala? 'know, be acquainted with'.
106 Tasaday ilib 'cave, shelter, house'.
    Blit ilib 'cave'; Klm ilib 'boulder, stone face of a cliff'.
    Blit lawi? 'field shelter'; Klm lawi 'temporary shelter';
        Blit, Klm daləsan 'house'.
107 Tasaday kumabus 'rib cage'.
    Blit kəmabus; Klm kumabus 'lower ribs'.
108 Tasaday məlawis 'tree'.
    Klm lawis 'sapling'; Blit, Klm kayu 'tree'.
109 Tasaday litay (-um-) 'walk the length of a fallen log';
        lumitay 'monkey'.
    Blit, Klm litay (-um-) 'walk the length of a fallen log';
        Blit, Klm ubal 'monkey'.
110 Tasaday məliton 'female'.
    Blit, Klm məliton 'old woman; married woman with children';
        Blit, Klm bayi 'female'.

111   Tasaday məlok 'chicken; bird'.
      Blit, Klm məlok 'wild chicken'; Blit, Klm manuk 'domesticated
         chicken; bird'.
112   Tasaday mətuluk 'stone'.
      Blit mətuluk 'kind of stone'; Blit, Klm batu 'stone'.
113   Tasaday sabaʔ (-an) 'hold in one's hand; grasp; get; receive'.
      Blit, Klm sabaʔ (-an) 'hold in one's hand; grasp'; Blit, Klm kuwa
         'get; receive'.
114   Tasaday səbaŋ 'moon'.
      Klm səbaŋ 'first quarter of the moon'; Blit, Klm bulan 'moon'.
115   Tasaday təpəs 'betel chew'; (-um-) 'to chew on, as betel,
         sugarcane'.
      Blit, Klm təpəs (-um-) 'to chew on, as sugar-cane';
         Blit, Klm mamaʔ 'betel chew'.
116   Tasaday ugah 'plaintain, wild banana, domesticated banana'.
      Blit ugah 'k.o. banana'; Blit, Klm sagiŋ 'banana, generic'.

Tasaday forms showing semantic narrowing
117   Tasaday daməs 'rain'.
      Blit, Klm daməs 'storm, wind and rain for several days'.
118   Tasaday lagas 'female genitals'.
      Klm lagas 'seed, fruit; female genitals (euphemism)'; Blit, Klm bətiʔ
         'female genitals'.

Tasaday forms showing semantic shift
119   Tasaday dompol (-um-) 'have intercourse'.
      Klm dumpal (-um-) 'collide with something, bang into something';
         Blit, Klm iyut (-um-) 'have intercourse'.
120   Tasaday əlaʔ[16] 'pain, injury'.
      Klm əlaʔ 'crack, as in wood, glass, cement, etc.'; Blit, Klm sakit
         (mə-) 'pain, sickness'; Blit ladu (-in-) 'feel sick'; Blit, Klm pali
         (-an) 'injury, wound'.
121   Tasaday ima (tig-) 'give'.
      Klm ima (əgpə-) 'feign to offer something to someone';
         Blit, Klm bəgay (əg-) 'give'.
122   Tasaday kəlamag (pə-) 'have intercourse (euphemism)'.
      Blit, Klm kəlamag 'wind'.
123   Tasaday ləkən 'tongue'.
      Klm ləkən 'shrink back, e.g., person anticipating attack, elastic after
         stretching'; Blit, Klm dilaʔ 'tongue'.
124   Tasaday lukəsan 'father'.
      Blit lukəs 'old man, married man', Klm lukəs 'old man, old woman';
         Blit, Klm əmaʔ 'father'.
125   Tasaday sagdig (-an) 'ear'; (-um-) 'hear, listen'[17].
      Blit, Klm sagdig (-um-, i-) 'lean against'; Blit, Klm təliŋa 'ear'.

126 Tasaday təbul 'water'.
    Blit, Klm təbulan 'spring, natural water source from ground';
        Blit, Klm wayəg 'water'.
127 Tasaday təliŋa (-um-) 'hear, listen'.
    Blit, Klm təliŋa 'ear'; Blit, Klm dinəg (-um-) 'hear, listen'.
128 Tasaday tigbas 'right hand'; (i-) 'to use one's right hand';
    (-um-) 'strike with a bolo'.
    Blit, Klm tigbas (-um-) 'strike with a bolo or other tool';
        Blit, Klm kuwanan 'right hand'.
129 Tasaday ukitan[18] 'trail, path, road'.
    Klm ukitan 'to pass by or through'; Blit, Klm dalan 'trail, path, road'.

Tasaday paraphrases and metaphorical extensions, post-1971

130 Tasaday baŋiʔ 'clothes', (-um-) 'wear clothes'.
    Cf. baŋiʔ 'k.o. ground orchid with wide leaves'.
131 Tasaday basag latiʔ 'coconut palm'.
    Cf. basag 'sago palm', latiʔ 'brush, small trees; vegetation outside rain forest'.
    Blit, Klm ləpoʔ 'coconut'; latiʔ 'brush, small trees'.
132 Tasaday bəgiyaŋ 'corn, maize'.
    Cf. bəgiyaŋ 'k.o. rain forest plant'.
    Blit, Klm kəlaŋ 'corn, maize'.
133 Tasaday bitog momoʔ dakəl 'canned sardines'.
    Cf. bitog 'tadpole', momoʔ dakəl 'Big Uncle'.[19]
134 Tasaday butuʔ basag latiʔ 'fruit of the coconut palm'.
    Cf. butuʔ 'lump, rounded thing' (see basag latiʔ above).
    Blit, Klm ləpoʔ 'fruit of the coconut palm'.
135 Tasaday daʔun kayu 'money'.
    Cf. daʔun 'leaf, kayu 'tree'.
    Blit, Klm pilak 'money'.
136 Tasaday hibatan 'mattress'.
    Cf. hibat 'lie down on one's back'.
    Blit tilam 'mattress'.
137 Tasaday kətilis mata 'to be drunk'.
    Cf. kətilis 'turn, spin', mata 'eye'.
    Blit, Klm məkəhilu 'to be drunk'.
138 Tasaday kudit (-um-) 'to write'.
    Cf. kudit 'k.o. plant with leaf markings'.
    Blit, Klm sulat 'to write'.
139 Tasaday kulinsuŋ 'flashlight'.
    Cf. kulinsuŋ 'fire drill'.
    Blit, Klm paslaʔit 'flashlight'.
140 Tasaday luyuŋ məlawis 'large brass gong'.
    Cf. luyuŋ 'hidden', məlawis 'wood, tree'.

Blit, Klm səlagi 'large brass gong'.

141 Tasaday maghalin 'lowlander; those who move the boundaries
     of the reservation'.
     Cf. Tag. maghalin 'to move'.
     Blit kristiano 'Christian settler, lowlander'.

142 Tasaday məbukəh balu't baŋag 'Caucasian'.
     Cf. məbukəh 'white', balu't baŋag 'hair of the head'.
     Blit amərikano 'Caucasian'.

143 Tasaday natək momoʔ dakəl 'husked or cooked rice'.
     Cf. natək 'palm starch', momoʔ dakəl 'Big Uncle'.
     Blit, Klm bəgas 'husked rice'.

144 Tasaday ninan 'Moslem'.
     Cf. Blit ninan 'word commonly used by Moslems'.

145 Tasaday paʔis tupasan 'shovel, pick, mattock'.
     Cf. paʔis 'tool', tupasan 'earth'.
     Blit pala 'shovel', sadul 'mattock'.

146 Tasaday pəlaʔpaʔ bəgiyaŋ 'corncob'.
     Cf. pəlaʔpaʔ 'growth (?)', bəgiyaŋ 'corn'.
     Blit tagbu 'corncob'.

147 Tasaday pəlaʔpaʔ ugah 'stalk of bananas'.
     Cf. pəlaʔpaʔ 'growth (?)', ugah 'banana'.
     Blit tagduk 'stalk of bananas'.

148 Tasaday puyut dugi 'shoe, slipper'.
     Cf. puyut 'cloth bag', dugi 'thorn'.
     Blit, Klm talumpaʔ 'shoe'.

149 Tasaday səkəg baŋag 'pillow'.
     Cf. səkəg 'support', baŋag 'head'.
     Blit dənanan, Klm dananan 'pillow'.

150 Tasaday taguʔan 'sheath of a bolo or knife'.
     Cf. taguʔan 'hiding place'.
     Blit, Klm gumaʔ 'sheath of a bolo or knife'.

151 Tasaday tinosoŋ məlawis 'mortar'.
     Cf. tinosoŋ 'hollowed', məlawis 'wood, tree'.
     Blit, Klm ləsuŋ 'mortar'.

152 Tasaday usa mətaʔəs lisən 'horse'.
     Cf. usa 'large animal', mətaʔəs 'long', lisən 'leg'.
     Blit kudaʔ 'horse'.

153 Tasaday usa paŋawan 'water buffalo'.
     Cf. usa 'large animal', paŋawan 'having horns'.
     Blit, Klm kalabaw 'water buffalo'.

Tasaday paraphrastic expressions, pre-1971

154 Tasaday amayan təbulan 'river'.
     Cf. amayan 'big', təbulan 'water+loc'.
     Blit dakəl wayəg 'river'.

155 Tasaday amayan haya?haya? 'thigh, upper leg'.
Cf. amayan 'big', haya?haya? 'leg'.
Blit, Klm bubun 'thigh, upper leg'.

156 Tasaday amayan ŋuŋut 'molar'[20].
Cf. amayan 'big', ŋuŋut 'tooth'.
Blit bi?əgaŋ, Klm bi?igaŋ 'molar'.

157 Tasaday aŋayan təbul 'fetch water'.
Cf. aŋayan 'go-for', tebul 'water'.
Blit səkədu 'fetch water', Klm səkədu 'bamboo water container'.

158 Tasaday balu't məluk 'feather'.
Cf. balu't 'hair-of', məluk 'bird'.
Blit, Klm bulbul 'feather'.

159 Tasaday balu't baŋag 'eyebrow'.
Cf. balu't 'hair-of', baŋag 'head'.
Blit, Klm kəleweŋ 'eyebrow'.

160 Tasaday balu't pəha?a 'eyelash'.
Cf. balu't 'hair-of', peha?a 'eye'.
Blit, Klm piləkpilək 'eyelash'.

161 Tasaday bəliboy lisaha?[21] 'nit'.
Cf. bəliboy 'child', lisaha? 'head louse'.
Blit kəliha?[22] 'nit'.

162 Tasaday buku haya?haya? 'knee'.
Cf. buku 'lump', haya?haya? 'leg'.
Blit buku lulud,[23] Klm lulud 'knee'.

163 Tasaday buku bətikənan 'ankle'.
Cf. buku 'lump', bətikənan 'lower leg'.
Blit sokil, pəniŋtiŋ 'ankle'.

164 Tasaday ilib sumakul[24] 'field shelter'.
Cf. ilib 'shelter', sumakul 'pound palm pith'.
Blit lawi?, Klm lawi 'field shelter'.

165 Tasaday limusaŋ lugabuan 'dew'.
Cf. limusaŋ 'sweat', lugabuan 'sky'.
Blit, Klm agmu? 'dew'.

166 Tasaday mətibulu lubad 'gall bladder'.
Cf. mətibulu 'lump', lubad 'liver'.
Blit, Klm pədu 'gall bladder'.

167 Tasaday nə?uyat idəŋ[25] 'orphan'.
Cf. nə?uyat 'dead', idəŋ 'mother'.
Blit, Klm nə?ilu 'orphan'.

168 Tasaday nə?uyat tinəlomin 'widow, widower'.
Cf. nə?uyat 'dead', tinəlomin 'spouse'.
Blit, Klm balu 'widow, widower'.

169 Tasaday səgoysoy pəha?a[26] 'tear'.
Cf. səgoysoy 'drip', pəha?a 'eye'.
Blit, Klm luha? 'tear'.

170 Tasaday suliʔ olom[27] 'answer'.
    Cf. suliʔ 'return', olom 'speech'.
    Blit, Klm sagbiʔ 'answer'.
171 Tasaday təbul lawawan 'sweat'.
    Cf. təbul 'body', lawawan 'water'.
    Blit, Klm limusəŋ 'sweat'.
172 Tasaday tosoŋ bəlitaŋ 'navel'.
    Cf. tosoŋ 'hole', bəlitaŋ 'umbilical cord'.
    Blit, Klm pusəd 'navel'.
173 Tasaday usa məʔidəb bələŋus 'pig'.
    Cf. usa 'large animal', məʔidəb 'pointed', bələŋus 'snout, nose'.
    Blit, Klm babuy 'pig'; usa 'deer'.

Manobo synonyms restricted in Tasaday
174 Tasaday, Blit, Klm amayan; Blit, Klm dakəl 'big'.
175 Tasaday, Blit, Klm bukeh; Blit, Klm bulaʔ 'white'.

Phonological shift
176 Tasaday dompol 'have intercourse'.
    Klm dumpal 'collide with something, bang into something'.
177 Tasaday pondol (mi-) 'go'.
    Blit, Klm panaw (mi-) 'walk'.

NOTES

1 Prepared in collaboration with the late Robert Fox, then Chief Anthropologist of the National Museum of the Philippines, and Director of the Research Center associated with a private project to assist national minorities, known as PANAMIN, established by Elizalde.

2 I am grateful to the University of Hawaii for granting me a full-time research position during the Spring and Summer, 1994, that enabled me to conduct the first stage of the project.

3 A paper reporting on this period of fieldwork, during which some of the tapes secretly recorded in the Tasaday caves in 1972 were transcribed and translated with the assistance of the Tasaday, was presented to the 4th Pan-Asiatic Linguistics Conference (Reid 1996).

4 The program used was Shoebox, a database program for linguists developed by members of the Summer Institute of Linguistics.

5 This phonological distortion by infixation of -əl- is identical to that used by Belayem in his pronunciation of the English word 'beginning' in the sitio name *nu bəliginiŋ* ('New Beginning'), as well as in other items such as *təligəsa* ('other') (no. 50), and a subsequently rejected variant of *kuʔkuʔ* cough (no. 91).

6 Both Tasaday pronunciations differ from the Blit and Kulaman forms, but at least *dikət* has cognates distributed widely throughout the Philippines, including other Manobo languages. Cognates with an initial bilabial stop (but usually voiceless) are also found throughout the archipelago (see Reid 1971: 140). The Tsd *d-* / Blt, Klm *l-* correspondence seen here is however also found in no. 7 *datək* ('leech'), where it is the *l-* initial form which has greater historical validity.

7 This Tasaday form may be a reflex of an older form of the Manobo cognates. Cf. Sml *labu*, and SubS *labuʔ* ('to fall').

8 Variant forms with loss of final *-l* were both recorded. This phonological process commonly occurs in both Blit and Tasaday.

9 Also recorded as *sandigan*.

10 Note Klm *subəŋ* ('handle of a tool').

11 In Bontok, *balliwəs* is ('dance in a circle'). The form of the first vowel and the doubled consonant following it indicates that it is probably borrowed from one of the Cagayan Valley languages in which *ə > a*, and reflects an earlier form *bəliwəs*.

12 Also recorded as *kəluʔkuʔ*, but this form was subsequently rejected.

13 Possibly a borrowing from Tboli.

14 Note that both Klm *kutu*, and Tsd *lisahaʔ ləgləg* have the extended meaning of 'sparks thrown off by a fire, flying ashes', implying that the Tasaday circumlocution here is a coinage of recent origin.

15 That this is not a borrowing from Tagalog or from some other language is suggested by the final *t*, probably a frozen genitive form found on certain other body parts in Tasaday, Blit and Kulaman, e.g. *balu't ulu* ('hair of head').

16 For example: duʔen   elaʔ   pehaʔa   ku
there.is   pain   eye   my
'My eye is painful'

17 See also Tsd *tum << liŋa* ('hear, listen').

18 Variant *nukitan*.

19 Ethnonym for Manuel Elizalde, Jr.

20 An alternative Tasaday term, *bəliʔəgaŋ* ('molar'), was subsequently elicited. However it should be noted that a number of circumlocutions for teeth appear in Errington and Errington's (1981) dictionary of the Kulaman dialect, for example: *ŋipən ulu* ('upper front teeth'; lit. teeth of head), *ŋipən bahaʔ* ('lower front teeth'; lit. teeth of chin), and *ŋipən tuyaŋ* ('eye teeth'; lit. teeth of dog).

21 This term may apply to the egg of the head louse. A different Tasaday term *kuwol* was subsequently elicited for 'nit'.

22 Or, Blit *keliha*.

23 Lit. lump of lower leg.

24 Temporary shelter for preparation of palm starch.

25 *telewon* ('orphan') was subsequently elicited.

26 Also recorded as *tebul pehaʔa* (lit. 'water of eye').

27 Also recorded as *subeŋan*.

REFERENCES

Berreman, G.D. 1992. The Tasaday: stone age survivors, or space age fakes? In *The Tasaday controversy: assessing the evidence*, T.N. Headland (ed.), 21–39. Special Publication No. 28, Scholarly Series. Washington, DC: The American Anthropological Association.

Boeles, J.J. 1963. Second expedition to the Mrabri of North Thailand ('Khon Pa'). *Journal of the Siam Society* 50, 133–160.

Elizalde, M. Jr. and R. Fox. 1971. The Tasaday forest people. A data paper on a newly discovered food gathering and stone tool using Manubo group in the mountains of South Cotabato, Philippines. Typescript. Washington, DC: Smithsonian Institute for Short-lived Phenomena. Published under the same title in *Readings on the Tasaday*, V.B. Dandan (ed.), 2–12. Publication No. 1. Manila: Tasaday Community Care Foundation.

Elkins, R.E. 1992. The Tasaday: some observations. In *The Tasaday Controversy: Assessing the evidence*, T.N. Headland (ed.), 117–29. Special Publication No. 28, Scholarly Series. Washington, DC: The American Anthropological Association.

Errington, R. and E. Errington. 1981. Cotabato Manobo dictionary. Unpublished computer printout. Manila: Summer Institute of Linguistics.

Headland, T.N. (ed.) 1992. *The Tasaday Controversy: assessing the evidence*. Special Publication No. 28, Scholarly Series. Washington, DC: The American Anthropological Association.

Johnston, E. Clay 1992. The Tasaday language: Is it Cotabato Manobo? In *The Tasaday Controversy: assessing the evidence*, T.N. Headland, (ed.), 144–56. Special Publication No. 28, Scholarly Series. Washington, DC: The American Anthropological Association.

Llamzon, T.A. 1989. The Tasaday language so far. In *Readings on the Tasaday*, V.B. Dandan (ed.), 54–64. Publication No. 1. Manila: Tasaday Community Care Foundation.

Molony, C.H. 1976. (with the collaboration of Dad Tuan) Further studies on the Tasaday language: texts and vocabulary. In *Further studies on the Tasaday*, D.E. Yen and J. Nance (eds.), 13–96. PANAMIN Foundation Research Series No. 2. Rizal, Philippines: Makati. Reprinted in *Readings on the Tasaday*, V.B. Dandan (ed.), 85–168. Publication No. 1. Manila: Tasaday Community Care Foundation.

Molony, C.H. 1992 The Tasaday language: evidence for authenticity? In *The Tasaday Controversy: assessing the evidence*, T.N. Headland (ed.), 107–16. Special Publication No. 28, Scholarly Series. Washington, DC: The American Anthropological Association.

Nance, J. 1988. *The Gentle Tasaday* (2nd edn). Boston: David R. Godine.

Reid, L.A. 1971. *Philippine Minor Languages: word lists and phonologies*. Oceanic Linguistics Special Publication No. 8. Honolulu: University of Hawaii Press.

Reid, L.A. 1976. *Bontok–English Dictionary, with English–Bontok Finder List*. Pacific Linguistics, Series C, No. 36. Canberra: Research School of Pacific Studies, Australian National University.

Reid, L.A. 1992. The Tasaday language: a key to Tasaday prehistory. In *The Tasaday Controversy: assessing the evidence*, T.N. Headland (ed.), 180–93. Special Publication No. 28, Scholarly Series, Washington, DC: The American Anthropological Association.

Reid, L.A. 1993. Another look at the language of the Tasaday. Keynote Lecture presented to the 3rd Annual Conference of the South-east Asian Linguistic Society, Honolulu, Hawaii, 10–17 May.

Reid, L.A. 1996. The Tasaday cave tapes. Paper presented to the 4th International Pan-Asiatic Linguistics Conference, Bangkok, Thailand, 8–10 January.

Rogel-Rara, A. and E.S. Nabayra. 1992. The genealogical evidence. *The Tasaday Controversy: assessing the evidence*, T.N. Headland (ed.), 89–196. Special Publication No. 28, Scholarly Series, Washington, DC: The American Anthropological Association.

Rischel, J. 1995. *Minor Mlabri: A hunter-gatherer language of Northern Indochina*. Copenhagen: University of Copenhagen, Museum Tusculanum Press.

Salazar, Z.A. 1971. Footnote on the Tasaday. *Philippine Journal of Linguistics* 2(2): 34–8.

Salazar, Z.A. 1973. Second footnote on the Tasaday. *Asian Studies* 11(2): 97–113.

13   Social networks and kinds of speech-community event

MALCOLM ROSS

INTRODUCTION

The disciplines of linguistics, archaeology, anthropology and genetics each have a bearing on the reconstruction of human prehistory, and it is hardly surprising that in their attempts to match findings across disciplinary boundaries the practitioners of one discipline sometimes do violence to the methodology of another. Historical linguists commonly present their findings in the shape of 'family trees', the very simplicity of which lends them to misinterpretation. Cavalli-Sforza *et al.* (1988) attempt to correlate trees of worldwide prehistory drawn on the basis of genetic and linguistic data. Quite apart from the content of their linguistic tree, which represents the position of extreme 'lumper' linguists, its use is questionable because it assumes that the kinds of continuity represented by trees in genetics and linguistics are qualitatively similar. The basis of this assumption is that ethnic groups, of which genetic markers and language are taken to be manifestations, have diachronic stability and speciation mechanisms of a kind which can be appropriately depicted as a tree.[1]

This assumption has been vigorously challenged by the anthropologist John Moore (1994a, 1994b), who seeks to replace the cladistic (branching, tree-like) model of ethnogenesis with the rhizotic (root-like) metaphor according to which 'each human language, culture, or population is considered to be derived from or rooted in several different antecedent groups' (1994b: 925). Whilst this seems to me, an anthropological layman, to be an eminently satisfactory approach to ethnogenesis, it entails a misapprehension similar, ironically, to Cavalli-Sforza's; namely, that glottogenesis and ethnogenesis can be described with parallel models. Moore (1994a: 16) reserves the term 'ethnogenesis' for rhizotically generated ethnic groups. If we reserve 'glottogenesis' for rhizotically generated languages, however, it will apply only to cases of pidginization and creolization – relatively rare events in linguistic diachrony (see pp. 251–3). Whilst the social network model I shall use here is neither cladistic nor rhizotic, I will show that it is reasonable to treat kinds of contact-induced language change other than pidginization and creolization as cladistic; that is, as maintaining genealogical continuity. Because pidginization and creolization occur only in special circumstances, the majority of cases of (rhizotic) ethnogenesis probably do not involve a corresponding glottogenesis (although it could be argued that the converse entailment is more often true).

Peter Bellwood (1995) points out that the rhizotic model of ethnogenesis is also very much alive among archaeologists, although not always in so many words. Where I work, in the Pacific, it is found in the work of John Terrell (Terrell 1986; Welsch et al. 1992). Whereas Moore grants that in certain respects language is cladistic (1994b: 928), Terrell apparently believes that the formation of both social groups and languages is fundamentally rhizotic, and to the degree that there is not necessarily any association at all between material culture and language. Welsch et al. (1992) is a statistical analysis which sets out to show that on the north coast of New Guinea, a group's linguistic genealogy is no predictor at all of its material culture (their analysis has, however, been called into question by Moore and Romney 1994). This position is in a sense the diametric opposite of Cavalli-Sforza's: he and his colleagues assert that trees from different disciplines match each other suffi-ciently to show significant patterns over the span of human prehistory, whilst Terrell and his co-researchers claim no matching at all.

Both positions seem to me to be overstated. In each case, language change is being modelled in the way favoured for the data with which it is being matched. When it is matched with genetic data, language change is modelled as a tree, but seemingly without the realization that a linguistic tree expresses a continuity which is less tidy than the continuity of a biogenetic tree. And when language change is matched with ethnic change, both kinds of change are assumed to be rhizotic, an assumption that does not do justice to such continuity as language does possess.

My concern here, then, is to outline a linguist's model of language change. For convenience's sake I label this model the 'social network model'. It has yet to acquire a conventional label in the linguistic literature, where it has emerged since the publication of Weinreich et al. (1968) and especially since the appearance of Lesley Milroy (1980/1987). More recent expositions of some of its concepts are found in James Milroy (1992, 1993).

In particular, I am interested in the reconstruction of sequences of linguistic and speech community events and their correlation with archaeologically reconstructed event sequences (cf. Spriggs 1994). In Ross (Volume II), I present a case study (henceforth 'the case study') illustrating the use of the linguistic comparative method to reconstruct a sequence of innovations in a group of languages, or 'linguistic events' as I call them there. Since a linguistic event often reflects a change in the life of the speech-community (e.g. division, growth, contact), it can be used to infer the occurrence and general nature of that 'speech-community event' (henceforth SCE). A recon-structed sequence of SCEs can then be related to the archaeological record, as I exemplify in the case study. But whereas the case study focuses on the *sequencing* of SCEs, my interest here is in the different *kinds* of SCE that can be reconstructed for the preliterate past from present-day language data.

Although the rhizotic model is presented by its proponents as an alternative to the cladistic, this misses the mark so far as language is concerned. Some kinds of SCE lend themselves to a rhizotic account, others to a cladistic approach, and yet others to a mixture of both, or to neither. The two models are not alternatives, and neither properly captures more than a small portion of the kinds of SCE that occur.

Another pair of seeming alternatives has been perpetrated by linguists themselves. Textbooks on historical linguistics persistently juxtapose the family tree model and the 'wave' model, creating the impression that these, too, are alternatives. But linguistic prehistorians do not generally use these two models to interpret the same sets of data. The family tree model is used to map the genealogies of language families, e.g. the internal relationships of Romance (the languages descended from Latin), Germanic, Slav, etc., and their relationships with each other, whilst the wave model was conceived to represent details of the internal structure and development of a single dialect continuum, such as the West Germanic continuum represented by the German and Dutch dialects of Austria, Switzerland, Germany, the Netherlands and Belgium.

None of these models – the cladistic/family tree model, the rhizotic, or the wave – is an alternative to either of the others. In other words, one cannot take the same set of language data and, by the application of different models, reconstruct alternative sets of linguistic events and SCEs. However, it is clumsy to operate with two or more models side by side, and the social network model is offered as a means of encompassing the various kinds of SCE which each model was designed to capture.

I shall approach the social network model via the family tree model. There are two reasons for this. The first is familiarity: the social network model is not yet widely used among linguistic prehistorians – at least among those to whom archaeologists are likely to have recourse – but the family tree model is. The second is that by relating the two models I hope to elucidate the linguistic assumptions implicit in the use of the tree.

The reader may have noted my preference for the terms 'linguistic prehistory' and 'linguistic prehistorian' rather than the more traditional 'historical linguistics' and 'historical linguist'. The reason for this is simple: the methods I am discussing here rely only on present-day linguistic data and do not require the use of older written texts which, of course, are non-existent in many parts of the world.

There is a bias in this chapter towards examples drawn from the Pacific. The only reason for this is that this is the region of the world I know best. However, since the societies of the Pacific islands were small-scale traditional agricultural societies until more intense European contact in the nineteenth and twentieth centuries, they are probably fairly typical of much of the world throughout the last few millennia.

THE FAMILY TREE MODEL, THE SOCIAL NETWORK MODEL AND THE SPEECH COMMUNITY

As the case study illustrates, the linguist compares a group of related present-day languages, reconstructs their common ancestor or 'proto-language', then analyses innovations characteristic of subgroups within the group. It is the patterning of these innovations and their locus in the language (e.g. in the vocabulary, in the sound system, in the grammar) that constitute linguistic evidence of different kinds of SCE.

Despite its apparent simplicity, the case study entails three different kinds of SCE. The first is represented by the fissure of Proto-Central Papuan from the rest of the Papuan Tip group. The second is the progressive break-up of a linkage of lects to form a group of separate languages, and the third is a major event which involved contact with speakers of another Oceanic Austronesian language. (I use the term 'lect' and the corresponding adjective 'lectal' to cover both 'language' and 'dialect' since there is no objective way to draw a boundary between the two.) Although the case study appears to be quite simple, its conclusions were based on a considerable body of fine-grained analysis, reported in Ross (1994b).

Of these three kinds of event, the first, language fissure, is the one that is recognized in the traditional family tree model. It is the SCE which occurs when speakers of a lect become geographically or socially isolated from other speakers of the same or closely related lects, thereby forming a new speech community. Diagrammatically, linguists have traditionally shown a language fissure in the two equivalent ways shown in Figure 13.1. There is no difference in meaning between these diagrams, and from this point on I shall only use the left-hand variety.

The second kind of event in the case study was lectal differentiation, the progressive break-up of a lectal linkage to form a group of separate languages. But when we depict lectal differentiation within the conventions of the family tree model, as in the left-hand portion of Figure 13.2, the resulting diagram is ambiguous between lectal differentiation and the fissure of A into seven lects.

As I noted in the case study, language fissure and lectal differentiation are different events which leave different patterns of innovation. Fissure is reflected in discrete bunches of innovations, differentiation in overlapping (bunches of) innovations. These two patterns reflect different SCEs. Language fissure is usually the result of a single event which divides one group of speakers into two, whilst lectal differentiation entails the (usually gradual) geographic spread of a group of speakers.

We can overcome the ambiguity inherent in the tree diagram if we adopt the convention (introduced in Ross 1988) that a linkage is shown as a double horizontal line with its title italicized, as in the right-hand portion of Figure 13.2.

If lectal differentiation stretches the bounds of the family tree model, then the third kind of SCE in the case study, contact with speakers of another,

Figure 13.1   Language fissure.

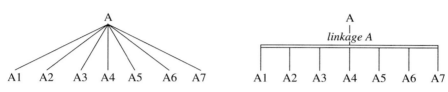

Figure 13.2   Lectal differentiation.

and distinct, language, bursts them altogether. Yet it is clearly just as important to the prehistory of the Central Papuan languages as the first two kinds
of event. The problem is that the family tree model is designed to represent
processes of language divergence, not language convergence. As is often the
case with models, however, this model has not only determined the graphic
depiction of linguistic prehistory but also the direction of research. It is only
in the last twenty or so years that linguistic prehistorians have become more
adept at recognizing that there are different *kinds* of linguistic divergence,
and that there are also varieties of linguistic *convergence*, reflecting community
contact and integration. Indeed, linguistic convergence has only re-entered
the scholarly limelight with the publication of Thomason and Kaufman (1988),
after perhaps seventy years of relative neglect.

   Despite its name, the metaphor in which the family tree model is rooted
is not so much human genealogy as species evolution, whereby each language
is treated as if it were a species and innovations in a language are treated as
if they generated new species of language (for discussions see Keller 1990;
Ross and Durie 1996). Although the model is isomorphic enough with a
wide-angle view of linguistic prehistory, it can be inimical to more narrowly
focused research.

   The alternative adopted here, the social network model, is founded on a
transparent fact that the species evolution metaphor ignores – that languages
have speakers, and that language resides in their minds. Speakers use language
to communicate with each other, and the model treats speakers as nodes in
a social network, such that each speaker is connected with other speakers by
social (and therefore communication) links.

   The social network concept gives a fresh lease of life to the traditional
sociolinguistic idea of the 'speech community', but also entails a new definition

of it. Although the speech community concept is generally taken for granted in linguistic literature, it has, I believe, never been rigorously defined. Conventionally, a speech community is simply taken to be coterminous with the speakers of a particular lect or language, but this definition is fraught with difficulties. One is that it is often hard to say linguistically (as opposed to politically or culturally) what group constitutes 'the speakers of a particular lect or language'. How different does one lect have to be from another for the difference to constitute a speech-community boundary? When, as a lect is differentiating into a lectal linkage, does one speech community become more than one speech community? And if people are bi- or multilingual or di- or polyglossic (speaking two or more lects regarded as belonging to the same language), which lect or language does one use to define their speech-community membership? I know of no satisfactory answers to these questions.

In practice linguists avoid the definitional problem by using 'speech community' primarily to refer to a social, not a linguistic, entity. This is what I have done both here and in the case study by making a distinction between a linguistic event (an innovation in a language) and a speech community event (a change in the life of that community). It seems sensible to bring theory into line with practice and to stop attempting to define 'speech community' linguistically. Grace, faced with multilingual communities in New Caledonia, gives a redefinition of 'speech community':

> In its modified form it might read, 'A speech community consists of those people who communicate with one another or are connected to one another by chains of speakers who communicate with one another.' But to be entirely satisfactory it would also need to recognize that community is a matter of degree.
>
> (Grace 1996: 172)

Grace redefines a speech community as a social network. A social network is a matter of extent and of degree. We can talk sensibly about the social network or the speech community of a village, and equally sensibly about the social network or the speech community of a larger area which subsumes a number of villages whose local networks are parts of the structure of the larger network.

A number of features of the social network model are relevant to the reconstruction of SCEs. I will return to each of these at greater length below, but mention them here to assist the reader's orientation. The first is the *size and structure of a network*. Structure comprises the patterning and the strength of the social links in the network. The second is the degree and distribution of *lectal differentiation* within it; that is, the degree to which the related lects of speakers and groups within the network differ one from another. The third feature is the place in the model of *innovations*. An innovation in a language begins its existence in the mouths and minds of one or more speakers and spreads from them to other speakers. In fact, innovations occur constantly in the speech of individuals, but an innovation becomes part of the history of the language only when it spreads through the network to become a stable feature in the speech of a group of speakers. I will show below that *speakers' attitudes* can favour the spread of certain innovations and disfavour others. The final feature is the degree and distribution of *bi- or multilingualism* in a network. From this point on I will use 'bilingual' to subsume 'multilingual'.

The remainder of this chapter is a discussion within this framework of the various kinds of SCE that can be reconstructed from linguistic evidence, and of the sorts of evidence which allow the reconstruction of a particular kind of event.

For the purposes of discussion, SCEs are divided into three broad categories based on the features mentioned above:

1   those which entail major changes in network size and/or structure;
2   those where social significance is attached to innovations, so that their spread or otherwise clues us in to events which motivate speaker attitudes;
3   those where contact and/or bilingualism has occurred.

I would have liked to indicate what the archaeological correlates of each kind of SCE might be, but this is mostly beyond my competence. It seems to me, though, that the major network reshapings discussed in the next section potentially have fairly obvious archaeological correlates, since they deal with the distribution of groups of speakers who share, or have shared, a common language and usually a common culture. We would expect archaeological reflexes of the geographical distribution of a culture to correspond with reconstructed linguistic geography. Because the kinds of SCE discussed later (see pp. 231–40) are motivated by speaker attitudes, their archaeological correlates are liable to be rather subtle, if not undetectable. As I observed in the case study, events involving contact between two languages (see pp. 240–50) are likely to correlate with archaeological reflexes of that contact.

If we want to reconstruct different *kinds* of SCE, then the social network model enjoys significant advantages over the family tree model. Unfortunately, its graphic conventions are less adaptable to depicting sequences of changes in network structure. These are more easily, if undiscriminatingly, presented in a family tree diagram (compare, for example, Figures 13.4 and 13.5 below). For this reason, I will continue to use tree diagrams where relevant to represent sequences of network structure changes, with the *caveat* that they are unavoidably unsubtle.

MAJOR RESHAPINGS OF NETWORK STRUCTURE

Before we can talk about reshapings of network structure, we need some terms with which to describe it. Lesley Milroy (1980: 20, 49–52, 139–44) describes network structure by characterizing the social links between speakers. She measures these links in terms of their *density* (the number of relation-

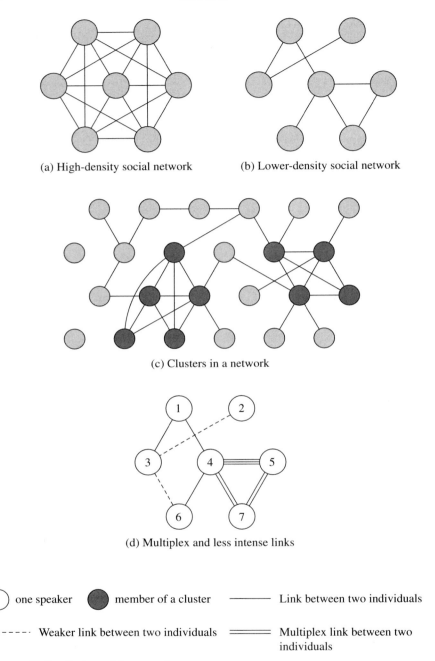

(a) High-density social network   (b) Lower-density social network

(c) Clusters in a network

(d) Multiplex and less intense links

◯ one speaker   ⬤ member of a cluster   ——— Link between two individuals

------- Weaker link between two individuals   ═══ Multiplex link between two individuals

Figure 13.3   Basic social network structures.

ships an individual has with other individuals) and their *clustering* (where a cluster is a network portion with relatively high density). These are illustrated schematically in Figure 13.3, which shows (a) a maximally dense segment of a network, (b) a much less dense segment, and (c) a larger portion of a network which contains two denser segments (i.e. clusters). Milroy also uses the measures of the *uniplexity/multiplexity* of a link (the number of purposes for which two people relate to each other), and its *intensity* (the amount of time two people spend together and the intimacy of that relationship). These are schematically represented in Figure 13.3(d), where the links between persons 2 and 3 and between 3 and 6 are weak, and those among persons 4, 5 and 7 are multiplex. Thus 4, 5 and 7 might represent a married couple with a child.

The Milroys apply these concepts to an urban setting, but they can readily be applied in other settings (cf. Le Page and Tabouret-Keller 1985; Schooling 1990). In traditional Melanesian villages, for example, there is little division of labour that is not gender-based, and most links are multiplex. There is no particular clustering (although generally relationships among closer kin are more intense than those among more distant kin), so that the network structure forms a homogeneous unit. Much the same will be true if there is a locally recognizable grouping of villages. Relationships within each village will be rather more dense than those between villages, but apart from this there will be little variation across the grouping. This is a very different situation from the complex network structure of a European country town or of the parts of the city of Belfast described by the Milroys.

In the tabulation below, *language* and *linkage* represent the two extremes of the clinal parameter of lectal differentiation: a language is what we have before lectal differentiation occurs; a linkage after. The other parameter is binary: a network, whether it is a language or a linkage, may undergo *division* or *reintegration*. Division entails a reduction in the homogeneity of network structure, whilst reintegration entails an increase.

Although lectal differentiation is a matter of degree, for ease of presentation I will generally discuss just the extremes, giving different labels to each of the four cells in the table, speaking, e.g., of 'language fissure' but 'linkage breaking':

	Division	*Reintegration*
Language	Fissure	Fusion
Linkage	Breaking	Rejoining

From a theoretical viewpoint, it would be logical first to discuss network growth, as this usually brings about lectal differentiation from language to linkage, and then to discuss the separate parameter of division/reintegration. But I will eschew logic here, and describe language fissure first, simply because this is the familiar staple of family tree diagrams, then move to the less familiar but essential concept of lectal differentiation before returning to the other three cells in the table.

All four reshapings are reconstructed from the patterning of innovations which have occurred since the reshaping. Unlike the SCEs discussed on pp. 231–40, the nature of the innovations themselves is here generally irrelevant. It is the way that innovations pattern (in discrete sets or in overlapping bunches) that enables the linguistic prehistorian to reconstruct SCEs of this kind.

Language fissures and innovation-defined subgroups

Language fissure is the SCE that is prototypically depicted in a family tree diagram. It occurs when a network which has functioned as a fairly homogeneous unit is broken into two (or more) networks; in other words, when a subset of the links in the network undergoes a sharp reduction in density. In a traditional Melanesian setting, this occurred when population growth induced part of a community to up sticks and seek a new location for dwelling, gardening, foraging and fishing. In this way a single community became two. This resulted in the division of a community into two communities on, say, separate islands some hours' voyage apart, as well as the eventual reduction in social contacts to an annual cycle of ceremonial and trading

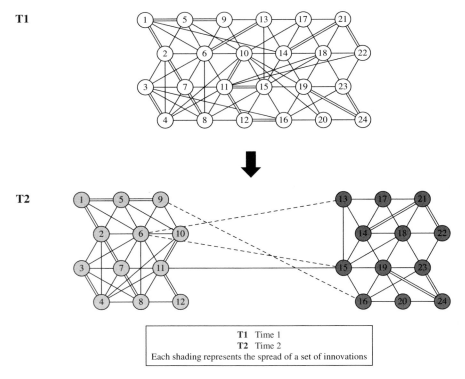

T1	Time 1
T2	Time 2
Each shading represents the spread of a set of innovations	

Figure 13.4   A social network representation of language fissure.

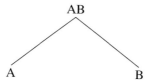

Figure 13.5   A family tree representation of language fissure.

visits, with a concomitant reduction in the density of links, a weakening in their intensity and a reduction in multiplexity. This is represented schematically in Figure 13.4, which shows the links among twenty-four speakers in a group before (at Time 1) and after (at Time 2) the separation of speakers 13–24 from speakers 1–12. In these circumstances language fissure is a likely outcome, as innovations (represented by shadings) occur in one or both lects which render them markedly different to their speakers' ears, if not mutually unintelligible. In this case the event shown in Figure 13.4 is very simply shown in a family tree representation as Figure 13.5.

Let us assume that after this fissure of B from A, there is a further fissure of B into, say, B1, B2 and B3. We may extend our diagram downwards. In conventional form this becomes Figure 13.6. If B1, B2, B3 and the descendants of A are the present-day lects, the linguist reconstructs the fissure of B from A by (a) reconstructing the proto-language AB on the basis of data from B1, B2, B3 and A's descendants and (b) determining that B1, B2 and B3 share a set of innovations in common relative to AB – innovations which are not reflected in A's descendants. These innovations are the linguistic events which serve as evidence that B1, B2 and B3 have a common ancestor B, since it is far more likely that the innovations have occurred once in a lect ancestral to B1, B2 and B3 (i.e. in B), than that they have occurred independently in each of the three lects (this statement is too simple, as it neglects the diagnostic substance of innovations, discussed below). Positing the common ancestor B in turn leads to the conclusion that AB underwent fissure into A and B.

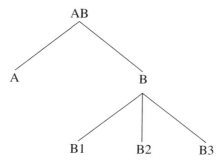

Figure 13.6   Innovation-defined subgroup.

When lects are found to be descended from a common interstage like B, they are said to constitute a subgroup. In practice, however, the term 'subgroup' is used by linguists in various ways, and so I will label a subgroup like B1, B2 and B3 an *innovation-defined subgroup*, since its membership is defined by shared innovations relative to a proto-language. In the case study the Central Papuan family is an innovation-defined subgroup within the larger Papuan Tip grouping.

It is worth reminding ourselves at this point that a linguist can only detect a SCE if that event has had an outcome in the shape of a linguistic event (i.e. an innovation in a language). If the community speaking AB had divided into communities speaking A and B, respectively, but B had undergone no innovations before dividing into B1, B2 and B3, then there would be no evidence of the fissure of AB into A and B. This SCE would remain linguistically undetected, and B1, B2 and B3 would not constitute an innovation-defined subgroup.

The innovations which a linguist uses to define a subgroup need to have 'diagnostic substance'; that is, to be innovations which are (a) not likely to have occurred independently in the lects of the putative subgroup, and (b) not likely to have been copied ('borrowed') from one lect into another, especially where their speakers perceive them as different languages. Certain sound changes, e.g. intervocalic stop lenition (for example, the stop p or b becomes the fricative v between vowels), are so 'natural' that they can easily occur independently in related lects. In general, changes in syntax (the order of words in a phrase and of phrases in a clause) and in lexicon (vocabulary) have little diagnostic substance by themselves, as they are often copied. Innovations which *do* have diagnostic substance include (a) sound changes which affect only some words in the lexicon, such as the unpredictable replacement of Proto-Malayo-Polynesian $\star m$ by (Proto-Oceanic) $\star m^w$ which is a defining feature of the Oceanic subgroup of Austronesian (Ross 1995: 87); (b) shared sequences of sound changes, like the sequence affecting Proto-Oceanic/Proto Papuan Tip $\star u$, $\star l$ and $\star \gamma$, which is one of the defining innovations of the Central Papuan subgroup in the case study; (c) changes in the form or use of bound morphemes (prefixes, suffixes, etc.), such as the use of $\star paN\text{-}$ as antipassive derivative which helps define the Malayo-Polynesian subgroup of Austronesian (Ross 1995: 69–70); and (d) changes in the form or use of paradigms of morphemes, like the innovation in pronoun forms which also helps define Malayo-Polynesian (Blust 1977).

Diagnostic substance is the probability that an innovation has been inherited into a set of lects from its common ancestor. It is the inverse of the probability that it has occurred independently in different lects and been copied from lect to lect. If we assume arbitrarily that for each of three mutually independent innovations X, Y and Z this probability is 0.4, then the probability of all three occurring independently in different lects or being copied is 0.4^3, or 0.064. Thus a collection of independently occurring innovations has far more diagnostic substance than any single innovation. Ideally, a subgroup is defined by a bunch of innovations, some of which have considerable diagnostic substance in their own right.

One of the best known innovation-defined subgroups is the Germanic subgroup of Indo-European. It is defined by a fairly complex set of innovations in Proto-Indo-European consonants encapsulated in Grimm's and Verner's Laws (for a textbook presentation, see Hock 1986: 37–42). However, although Grimm's Law had survived inspection since 1822, in the 1970s it was called into question by proponents of the 'glottalic theory'. They claim that the conventional reconstruction of Proto-Indo-European consonants is implausible and propose a new one. The new reconstruction, however, has the effect of turning Indo-European subgrouping on its head, doing away with Grimm's Law because it is claimed that the Proto-Indo-European consonant system was rather similar to that of Proto-Germanic, and instead creating other innovation-defined subgroups. (For a popular presentation of the glottalic theory, see Gamkrelidze and Ivanov 1990; for summaries of counter arguments see Hock 1986: 621–6 and Szemerényi 1990: 159–62.)

This controversy highlights a weakness in the linguistic comparative method; namely, that subgrouping is dependent on innovation, innovation on reconstruction of a proto-language. If the reconstruction is wrong, innovations will be mis-stated and consequently subgroups will be erroneous – and this is what the glottalic theorists claim for conventional Proto-Indo-European reconstruction. The grounds on which the glottalicists stake their claim are typological. Since the 1960s linguists have focused more and more on typological issues, investigating the parameters along which languages vary from each other and the covariation of these parameters. At the same time, linguistic prehistorians have looked into the parameters of sound *change*. The outcome of this research is a growing consensus, for example, about (a) the kinds of consonant systems which are likely to occur in human languages and those which are not, and (b) the kinds of sound change that occur and those which do not. On the basis of such research, the glottalicists claim that the conventionally reconstructed Proto-Indo-European consonant system is implausible, and propose one which they say is typologically plausible. Even a brief survey of the relevant literature, however, suggests that the growing consensus is incomplete, and that the jury is still out on the question of Proto-Indo-European consonants.

Lest the non-linguist reader infer from the glottalic problem that the comparative method of subgrouping is hopelessly flawed, I should say two things in its defence. Firstly, typological plausibility allows us to resolve perhaps 80–90 per cent of reconstructive questions without controversy (it is simply unfortunate that Proto-Indo-European belongs to the other 10 or 20 per cent). Secondly, for most reconstructive questions there is also *external* evidence. In Figure 13.6, for example, the reconstruction of B's sounds would be based not only on the sounds of B1, B2 and B3, but also on a consideration of what A's sounds (or its descendants') tell us about AB's and therefore indirectly also about B's. But until such time as we have a sound

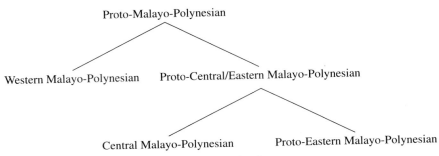

Figure 13.7 Segment of the Austronesian family tree.

reconstruction of Proto-Indo-European's nearest relatives, there will be no external evidence to bring to bear on the glottalic problem. There are linguists working on the reconstruction of Proto-Nostratic (of which Proto-Indo-European is claimed to be a descendant) who hold that this evidence is already available, and that it supports the glottalic theory. Sadly they are not united in their interpretation of the data in this regard (Bomhard and Kerns 1994: 12–19), and there are conflicting versions of the Nostratic theory, not to mention plenty of linguistic prehistorians who reject it altogether.

One family-tree pitfall for the unwary is illustrated in Figure 13.7, which shows part of Blust's (1977) Austronesian family tree. The Central/Eastern and Eastern Malayo-Polynesian groups of languages are each defined by a clear set of innovations (Blust 1978, 1993) – that is, each is an innovation-defined subgroup descended from a reconstructible proto-language. For the languages labelled 'Western Malayo-Polynesian', however, there are no innovations shared by all (or even most) of the group: it is *not* an innovation-defined subgroup. Instead, it is negatively defined: it consists of all Malayo-Polynesian languages other than the Central/Eastern Malayo-Polynesian group. Whereas Proto-Central/Eastern Malayo-Polynesian can be reconstructed because Central/Eastern Malayo-Polynesian is an innovation-defined subgroup, the Western Malayo-Polynesian languages do not constitute a subgroup and no 'Proto-Western Malayo-Polynesian' is reconstructible. (The same is perhaps true of the Central Malayo-Polynesian languages, but these at least form an innovation-*linked* subgroup in the sense described in the next section (see pp. 224–5). These cases are discussed in more detail in Ross (1995: 72–84.)

The pitfall here, then, is that, if one branch of a binary node is the proto-language of an innovation-defined subgroup, it is all too easy to assume that the other branch is one too. But this is an artefact of the vagueness which bedevils family tree diagrams.

Network growth, lectal differentiation and innovation-linked subgroups

Genuine language fissure is probably a relatively rare event in the world's linguistic history. A far more common scenario, at least in parochial traditional communities, is *lectal differentiation*. As a community grows, it establishes new settlements which remain in contact with each other, contact being naturally greatest with the geographically most accessible sister settlements. There is an increase in structural heterogeneity, but, unlike language fissure, it does not entail a sharp reduction in the density of links so that one unit becomes two but rather a gradual reduction in intensity and multiplexity which shades into a reduction in network density. This is illustrated in Figure 13.8, where the community at Time 1 differentiates into four groups at Time 2. The links between these groups show much less diminution in density than in Figure 13.4. The language of the founder community continues to be spoken in the new settlements, but innovations occur in local lects, and links are still dense enough for some innovations to spread from one lect to its neighbours. The result is the differentiation of the lect of the founder community into a linkage of lects in which, say, as in Figure 13.8, lects A1 and A2 reflect one bunch of innovations, lects A2 and A3 another bunch, and lects A3 and A4 yet another. This is the kind of process which the 'wave' model was designed to capture. Over time, lects may come to differ from each

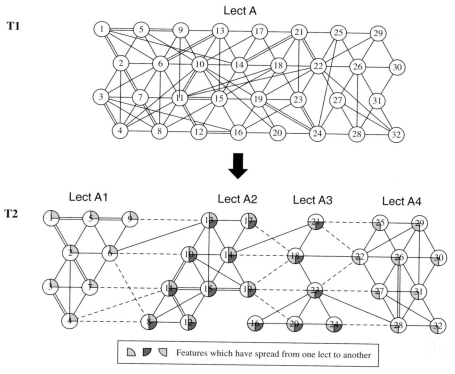

Figure 13.8 A social network representation of the differentiation of a lect into four lects.

other enough for us to speak of them as 'separate languages', but the over-lapping pattern of innovations remains. Such a linkage I will call an *innovation-linked subgroup*.[2] The linguist uses this overlapping pattern of inno-vations to detect the fact that the lects of the subgroup are the outcome of a process of lectal differentiation reflecting the gradual geographic extension of their speakers' habitat.

Probably the best known and most researched innovation-linked subgroup in the literature is the West Germanic (German plus Dutch) lectal continuum, which displays a plethora of overlapping innovations (König 1978: 140–229; Barbour and Stevenson 1990: 77–99) such that there are no major linguistic boundaries corresponding with the borders of the Netherlands, Belgium, Germany, Austria or Switzerland, but numerous other boundaries which divide an area across which an innovation has spread from one where it has not. These boundaries are known as 'isoglosses'.

Renfrew (1987) has claimed that the early spread of Indo-European speakers took the form of gradual agricultural expansion. If he is right, then we would expect the major subgroups of Indo-European to be connected by the pattern of overlapping innovations that is typical of lectal differentiation, and there is indeed evidence that the early diversification of Indo-European took this form (Hock 1986: 451–5). However, although this is a necessary condition for a linguistic confirmation of Renfrew's hypothesis, it is far from being a sufficient one.

As I noted earlier (see p. 213), the differentiation of A into a linkage consisting of lects A1 to A7 can be shown as in Figure 13.9. It is also possible, however, for a subgroup to be both innovation-defined *and* innovation-linked. Consider Figure 13.10. If B underwent a set of innovations before differen-tiating out into the linkage B1 to Bn, then, ideally, the lects B1 to Bn will all reflect those innovations and thereby comprise an innovation-defined subgroup. But if B became the linkage B1 to Bn by a process of lectal differ-entiation, then there is a strong likelihood that during this process innovations have arisen in various lects and spread to their neighbours, also giving the overlapping pattern of innovations characteristic of an innovation-linked subgroup. Given this double pattern of innovations – some shared by all lects, some forming an overlap pattern – the linguist infers that the lects B1 to Bn are descended from a single interstage language B *and* that B became B1 to Bn by a process of lectal differentiation. So B1 to Bn constitutes a subgroup which is both innovation-defined and innovation-linked.

There is a potential pitfall here. An innovation may arise in one lect and spread to *all* other lects of the linkage. Since this innovation is now shared by all lects, the linguist may conclude that this is an innovation-defined subgroup, that is, that the innovation occurred in the common ancestor of the linkage. This conclusion would be false. However, this pitfall is not as great as it may seem. Firstly, as I noted earlier (see pp. 220–1), an innova-tion-defined subgroup should be defined by a diagnostically substantial *bunch* of innovations. By definition, this must include innovations which are unlikely

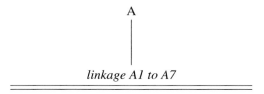

linkage A1 to A7

Figure 13.9   A family tree representation of lectal differentiation into an innovation-linked subgroup.

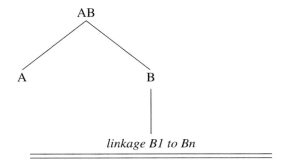

linkage B1 to Bn

Figure 13.10   Innovation-linked and innovation-defined subgroup.

to be copied from lect to lect. If this condition is not satisfied, then it is unwise to infer the prior existence of the common ancestor of an innovation-defined subgroup. Secondly, the circumstances in which an innovation with diagnostic substance is copied to *all* other lects of a linkage are limited. The linkage needs to be close-knit. By this I mean that speakers of each lect are in regular contact with speakers of at least one other lect *and* the lects are perceived by their speakers as 'the same language'. These circumstances are likely to occur only rather early in a process of differentiation, so that the linguist's inference of a common ancestor is likely to be correct.

The reader may well wonder how an innovation-linked subgroup can arise without also being innovation-defined. One way in which this can happen is simply that no (defining) innovations occur before B differentiates out into a linkage. Another is covered in the next section.

Linkage breaking
For practical purposes, two processes can be recognized in the formation of innovation-linked subgroups. The first is lectal differentiation (see pp. 222–3). The second I label *linkage breaking*.

Linkage breaking is the event in a linkage which corresponds to fissure in a single language. It occurs when part of the network making up the linkage

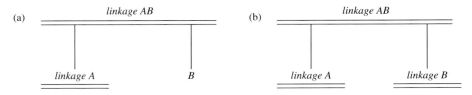

Figure 13.11   Two linkage-breaking scenarios.

becomes geographically or socially isolated from the rest of the network (i.e. there is a sharp drop in the density of the links where the new boundary has arisen), so that innovations no longer spread across that boundary. The fact that the lects under scrutiny once formed a single linkage is revealed by a pattern of overlapping bunches of innovations like that described previously (see pp. 223–4) across the whole set of lects, whilst breaking is manifested by different patterns of later innovations on either side of the new boundary. (This presupposes that innovations can be ordered, as exemplified in the case study.)

It is convenient to discuss the geographic and social varieties of linkage breaking separately. Geographic linkage breaking occurs when the speakers of a single lect part company from the rest of the linkage or when the speakers of several lects of AB migrate away from the speakers of other lects of AB, forming linkage B and leaving the stay-at-home lects as linkage A. These two scenarios are shown in Figure 13.11. Among parochial traditional societies the kind of linkage breaking in Figure 13.11(a) has probably been repeated over and over again in traditional village societies and can be characterized as follows.

AB is a linkage. Some AB speakers leave one of its villages, settling far enough away to prevent ongoing contact between the speakers who have founded the new village and those who remain in the old one (or in any other AB-speaking village). Over time, the lect of the new village, B, undergoes various innovations which render it rather different from the lect of the old village and from other lects of the AB linkage, which we will now call 'A'. Because the speakers who have remained in the old village have continued in contact with speakers of other lects of A, their lect has undergone far fewer innovations than B. The few innovations it has undergone it tends to share with neighbouring lects of A. What was once the linkage AB has become the linkage A and the language B. The clues from which we infer this situation are of two kinds: firstly, B shares innovations with some lects of A; secondly, B is characterized by innovations not found in any lect of A. This scenario is exemplified by the Tokalau Fijian linkage and Proto-Polynesian below (Figure 13.12).

The scenario in Figure 13.11(b) is unlikely a priori to result from migration, as it requires that the speakers of several lects move to a new location, yet maintain enough cohesion to continue as linkage B. In my studies of

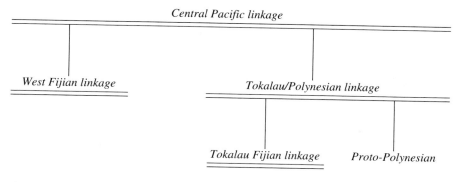

Figure 13.12   Linkage breaking in the Central Pacific linkage.

Oceanic Austronesian languages I have only encountered one case where this scenario may fit. This is the Bel linkage, which consists of languages scattered in tiny enclaves along the north coast of the Papua New Guinea mainland. The linkage today falls into two parts, east and west (Ross 1988: 161). There is evidence from oral history and vulcanology that this division is the result of a volcanic eruption which destroyed an island situated between Bagabag and Long Islands and scattered the speakers of Bel lects to their present locations.

Another example of this scenario is the early history of the Fijian lects, as reconstructed by Geraghty (1983) and shown in Figure 13.12. He infers that Proto-Central Pacific, an Oceanic Austronesian language whose speakers occupied the Fijian archipelago sometime around 1000 BC (Spriggs 1994), diversified into the Central Pacific linkage (my term), consisting of lects scattered across the archipelago. As the result of weakening social links between some settlements on the large mountainous island of Viti Levu, the linkage separated at quite an early stage into the Western Fijian and Tokalau/Polynesian linkages (Geraghty 1983: 348–51, 381). The Tokalau/Polynesian linkage occupied the eastern part of the Fijian archipelago and is thus named because it is ancestral not only to the lects of eastern Fiji ('Tokalau' = east, east wind) but also to all the Polynesian languages. The latter are all descended from a unitary language, Proto-Polynesian, which came into being when speakers of a Tokalau/Polynesian lect migrated from their home in the north-eastern part of the Fiji archipelago to Tonga probably sometime between 1000 and 800 BC.

Thus Geraghty reconstructs a sequence of two linkage breakings. The first is social, and breaks the Central Pacific linkage into two linkages as in Figure 13.11(b), Western Fijian and Tokalau/Polynesian, whilst the second is geographic and takes the form in Figure 13.11(a), when Proto-Polynesian broke away from Tokalau/Polynesian. As Geraghty (1983: 381) says, this account matches the archaeology well, although there is no obvious archaeological reflex of the Central Pacific linkage breaking. The analysis of pottery style, however, lends some support to a west-to-east spread in the Central Pacific region (Fiji, Tonga, Samoa; Matthew Spriggs, pers. comm. and 1994). Seemingly as a result of the remarkable speed (on archaeological evidence) with which the Central Pacific area was settled, there is no set of innovations which is reflected in all the lects descended from the putative Central Pacific linkage. Equally, though, there is no linguistic evidence to suggest that the Central Pacific linkage was the outcome of more than one original immigration. There is ample evidence in the form of overlapping patterns of innovations for the Western Fijian and Tokalau/Polynesian linkages (Geraghty 1983: 277–346), and shared innovations indicate that Proto-Polynesian has its origin somewhere in the Tokalau/Polynesian linkage (Geraghty 1983: 366–78).

Earlier I touched on the question of how an innovation-linked subgroup can arise without also being innovation-defined (see p. 225). Another way in which this can happen is encapsulated in Figure 13.11(b). If we assume that the linkage AB is descended from a language Proto-AB, which underwent certain innovations before diversifying into a linkage, then all lects of AB reflect a common set of innovations (i.e. AB is an innovation-defined subgroup). After linkage breaking, new innovations occur in various parts of linkage A creating the overlapping pattern of innovations that is typical of a linkage. But the only innovations shared by all lects of A are also reflected in B. That is, there are no innovations which define A, only innovations that link its lects together.

Language fusion and linkage rejoining

Language fusion and linkage rejoining are the reverses of language fission and linkage breaking. They occur when links between two or more networks (or parts of a network) are (re-)established, eventually becoming as dense as links elsewhere in the network(s); that is, the process in Figure 13.4 is reversed and, as a result, innovations begin to pass via the new links from one lect to another across the former gap. Of course, this movement can only take place if the lects on either side of the gap are related and sufficiently similar for features from a lect on one side of the gap to be adopted by speakers of a lect on the other side.[3]

Lynch and Tepahae (in press) describe a case of probable language fusion on the island of Aneityum (Vanuatu). Here, radical population decrease following contact with Europeans appears to have resulted in the speakers of two (or more) related languages from separate communities coming together as a single community and pooling their lects to form a single new lect, Anejom. The pre-fusion lects had undergone different morphological innovations, so that, for example, the Proto-Oceanic article *na had become accreted to its noun as in- in one lect and as nV- (where -V- is a vowel) in the other. Anejom reflects these forms in different nouns with no predictable pattern, and displays equally unpredictable alternations in other areas of its vocabulary. (A special kind of fusion occurs with koineization; see pp. 236–8.)

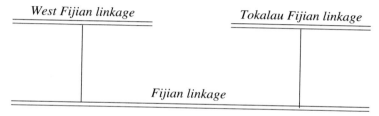

Figure 13.13   Linkage joining in Fiji.

Language fusion represents one extreme of a continuum of linguistic reintegration; at the other end lies linkage rejoining. Whereas the innovations of
pre-fusion lects end up side by side in the new fused lects, the likelihood is
that the innovations of pre-joining linkages will largely stay put in different
lects of the newly rejoined linkage.

The best-documented case of linkage rejoining that I know of in the literature has (again) occurred in Fiji. In Figure 13.12 I diagrammed the history
of the Central Pacific linkage. The next instalment of that history is shown
in Figure 13.13. After the geographic separation of Pre-Proto-Polynesian from
the Tokalau/Polynesian linkage, the growing population filled up the coastal
strip of Viti Levu and spread up the mountain valleys, so that the West Fijian
linkage and the Tokalau Fijian linkages were gradually rejoined and innovations again began to spread across the mountain barrier between the two
linkages (Geraghty 1983: 379–86). The net result is that there are innovations linking the lects of the former West Fijian linkage, innovations linking
the lects of the former Tokalau/Fijian linkage with the Polynesian languages,
as well as innovations linking the lects of the present-day Fijian linkage to
the exclusion of the Polynesian languages. The sorting out and interpretation of these patterns of innovation is one of Geraghty's major achievements.

It is worth noting, incidentally, that linkage rejoining is only detectable
linguistically if we have clear evidence of former linkage breaking. In the
Fijian case, we only know that the innovations characteristic of the Fijian
linkage have occurred after linkage rejoining because its members reflect other
innovations which bear witness to earlier linkage breaking.

I said above that the lects on each side of the gap between the two linkages must be related if linkage rejoining is to occur. I suspect linkage rejoining
is a process that has occurred much more often in prehistory than our largely
divergence-oriented linguistic theories have allowed us to recognize, but it
is one that has received little study. As a result, I do not know how similar
the lects on either side of the gap need to be for linkage rejoining to occur,
nor what parameters of similarity are relevant to it. It does seem, though,
that linkage rejoining can occur in cases where the lects have diverged considerably more than they had in Fiji, as an example from the south-west Pacific
shows.

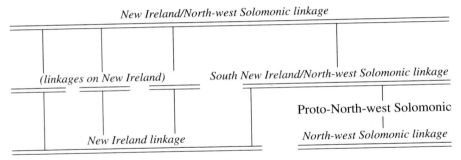

Figure 13.14   Linkage joining and breaking in New Ireland.

The island chain formed by New Ireland and the north-western part of the Solomons chain (Bougainville, Choiseul, the New Georgia group, Santa Isabel) and their offshore islands evidently has a rather complex linguistic history, diagrammed in Figure 13.14 (this is a revision of part of the diagram in Ross 1988: 258; for a map, see Ross 1988: 259). It was once occupied by a linkage of Western Oceanic lects, the New Ireland/North-west Solomonic linkage. On New Ireland, which is long and narrow, with a steep ridge forming a backbone along much of the island, these lects diversified early into a number of quite varied languages, each of which then differentiated into a linkage of its own. The languages of the north-west Solomons formed a linkage with those around the mountainous southern end of the New Ireland backbone, so that southern New Ireland and the north-west Solomons exclusively share certain innovations (Ross 1988: 307–13). As populations built up on the islands, however, three things happened. One was that links across the ocean expanse between New Ireland and Buka (the north-westernmost island of the Solomons archipelago) diminished in multiplexity and density towards today's once-a-year voyages. The second was that links between the linkages on New Ireland, including its southern lects, regrew and innovations again spread across the former gaps. The third was that with the expansion of population in the north-west Solomons (probably initially on Buka and Bougainville), Proto-North-west Solomonic speakers carried with them the innovations which today characterize the North-west Solomonic linkage (Ross 1988: 218), which is both innovation-linked and innovation-defined.

   The patterning of innovations in the New Ireland/north-west Solomons area is rather similar to that in Fiji, in that it defines two different linkage configurations at different stages of linguistic prehistory. New Ireland differs from Fiji, however, in that present-day evidence implies much greater diversity among New Ireland and north-west Solomons lects than in Fiji when linkage rejoining occurred. It seems probable that the greater the diversity of lects, the more limited the potential for the spread of innovations.

It is obvious that the SCEs described here do not fit into a standard family tree (although they fit into a tree with extended conventions well enough, as I have shown). In a sense, they fit Moore's definition of a rhizotically derived language: 'derived from or rooted in several different antecedent groups' (1994b: 925). But note that even the Aneityum case is hardly one of glottogenesis: there is continuity through the generations.

SOCIALLY RELEVANT INNOVATIONS

The linguistic evidence for the changes in network structure discussed on pp. 215–30 resides largely in the *distribution* of innovations. Here, and on pp. 240–50, the evidence is of a different kind: the *nature* of the innovation provides fairly direct information about the SCE that caused it.

Before we can look at these events, a brief excursus is needed into the tricky matter of the causes of language change. Since a social network is made up of speakers, every change in the language must begin with one or more speakers adopting an innovation. If that innovation is copied by other speakers, then it may become what the linguist observes as a language change. If not, it eventually disappears (Milroy and Milroy 1985).[4]

Keller (1990) argues brilliantly that language change is usually an 'invisible hand process'. An invisible hand process occurs, for example, when a number of passers-by stop to watch a fight, forming a circle around the combatants. None of the passers-by intended to form the circle. It is the collective result of their individual attempts to get the best possible view of the fisticuffs. Another example consists of many people taking the same short cut over a grassed area, with the unintended result that they trample a track across it. The essentials of an invisible hand process are that members of a population each act in a similar way with similar intentions, yet their collective acts have a result they did not envisage. Invisible hand processes are, of course, very much the stuff of which economic systems are made, and it was in this context that the term was coined by the eighteenth-century economist and philosopher Adam Smith.

Since the individual acts which form the basis of an invisible hand process are performed with similar intentions, we can predict that a performer will often follow someone else's example: A sees B taking a short cut and follows him, or A sees the beginnings of the trampled track, recognizes its use, and follows it. This is evidently the way a speaker innovation diffuses through a social network to become a language change. A classic case occurred in seventeenth-century French, where speakers imitated the prestigious lect of Paris by replacing their tongue-tip trilled /r/ with the uvular (top of the throat) /r/ which still characterizes standard French. This feature, adopted by non-Parisian speakers in order to identify with Parisian prestige, was copied right across northern and eastern France and the French-speaking parts of Belgium and Switzerland, with the unintended result that it became a language change throughout much of the French-speaking region of Europe (Chambers and Trudgill 1980: 186–92).

Explaining an invisible hand process is always a complex business. If what we are seeking to explain is the language change, then its immediate efficient cause is the innovation's cumulative adoption by a sufficient number of speakers. But this adoption, as in the French /r/ case, often has to be explained in terms of a final cause, the speakers' motive(s) for adopting the innovation.

Keller seems to assume that the adoption of an innovation *always* depends on final cause, but this cannot be true. Sound changes like those described in the case study have their origins in physical and cognitive constraints on pronunciation and perception (for a brief overview and references, see Ross and Durie 1996), whilst cognitive factors account for the innovations which result from bilingualism (see pp. 241–5). Their spread through the social network entails a measure of copying, but there is not necessarily a socially significant motivation for it. The innovations discussed below, however, do entail a recognizable and specific social motivation. That is, their adoption does depend on final cause.

Innovations constantly occur in the language(s) of any social network. An innovation – or more precisely, the feature resulting from the innovation – becomes *socially relevant* in one of two ways. First, as with the association of uvular /r/ with Parisian speakers, a feature may become associated with a particular group of speakers either in the minds of those speakers or of the speakers of other lects (or both). This may lead to speakers of other lects making an 'act of identity' (Le Page and Tabouret-Keller 1985), either adopting (see below) or rejecting (see p. 238) a feature because of its social significance. Second, the simplifying or complicating effect of the feature on the structure of the language may itself lead to its acceptance or rejection by a group of speakers (see pp. 238–40).

In each case where an innovation is accepted or rejected because of its social relevance, the SCE which is reflected thereby involves a change in speakers' values. It may also involve changes in network structure, but does not necessarily do so. SCEs of this kind are somewhat difficult to characterize accurately, and I approach them in the following sections via the linguistic events that express them.

Emblematic features and acts of identity

When a feature becomes associated with a particular group of speakers, it is said to be 'emblematic' of that group. The immense language diversity of the Pacific region is associated with the fact that Pacific societies are usually tiny and speakers have therefore tended to seize on accidentally generated innovations as linguistic emblems of their local community, with the result that the language of each tiny society becomes quite rapidly differentiated from that of its neighbours (Grace 1975). I take it that such acts of identity can also hasten the processes of language fissure (see pp. 218–22) and lectal differentiation (see pp. 223–4), although it is generally impossible to reconstruct the motivation itself.

When emblematicity results in the *spread* of an innovation, however, its motivation is more readily inferable. Much modern work in dialectology by Labov (e.g. 1980, 1981, 1986), by the Milroys (James Milroy and Lesley Milroy 1985, Lesley Milroy 1980/1987, Lesley Milroy and James Milroy 1992, James Milroy 1993) and by Trudgill (e.g. 1986) focuses on the spread of innovations across social networks in which dialects of the same language are spoken. This spread happens in a variety of often rather complex ways, and it has generated an equally complex literature. Our concern here, however, is with those cases where it is reasonably clear that innovations have spread from a particular geographic area – a *centre of innovation*.

Trudgill (1983: 73–8; 1986: 44–57) enumerates a number of changes which have occurred in the English dialects of East Anglia and which have clearly been adopted from London, to the south. He argues that such innovations spread generally as the result of face-to-face interaction between London and East Anglian speakers, and makes the point that one reason for the uni-directional spread of innovations is quite simply that there are far more Londoners than East Anglians, so that the probability of an East Anglian having a conversation with a Londoner and accommodating her/his speech to the Londoner's is far higher than the opposite. He also shows, however, that there are grounds to infer that the spread of innovations is not only determined by demography but also by emblematicity. London speech is a prestige variety to the ears of Norwich teenagers, and London is a centre of innovation whose language forms are being adopted by speakers across the social network of eastern and south-eastern England. Generally, innovations are adopted in towns first, then spread from them to the surrounding countryside.

The spread of an emblematic feature *e* from speakers in a centre of innovation C to other speakers in the network with whom they have links is shown schematically in Figure 13.15. The assumption is made here that *e* has only recently begun to be adopted by speakers outside C, but is already occurring in the speech of individuals who have no direct contact with C speakers. In a corresponding diagram representing a later time we would expect *e* to have spread further among speakers outside C. The reader will note the qualitative difference between this diagram and Figures 13.4 and 13.8. Whereas the latter depict *structural* changes in a network, Figure 13.15 depicts feature spread without an alteration in network structure.

Emblematic feature spread leads to a certain levelling of lectal differences, as speakers adopt what for them are salient forms from a nearby centre of innovation. Such processes have been going on in France, Spain, Portugal and Italy for a long time. Apart from certain small enclaves, the languages of these countries are all descended from the spoken Latin of the late Roman Empire. However, this descent has not taken the form of fissure that is often implied in textbook family tree diagrams. Instead, lectal differentiation occurred right across the region, resulting in a vast linkage of Romance lects.

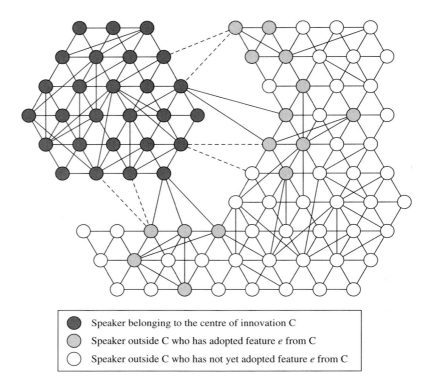

Figure 13.15 Spread of an emblematic feature *e* from a centre of innovation C.

There was an enormous variety of lects within each of these countries (throughout much of the region, there still is), and originally no marked breaks in the linkage where the present national borders run.

Over time, however, with the establishment of increasingly large states, there has been a pattern whereby lects have 'focused' (the term is from Le Page and Tabouret-Keller 1985) around the capital city of the state. That is, speakers have adopted salient forms from the capital, so that their lects have become more like that of the capital. Thus at the time the Arabs were driven out of the Iberian Peninsula, Iberian Romance lects had focused around a number of regional centres, each the capital of a local state (Harris 1988: 6–8). With the agglomeration of these states into today's nation-states, the lects of the south-west became the basis of Portuguese, whilst Leonese and Aragonese were heavily influenced and partly absorbed by Castilian (the basis of modern Spanish), Catalan surviving as a separate language because of the size, power and prestige of the city of Barcelona (Harris 1988: 13). The linguistic history of the Romance lects in France is similar, with the lects of local states like Gascon (a lect of Occitan, not French) surviving until the

Revolution. The diversity of lects continues strongly in Italy, because Italian political unification occurred only in the late nineteenth century.

In the West Germanic lectal continuum, the lects of the Netherlands focused into a separate language, Dutch, after it became an independent state in the early seventeenth century (Barbour and Stevenson 1990: 39–40). Although the lects of modern Germany have been adapting increasingly towards standard High German, there are still cases where a boundary between lects more or less follows the border of a medieval princedom (König 1978: 142).

I noted above the spread of uvular /r/ in northern French. Interestingly, however, prestige-driven adoptions of salient features can cross significant linguistic boundaries, and French uvular /r/ was adopted not only by speakers of French lects but also into the lects of much of Germany and Denmark, and into the urban lects of parts of the Netherlands, southern Norway and Sweden, and north-western Italy (Chambers and Trudgill 1980: 186–92).

These examples all show that the spread of an emblematic feature reflects something of the social (especially prestige) relations that prevailed at the time of the spread. In each of these cases, however, we also have historical records to tell us about these relations. Since (apart from borrowed vocabulary), however, the only features which appear to spread across language boundaries in the absence of widespread bilingualism are salient, emblematic features, we can use the reconstruction of such a spread to make an inference about the social relations that gave rise to it.

Just such an innovation occurs in three languages in the New Ireland linkage shown in Figure 13.14. These languages are located around the St George's Channel, which divides southern New Ireland from the Gazelle Peninsula of New Britain. Here, we are looking at a fairly recent period, well after the events diagrammed in Figure 13.14, when the southern part of the New Ireland linkage has further diversified into a number of small, localized linkages. We are concerned here with three of these, which I will label A, B, and C. Their member languages (mapped in Ross 1988: 260) are as follows:

A Patpatar, Minigir, Tolai.
B Label, Bilur.
C Kandas, Ramuaaina (formerly known as 'Duke of York').

The members of each linkage are closely related to each other, but there is a curious innovation which cuts across the three groups: in Tolai, Bilur and Ramuaaina, *s has been completely lost. At some time in the past speakers of lects ancestral to Minigir, Tolai, Bilur and Ramuaaina emigrated from New Ireland, the first three to New Britain, and Ramuaaina to the Duke of York Islands in the St George's Channel. Thus they have become somewhat isolated from their former close neighbours, speakers of the lects ancestral to Patpatar, Label and Kandas. The ancestors of Minigir and Tolai speakers, according to Tolai oral history (Salisbury 1972), crossed to New Britain sometime (probably some centuries), after the volcanic eruption which devastated the Gazelle

Peninsula around AD 600 (Walker *et al.* 1981). The Pre-Minigir moved further west, became separated by a stretch of water from the Pre-Tolai (Ross 1988: 259), whilst the Pre-Tolai expanded into the fertile country along the north coast of the peninsula and became the major group in the area. The Bilur (who occupy a small coastal enclave) and the Ramuaaina probably arrived from New Ireland somewhat later.

How has it come about that *s*-loss has affected these three languages, despite substantial lexical and morphosyntactic differences among them? In the case of Bilur speakers, it is known that they identify with the Tolai and even call themselves Tolai (it is probably for this reason that the Bilur language remained unrecorded until 1974; Ross 1988: 259, 423). In other words, they have become so integrated into the Tolai social network that there is no longer any qualitative or quantitative difference between the links connecting Bilur-speaking and Tolai-speaking villages and the links among Tolai-speaking villages. It seems that *s*-loss occurred first in Tolai and, being a rather striking feature of Tolai phonology, was taken as emblematic of 'being Tolai' and thus spread through the network into Bilur-speaking villages too. One may infer that a similar process occurred in Ramuaaina-speaking villages.

Koineization

The processes referred to in the previous section result in lectal levelling (i.e. in lects becoming more similar to each other), because speakers adopt the emblematic features of another lect with whose speakers they identify (or want to identify). *Koineization* is also a levelling process, but its motivation seems to be almost the opposite − namely, the avoidance of emblematic features.

The classic case of koineization is the Hellenistic Koine of the Macedonian Empire. Ancient (pre-Koine) Greek formed a fairly complex and varied linkage of lects, one of which was Attic, the lect of Athens. During the Macedonian period, a form of Attic came to be used as the *lingua franca* of the empire, and continued in this function in the eastern Roman Empire. It was, however, in Hock's words 'de-atticized Attic' (Hock 1986: 485). Its emblematically Attic forms were eliminated in favour of forms that were emblematic of no particular lect.

Koineization usually occurs when there is a radical realignment of a social network consisting of a linkage of lects. In the Greek case, each lect had been used in a relatively closed social network in the age of city states. With the arrival of the Macedonian Empire, however, new ties between the various lectal areas were established, speakers were uprooted and moved to new loca-tions, and the lectal emblematicity associated with each city-state lost its significance. The language of the new, larger-scale, more integrated network was the Hellenistic Koine.

In other cases of koineization, a collection of related lects were transported to new locations, so that they came to be in a totally new relation to each other in social network terms. Trudgill (1986: 129–48) argues that Australian

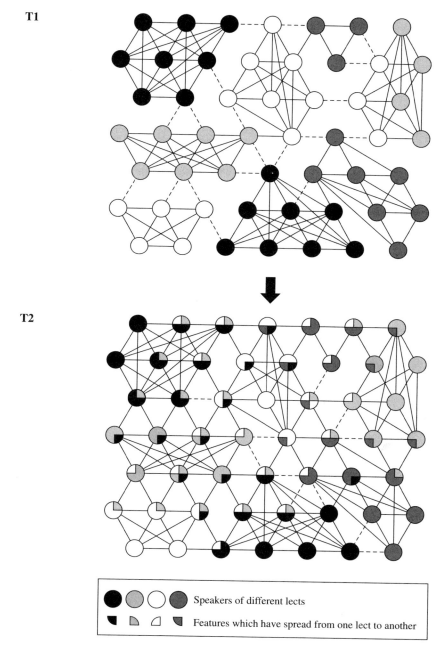

Figure 13.16   A social network representation of koineization.

English also bears the marks of koineization, based on lects from south-eastern England and from Ireland. But perhaps the best-documented modern koine is Fiji Hindi, which represents a levelling of the emblematic features of a number of languages of the north Indian Indo-Aryan linkage (Moag 1977; Trudgill 1986: 99–102; Siegel 1987: 185–210). These languages found their way to Fiji with indentured labourers in the nineteenth century, whose descendants now make up almost half of Fiji's population.

Figure 13.16 is a highly schematized diagram of a koineization process. At Time 1, speakers of four different lects have been planted in proximity to each other; the diagram assumes maximally dense and intense links among adjacent speakers of the same lect, but much less dense and less intense links between speakers of different lects. At Time 2, links between speakers of different lects have grown in density and intensity (I have assumed that links among speakers of the same lect remain maximal, but this is not a necessary assumption) and features have begun to pass from lect to lect. It is reasonably easy to see that if the process were continued, levelling would soon occur.

Koineization is not only an act of identity that rejects emblematic features; it is also a special case of reintegration (see pp. 217, 228), somewhere on the cline between language fusion and linkage rejoining, and one where some post-reintegration innovations are motivated by avoidance of emblematicity. I am not aware of a case in which a linguistic prehistorian has reconstructed koineization, and it is difficult to know how readily one would recognize it without additional (e.g. historical) evidence. Its identifying marks would be the irregular reflexes of proto-forms that result from mixing lectal forms that reflected the proto-language differently (i.e. as for language fusion), combined with the reduction in irregular grammatical forms that seems to be typical of koineization.

Hines (1990, 1995) suggests that after the settlement in the fifth and sixth centuries of parts of England by Angles, Saxons and Jutes – who would have spoken a variety of north-west Germanic lects – a koineization occurred (the term is mine, not his) that levelled many of the differences between these lects to give a common 'Anglo-Saxon', which in its turn differentiated into the well-known regional dialects of Old English. His proposal is based on archaeological evidence of the different immigrant groups, combined with the *absence* of reflexes of the expected linguistic differences among them, and is therefore not really an exercise in *linguistic* prehistory: this remains to be done.

Exoterogeny and esoterogeny

If a community has extensive ties with other communities and their emblematic language is also spoken as a contact language by members of those communities, then they will probably value their language for its use across community boundaries. In the terminology of Thurston (1989: 556–7), it will be an 'exoteric' lect. Its use by a wider range of speakers means that an exoteric lect is subject to considerable variability, and innovations leading to greater simplicity are liable to be preferred (and those leading to greater complexity disfavoured). This simplifying process Thurston calls 'exoterogeny': it reduces phonological and morphological irregularity or complexity, and makes the language more regular, more understandable and more learnable. The outcome of this process is what Platt (1975), seeking a term to describe the less 'educated' forms of Singapore English, called a 'creoloid'.

Another creoloid is Afrikaans, whose history illustrates that exoterogeny may have simplifying effects but is not itself necessarily a simple process. Roberge (1993) shows that the variability out of which modern Afrikaans developed in the late eighteenth century was probably a continuum reaching from a Cape Dutch Creole (see p. 253) through to a Cape Dutch which was still a dialect of eighteenth-century Netherlands Dutch.

Exoterogeny differs from koineization in an important respect. Both koineization and exoterogeny result in simplification, but koineization also entails the elimination of the emblematic features of its contributing lects (i.e. levelling). Exoterogeny does not necessarily involve more than one lect, so that levelling need not apply.

Esoterogeny is the opposite process. If the members of a community have few ties with other communities and their emblematic lect is not usually known to outsiders, then they may use it as an 'in-group' code, an 'esoteric' lect from which outsiders are consciously excluded. Innovations leading to increased complexity and to differences from neighbouring lects will be favoured. Because the social network is small and norm enforcement can accordingly be strong, irregular variants are accumulated and elision and assimilation result in phonological compactness, in allophony and in allomorphy (Thurston 1987: 55–60). The lexicon is elaborated with numerous near synonyms, often by borrowing, and the frequency of opaque idioms increases (Thurston 1989: 556). As a result, the lect becomes increasingly difficult for one's neighbours to understand or learn.

Thurston's examples of esoterogeny are drawn from the Melanesian island of New Britain. A set of European examples is given by Andersen (1988), who describes the development of 'parasitic' consonants out of the offglide occlusion of long high vowels. Thus the German lect of Waldeck in Hesse has *iks* 'ice' from earlier *$\star$i:s* (Standard German *Eis*), *likp* 'body' from *$\star$li:p* (Standard German *Leib*), *fukst* 'fist' from *$\star$fu:st* (Standard German *Faust*), and so on (Andersen 1988: 65). This unusual sound change has been recorded in a number of lects, including lects of Rhaeto-Romance and Upper Rhône lects of Provençal (both spoken in remote Swiss Alpine valleys), Low and Middle Franconian lects of Dutch/German (in areas which were politically fragmented in the Middle Ages), the small island Rømø and Samsø lects of Danish, and Maru, a lect of the mountainous Kachin region of northern Burma, closely related to Burmese (Burling 1966). All of these are quite closely related to lects which lack parasitic consonants, and in each case their development seems to reflect esoterogeny fostered by geographic or political isolation.

Exoterogeny and esoterogeny cannot readily be captured in a social net-work diagram because it is not the distribution or the spread of innovations which is significant, but the *kind* of innovation. The products of exoterogeny and esoterogeny – simplification and complication – are recognizable for the linguistic prehistorian precisely because they do *not* correspond with either their relatives or their neighbours. Thurston (1989) infers from its simplifi-cation that Lusi of New Britain has undergone exoterogeny, whilst I have inferred esoterogeny as part of the convoluted history of Maisin of south-east Papua on the basis of certain kinds of complication (Ross 1996).

CONTACT-INDUCED CHANGE, LANGUAGE SHIFT, AND CULTURE CONTACT

In this section we are concerned first with those kinds of language change which result from and allow us to reconstruct language contact. I am using the term '*language contact*' – and by extension, the term '*contact-induced change*' – in the narrow sense introduced by Weinreich ([1953] 1963), to refer to situations in which enough members of a community are bilingual for their bilingualism to bring about innovations in their emblematic language.

It is important to distinguish between language contact, in this narrow sense, and *culture contact*, which does not necessarily involve widespread bilingualism. In culture contact, culture A has a sufficiently powerful effect on culture B to leave its mark on the language of culture B, but this mark is not the same as the marks left by language contact.

When bilingualism occurs in traditional societies, it is often the case that one language is emblematic of its speakers' ethnicity, whilst the other is an inter-community language (this may have just local use or be a more widespread lin-gua franca). It may well happen that many speakers are more at home in the inter-community language than in their emblematic language. When this occurs, it is quite likely that speakers will progressively adapt the semantic and morphosyntactic patterns of their emblematic language in the direction of the patterns of the inter-community language. They will probably also speak the inter-community language with the 'accent' of their emblematic language (that is, they will use a phonology and phonetic realizations in the inter-community language which approximate those of their emblematic language). Again (see above) because it is the *kind* of innovation reflected in the data that enables the linguist to reconstruct contact-induced change, the process cannot conveniently be represented in a social network diagram.

Contact of this kind has two major kinds of outcome. Either bilingualism continues and the emblematic language is progressively restructured, or the community progressively abandons its emblematic language in favour of the inter-community language and *language shift* occurs.

Culture contact, on the other hand, results in the borrowing of vocabu-lary from the language of culture A by the language of culture B, but not in the restructuring that marks contact-induced change or the change in pronunciation that marks language shift.

It is easy to entertain the thought that contact-induced change and language shift are rhizotic rather than cladistic processes. However, the crucial point here is that neither entails a break in linguistic continuity. The processes described in the next section proceed gradually over the generations, and there is no good, and certainly no principled, reason to say that a language undergoing metatypy shifts from one language family to another, any more than there is reason to say that a language that undergoes radical change for other reasons has somehow ceased to be a member of its family. The case of language shift is a little different. However, whilst there may be grounds for a rhizotic analysis of the *ethnicity* of a group that shifts lg, the continuity of the language itself is not in question.

Contact-induced change

The class of language changes which is diagnostic of contact-induced change includes (a) the reorganization of a language's semantic patterns and 'ways of saying things', and (b) the restructuring of its syntax (i.e. the patterns in which morphemes are concatenated to form words, phrases, clauses and sentences). This reorganization and restructuring is truly diagnostic of contact-induced change only if we can show that the new patterns bring the language closer to the patterns of a putative inter-community language. I have coined the term 'metatypy' for this reorganization and restructuring (Ross 1996), as this kind of language change leads to a metamorphosis in structural type. Traditionally, the inter-community language has been referred to as a 'superstratum', but there has been no term for the actual process of change. Thomason and Kaufman (1988: Ch. 3) label it 'borrowing', but this term has a much wider meaning for most linguists.

We can readily infer how metatypy comes about. Every language carries with it a conventional way of construing reality. To take an elementary example, the English speaker says *I am cold*, but the French speaker says *J'ai froid* 'I have cold', the German *Mir ist kalt* 'To me is cold'. When speakers are using two different languages side by side more or less continuously, there is a strong tendency for them to reduce the cognitive and linguistic processing burden by bringing their two languages' construals of reality into line with each other. That is, they use words and phrases in the two languages so that the literal translation from language A to language B increasingly becomes the natural free translation. This process is known as 'calquing'. It means that the idioms of the two languages become more literally inter-translatable, the range of meaning of words in each language becomes closer to the other, and finally that the way events are structured into predicates and arguments also becomes closer (Grace 1981: 43–5, 124). This results in the reorganization of the semantic patterns of the emblematic language and then in the restructuring of its syntax. The *forms* of words remain unchanged, however. If English were ever to be remodelled metatypically along French lines, the

English speaker would adopt the French pattern and say 'I have cold', but he would not replace the English form *cold* with French *froid*.

This makes metatypy relatively easy to spot, as the *forms* of the language which has undergone metatypy remain largely unchanged, whilst its *semantics* and its *syntax* change in the direction of its metatypic model.

I have reconstructed metatypy in the prehistories of the Papua New Guinea Austronesian languages Takia and Maisin in Ross (1996), where there is also a far more detailed exploration of contact-induced change and metatypy with references to relevant literature. Takia speakers share Karkar Island with speakers of Waskia, a Papuan language. The two languages are thus unrelated. Takia phonology and vocabulary are clearly Oceanic Austronesian, but its semantics and its syntactic structures follow closely the patterns of Waskia. Many Oceanic Austronesian languages in the south-west Pacific reflect the patterns reconstructible for Proto-Oceanic; namely, Subject–Verb–Object (or possibly Verb–Subject–Object) clause order, Preposition–Noun Phrase order in adpositional phrases, and Determiner–Noun and Possessed–Possessor noun phrase order. Takia, however, follows Waskia and other nearby Papuan languages in displaying the orders Subject–Object–Verb, Noun Phrase–Postposition, Noun–Determiner and Possessor–Possessed. The interesting thing is that Takia and Waskia speakers are today *not* bilingual in each other's languages. They communicate with each other in Tok Pisin, Papua New Guinea's English-based pidgin lingua franca. But the changes which have occurred in Takia indicate that pre-Takia speakers were at one time bilingual in an inter-community Papuan language, quite possibly Waskia.

I am aware of three documented European cases of metatypy. One is Haase's (1992) careful and detailed account of the effects of Romance languages on the Mixe dialect of Basque over two thousand years. Mixe shows plentiful evidence of metatypy on the model of Gascon as a result of Basque/Gascon bilingualism.

The second case is the Rhaeto-Romance lects which make up Romansch, the 'fourth language' of Switzerland. Haiman (1988) shows repeatedly that there are differences between the Swiss and the Italian lects of Rhaeto-Romance resulting from the different bilingualisms of their speakers. The Swiss lects differ from their Italian sisters in having verb-second order in independent clauses, lacking pro-drop, using dummy impersonal subjects, having a special impersonal pronoun, and so on, matching Germanic languages, medieval French (itself the product of metatypy on the model of Germanic lects) and 'practically no other language on earth' (Haiman 1988: 384). Romansch is thus the product of the metatypy of Rhaeto-Romance on a Swiss German model.

Not far to the south is the third case, Sauris, one of the German-speaking enclaves of northern Italy, where Denison (1977, 1988) describes a German lect that has undergone metatypy on the model of a (Rhaeto-Romance) Friulian lect and to a lesser extent of standard Italian.

The linguist reader will recognize that the Takia/Waskia, Mixe Basque/ Gascon, Romansch/Swiss German and Sauris German/Friulian pairs each form a small *Sprachbund* ('language alliance'). Probably the best-known *Sprachbund* consists of modern Greek, Albanian, Romanian, and the southern Slav languages Macedonian, Bulgarian, Serbian and Croatian, which through centuries of contact have undergone metatypy to the extent that there are very close semantic and syntactic parallels among these languages. Because the members of this, the Balkan *Sprachbund,* are all Indo-European languages, however, it is difficult to identify the language which has been a metatypic model for the others (Joseph 1983), and in any case it is probable that there have been various bilingualisms over time which have contributed to Balkan metatypy.

It is easy to see that in a social network structure like that of pre-Takia/Papuan bilingualism, there must have been quite dense links between speakers of the emblematic language (pre-Takia) and non-Takia speakers of the Papuan inter-community language, otherwise there would not have been the need for the regular and continuing bilingualism that brought about Takia metatypy. At the same time, the fact that Takia has remained as the emblematic language of its speakers indicates that they have maintained their identity as a group and that links among them must always have been somewhat stronger than links with speakers of the inter-community language. This kind of network structure must also have occurred in the history of the Balkan *Sprachbund.*

There are degrees of metatypy: larger patterns tend to be affected first (i.e. inter-clausal structures), then clause structure, then phrase structure, and finally word structure. In Takia, metatypy reaches as far as phrase structure, whilst in the Balkan *Sprachbund* it has reached some word structures (thus the definite article is an enclitic in Balkan languages). The furthest-reaching case of metatypy reported, but not well documented, is from Kupwar, a village on the border between the Indo-European and Dravidian language families in India, where local dialects of three languages, Urdu, Marathi (both Indo-European) and Kannada (Dravidian) have developed almost identical syntactic structures. The grammatical structures of Kupwar Urdu and Kupwar Kannada have been largely replaced by the grammatical structure of Marathi, with some movement of Kupwar Urdu and Kupwar Marathi towards Kannada (Gumperz and Wilson 1971; Grace 1981: 23–32 has an insightful discussion).

Exactly what parameters determine the degree of metatypy is unclear. Time-depth is undoubtedly one. Another is probably the initial structural similarity of the languages involved. This is suggested by what happens when the members of a *Sprachbund* are also closely related. Grace describes such a situation in southern New Caledonia (Grace 1996). What apparently happened here was that the community divisions between speakers of several different but quite closely related Austronesian languages became blurred, and people were often bilingual (the details of who was bilingual in what and of which language(s) had an inter-community function are probably not recoverable).

Because of the family relationship between the languages, the semantic and syntactic differences among them were presumably not very great, but those that existed were largely eliminated by metatypy. Any differences between the phonological systems of the languages were also levelled over time, but the diverse *forms* of words were evidently retained because of their emblematic value. One might expect that this would be the end of the story: words would simply be retained in the New Caledonian languages as they have been in Takia and in the Balkans – but this has not happened. Instead, words often have unexpected forms. Because the south New Caledonian languages were closely related, there were once regular sound correspondences between their vocabularies. Where speakers regularly used two or more lects, they had an intuitive grasp of some of these correspondences and used them to convert the phonological shapes of words from one lect to another. However, the speakers' intuitive correspondences and the real correspondences resulting from historical change often differed from each other (because the converted word had been the object of a lexically diffused change or because it included the reflex of a proto-phoneme which had merged with another proto-phoneme in the 'donor' but not in the 'recipient' language). As a result, the output of the bilingual's conversion was often not the same as if the word had been directly inherited into the recipient language. As conversions of this kind occurred over centuries and words were also sometimes copied from one language into another, the 'original' sound correspondences were completely lost, as Grace found when he tried to apply orthodox comparative procedures to the south New Caledonian languages. The linguistic clues to this kind of long-term interaction between related lects are thus (a) close similarities in phonology and syntax; (b) vocabularies in which relationships between languages remain recognizable, but in which the sound correspondences between related words in different languages are impossibly confused.

Similar situations to the one described for New Caledonia also occur in parts of Australia. In traditional aboriginal Australia each person belonged to an exogamous patriclan and spoke its emblematic patrilect. However, aboriginal Australians moved around hunting and gathering in bands whose members belonged to different patriclans. A number of patrilects, often quite closely related to each other, were typically represented in a band, and band members spoke their own and other members' patrilects. Their vocabularies seem to have been affected in much the same way as those of the south New Caledonian lects (Boretzky 1984; Johnson 1990). The notable feature of each of these situations is, as Grace points out, that the speech community is not coterminous with the speakers of a single language.

The kind of account offered by Grace also fits the data from EKoti, Mozambique, presented by Schadeberg (1994). EKoti has elements from two structurally similar Bantu languages, the widely spoken KiSwahili and nearby EMakhuwa. Basic EKoti vocabulary is drawn from one or other of these two languages, as the consonant correspondences show. Some items, however, are clearly from KiSwahili but with certain consonants converted to the corresponding EMakhuwa. This can be attributed to conversion in line with speakers' intuitive correspondences, as in south New Caledonia. Productive grammatical morphemes, on the other hand, are mostly of EMakhuwa origin. Thus EKoti seems to be the product of an originally EMakhuwa-speaking community which acquired KiSwahili members and many of whose speakers were bilingual in the two languages. Since neither language was more emblematic of the community than the other, contact-induced change of the kind described by Grace occurred.

I said above that metatypy entails copying syntactic structure from one language to another, but not actual words or morphemes. There are two exceptions to this generalization. One is the *Sprachbund* of closely related languages I have just described. The other occurs when the emblematic language simply does not have a class of morphemes to serve as the translation equivalent of a morpheme class in the metatypic model. In such a case the forms themselves may be copied from the model to the emblematic language. Thus certain Papua New Guinea languages have copied Tok Pisin modal auxiliary morphemes (e.g. *mas* 'must, have to', *ken* 'can', *inap* 'be able to') where they formerly expressed these concepts by a variety of elements that did not constitute a morpheme class (Ross 1985). This copying of forms to expedite metatypy usually occurs only where morphemes are independent, not when they are bound (i.e. prefixed, suffixed, cliticized).

Where languages in contact belong to different families with different cultures, it is likely that the material cultures of the two groups of speakers were once distinct and that this will show up in the archaeological record. Such a correlation occurs on Halmahera and its offshore islands (eastern Indonesia), where the northern part of the area is occupied by speakers of Papuan languages, the southern by Austronesian speakers. Voorhoeve (1994) has shown that the Papuan languages have undergone metatypy, from which one can infer their speakers' bilingualism in an Austronesian inter-community language. Bellwood (in press) discusses the archaeological correlates of this contact. He suggests that Papuan speakers were in the islands before Austronesians, who arrived around 1500 BC. This arrival heralded technological advances (pottery, stone axes), and this fits well with the linguistic inference that an Austronesian language served as the inter-community lingua franca.

Language shift

When bilingualism continues over a long period in a traditional society with no strong language maintenance norms, the outcome may be either contact-induced change or language shift. Language shift occurs when bilinguals use their version of the inter-community language more and more, finally abandoning their old emblematic language. Since people tend to adapt the phonology of their 'second' language to that of their emblematic language (i.e. they speak it with 'an accent'), the most likely mark that language shift will leave on a language is that it will be spoken with a phonology resembling that of the abandoned emblematic language.

Obviously, it is easiest for the linguistic prehistorian to detect a lect which is the outcome of language shift if s/he has for comparison data from a lect closely related to the old emblematic language *and* data from a lect closely related to the lect to which the suspected shift has been made. The (Austronesian) Madak language on New Ireland provides a nice fulfilment of these conditions (Ross 1994a). All the languages spoken on New Ireland today are, with one exception, Austronesian. The exception is Kuot, which survives today as a Papuan isolate. The interesting point about Madak (and closely related Lavatbura-Lamasong) is that it has a phonology quite unlike any other Austronesian language on New Ireland (or anywhere else in Oceania, for that matter). A feature of Madak phonology is that a number of rules apply to phrases rather than to words, with some odd morphophonemic effects. Madak is, however, not alone in possessing this unusual phonology: it is shared by its unrelated neighbour, Kuot. The inferences that can be made from this constellation of facts are (a) that the ancestors of today's Madak speakers spoke a Papuan language rather similar to Kuot; (b) that they also spoke a local Austronesian inter-community language with a strong Kuot-like accent; and (c) that they then shifted to the inter-community language, their version of which became Madak.

It is also interesting that in this case there are fairly clear archaeological correlates of the reconstructed linguistic history. One can infer that there were once other Papuan languages spoken on New Ireland, as there is quite widespread evidence of pre-Austronesian habitation. The island was then overrun by Austronesian speakers (archaeologically, the Lapita culture), some of whose lects became inter-community languages because of their superiority as seafarers and traders. Over time, Papuan speakers were either absorbed into Austronesian speaking communities or shifted to Austronesian languages, leaving Kuot (now in decline) as the only Papuan language on the island. The archaeology of this process has been well recorded in several reports in Allen and Gosden (1991).

A somewhat controversial case where language shift has been reconstructed is early Indo-Aryan (i.e. Indo-European in India). Here the main marker of contact is the dental/retroflex distinction in the phonology of Indo-Aryan languages. Burrow (1971) shows that the introduction of retroflex consonants into Indo-Aryan cannot be explained by internally motivated change. Since these consonants are characteristic of Dravidian languages, it is reasonable to infer that their presence in Indo-Aryan is the result of pre-Indo-Aryan being spoken with a Dravidian accent prior to language shift.

A European example of language shift is provided by the Romance language Gascon, where a number of phonological features are attributable to the shift of Basque speakers to a lect of Occitan, the earlier Romance language of southern France (Haase 1993).

A fundamental point in the reconstruction of language contact is that metatypy is evidence of change within the emblematic language whilst phonological restructuring is evidence of language shift. Thomason and Kaufman's (1988) study represents the most thorough attempt so far to collect together and classify documented cases of contact-induced change and to record their sociolinguistic correlates. But as they note, sociolinguistic conditions often go undocumented, and Thomason and Kaufman are themselves often reduced to making sociolinguistic inferences from structural and formal features. Some of these inferences seem poorly founded. For example, speakers of Burushaski (a genetic isolate in mountainous northern Pakistan) are said to have shifted to the Indo-Aryan (Dardic) language Shina. Shina shows some clear cases of morphosyntactic calquing on the model of Burushaski. In summarizing Lorimer's (1937) account of this case, Thomason and Kaufman (1988: 136) write, 'native Shina morphemes combined in Burushaski ways, *as is typical in interference through shift*' (emphasis added), and again (1988: 139): 'The argument that the mechanism of interference was shift can be disputed; but we find Lorimer's discussion of this point cogent, and *the fact that the relevant grammatical morphemes themselves are native to Shina suggests interference through shift rather than borrowing*' (emphasis added). That is, Thomason and Kaufman assume that calquing is a feature of shift, but they present no argument in support of this assumption. Unless the shift is abrupt (see pp. 252–3), shifting speakers are very unlikely to impose features of their emblematic language onto their inter-community language, as this would run counter to its use as an inter-community language. If the model I have presented here is even roughly accurate, Shina is not an outcome of shift, but is a Dardic language that has undergone metatypy as a result of its speakers' being bilingual in Burushaski.

Culture contact

Evidence of culture contact takes the form of words borrowed by speakers of culture A's language from culture B's, often for items and concepts for which the former has no direct translation equivalent. The classic case of modern culture contact is Japanese, which borrowed English words extensively at a time when few Japanese were bilingual in English. A somewhat older and more extreme case is Maltese, with its large component of Italian vocabulary (Drewes 1994). In these two cases, we also have independent evidence of culture contact. However, we can also use borrowed vocabulary to reconstruct culture contact. One example is the third SCE in the case study, where the evidence consists entirely of borrowed words. Another is Napolskikh's (1994) reconstruction of contact between (pre-)Tocharian and early Uralic in the 2nd millennium BC.

Although the basic mark of culture contact is vocabulary borrowing, however, extensive borrowing can also have an impact on the morphology and phonology of the recipient language. The impact on the morphological system occurs when a number of pairs of words are borrowed, one of which consists of a root, the other of the root plus a derivational morpheme. English -*tion* entered the language in this way via French and Latin borrowings and the incorporation into the English lexicon of pairs like *act/action* and *perfect/perfection*.

Borrowing impacts a language's phonological system as speakers try to approximate the phoneme distinctions in borrowed words. Thus Tagalog, now the (Austronesian) national language of the Philippines, had just three vowels /i a u/ before contact with the West, but under the impact of Spanish (and now also English) borrowings it now has the five-vowel system of Spanish: /i e a o u/. This in turn has complicated Tagalog's verbal morphophonemics. Other cases where borrowing has affected phonology include Medieval English (where the phonemes /v ð z ǰ/ entered the system through borrowings from French (Pyles 1971: 125–6, 159–60), twentieth-century Japanese (through English borrowings), Soviet Eskimo (through Russian borrowings), southern Welsh (through English borrowings) (Thomason and Kaufman 1976, Thomason and Kaufman 1988: 33, 38, 54, 102, 124) and Fagauvea (a Polynesian language which has borrowed heavily from Iaai, an Austronesian language of the Loyalty Islands; Ozanne-Rivierre 1994). The Nguni and Sotho-Tswana groups of Bantu languages have click phonemes, evidently as a result of extensive borrowing from neighbouring Khoisan languages (Alexandre 1977: 35).

Complex contact histories

I have treated metatypy and culture contact as separate phenomena because they can and do occur independently of each other: Takia, for example, displays metatypy but relatively little borrowed vocabulary, whilst Japanese has borrowed vocabulary without widespread bilingualism. My view of metatypy and culture contact as independent phenomena is thus somewhat different from Thomason and Kaufman's (1988: 66–76), who take calquing and borrowing to be different points on a cline of 'language maintenance'.

Since metatypy and language shift are alternative outcomes of bilingualism, they cannot affect a single language simultaneously. However, there is sometimes evidence that a language has been affected by both processes at different periods of its history. A likely instance of this is Megleno-Rumanian (northwest of Salonica, Greece). Petrovici (1957: 43–4) argues that all forms of Rumanian (i.e. Balkan Romance) except Istro-Rumanian (north-west Croatia) have acquired an essentially Slav phonological system as the result of the shift of speakers of Slav lects, especially Old or Middle Bulgarian, to Romance speech. This shift must have occurred after the separation of Istro-Rumanian from other lects but before the separation of Daco-Rumanian (ancestor of the language of modern Rumania) from Megleno-Rumanian and Arumanian (spoken in enclaves in north-eastern Greece, Albania and Macedonia), probably sometime between the tenth and twelfth centuries (Rosetti 1973: 169).

At some later date, Megleno-Rumanian copied Bulgarian verbal suffixes, giving Megleno-Rumanian *aflum* 'I find', *afliš* 'you (something.) find' where Daco-Rumanian has *aflu*, *afli* (Thomason and Kaufman 1988: 98, cited from Sandfeld 1938: 59). It is highly unlikely that this is the result of language shift, as shifting speakers typically do not copy the morphology of their emblematic language into their inter-community language (this would impede the very communication for which the inter-community language is used). Rather, this seems to be a case rather like that in southern New Caledonia (see pp. 243–4) where a speech-community uses two or more closely related and structurally congruent languages and there is ongoing metatypy and copying. Speakers treated Megleno-Rumanian and Bulgarian as related lects and used the affixes in the 'wrong' lect (Křepinský 1949; Weinreich [1953] 1963: 32).

One of the best known cases of 'language mixing' in the literature is Ma'a of Tanzania (Goodman 1971; Tucker and Bryan 1974). Ma'a is intriguing, because two rather different accounts of it exist.

Thomason (1983) argues that Ma'a is a South Cushitic language whose speakers migrated south into a Bantu-speaking area, where they became bilingual in the Bantu languages Pare and Shambaa. Forms which mark Ma'a as Cushitic are its pronouns, its possessor suffixes, and the South Cushitic verb 'have' (where Ma'a's Bantu neighbours use a comitative construction). Morphosyntactic features attributable to Bantu are Subject–Verb–Object order (Cushitic order is verb-final) and prepositions (derived from South Cushitic verbs). Thus far, Thomason seems to be describing a paradigm case of metatypy. But Ma'a also has Bantu noun classifier prefixes and verbal agreement prefixes. Thomason suggests that the classifiers have been borrowed with the nouns they are attached to. Since verbal agreement prefixes in Bantu match the nominal classifier prefixes in form, their borrowing would also be a consequence of the borrowing of nouns. Ma'a also shows phonological features which seem due to the borrowing of Bantu vocabulary, having phonemic tone and contrasts between prenasalized and plain voiced stops and between voiced stops and voiced fricatives (Thomason 1983: 202–4).

Recent research by Mous (1994), however, shows a different picture. Ma'a is evidently a register of the Mbugu language, itself a Bantu language closely related to Pare. A register is a speech style used by speakers in particular circumstances. In this case, all speakers of Ma'a are native speakers of Mbugu, but switch to Ma'a among themselves. Ma'a is the Bantu language Mbugu with much of its vocabulary replaced by Cushitic items. Mous infers that Ma'a is a consciously created register, used by its speakers 'to set themselves apart from their neighbours'. He does not say much more about the origins of Ma'a, but one is left to infer that the ancestors of the Ma'a may have spoken a Cushitic language, and then gradually shifted to a Bantu lect. Despite the shift, however, they maintained their identity by using an emblematic register of Mbugu with vocabulary from their old emblematic language.

The Ma'a case is salutary: Thomason (and I, when I first read her account) sought to explain away the presence of Bantu morphology and phonology, as it is inconvenient for an explanation based on metatypy, but Mous's on-the-spot research generated a rather different account. Although the two accounts assume much the same underlying history of ethnic contact, their interpretations of the data say quite different things about the genesis of Ma'a. The language's significant feature is that it consists essentially of Bantu syntax, morphology and phonology, but Cushitic vocabulary. This constellation of features does not reflect language shift, although shift probably occurred. The function served by the vocabulary in this constellation is emblematic: it serves as a link with traditional ethnicity, and also asserts its speakers' difference from their neighbours as an esoteric lect does (see p. 239). There is some evidence that Media Lengua of Ecuador, basically Quechua with Spanish vocabulary, is a similar phenomenon: it is emblematic of a group of Indians who find themselves midway between rural Quechua and urban Spanish cultures (Muysken 1994).

Having drawn attention to the need for good data and on-the-spot research, I will resist the temptation to interpret any more cases of contact-induced change. It should be noted, however, that many languages show the marks of contact, neglected though these have been by the linguistic comparative method. The contributors to Bakker and Mous (1994) describe thirteen more 'mixed languages' in addition to Ma'a and Media Lengua, not to mention the numerous cases referred to by Thomason and Kaufman (1988), and each of them has a story to tell about its speakers.

ESTABLISHING THE EXISTENCE OF A PHYLUM

Much of the preceding discussion of the use of linguistic evidence to reconstruct SCEs presupposes the concept of the 'phylum', i.e. a set of related languages descended from a proto-language like Proto-Indo-European or Proto-Austronesian (and not definitely known to be related to any language outside the phylum). Language fissure, lectal differentiation and linkage breaking are the events through which a proto-language diversifies into a phylum. Linkage rejoining, emblematic feature spread, and koineization each depend on the affected lects being members of the same phylum. Esoterogeny often takes place because a lect's speakers want to separate themselves off from speakers of related lects, and we have seen that contact-induced change takes a somewhat different form from usual when the lects in which speakers are bilingual are closely related.

It thus comes as something of a shock to recognize that the question of how we demonstrate that a group of languages constitutes a phylum is still controversial. We can see the fundamental difficulty in establishing a phylum if we refer back to Figure 13.6. The relationship of B1, B2 and B3 is established by the innovations which they share relative to AB, but the relationship of A and B cannot be established by innovations relative to anything, as there is only one node above them – namely, AB itself. That is, a phylum, however small, is not an innovation-defined subgroup. Of course, it can be assumed that the proto-language at the top of a family tree is descended from some other unknown, as yet unreconstructed, language, but this is of no help in establishing the relatedness of the languages in a phylum. So how does the linguistic prehistorian establish a phylum?

A traditional answer – and the one on which Indo-European was founded – is that a phylum is initially established by finding morphological paradigms which occur in each language and which are all regularly descended from the morphological paradigms of a common proto-language. In Indo-European languages, such paradigms are the verb suffixes which mark the person and number of the subject, or the noun suffixes which mark a noun's case and number. However, this answer is necessarily incomplete, since some Indo-European languages have evidently lost the relevant suffixes but no one doubts that they are Indo-European, and since in some phyla, especially in east and south-east Asia, all or many member languages have no morphological paradigms at all.

Nichols (1996) points out that the significant feature of a morphological paradigm is that it is 'individual-identifying'; in other words, 'its probability of multiple independent occurrence among the world's languages is so low that for practical purposes it can be regarded as unique and individual'. Thus any individual-identifying evidence is diagnostic of phylic relationship. Although English has lost much of the morphological apparatus that uniquely identifies Indo-European, it retains enough morphology to provide individual-identifying evidence of its phylic membership. In some Asian languages, with little or no morphology and with basic forms of just one syllable, the only individual-identifying evidence that can be produced to demonstrate relationship consists in large sets of regularly related words, especially in basic vocabulary. Whilst such evidence of relationship is generally accepted, it is weaker than morphological evidence simply because words are more subject to borrowing than are bound morphemes (prefixes, suffixes, vowel alternations like *sing/sang/sung*, etc.).

Once a phylum has been established, we often find that new member languages are progressively discovered by linguists as the number of recognized individual-identifying features grows. We also need to recognize, however, that the evidence for some macro-phyla is quite unconvincing because it does not meet the criterion of being individual-identifying. Collections of supposedly related words which show superficial similarity but which do not show regular semantic and sound correspondences fail to meet the individual-identifying criterion because they can arise by chance (Ringe 1992). (For a different view, see Ruhlen 1994.)

PIDGINIZATION AND CREOLIZATION

A great deal has been written in recent years about pidginization and creolization, and they are often inappropriately invoked to explain phenomena which are due to bilingualism (see pp. 240–7). We have seen here that contact phenomena usually entail gradual change, so that even when language shift occurs there is still continuity from one variety/stage of the language to the next. There are, however, circumstances in which glottogenesis (see pp. 209–10) does occur; that is, a new language is generated abruptly. These take several forms.

One of these is illustrated by Pacific Pidgin, whose reconstructible history is roughly as follows. During the late eighteenth and early nineteenth centuries, Pacific islanders served on merchant vessels plying the Pacific. They acquired varieties of the unstable English-based nautical jargon used on these ships, as well as something of the pidgin used between Australian aborigines and whites in Sydney, and out of these developed early Pacific Pidgin, used at various trading posts and plantations in the Pacific. When Pacific islanders were recruited (in some cases virtually abducted) to work on plantations in Queensland and Samoa from around 1865, these jargon varieties were used for communication between speakers of different languages. In the course of their use between speakers of different Oceanic Austronesian languages, first from Vanuatu, then from the Solomons and the New Guinea islands, these varieties stabilized into a form whose grammar was a simplified version of the morphosyntactic structures of north and central Vanuatu and south-east Solomons languages and whose vocabulary was from seamen's jargon and (directly or indirectly) English. The resulting 'Pacific Pidgin' was taken home by returning labourers and underwent language fissure, so that Pacific Pidgin has today become a number of languages: Tok Pisin, Solomons Pijin, Vanuatu Bislama, and Torres Straits Broken. The basic sources of this account (which is not entirely uncontroversial) are Clark (1979), Keesing (1988) and Goulden (1990).

This history is often labelled the 'pidginization' stage. It has been followed by 'creolization'; that is, each version of Pacific Pidgin has become the native language of some speakers. It sometimes seems to be assumed that stabilization takes place when the language is creolized/'nativized', but this is not true of Pacific Pidgin, which had already stabilized by the beginning of the twentieth century. It is true, however, that creolization has probably been the spur to the development of mechanisms to generate new vocabulary from existent resources (Mühlhäusler 1979).

Thomason and Kaufman (1988: 48) speak of cases of 'abrupt creolisation' where the language did not develop from a pidgin but from 'extreme unsuccessful acquisition of a T[arget] L[anguage]'. The faster the shift, they argue, the greater the likelihood of imperfect learning of the target language and the imposition upon it of features of speakers' native languages (1988: 41, 47). Most known cases of abrupt creolization have arisen in slaving situations, where people found themselves unable to use or limited in their use of their native languages and were compelled to use the language of their masters, to which, however, they had only limited access. The resulting contact language becomes the primary language of the community without ever stabilizing as a pidgin (i.e. as a functionally restricted inter-community language) (1988: 150). In such cases various demographic factors have important effects on the structure of the resulting creole (1988: 155–8). The Portuguese-based creoles of the Gulf of Guinea are probably cases of abrupt creolization (for details see Ferraz 1976, 1983; Thomason and Kaufman 1988: 151–8).

Whatever the exact process by which creolization occurs, the SCE it reflects entails the cataclysmic removal of people from their social networks into a situation where a new social network is formed among speakers who have no common language and who are forced by circumstances to draw for their medium of communication either on a current jargon or on the fragments of a language that they share in common (cf. Mühlhäusler 1985; Whinnom 1971). The features from which creolization can be reconstructed are a combination of the structure and phonology of two or more languages, together with simplification and regularization, and vocabulary from a third language. At first sight, this is difficult to distinguish from the effects of metatypy, where vocabulary has one source, morphosyntactic structure another – and this is why creolization has sometimes been inappropriately invoked in the reconstruction of language change. But the morphosyntactic structure of a pidgin/creole undergoes simplification and regularization, whereas, for example, Takia verbal morphology shows no such signs of simplification. A particularly subtle reconstruction of creolization is given by Roberge (1993), who argues on the basis of features which survive in the Orange River Afrikaans lect that there was once a Cape Dutch Creole, whose structure owed some of its features to (African) Khoisan languages.

Before I leave this topic, I will note that Pacific Pidgin illustrates nicely that a developed pidgin or a creole can father a language phylum just as readily as any other language can. It can also be the inter-community language in metatypy (see p. 245) and language shift (see p. 252).

CONCLUDING OBSERVATIONS

The social network model allows us to capture within one framework the various kinds of reconstructible SCE: reshapings of network structure (see pp. 215–31), the adoption or avoidance of socially significant features (see pp. 231–40), the effects of the use of more than one language within a network (see pp. 240–50), and abrupt language generation (see pp. 251–3). Each event type is detectable by different kinds of language change, and I hope I have shown that the linguistic prehistorian has the tools to reconstruct quite an inventory of SCEs. This inventory includes a number of SCEs which one might describe as 'rhizotic': the transmission of innovations across lectal boundaries (see pp. 222–5, 232–8), reintegration of lects and linkages (see pp. 228–31, 236–8), changes due to bilingualism (see pp. 240–50), and glottogenesis (see pp. 251–3). Of these, only the last is indisputably rhizotic. But the social network analysis presented here shows that there are marked differences among these processes, and the issue of whether they are 'cladistic' or 'rhizotic' boils down quite simply to the definition of terms – and this is a fruitless endeavour, given that the social network approach provides a much finer grained classification of SCEs than this simple dichotomy can.

There are a number of issues in the reconstruction of linguistic prehistory in a social network framework which I have not addressed here, and which need to be addressed. It is known, for example, that community size and social network structure affect the enforcement of linguistic norms (Milroy 1980/1987: Ch. 7) and that linguistic innovators occupy particular kinds of position in the social network (Milroy and Milroy 1985). Related to this is the apparent fact that linguistic change is correlated with social upheaval, so that the languages of groups whose social networks remain *in situ* and undergo little structural change tend to be conservative. I say 'apparent fact' because this point has received little attention and little acceptance, powerful though it can be in reconstructing a sequence of SCEs (Ross 1991 is an example of its application).

It is obvious that the social network diagram cannot replace the family tree as a means of representation. A social network diagram presents a single SCE; a tree represents an event sequence. A well-supported family tree drawn according to explicit conventions has important functions beyond the presentation of event sequences and of the subgroups that are their outcomes. Without the subgrouping hypothesis that a tree represents, we cannot determine what words are reconstructible in the proto-language. Thus in Figure 13.17 we would reconstruct a word in AB only if it were reflected in one of the languages A1, A2, A3 *and* in one of B1, B2, B3. But if we did not know how these six languages subgrouped, we could make the error of reconstructing a word in AB on the basis of, say, reflexes from A1 and A3, from which we should be reconstructing the word only in A.

An inspection of the distribution of reflexes of reconstructed roots given by Bird (1982) shows how this problem bedevils Indo-European. Some of the root distributions given in his Table 2 cannot satisfy the criteria for reconstructing a Proto-Indo-European word, but without a subgrouping we cannot tell which distributions. (In fairness to students of Indo-European

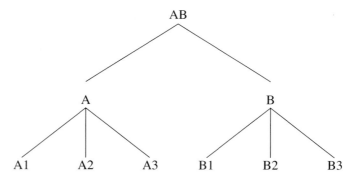

Figure 13.17 A subgrouping example.

linguistic prehistory, it should be recalled from p. 224 that Proto-Indo-European may well have differentiated into a linkage, and this complicates the setting of criteria for reconstructive adequacy.) Obviously, knowing what is and is not reconstructible in a proto-language has vital relevance to the *Wörter und Sachen* technique.

A well-argued tree is also crucial to locating the homeland of a proto-language. The first node of the Austronesian family tree splits into several groups of languages spoken on the island of Taiwan and a single group, Malayo-Polynesian, comprising the hundreds of Austronesian languages spoken outside Taiwan. If one accepts the tree, then it is a reasonable inference that Proto-Austronesian was spoken on Taiwan (Ross 1995). By similar reasoning, Goddard (1994) has argued for an Algonquian homeland well to the west of the Great Lakes, where Blackfoot is spoken today, rather than on the lakes themselves, where Siebert's (1967) application of the *Wörter und Sachen* approach would put it. Goddard's conclusion is apparently borne out by the archaeological evidence (Denny 1991). The Austronesian and Algonquian cases exemplify a long-recognized rule of thumb: the area of a phylum which shows the greatest diversity is likely to be its homeland (Dyen 1956; Sapir 1916).

Whether or not the social network model stands the tests of time and use in the form presented here, the fundamental point that there is a causal relationship between particular kinds of SCE and particular kinds of patterning of linguistic innovations is vital to the practice of linguistic prehistory. It is this causality that allows the linguistic prehistorian to diagnose a SCE from linguistic evidence. Because this is so, it is important that further research take place into determining the relationships between various SCEs and linguistic innovations within the framework of an integrated social and socio-linguistic model – otherwise we shall find ourselves describing changes in language and merely guessing at the SCEs behind them.

As an important adjunct to this programme, the linguistic prehistorian needs to know from the archaeologist what the archaeological reflexes of various SCEs might be. In some cases, the answers are fairly obvious; in others, they are less so. But the relationship between linguistic prehistory and archaeology is not simply one of correlation; it may also be one of complementation. The reconstruction of SCEs can provide information about those communities which is less available to the archaeologist, and vice versa.

NOTES

1 I am grateful to Peter Bellwood, Roger Blench, John Lynch, Andrew Pawley and Matthew Spriggs for their comments on an earlier draft of this chapter.
2 The terms 'innovation-defined' and 'innovation-linked' were originally devised to characterize the subgroups of Oceanic Austronesian languages (Pawley and Ross 1995). Elsewhere I have used the terms 'family' and 'linkage' (with 'chain' and 'network' as configurations of linkage), respectively, for an innovation-defined and

an innovation-linked subgroup (Ross 1988: 8), but these terms have other connotations for linguists; 'innovation-defined' and 'innovation-linked' are more transparent, even if a little clumsy. I retain 'linkage' as shorthand for an innovation-linked subgroup, avoiding the term 'network', since the latter has received a new lease of life as an abbreviation of 'social network'.

3 I am grateful to John Lynch for making me recognize that language fusion *does* occur: I had omitted it from earlier drafts of this chapter.

4 The Milroys distinguish between speaker 'innovation' and language 'change'. Substantively, this is an important distinction, but I have not adopted their terms as this would entail a redefinition of 'innovation', a basic term in historical linguistics.

REFERENCES

Alexandre, P. 1977. *An Introduction to Languages and Language in Africa.* (trans. F.A. Leary). London: Heinemann.

Allen, J. and C. Gosden (eds). 1991. *Report of the Lapita Homeland Project.* Occasional Papers in Prehistory 20. Canberra: Department of Prehistory, Research School of Pacific Studies, Australian National University.

Andersen, H. 1988. Centre and periphery: adoption, diffusion and spread. In *Historical Dialectology*, J. Fisiak (ed.), 39–85. Berlin: Mouton de Gruyter.

Bakker, P. and M. Mous (eds). 1994. *Mixed Languages: 15 Case Studies in Language Intertwining.* Studies in Language and Language Use 13. Amsterdam: Institute for Functional Research into Language and Language Use (IFOTT).

Barbour, S. and P. Stevenson. 1990. *Variation in German: a critical approach to German sociolinguistics.* Cambridge: Cambridge University Press.

Bellwood, P. 1995. Ethnogenesis: the significance of scale. Unpublished ms.

Bellwood, P. in press. The archaeology of Papuan and Austronesian prehistory in the northern Moluccas, Eastern Indonesia. In *Archaeology and Language II*, Roger Blench and Matthew Spriggs (eds). London: Routledge.

Bird, N. 1982. *The Distribution of Indo-European Root Morphemes: a checklist for philologists.* Wiesbaden: Harrassowitz.

Blust, R.A. 1977. The Proto-Austronesian pronouns and Austronesian subgrouping: a preliminary report. *University of Hawaii Working Papers in Linguistics* 9(2), 1–15.

Blust, R.A. 1978. Eastern Malayo-Polynesian: a subgrouping argument. In *Second International Conference on Austronesian Linguistics: proceedings*, S. A. Wurm and L. Carrington (eds), 181–234. Canberra: Pacific Linguistics C-61. Australian National University.

Blust, R.A. 1993. Central and Central-Eastern Malayo-Polynesian. *Oceanic Linguistics* 32, 241–93.

Bomhard, A.R. and J.C. Kerns. 1994. *The Nostratic Macrofamily: a study in distant linguistic relationship.* Berlin: Mouton de Gruyter.

Boretzky, N. 1984. The Indo-Europeanist model of sound change and genetic affinity, and change in exotic languages. *Diachronica* 1, 1–51.

Burling, R. 1966. The addition of final stops in the history of Maru (Tibeto-Burman). *Language*, 42: 581–6.

Burrow, T. 1971. Spontaneous cerebrals in Sanskrit. *Bulletin of the School of Oriental and African Studies* 34, 538–59.

Cavalli-Sforza, L.L., A. Piazza, P. Menozzi and J. Mountain. 1988. Reconstruction of human evolution: bringing together genetic, archaeological and linguistic data. *Proceedings of the National Academy of Science of the USA* 85, 6002–6.

Chambers, J.K. and P. Trudgill. 1980. *Dialectology*. Cambridge: Cambridge University Press.

Clark, R. 1979. In search of Beach-la-Mar: towards a history of Pacific Pidgin English. *Te Reo* 22, 3–64.

Denison, N. 1977. Language death or language suicide? *International Journal of the Sociology of Language* 12, 13–22.

Denison, N. 1988. Language contact and language norm. *Folia Linguistica* 22, 11–35.

Denny, J.P. 1991. The Algonquian migration from Plateau to Midwest: linguistics and archaeology. In *Papers of the 22nd Algonquian Conference*, W. Cowan (ed.), 103–24. Ottawa: Carleton University.

Drewes, A.J. 1994. Borrowing in Maltese. In *Mixed languages: 15 case studies in language intertwining*, P. Bakker and M. Mous (eds), 83–111. Studies in Language and Language Use 13. Amsterdam: Institute for Functional Research into Language and Language Use (IFOTT).

Dyen, I. 1956. Language distribution and migration theory. *Language* 32, 611–26.

Ferraz, L. 1976. The substratum of Annabonese Creole. *International Journal of the Sociology of Language* 7, 37–47.

Ferraz, L. 1983. The origin and development of four creoles in the Gulf of Guinea. In *The Social Context of Creolization*, E. Woolford and W. Washabaugh (eds), 120–5. Ann Arbor, Mich.: Karoma.

Gamkrelidze, T.V. and V.V. Ivanov. 1990. The early history of Indo-European languages. *Scientific American* 262(3), 82–9.

Geraghty, P. 1983. *The History of the Fijian Languages*. Oceanic Linguistics special publication No. 19. Honolulu: University of Hawaii Press.

Goddard, I. 1994. The west-to-east cline in Algonquian dialectology. In *Actes du vingt-cinquième congrès des Algonquinistes*, W. Cowan (ed.), 187–211. Ottawa: Carleton University.

Goodman, M. 1971. The strange case of Mbugu. In *Pidginization and Creolization of Languages*, D. Hymes (ed.), 243–54. Cambridge: Cambridge University Press.

Goulden, R.J. 1990. *The Melanesian Content in Tok Pisin*. Pacific Linguistics B-104. Canberra: Australian National University.

Grace, G.W. 1975. Linguistic diversity in the Pacific: on the sources of diversity. Paper presented to the Thirteenth Pacific Science Congress, Vancouver.

Grace, G.W. 1981. *An Essay on Language*. Columbia, SC: Hornbeam.

Grace, G.W. 1996. Regularity of change in what? In *The Comparative Method Reviewed: irregularity and regularity in language change*, M. Durie and M.D. Ross (eds), 157–79. New York: Oxford University Press.

Gumperz, J.J. and R. Wilson. 1971. Convergence and creolization: a case from the Indo-Aryan/Dravidian border. In *Pidginization and Creolization of Languages*, D. Hymes (ed.), 151–68. Cambridge: Cambridge University Press.

Haase, M. 1992. *Sprachkontakt und Sprachwandel im Baskenland: Einflüsse des Gaskognischen und Französischen auf das Baskische*. Hamburg: Buske.

Haase, M. 1993. *Le Gascon des Basques: contribution à la théorie des substrats*. Arbeiten zur Mehrsprachigkeit 50. Arbeitsstelle Mehrsprachigkeit, Germanisches Seminar, Universität Hamburg, Hamburg.

Haiman, J. 1988. Rhaeto-Romance. In *The Romance Languages*, M. Harris and N. Vincent (eds), 351–90. London: Croom Helm.

Harris, M. 1988. The Romance languages. In *The Romance Languages*, M. Harris and N. Vincent (eds), 1–25. London: Croom Helm.

Hines, J. 1990. Philology, archaeology and the *adventus Saxonum vel Anglorum*. In *Britain 400–600: language and history*, A. Bammesberger and A. Wollmann (eds), 17–36. Heidelberg: Carl Winter.

Hines, J. 1995. Focus and boundary in linguistic varieties in the North-West Germanic continuum. In *Friesische Studien II: Beiträge des Föhrer Symposiums für Friesische*

Philologie vom 7.-8. April 1994, V.F. Faltings, A.G.H. Walker, and O. Wilts (eds), 35–62. North-Western European Language Evolution Supplement 12. Odense: Odense University Press.

Hock, H.H. 1986. *Principles of Historical Linguistics*. Berlin: Mouton de Gruyter.

Johnson, S. 1990. Social parameters of linguistic change in an unstratified Aboriginal society. In *Linguistic Change and Reconstruction Methodology*, P. Baldi (ed.), 419–33. Berlin: Mouton de Gruyter.

Joseph, B.D. 1983. *The Synchrony and Diachrony of the Balkan Infinitive: a study in areal, general and historical linguistics*. Cambridge: Cambridge University Press.

Keesing, R.M. 1988. *Melanesian Pidgin and the Oceanic Substrate*. Stanford: Stanford University Press.

Keller, R. 1990. *Sprachwandel*. Tübingen: Francke.

König, W. 1978. *dtv-Atlas zur deutschen Sprache*. München: Deutscher Taschenbuch Verlag.

Křepinský, M. 1949. Réponse à la Question IV. In *Actes du Sixième Congrès Internationale des Linguistes*, Paris: Klincksieck.

Labov, W. 1980. The social origins of sound change. In *Locating Language in Space and Time*, W. Labov (ed.), 251–65. New York: Academic Press.

Labov, W. 1981. Resolving the Neogrammarian controversy. *Language* 57, 267–308.

Labov, W. and W. Harris. 1986. De facto segregation of black and white vernaculars. In *Diversity and Diachrony*, D. Sankoff (ed.), 1–24. Amsterdam: John Benjamins.

Le Page, R.B. and A. Tabouret-Keller. 1985. *Acts of Identity: creole-based approaches to language and ethnicity*. Cambridge: Cambridge University Press.

Lorimer, D.L.R. 1937. Burushaski and its alien neighbours: problems in linguistic contagion. *Transactions of the Philological Society*, 63–98.

Lynch, J. and P. Tepahae in press. Digging up the linguistic past: the lost language(s) of Aneityum, Vanuatu. In *Archaeology and Language III*, R. Blench and M. Spriggs (eds). London: Routledge.

Milroy, J. 1992. *Linguistic Variation and Change: on the historical sociolinguistics of English*. Oxford: Blackwell.

Milroy, J. 1993. On the social origins of language change. In *Historical linguistics: problems and perspectives*, C. Jones. (ed.), 215–36. London: Longman.

Milroy, J. and L. Milroy. 1985. Linguistic change, social network and speaker innovation. *Journal of Linguistics* 21, 339–84.

Milroy, L. 1980. *Language and Social Networks*. Oxford: Basil Blackwell.

Milroy, L. 1987. *Language and Social Networks* (2nd edn). Oxford: Blackwell.

Milroy, L. and J. Milroy. 1992. Social network and social class: toward an integrated sociolinguistic model. *Language in Society* 21, 1–26.

Moag, R.F. 1977. *Fiji Hindi: a basic course and reference grammar*. Canberra: Australian National University Press.

Moore, C.C. and A.K. Romney. 1994. Material culture, geographic propinquity, and linguistic affiliation on the north coast of New Guinea: a reanalysis of Welsch, Terrell, and Nadolski (1972). *American Anthropologist* 96, 370–96.

Moore, J.H. 1994a. Ethnogenetic theory. *Research and Exploration* 10, 10–23.

Moore, J.H. 1994b. Putting anthropology back together again: the ethnogenetic critique of cladistic theory. *American Anthropologist* 96, 925–48.

Mous, M. 1994. Ma'a or Mbugu. In *Mixed Languages: 15 case studies in language intertwining*, P. Bakker and M. Mous (eds), 175–200. Studies in Language and Language Use 13. Amsterdam: Institute for Functional Research into Language and Language Use (IFOTT).

Mühlhäusler, P. 1979. *Growth and Structure of the Lexicon of New Guinea Pidgin*. Pacific Linguistics C-52. Canberra: Australian National University.

Mühlhäusler, P. 1985. Patterns of contact, mixture, creation and nativization: their contribution to a general theory of language. In *Developmental Mechanisms of*

Language, C.-J. N. Bailey and R. Harris (eds), 51–88. Oxford: Pergamon Press.

Muysken, P. 1994. Media Lengua. In *Mixed Languages: 15 case studies in language intertwining*, P. Bakker and M. Mous (eds), 207–11. Studies in Language and Language Use 13. Amsterdam: Institute for Functional Research into Language and Language Use (IFOTT).

Napolskikh, V.V. 1994. Uralic and Tokharian: evidence and archaeological data. Paper presented to the WAC-3, New Delhi.

Nichols, J. 1996. The comparative method as heuristic. In *The Comparative Method Reviewed: irregularity and regularity in linguistic change*, M. Durie and M. D. Ross (eds), 39–71. New York: Oxford University Press.

Ozanne-Rivierre, F. 1994. Iaai loanwords and phonemic changes in Fagauvea. In *Language Contact and Change in the Austronesian World*, T. Dutton and D. Tryon (eds), 523–49. Berlin: Mouton de Gruyter.

Pawley, A.K. and M.D. Ross. 1995. The prehistory of Oceanic languages: a current view. In *The Austronesians: historical and comparative perspectives*, P. Bellwood, J. Fox, and D. Tryon (eds), 39–74. Canberra: Department of Anthropology, Research School of Pacific and Asian Studies, Australian National University.

Petrovici, E. 1957. *Kann das Phonemsystem einer Sprache durch fremden Einfluß umgestaltet werden*? The Hague: Mouton.

Platt, J.T. 1975. The Singapore English speech continuum. *Anthropological Linguistics* 17, 363–74.

Pyles, T. 1971. *The origins and development of the English language* (2nd edn). New York: Harcourt, Brace, Jovanovich.

Renfrew, C. 1987. *The Puzzle of Indo-European Origins*. Cambridge: Cambridge University Press.

Ringe, D.A. 1992. On calculating the factor of chance in language comparison. *Transactions of the American Philosophical Society* 82(1), 1–110.

Roberge, P.T. 1993. *The Formation of Afrikaans. Stellenbosch Papers in Linguistics 27*. Stellenbosch: Department of General Linguistics, University of Stellenbosch.

Rosetti, A. 1973. *Brève histoire de la langue roumaine des origines à nos jours*. The Hague: Mouton.

Ross, M.D. 1985. Current use and expansion of Tok Pisin: effects of Tok Pisin on some vernacular languages. In *Handbook of Tok Pisin (New Guinea Pidgin)*, S.A. Wurm and P. Mühlhäusler (eds), 539–56. Pacific Linguistics C-70. Canberra: Australian National University.

Ross, M.D. 1988. *Proto Oceanic and the Austronesian Languages of Western Melanesia*. Pacific Linguistics C-98. Canberra: Australian National University.

Ross, M.D. 1991. How conservative are sedentary languages? Evidence from western Melanesia. In *Currents in Pacific Linguistics: papers on Austronesian languages and ethnolinguistics in honour of George W. Grace*, R.A. Blust (ed.), 443–51. Pacific Linguistics C-119. Canberra: Australian National University.

Ross, M.D. 1994a. Areal phonological features in north central New Ireland. In *Language Contact and Change in the Austronesian World*, T.E. Dutton and D.T. Tryon (eds), 551–72. Berlin: Mouton de Gruyter.

Ross, M.D. 1994b. Central Papuan culture history: some lexical evidence. In *Austronesian Terminologies: continuity and change*, A. Pawley and M. D. Ross (eds), 389–479. *Pacific Linguistics* C-127. Canberra: Australian National University.

Ross, M.D. 1995. Some current issues in Austronesian linguistics. In *Comparative Austronesian Dictionary* 1, D.T. Tryon (ed.), 45–120. Berlin: Mouton de Gruyter.

Ross, M.D. 1996. Contact-induced change and the comparative method: cases from Papua New Guinea. In *The Comparative Method Reviewed: irregularity and regularity in language change*, M. Durie and M.D. Ross (eds), 180–217. New York: Oxford University Press.

Ross, M.D. in press. Sequencing and dating linguistic events in Oceania: the linguistics/archaeology interface. In *Archaeology and Language II*, R. Blench and M. Spriggs (eds). London: Routledge.

Ross, M.D. and M. Durie. 1996. Introduction. In *The Comparative Method Reviewed: irregularity and regularity in language change*, M. Durie and M.D. Ross (eds). New York: Oxford University Press.

Ruhlen, M. 1994. *The Origin of Language: tracing the evolution of the mother tongue*. New York: John Wiley.

Salisbury, R.F. 1972. The origins of the Tolai people. *Journal of the Papua and New Guinea Society* 6, 79–84.

Sandfeld, K. 1938. Problèmes d'interférences linguistiques. In *Actes du Quatrième Congrès Internationale de Linguistes*, 59–61. Copenhagen: Einar Munksgaard.

Sapir, E. 1916. *Time Perspective in Aboriginal American Culture*. Anthropological Series 13, Memoir 90. Geological Survey, Department of Mines, Ottawa. [Reprinted in D.G. Mandelbaum (ed.) 1949. *Selected Writings of Edward Sapir in Language, Culture and Personality*. Berkeley: University of California Press, pp. 389–462.]

Schadeberg, T.C. 1994. EKoti: between KiSwahili and EMakhuwa. Paper presented to the WAC-3, New Delhi.

Schooling, S. 1990. *Language Maintenance in Melanesia: sociolinguistics and social networks in New Caledonia*. Publications in Linguistics 91. Dallas/Arlington: Summer Institute of Linguistics/University of Texas at Arlington.

Siebert, F.T. 1967. The original home of the Proto-Algonquian people. In *Contributions to Anthropology: Linguistics I (Algonquian)*, A.D. DeBlois (ed.), 13–47. Bulletin 214. Ottawa: National Museum of Canada.

Siegel, J. 1987. *Language Contact in a Plantation Environment: a sociolinguistic history of Fiji*. Cambridge: Cambridge University Press.

Spriggs, M. 1994. From Taiwan to the Tuamotus: absolute dating of Austronesian language spread and major subgroups. Paper presented to the WAC-3, New Delhi.

Szemerényi, O. 1990. *Einführung in die vergleichende Sprachwissenschaft* (4. durchgesehene Auflage). Darmstadt: Wissenschaftliche Buchgesellschaft.

Terrell, J. 1986. *Prehistory in the Pacific Islands*. Cambridge: Cambridge University Press.

Thomason, S.G. 1983. Genetic relationship and the case of Ma'a (Mbugu). *Studies in African Linguistics*, 14: 195–231.

Thomason, S.G. and T.S. Kaufman. 1976. Contact-induced language change: loanwords and the borrowing language's pre-borrowing phonology. In *Current Progress in Historical Linguistics: Proceedings of the Second International Conference on Historical Linguistics, Tucson, Arizona, 12–16 January 1976*, W.M. Christie (ed.), 167–79. Amsterdam: North Holland.

Thomason, S.G. and T.S. Kaufman. 1988. *Language Contact, Creolization and Genetic Linguistics*. Berkeley: University of California Press.

Thurston, W.R. 1987. *Processes of Change in the Languages of North-western New Britain*. Pacific Linguistics B-99. Canberra: Australian National University.

Thurston, W.R. 1989. How exoteric languages build a lexicon: esoterogeny in West New Britain. In *VICAL 1, Oceanic Languages: papers from the Fifth International Conference on Austronesian Linguistics*, R. Harlow and R. Hooper (eds), 555–79. Auckland: Linguistic Society of New Zealand.

Trudgill, P. 1986. *Dialects in Contact*. Oxford: Blackwell.

Tucker, A.N. and M.A. Bryan. 1974. The 'Mbugu' anomaly. *Bulletin of the School of Oriental and African Studies* 37, 188–207.

Voorhoeve, C.L. 1994. Contact-induced change in the non-Austronesian languages in the north Moluccas, Indonesia. In *Language Contact and Change in the Austronesian World*, T. Dutton and D. Tryon (ed.), 649–74. Berlin: Mouton de Gruyter.

Walker, G.P.L., R.F. Heming, T.J. Sprod and H.R. Walker. 1981. Latest major eruptions of Rabaul volcano. In *Cooke-Ravian Volume of Volcanological Papers*, R.W. Johnson (ed.), 181–93. Geological Survey of Papua New Guinea Memoir 10.

Weinreich, U. [1953] 1963. *Languages in Contact*. The Hague: Mouton. [Originally published 1953 by the Linguistic Circle of New York.]

Weinreich, U., W. Labov and M. Herzog. 1968. Empirical foundations for a theory of language change. In *Directions for Historical Linguistics*, W.P. Lehmann and Y. Malkiel (eds), 95–195. Austin: University of Texas Press.

Welsch, R.L., J. Terrell and J.A. Nadolski. 1992. Language and culture on the north coast of New Guinea. *American Anthropologist* 94, 568–600.

Whinnom, K. 1971. Linguistic hybridization and the 'special case' of pidgins and creoles. In *Pidginization and Creolization of Languages*, D. Hymes (ed.), 91–115. Cambridge: Cambridge University Press.

14   Linguistic similarity measures using the minimum message length principle

Anand Raman and Jon Patrick

INTRODUCTION

It is now generally accepted that French and Spanish are both descended from Latin. But is it possible to specify in any objective manner which of these is closer to Latin and by how much? In this chapter,[1] we look at the general problem of deriving (dis)similarity measures between natural languages. Obviously, our results are not intended to be conclusive assertions about such issues, but are only meant to serve as impetus for further study of subgrouping techniques. The method employed is to first form an inductive hypothesis explaining the derivation of words in a child language from those of its parent. The inductive hypothesis is suitably encoded along with its exceptions in observational data, in our case using Probabilistic Finite State Automata (PFSA). We assume that more complex automata are needed to explain the phonological changes between less similar languages. Thus a measure of the complexity of the PFSA would be indicative of the amount of phonological dissimilariy between the languages under consideration.

We also illustrate our technique by applying it to the languages Later North-West Germanic (LNWG), Old Frisian (OF) and Old High German (OHG). The LNWG reconstructions for the OF and OHG words we use are taken from Voyles (1992). The diachronic rules applied to derive OF and OHG forms from the reconstructed ancestor are also taken from the same work.

PREVIOUS WORK

Mathematical methods seeking to quantify one or more aspects of languages are not particulary new. Embleton (1991) describes many earlier approaches along these lines. For example, in Kroeber and Chrétien (1937) we find a quantitative classification of Indo-European languages based on a technique used in ethnography and physical anthropology. The degree of association,

Q, between two languages L1 and L2 is given by:

$$Q = \frac{ad - bc}{\sqrt{[(a+b)(c+d)(a+c)(b+d)]}}$$

where a is the number of features exhibited by both, d is the number of features exhibited by neither, b is the number of features exhibited by L1 and not L2, and c is the number of features exhibited by L2 and not L1. The above formula is called the tetrachoric correlation coefficient or Karl Pearson's tetrachoric R'. The values of Q thus computed allow us to rank the closeness of relationship between L1 and L2. Obviously, the presence or absence of the features under consideration (such as word-final-consonant-devoicing in German) must be unambiguously decidable and it is of importance for statistical significance that the features also be independent of each other. These, coupled with the additional problem of reconstructing features in the proto-language in order to determine the value of d, beset the method with practical and conceptual difficulties and other methods were suggested to overcome these problems. Embleton reviews a related technique in Ross (1950) which was shown to be a disguised variation of the Kroeber model that did not account for d.

Other lexicostatistical methods which attempt to reconstruct family trees have also been proposed. A common thread that links these methods is the use of cognate (words with a common ancestor in two or more languages) counts to derive a degree of relatedness. An instance of such an approach applied to linguistics can be found in Henrici (1973); it employs hierarchical cluster analysis, a method popular in numerical taxonomy. A family tree is reconstructed for a set of languages based upon the number of cognate and non-cognate items each has in a given word list. The motivation for this word list itself comes from earlier work by Morris Swadesh who popularized a technique called glottochronology for linguistic subgrouping. Stimulated by the achievements of the radiocarbon dating technique in archaeology, Swadesh undertook studies of rate of vocabulary change. Swadesh (1952) suggested that it was possible to date the separations of languages by incorporating the idea of radioactive decay into the process of vocabulary turnover.

Although glottochronology seems to have fallen into disrepute now, as expounded originally by Swadesh, it still remains one of the earliest mathematical methods that attempted to classify languages with a reasonable degree of success. It is noteworthy, however, that its origin goes back much earlier than 1951. It is likely that Swadesh himself developed it from a suggestion originally made by his teacher Edward Sapir (1916): 'The greater the degree of linguistic differentiation within a stock, the greater is the time that must be assumed for the development of such differentiation.'

Hymes (1971) traces anticipations of this technique even further back to Captain J. Dumont d'Urville (1790–1842), a French explorer who chanced to come upon the work of a certain self-styled professor called Constantin

Rafinesque (1783–1840). D'Urville was part of a committee to decide the best paper for a competition on the topic of 'The origin of the Asiatic Negroes'. Rafinesque had mailed d'Urville a paper titled 'Languages do not lie' and a subsection of it outlined:

> *a procedure by which to appreciate at a glance the diverse degrees of identity and affinity that can be established between two languages, of which a certain number of words common to both are known.*

Here then, we have one of the earliest foretastes of the glottochronological technique. Its subsequent refinement by Swadesh had led to some degree of success in dating language separations, which caught the attention of a good many contemporary linguists. Sarah Gudchinsky, who gave one of the clearest expositions of the technique, hails it as novel and useful (Gudchinsky 1956). Essentially, glottochronology makes the following basic assumptions:

- some parts of a vocabulary (core-words) change less rapidly than others (Swadesh 1951);
- the rate of replacement of words in this core-word list is constant through time;
- the rate of loss of items from this list is the same for all languages.

Given these assumptions, it is reasonably easy to derive the relation in Lees (1953)

$$t = \frac{\log c}{2 \log r}$$

where t is the time-depth of separation in millennia, r is the rate of retention of words in any core-word list (assumed constant at 85 per cent per millennium), and c is the percentage of common cognates in two given core-word lists. An example will serve to clarify this further. Let us assume that the five-word lists given in Table 14.1 are used for English and German. This gives us a 60 per cent agreement in the two word lists, allowing us to calculate $t = 1.561$ millennia. That is, German and English started diverging from each other approximately 1,561 years ago, around AD 433.

This is remarkable indeed, or so it was considered for a while. But the premises are not indisputable and glottochronology has come under heavy criticism from many quarters. A devastating critique of its fundamental postulate

Table 14.1 Comparison of English and German

English	German	Score
Animal	Tier	✗
Four	Vier	✓
Head	Kopf	✗
I	Ich	✓
Sun	Sonne	✓

that the rate of change of items in the basic vocabulary is the same for all languages was published in Bergsland and Vogt (1962), and Chrétien (1962) strongly criticized the mathematics originally examined by Lees (1953). But several other approaches have been more forgiving. Particularly relevant to our chapter are criticisms levelled at the technique which seek to modify one or more aspects of it to make it more acceptable. Among these may be included Gleason (1959) and Sankoff (1972) which sought to modify the mathematics involved. Ultimately, this resulted in a revised formula which incorporated stochasticity into the model and allowed for chance cognation and borrowing into the test list. Embleton (1981) also concerns itself with incorporating borrowing of items into the original core-word list. But glottochronology was now deviating more and more from its original simple formulation and it is noteworthy that Sankoff observed that more complex models offered little or no predictive advantage over the simpler ones. Thus a fallback to earlier proposals or the introduction of fundamental revisions was inevitable.

Our technique, which it is appropriate to introduce now, is one such revision. It more closely resembles the work of Kroeber and Chrétien outlined earlier than glottochronology as it stands, but it borrows important aspects from both of them while enhancing the basic approach. It is based on the assumption that more distant languages are correspondingly likely to be phonologically dissimilar in their cognates. In other words, we attempt to quantify the amount of phonological dissimilarity between cognates and their ancestors in two languages and use this measure to suggest language kinships.

The procedure involved is this: given a pair of related languages L1 and L2, and a set of diachronic phonological rules deriving phonemes in L2 from those in L1, we collect a finite sample of word transformations[2] from L1 to L2. The words chosen for this purpose come from Swadesh's basic vocabulary for L1. The fact that we use the Swadesh list for this instead of an arbitrary list of words is significant. The choice guarantees (assuming Swadesh's conjectures) that the changes affecting the words in the list are as a result of internal effects and not likely to be due to borrowing. Hence it is more likely that our derivations using diachronic rules are correct.

Using this finite sample of transformations, we extrapolate and construct an inductive hypothesis H that tries to explain a general way in which words in L2 can be derived from corresponding ones in L1. The size of the hypothesis H when encoded using a suitable scheme indicates to a reasonable extent its complexity and hence the distance between L1 and L2.

In the case of two languages L2 and L3, both related to a common parent L1, it is possible using our method to get a reasonable estimate of the relative closeness of either language to the parent by deriving H12 and H13, two hypotheses which explain the phonological evolutions between each pair of languages L1, L2 and L1, L3 and comparing their sizes. Here, it is important that we use the same set of words in both models. It will guarantee a greater accuracy of comparison. We demonstrate this empirically for Old Frisian, Old High German and Later North-west Germanic later in this chapter. Unfortunately, however, the Swadesh list for OF, OHG and a reconstructed one for LNWG were not completed at the time of writing. Thus the choice of words used is somewhat arbitrary, though identical, in the two examples. Nevertheless, they represent a variety of combinations of consonants and vowels and serve to illustrate well the procedure involved in constructing such a model.

MODELLING INDUCTIVE HYPOTHESES

As the task at hand involves the modelling of an inductive hypothesis derived from a finite sample of word transformations, it remains to be explained just how such inductive hypotheses may be modelled. To do this, we first consider the nature of hypotheses in general. An inductive hypothesis can be said to be an abstraction of a set of observations. The problem of abstracting such a structure (a pattern of occurrence) from a given set of observations is ancient and fundamental (Gaines 1976), but the process itself has undergone little conceptual change in centuries. The abstraction, in general, consists of two parts (Georgeff and Wallace 1984):

- a statement of the hypothesis itself encoded in a suitable language, and
- a specification of the data given this hypothesis.

Under normal circumstances, the data specification part is dominated by exceptions to the hypothesis because confirmations, which are already implicit in the hypothesis, can typically be stated succinctly. It may be that the hypothesis is accurate and that there are no exceptions to it, in which case the data specification part will be very concise. In general, a good hypothesis will minimize the second component of the abstraction.

One of the ways in which the hypothesis can be stated is as a list of the probabilities of occurence of each data item. The data items can then be specified using these probabilities, assigning the shortest code to the most probable symbol in the data and the longest code to the least probable symbol. Assuming that the symbols are encoded using an alphabet with n unique symbols, information theory guidelines (Shannon and Weaver 1963) suggest that the optimal codelength for a symbol representing data item i is $-\log_n p_i$ bits where p_i is the probability of occurrence of the symbol. Huffman encoding, described in Gallager (1968), achieves this in practice with a prefix code over a binary alphabet. A code has the prefix property if the encoded symbols are self-delimiting. This is important so that the codes can be unambiguously discerned from a stream of concatenated encodings. The fact that $-\log_n p_i$ may not always be a whole number means that there will always be some redundancy as the number of bits will have to be rounded away from zero. However, this is not a major concern in coding as other coding schemes, notably arithmetic coding (Witten et al. 1987) allow us to achieve this theoretical optimum per-symbol length.

A variation of this approach encodes the abstraction in the form of a Probabilistic Finite State Automaton (PFSA). A PFSA is a state-determined machine with a stochastic transition function. That is, moves from one state to another are governed by probabilities. Gaines (1971) adopted this approach with regard to the problem of developing a behavioural account of human behaviour. This was further developed by Wallace and Georgeff (1983) who looked at the general problem of inferring a structure for a PFSA from a given string with zero or more embedded delimiters.

PFSAs, in general, can code any hypothesis that can be coded using our earlier scheme, but somewhat more intuitively. To see how, consider the following scenario. Four events A, B, C and D are observed to occur in that order a large number of times, say $n \gg 1$. Eventually, a biased observer (it is important that some kind of bias exists (Hanson 1958) for an inductive hypothesis to take shape) will begin to form a generalization about the environment in which these events occur, and the generalization is then formally stated. Let us see how the hypothesis may be coded using each scheme. Since temporal information allows us to capture the sequence of occurrence of the four events, the sequence itself can be viewed as a single event, say X. This is a result of Shannon's noiseless coding theorem (Abramson 1963) which allows us to improve coding efficiency by grouping source symbols where such grouping information is available. X being the only event known to occur, it will now be assigned the shortest code, say C1, in accordance with Huffman (1952). Thus the hypothesis specification will code the probability of occurrence of X and the data specification will be n repetitions of this code, which will be concise as C1 is small. The entire abstraction will look as in Figure 14.1.

Suppose now, that the sequence was disturbed abruptly by the sudden occurrence of an unexpected event B' after the mth A $(m < n)$, which is followed by C and D. Assuming that our coding algorithm dictates that the sequence A, B', C, D be viewed as a single event Y and assigned a code C2 longer than C1, the abstraction will now look as in Figure 14.2. This will

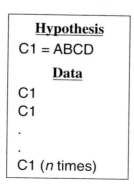

Figure 14.1   A coding of the explanation for events ABCD.

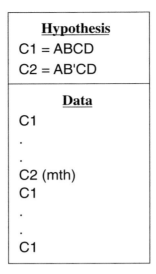

Hypothesis
C1 = ABCD
C2 = AB'CD

Data
C1

.

.

C2 (mth)
C1

.

.

C1

Figure 14.2 A coding of the explanation of the events ABCD with an exception B'.

be longer than the size of the first explanation as $|C2| > |C1|$. The sizes of C1 and C2 in this hypothesis are determined by the probabilities of occurrences of the event sequences A, B, C, D and A, B', C, D respectively. Accordingly, C1 is $\log(n) - \log(n-1)$ symbols long and C2 is $\log(n)$ symbols long, where the base of the logarithm is the number of unique symbols in the alphabet.

If we decided to code the hypothesis explaining the first dataset as a PFSA, we would construct a state-determined machine (see Figure 14.3) which simulates the sequence of occurrence of the events A, B, C and D, in that order. We would consider a five-state machine, in which event A takes it from state 0 to 1, event B takes it from 1 to 2 and so on. Also, we would specify the transition probabilities for each symbol. We could do this indirectly by specifying the frequencies of occurrences of the symbols, as the probabilities are directly computable given the frequencies of all outgoing transitions from a state.

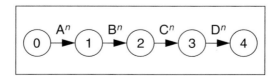

Figure 14.3 A PFSA coding of the explanation for events $(ABCD)^n$.

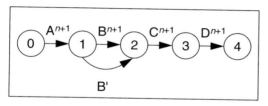

Figure 14.4 A PFSA coding of the explanation for events (ABCD)^n with exception AB'CD.

Non-diagramatically, a PFSA is a set of 4-tuples $< S1, S2, M, P>$ where S1, S2 ø a finite set of states, M ø a finite set of output symbols, and $0 < P < = 1$ is the probability of transiting on M from S1 to S2. Alternatively, P ø W, in which case it stands for the frequency of transitions on M in that 4-tuple. $\{< 0, 1, A, n >, < 1, 2, B, n >, < 2, 3, C, n >, < 3, 4, D, n >\}$ would be an ASCII representation of the PFSA just considered.

With the anomalous event B', a PFSA encoding would be as in Figure 14.4. The number of states of the automaton has not increased in this case, but this may not always be so. The extra transition from state 1 to 2 accounts for the anomalous event B'. Accordingly the ASCII representation of this PFSA will be slightly longer than the previous one and will be $\{< 0, 1, A, n >, < 1, 2, B', 1 >, < 1, 2, B, n-1 >, < 2, 3, C, n >, < 3, 4, D, n >\}$.

INFORMATION MEASURES AND MML CODES

At this stage, it is worth pointing out that every set of observations has at least one hypothesis purporting to explain it. As proof of this statement, we may consider the trivial null theory which claims to explain any given dataset, which however has as exceptions to it all the observed data and no confirmations whatsoever. Thus the problem of modelling an inductive hypothesis from a body of data really becomes one of choosing between competing models. Georgeff and Wallace (1984) propose the Minimum Message Length (MML) principle to help make such a decision. It states that the best hypothesis for explaining a set of data is one which minimizes the sum of

- the description length of the hypothesis, and
- the description length of the data when encoded using this hypothesis.

The technique has its origins in Wallace and Boulton (1969) where it is fairly obvious that the MML criterion is being considered as a general purpose inductive tool. Solomonoff (1964: 1), Chaitin (1966) and Kolmogorov (1965) had already looked at the problem of obtaining complexity measures for descriptions, and Solomonoff (1964: 2) had suggested its use in choosing between rival inductive hypotheses.

The MML principle has been applied with some success in Patrick (1978) to choose between proposed shapes of the Megalithic stone geometries in the British Isles. Muggleton *et al.* (1991) uses the similar Minimum Description Length (MDL) principle of Rissanen (1978) within the framework of Inductive Logic programming, and Quinlan and Rivest (1989) apply it to infer decision trees. Wallace and Patrick (1993) correct a derivation error in the latter paper and apply the MML criterion to the decision tree inference problem.

If the hypothesis and the data are stated in the form of a PFSA as discussed in the earlier section, the following formula gives the size of MML encoding the PFSA description.

$$
\sum_{j=1}^{N} \left\{ \log \frac{(t_j + V - 1)!}{(V-1)! \prod_{j=1}^{V} n_{ij}!} + m_j \log N \right\} - \log (N-1)!
$$

where t_j is the number of times the jth state is visited; V is the cardinality of the alphabet; n_{ij} is the number of times the ith symbol is produced from the jth state, m_j is the number of different transitions from the jth state; and N is the number of states.

For a consistent PFSA, the total number of incoming transitions into a state must equal the total number of outgoing ones. That is,

$$
t_j = \sum_{i=1}^{V} n_{ij}
$$

To find the number of ways that t_j transitions can be distributed among V symbols, we find the number of ways that $V-1$ partitions can be inserted into a pool of t_j transitions, the transitions within each partition being indistinguishable. This is given by

$$
\frac{(t + V - 1)!}{(V - 1)! \prod_{i=1}^{V} n_{ij}!}
$$

The log of this quantity, to the base 2 will give the number of bits that will nominally be required to code the outgoing transition distribution for the state. Log$N$ gives the number of bits required to specify one of N states and $m_j$log$N$ gives the number of bits required to specify the destination state of each of the m_j transitions out of the jth state. Since the specific numbering of states by the sender is irrelevant to the receiver, the length of specifying the actual state numbers, $\log (N-1)!$, is subtracted from the total which included it.

The formula is used in Patrick and Chong (1987) where it is stated with two typographical errors (the factorials in the numerators are absent). It is itself a correction (through personal communication) of the formula in Wallace and Georgeff (1983). The derivation follows on from work in numerical taxonomy (Wallace and Boulton 1968) which applied the MML principle to derive information measures for classification.

The MML of the PFSA (hereafter referred to simply as MML) is the length of MML encoding the hypothesis and the data in this form. As before, the base of the logarithm is the cardinality of the coding alphabet. If a binary code was used, the logs will be to the base 2 and the MML will expressed as a number of bits. On the other hand, if the base of the logarithm is assumed to be e, as Wallace does, then the MML is computed in nits (probably a contraction of natural bits), a term used by Wallace and Boulton to indicate that natural logs were used instead. Abramson (1963: 12) uses the synonymous term 'nats' for a similar measure.

The MML, thus computed, may be used to choose between competing hypotheses. Such an approach has been used once before in Patrick and Chong (1987) to analyse the behaviour of players in an Australian rules football game with encouraging results. This is the technique we use to encode our hypothesis to explain the evolution of sounds from one language to another.

MODELLING LANGUAGE SIMILARITIES

Suppose we want to encode the degree of relatedness between a parent language L1 and a child language L2, one method will be as follows: we consider a message encoding two sets of words – W1 and W2, one from each language. Let the words in each set be $\{x1..xn\}$ and $\{y1..yn\}$. Where a derivation di exists between xi and yi, it will be possible to code yi simply as di with a flag indicating the fact that it is coded as a derivation. If the derivation di occurs sufficiently frequently, as is the case with regular correspondences, then di can be coded concisely and the resultant encoding of the two word sets will be smaller than if the actual words were specified. Thus, the conciseness of coding W1 and W2 will be indicative of the degree of relatedness between L1 and L2.

In comparing closeness between the languages in two or more language pairs, the length of the message encoding the words in the parents will cancel out provided the same set of words is used. Thus the significant factor in comparison will be only the derivations where they exist and the actual words in the child language where derivations could not be found.

Equivalently, a PFSA encoding this model would represent all the derivations and underivable words with suitably costed arcs. For example, underivable words could be represented as arcs that trace their derivations from null phonemes without provision for exploiting structure within them. This is, however, just one possibility worthy of investigation. Our own examples do not account for underivable words at this stage. The following two examples demonstrate the application of our method to the two language

Table 14.2 *LNWG to OF

	English	*LNWG	OF	Path[3]
1	father	fađer	feder	A – α
2	moon	mēnōÚ	mōna	D–β–Y–B
3	stone	stainaz	stēn	E–H1–H2–L
4	staff	staƀ	stef	G–χ
5	field	akker	ekker	G
6	lamb	lamb	lamb	#
7	night	naxt	naxt	#
8	apple	appel	appel	#
9	bone	bain	bēn	H3–H5
10	tree	baum	bām	H1–H2
11	bed	badja	bed	I1–d–L–L
12	gap	klufti	kleft	I2–I3–I4–L
13	skin	hūdi	hēd	I2–I3–I4–L
14	power	maxti	maxt	L
15	day	daga	dei	J–L–G–δ
16	guest	jesti	jest	L
17	word	wordu	word	L
18	brother	brōθer	brōđer	R
19	man	man	man	#
20	grass	gres	gers	Z

pairs, Later North-west Germanic and Old Frisian and Later North-west Germanic and Old High German.

EXAMPLE: MODELLING *LNWG TO OF

Table 14.2 shows the derivation of a list of twenty Old Frisian (OF) words from corresponding reconstructed Later North-west Germanic (*LNWG) words. Unfortunately, the words do not all come from the Swadesh list as such a list with its reconstruction in LNWG was not completed at the time of writing. However, these words will suffice to illustrate some of the procedures involved in constructing the model using our method. The path column represents the (hyphen separated) sequences of diachronic rules that are applied to the *LNWG words to transform them into OF. The actual rules the labels in the path represent can be found in Appendix 1 (see p. 276). Obviously, the order of application of rules is significant in the determination of the paths. We have followed the order set out in Voyles (1992). Where such an order was not specified, we apply the rules in the order they appear in the work.

A PFSA derived from the data in Table 14.2 is given in Figure 14.5. It can be regarded as an explanation for the evolution of words in OF from *LNWG. The labels on the arcs indicate the rules that were applied in tran-

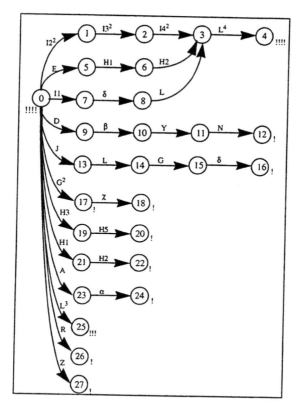

Figure 14.5 PFSA for *LNWG > OF derivation (MML = 354 nits).

siting from one state to another. Their superscripts represent the frequency of their application. One or more exclamation marks (!) subscripting a state means that there exist that many paths from that state to the start state. That is, a word delimiter was encountered at that state.

EXAMPLE: MODELLING *LNWG TO OLD HIGH GERMAN

Table 14.3 shows the derivation of twenty Old High German (OHG) words from corresponding reconstructed Later North-west Germanic (*LNWG) words. The path column represents the sequences of diachronic rules that are applied to the *LNWG word to transform it into OHG. The actual rules the labels in the path represent can be found in Appendix 2 (see p. 277).

The PFSA derived from the data in Table 14.3 is shown in Figure 14.6. It can be regarded as an explanation for the evolution of words in OHG

Table 14.3 *LNWG to OHG

	English	*LNWG	OHG	Path[4]
1	father	faðer	fater	A–P
2	moon	mēnō̃	māno	α–I–β
3	stone	stainaz	stein	E–C–F–D
4	staff	stab	stab	O
5	field	akker	akkar	b
6	lamb	lamb	lamb	#
7	night	naxt	naxt	#
8	apple	appel	apful	K–χ
9	bone	bain	bein	C–D
10	tree	baum	boum	C–D
11	bed	badja	betti	L–T–F–P–J
12	gap	klufti	kluft	F
13	skin	hūdi	hūt	F–P
14	power	maxti	maxt	F
15	day	daga	tage	F–P–O
16	guest	jesti	gast	F–β–δ
17	word	wordu	wort	F
18	brother	brōθer	bruoder	W
19	man	man	man	#
20	grass	gres	gras	O–δ

from *LNWG. See the text on pp. 272–3, concerning Figure 14.5, for a fuller description of the symbols used.

CONCLUSION

In our examples using Old Frisian, Old High German, and reconstructed Later North-west Germanic, we have shown that the length of the hypothesis required to explain the derivation of words from *LNWG to Old Frisian is 354 nits, whereas that required to explain a similar derivation from *LNWG to OHG is only 329 nits. This difference can be interpreted in the following way: If two structures have a difference in their MMLs of, say d nits, this can be approximately equated to an odds ratio $1 : e^d$. This means that any value of d greater than about 4.61 nits signifies that there is less than a 1 per cent chance that they are the same.

Also, we need to draw a distinction between the two levels of MML differences we are concerned with. In searching for a minimum PFSA modelling the derivation of words in a given language from its parent, d is a measure by which to choose one PFSA solution over another. However our real interest is in the MML differences between the derivation models for two or more languages. This is the difference which bears linguistic significance for us. In the above example, the difference signifies that OHG has diverged less from LNWG than OF.

It happens that such an inference is consistent with the chronological order of separation of these languages from LNWG as the OF words we used date from around AD 1200 and the OHG words from around AD 830. But we draw no specific conclusion based on this small test sample for the following reasons: first, the words we used were purely for the purposes of illustrating our method and not all taken from the Swadesh list; second, the heuristics we used to construct the PFSAs were tentative and needed refinement which we reserve till a later stage of this work. Finally, we haven't mentioned anything about the extent of chronological separation between the two languages. Whether there is a functional dependence between an MML computed for a PFSA and the amount of time the child language has been separated from its parent is questionable and needs to be addressed separately. We have, however, provided a framework within which sensible numeric figures indicative of language (dis)similarities can be derived.

APPENDIX 1: DIACHRONIC RULES FOR LATER NORTH-WEST GERMANIC TO OLD FRISIAN

The following are the diachronic rules used in deriving the Old Frisian words of about AD 1200 from Later North-west Germanic of about AD 400. They are taken from Voyles (1992). We retain the numbering used by him. Only rules that are actually used in our example are reproduced. As a result, the numbering may not be sequential. Each rule label is followed by the corresponding rule's number, its name as given by Voyles, and then the statement of the actual rule. In the occasional event when no rule in Voyles was found to account for a change, we made up our own rather tentative one as a stop-gap measure. Such rules are designated with Greek-letter labels. The following set is only rough guide. See Voyles (1992) for a more comprehensive discussion of each.

Table A.1 ⋆LNWG to OF rules

Label	No.	Name	Rule
A	7.1.1	đ to d	đ > d
D	7.1.4	ã to õ	[ą̄ + str] > ǭ
E	7.1.5	z-dele	z > Ø /_##
G	7.1.7	a to e	[a + str] > e /closed syllable
H1	7.1.8	ai/au change	ai, au > ǣ, ō/open syllable
H2	7.1.8	ai/au change	ǭ,o > a; a > e /_Ci(:), j; closed syllable
H3	7.1.8	ai/au change	ai > ǣ /closed syllable
H4	7.1.8	ai/au change	ǣ > a /_ x, p.b.m or w
H5	7.1.8	ai/au change	ε > e
I1	7.1.9	i/j umlaut	[V + str + low] >[−back,−low] / _Ci(:), j

Table A.1 – *cont.*

Label	No.	Name	Rule
I2	7.1.9	i/j umlaut	[V + str] > [− back, − low] /_ Ci(:), j
I3	7.1.9	i/j umlaut	a(:), o(:), u(:) > e ɛ, e ɛ, i(:) /_Ci(:), j
I4	7.1.9	i/j umlaut	a(:), o(:), u(:) > e, ɛ /_Ci(:), j
J	7.1.10	Palatalization	k > c, g > j /##_[V, − back]
L	7.1.12	Unstr. short.V dele	[V − long − str −nasal] > Ø /[_− high]##
N	7.1.14	Unstr. V short	[V + long −str −nasal] > [−long] /_##
R	7.1.18	Obstr. Voi/Devoi	[C + obs +cont] > [− voi] / _[− voi or ##]
Y	7.1.25	n-dele	opt. n > Ø /[V − str]_##
Z	7.1.26	r-metathesis	r [V + str] > [V + str] r / C _ [C + coronal or x C]
a	–	(*ad hoc*–1)	[a + str] > e /open syllable
b	–	(*ad hoc*–2)	ọ̄ > ā̤ /_##
c	–	(*ad hoc*–3)	ƀ > f
d	–	(*ad hoc*–4)	j > i /V_V

APPENDIX 2: DIACHRONIC RULES FOR LATER NORTH-WEST GERMANIC TO OLD HIGH GERMAN

The following are the diachronic rules that were used in deriving the Old High German words of about AD 830 from the Later North-west Germanic of about AD 400. See Appendix 1 for a fuller description of the table contents.

Table A.2　★LNWG to OHG rules

Label	No.	Name	Rule
A	9.1.1	đ to d	đ > d
C	9.1.3	ai/au changes	ai, au > ɛ̄, ō
D	9.1.4	Str.ē/ō-to-ie/uo	[ē, ō + str] > ie, uo
E	9.1.5	z-dele	z > Ø/[V, − str]_## or [V − back + str]_[+ obs]
F	9.1.6	Unstr short V dele	[V − long − str − nas] > Ø / _[− high]##
I	9.1.9	Unstr V short	[V + long − str − nas] > [− long] /_##
J	9.1.10	WG Gem	C > CC (C¹ r, q, z) /[V − long or − str]_j p, t > pp, tt /[V − long] _ l or r k > kk [V − long] _ r or w
K	9.1.11	2nd SS	[C + obs − cont − voi + asp] > pf, tz /## or C [_ − back] [C + obs − cont − voi + asp] > ff, zz, xx /V _

Table A.2 – *cont.*

Label	No.	Name	Rule
L	9.1.12	i/j umlaut	[V + low + back − long + str] > [− low − back] /_Ci(:), j
O	9.1.15	b̶, g̶ to b, g	b̶, g̶ to b, g
P	9.1.16	d to t	d > t /_##, in gemination, [+ son − voc]_V, opt.V_[+ son] or opt.##_
T	9.1.20	j to i	j > i /C_V
W	9.1.23	q to d	q > d /opt.##_ or obligatory
a	–	(*ad hoc* − 1)	ǫ − str] > ō
b	–	(*ad hoc* − 2)	e > a
c	–	(*ad hoc* − 3)	e > u
d	–	(*ad hoc* − 4)	j > g

NOTES

1   We are indebted to Dr John Newman, Department of Linguistics and Second Language Teaching, for his help with the linguistic aspects of this chapter and his many valuable suggestions which have mostly been incorporated into it. Thanks also to Dr Peter Kay, Department of Computer Science, for his careful and critical examination of the chapter and Charlie Clelland, Department of Computing and Maths, Deakin University, for his thorough help with the PFSA constructions and MML calculations. Chris Wallace, Department of Computer Science, Monash University, offered useful advice on the application of the MML technique to studying language similarities. Dr Peter Christian of Goldsmith's College, London, gave us a comprehensive review and several constructive comments for which we are very grateful. We have endeavoured to keep them in mind during the time this chapter was rewritten.
2   Originally it was assumed that our derivations were more likely to be correct if the words were chosen from the Swadesh list for L1. But it has been pointed out by Dr Peter Christian of Goldsmith's College, London, who reviewed our chapter, that whether or not the words come from the Swadesh list is irrelevant. What the Swadesh list guarantees is only that the words in it are less likely to be semantically different from their cognates. Our method only needs a list of words in one language and their cognates in another, regardless of their semantic differentiation. For instance, the Swadesh list would have 'dog' and 'hund' and 'flower' and 'fleur' as non-cognates. But we could use 'hound' and 'hund' and 'fleur' and 'blossom' for our method.
3   See Appendix 1 for ★LNWG to OF rule key.
4   See Appendix 2 for ★LNWG to OHG rule key.

REFERENCES

Abramson, N. 1963. *Information Theory and Coding*. New York: McGraw-Hill.
Bergsland, K. and H. Vogt. 1962. On the validity of glottochronology. *Current Anthropology* 3(2), 115–53.
Chaitin, G.J. 1966. On the length of programs for computing finite binary sequences. *Journal of the Association for Computing Machinery* 13, 547–69.

Chrétien, C.D. 1962. The mathematical models of glottochronology. *Language* 32, 11–37.

Embleton, S.M. 1981. Incorporating borrowing rates in lexicostatistical tree reconstruction. Ph.D. Thesis, University of Toronto.

Embleton, S.M. 1991. Mathematical methods of genetic classification. In *Sprung from Some Common Source*, S. Embleton (ed.), 365–88. Stanford: Stanford University Press.

Gaines, B.R. 1971. Axioms for adaptive behaviour. *International Journal of Man–Machine Studies* 4, 169–99.

Gaines, B.R. 1976. Behaviour structure transformations under uncertainty. *International Journal of Man–Machine Studies* 8, 337–65.

Gallager, R.G. 1968. *Information Theory and Reliable Communication*. New York: Wiley.

Georgeff, M.P. and C.S. Wallace. 1984. A general selection criterion for inductive inference. In *ECAI-84: Advances in Artificial Intelligence*, T. O'Shea (ed.), 473–81. North Holland: Elsevier.

Gleason, H.A. Jr. 1959. Counting and calculating for historical reconstruction. *Anthropological Linguistics* 2, 22–32.

Gudchinsky, S. 1956. The ABC's of lexicostatistics (glottochronology). *Word* 12, 175–210.

Hanson, N.R. 1958. *Patterns of Discovery*. Cambridge: Cambridge University Press.

Henrici, A. 1973. Numerical classification of Bantu languages. *African Language Studies* 14, 82–104.

Huffman, D.A. 1952. A method for the construction of minimum redundancy codes. *Proceedings of the Institute of Radio Engineers* 40, 1098–1101.

Hymes, D.E. 1971. Lexicostatistics and glottochronology in the nineteenth century. In *Proceedings of the Yale Conference on Lexicostatistics in Genetic Linguistics*, I. Dyen (ed.), 122–76. New Haven, Conn.: Yale University Press.

Kolmogorov, A.N. 1965. Three approaches for defining the concept of information quantity. *Problems of Information Transmission* 1, 1–7.

Kroeber, A.L., and C.D. Chrétien. 1937. Quantitative classification of Indo-European languages. *Language* 13, 83–103.

Lees, R.B. 1953. The basis of glottochronology. *Language* 29, 113–27.

Muggleton, S., A. Srinivasan and M. Bain. 1991. *MDL Codes for Non-monotonic Learning*. Glasgow: Turing Institute Research Memorandum (TIRM-91-049).

Patrick, J.D. 1978. An information measure comparative analysis of megalithic geometries. Ph.D. Thesis, Monash University.

Patrick, J.D. and K.E. Chong. 1987. Real time inductive inference for analysing human behaviour. In *Proceedings of the Australian Joint AI conference*, J. Gero. (ed.), 305–22. Sydney: University of Sydney Press.

Quinlan, J.R. and R.L. Rivest. 1989. Inferring decision trees using the minimum description length principle. *Information and Computation* 80, 227–48.

Rissanen, J. 1978. Modelling by shortest data description. *Automatica* 14, 465–71.

Ross, A.S.C. 1950. Philological probability problems. *Journal of the Royal Statistical Society, Series B* 12, 19–59.

Sankoff, D. 1972. Mathematical developments in lexicostatistic theory. *Current Trends in Linguistics* 11, 93–113.

Sapir, E. 1916. *Time Perspectives in Aboriginal American Culture: a study in method*. Geological Survey of Canada, Memoir 90, Anthropological Series No.13, Ottawa.

Shannon, C.E. and W. Weaver. 1963. *The Mathematical Theory of Communication*. Urbana: University of Illinois Press.

Solomonoff, R.J. 1964. A formal theory of inductive inference: parts 1 and 2. *Information and Control* 7, 1–22 (descriptional complexity) and 224–54 (application to induction).

Swadesh, M. 1951. Diffusional cumulation and archaic residue as historical explanations. *South-western Journal of Anthropology* 7, 1–21.

Swadesh, M. 1952. Lexicostatistic dating of prehistoric ethnic contacts. *Proceedings of the American Philosophical Society* 96, 452–63.

Voyles, J.B. 1992. *Early Germanic Grammar*. San Diego: Academic Press.

Wallace, C.S. and D.M. Boulton. 1968. An information measure for classification. *Computer Journal* 11(2), 185–94.

Wallace, C.S. and D.M. Boulton. 1969. The information content of a multistate distribution. *Journal of Theoretical Biology* 23, 269–78.

Wallace, C.S. and M.P. Georgeff. 1983. *A General Objective for Inductive Inference*. Computing Science Tech Report, TR-32, Monash University.

Wallace, C.S. and J.D. Patrick. 1993. Coding decision trees. *Machine Learning* 11, 7–22.

Witten, I.H., M.N. Radford and J.G. Cleary. 1987. Arithmetic coding for data compression. *Communications of the Association for Computing Machinery* 30(6), 520–38.

Part IV

ORAL TRADITIONS

15   Ancient migrations in the northern sub-Urals: archaeology, linguistics and folklore

LIDIA ASHIKHMINA

INTRODUCTION

From ancient times the northern sub-Urals has been the territory of the Permian branch of Finno-Ugric community formation: the Udmurt, the Komi-Zyryan and the Komi-Permyak peoples. An interesting and complicated period in the genesis of these peoples is the Bronze and Early Iron Ages, when mass migrations are observed in the region. This chapter follows these migrations and their reflection in Bronze and Iron Age archaeological materials, linguistic and folklore data. Across the European north-east in the second half of the 2nd millennium BC there are marked changes in ceramic forms. Vessels with a half-egg form of the Eneolithic (=Chalcolithic) period gave way to those with well-profiled necks. These sequences do not represent internal evolution but are the result of multiple migrations across the vast expanses of Eurasia in the Bronze Age in the first half of the 2nd millennium BC. This chapter[1] describes these pottery sequences and attempts to interpret them both in terms of house-forms known from excavation and some of the extensive folklore of the region.

MIGRATIONS OF THE INDO-EUROPEANS TO THE NORTHERN SUB-URALS, ACCORDING TO ARCHAEOLOGICAL DATA

The appearance of tribes with other cultures in the region is closely related to the movement of Seyma-Turbino groupings from Siberia and appearing after that in the Pechora river basin, on the middle Kama and lower Oka and Kama rivers (Chernykh and Kuz'minykh 1989: 215–21, 275). Penetration of the Seyma-Turbino tribes into these regions was followed by radical changes and a major redistribution of the ethnic map (Figure 15.1[2]). According to features of vessel-form, and elements and composition of their patterns, it is possible to assign them to different Indo-European cultures of the Bronze

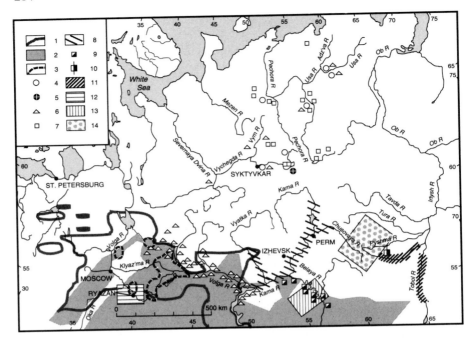

Figure 15.1   Map of Abashevo, Fatyanovo and Pozdnyakovo sites and settlements
with mixed ceramics of the Bronze Age.

Key: 1 territory of Fatyanovo tribes; 2 territory of Abashevo population community; 3 territory of Pozdnyakovo sites distribution; 4 settlements with hexagonal dwellings; 5 sanctuary-
observatory (?): Vomynyag on the Upper Vychegda river; 6 settlements with mixed types of
ceramics in the Volga–Kama region and in the European north-east; 7 territories in the Vychegda
and Pechora basin, occupied by the population of the Final Bronze Age (Lebyazhskaya culture);
8 territory in the Kama basin, occupied by the population with mixed ceramics (Maklasheevo
type); 9 territory occupied by the population of the Curmantau culture in the Belaya river
basin; 10 locality of Prygovskoe hillfort; 11 territory occupied by the population with ceramics
of Prygovskoe hillfort type; 12 ancient Iranian hydronyms of Ryazan' type; 13 Iranian
hydronyms in the basins of the Ik and Belaya rivers (Bashkiria); 14 Iranian hydronyms in the
basins of the Iset', Pyshma and Chusovaya rivers.

Age: the Fatyanovo (descendants of tribes using corded ware and bored battle
axes) (Krajnov 1987), Pozdnyakovo (Bader and Popova 1987) and Abashevo
(Pryakhin and Khalikov 1987). I argue that the Fatyanovo peoples were Proto-
Balts, and that the Pozdnyakovo and Abashevo were Indo-Iranian speakers.

In Fatyanovo, Abashevo and Pozdnyakovo vessels it is possible to distinguish traits more often observed in mixed complexes. Thus, Fatyanovo vessels
are characterized by a straight (Figure 15.2 – 1–7, 8) or everted (Figure 15.2
– 2–6, 9–14) neck with a smooth (Figure 15.2 – 6, 10, 11) or more often
sharp (Figure 15.2 – 1–5, 7–9, 12–14) transition to a globular (Figure 15.2
– 1–14), often ball-like body (Figure 15.2 – 1, 4–6, 9–11). There can be a

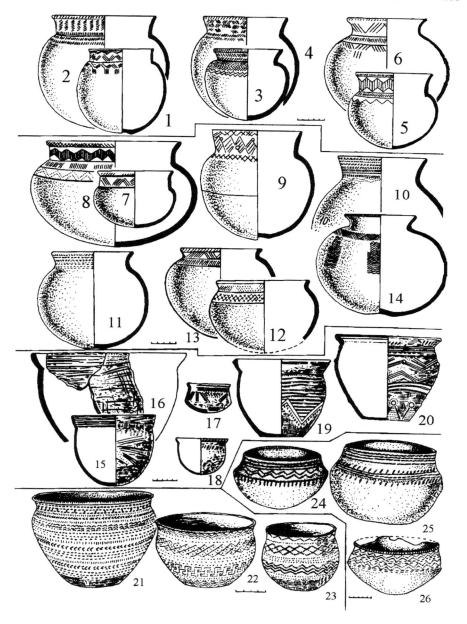

Figure 15.2   Some types of Fatyanovo (1–4), Abashevo (15–20) and Pozdnyakovo (21–6) vessels.

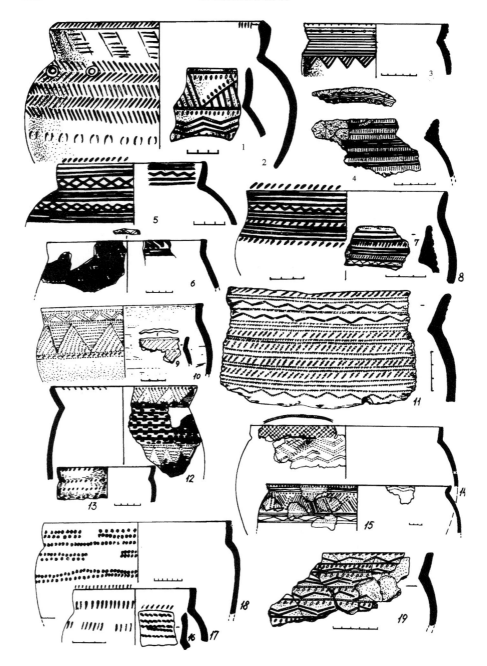

Figure 15.3 Hybrid ceramics with Fatyanovo, Abashevo and Pozdnyakovo features from settlements in the Volga–Kama region and the European north-east: settlements of Sakhtysh III (2), Sakhtysh II (2, 16, 17), Zajmizhche III (3), Vis II (4, 6), Sakhtysh I (5, 8), Veksa I (7, 11), Chudgudoryag (9, 10), Kubashevo (13), Niremka I (14, 15), Atamannyur 1, dwelling 6 (18), Yagyel' (19) and Seyma burial ground (13).

sharp edge in the interior at the junction of the neck and body (Figure 15.2 – 1–5, 7–9) and a characteristic dislocation of patterns among horizontal bands (Figure 15.2 – 1–9, 12, 13). Such traits as a marked eversion with a weakly globular body (Figure 15.2 – 15, 16, 18–20), an arch-like configuration of the neck, extremely simple *and* complex decorative elements can be linked to Abashevo traditions: from horizontal lines (Figure 15.2 – 5, 16, 18) to different combinations of triangles (Figure 15.2 – 17, 19, 20). Pozdnyakovo pottery can be characterized by a smoother profile (Figure 15.2 – 21–3), a short (Figure 15.2 – 21–3) or absent (Figure 15.2 – 24–6) neck; ornaments more often consist of two or three repeated pattern elements (Figure 15.2 – 21, 23–6).

Fatyanovo–Abashevo characteristics (Figure 15.3 – 12, 13) are observed on the vessels from the sites of the so-called Chirkovo-Seyma or Chirkovo culture, eighth to sixteenth centuries BC, found mainly at the mouths of the Oka and Volga (Khalikov 1987). Abashevo traits can be distinguished on the vessels (Figure 15.3 – 3) of the early period (fifteenth to sixteenth centuries BC) of the Prikazan' culture in the submouth of the Kama river (Khalikov 1980).

Finds of ceramics in the dwelling sites of the Northern sub-Urals make it possible to follow further movement of Indo-Europeans, probably together with the Seymins. Pottery forms mixed with elements of the Fatyanovo, Abashevo and Pozdnyakovo cultures are recorded in the basin of the North Dvina – Veksa I (Figure 15.3 – 7, 11) site (Oshibkina 1987, Figure 76 – 15, 16, 18, 19) and its large tributary the Vychegda river – Vis I and II (Figure 15.3 – 4, 6) sites (Burov 1967: Tables XXII, XXIII), Niremka I (Figure 15.3 – 14; Kosinskaya 1986, Figures 5–6), Chudgudoryag (Figure 15.3 – 9, 10; Loginova 1993, Figure 15.2 – 5, 6; 15.3 – 1, 2, 6, 7), in the basin of the Pechora river – Atamannyur I (Figure 15.3 – 18), Shikhovskaya I, Yagjel' (Figure 15.3 – 19), Adz'va II (Stokolos 1988, Figures 35, 42, 50, 56–58; Tables 25 – 10, 11; 35 – 1, 4; 36 – 15). In the Volga-Klyaz'ma interbasin region similar ceramics are found in abundance (Figure 15.3 – 1, 2, 5, 8, 16, 17) dated to the third quarter of the 2nd millennium BC. Most researchers link the appearance of the population with a hybrid ceramic tradition in the northern sub-Urals (Kosinskaya 1986; Stokolos 1988; Loginova 1993) to this time. The period of transition from the Eneolithic to the Bronze Age in the north-east of Europe is poorly studied. It is quite probable that purer (i.e. unmixed) complexes of Indo-Europeans can be found and the time of their appearance on the territory under investigation may be the middle 2nd millennium BC (Burov 1986; Ashikhmina 1993b, 1993c).

HEXAGONAL CONSTRUCTIONS IN THE EUROPEAN NORTH-EAST

The discovery and excavation of dwelling sites with the remains of hexagonal half-mud huts was quite unexpected. At present, similar constructions

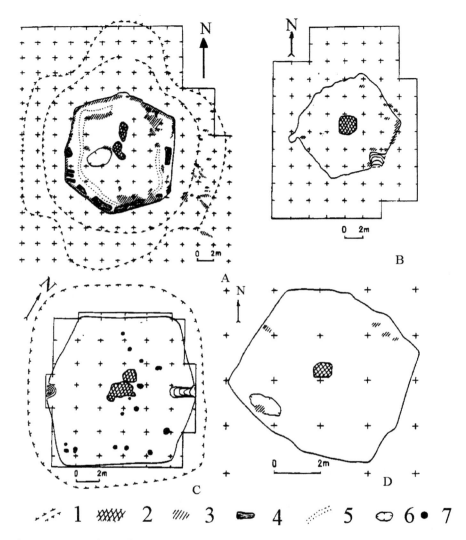

Figure 15.4   Plans of hexagonal semi-mud huts from sites in the Middle Vychegda (A) and Pechora (B, C, D) basins: A – dwelling site of Chudgudoryag; B – dwelling site of Atamannyur 1, dwelling 9; C – dwelling site of Shikhovskaya 1; D – dwelling site of Atamannyur 1, dwelling 7.

Key: 1 remains of bank-like surrounding; 2 hearth; 3 ochre; 4 burnt wood construction remains; 5 remains of the partitions within the dwelling (?); 6 pit; 7 post pit.

are found on the Middle and Upper Vychegda: Chudgudoryag (Figure 15.4 – A; Loginova 1993: Figure 1), and Vorkeros II dwelling sites (Ashikhmina 1993a: 14, Figure 3) and in the basin of the Pechora: dwelling sites of Atamannyur I (Figure 15.4 – B, D) Shikhovskaya I (Figure 15.4 – C), Adz'va II, Yagyel' (Stokolos 1988, Figures 39, 43, 45, 46, 55). Such constructions are not characteristic of the local population of the northern sub-Urals. In the half-mud huts fragments of pottery bearing the traits of the cultures mentioned above were found, but whether the two can be associated remains uncertain.

A unique monument at Vomynyag on the Upper Vychegda can be attributed to this period. On the hill there are six pits (diameter of 4.5–5 m and 0.4–0.5 m deep) laid out like the constellation of the Great Bear. A smaller pit fixed between the fifth and sixth pits may correspond to the star Alkor in the Great Bear. The 'scoop' of the constellation is oriented to the south. On the passageway from the 'scoop' to the 'handle' there is a big pit (diameter 17–18 m) with a noticeable bank around it, open to a water body. This pit may be the remains of an ancient sanctuary. One of the pits was excavated – the 'star' in the 'scoop' of the constellation – and the remains of a hexagonal wooden construction were found. At the rim of the hexagonal 'wheel' there is a felly up to 10 cm wide with some twenty-eight 'spokes', presumably representing days, radiating from it to the centre (Figure 15.5). A hexagonal construction with equal sides closely approximates a circle and may be a symbol of the sun, or perhaps a solar chariot and a lunar calendar.

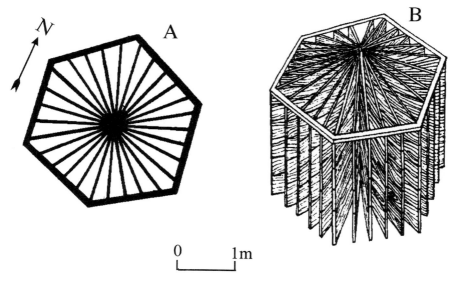

Figure 15.5 Sanctuary–observatory (?) of Vomynyag: A – plan reconstruction of investigated pit remains 2 in 'the scoop of the Great Bear'; B – preliminary reconstruction of lunar calendar (the second pit of 'the scoop').

This monument may combine the functions of an observatory (?) and sanctuary (Ashikhmina 1993a: 5–6, Figures 1, 2; 1993b: 74). Most probably the dwelling sites with hexagonal half-mud huts and the sanctuary-observatory (?) belong to the group of monuments which appeared in the north-east of Europe as a result of the arrival of Indo-Europeans.

HEXAGONAL CONSTRUCTIONS, A LEGEND OF A SIX-LEGGED ELK, THE GREAT BEAR AND THE LEGENDARY *SHARABKHA*

The hexagonal constructions are of great interest and almost certainly relate to the observation of celestial bodies. Such observations seem to form the basis of life-cycle ceremonies for local populations. The sky, with its numerous stars, led to astral myths, of which the Great Bear and its image were the most popular. Ancient cattle-breeders personified this constellation as a chariot or cart. Northern hunters thought of it as a celestial elk, as is shown by names for elk in the Khanty, Ket and Selkup languages. Personification of the constellation with the image of the elk resulted in numerous legends and traditional stories.

The hexagonal form of dwellings, the Great Bear calendar and a symbolism of the number six are linked to one of the legends of the Ob-Ugric people about a six-legged elk. At first this elk inhabited the sky, but the god of the Upper World learnt that the elk had become proud of his strength and speedy racing and sent a sky giant to punish the animal. After a long chase this wonderful hunter managed to catch the elk, cut off its two hind legs and threw them down to the Earth. Since that time the elk has become a common hunted animal and the six-legged elk remained in the sky as the Great Bear (Gondatti 1888).

Analysis of works depicting the elk from the territory of the northern sub-Urals showed that its ancient inhabitants thought of the universe as a female elk, and a dwelling was personified with the same image (Ashikhmina 1992a, 1992b). A six-legged symbol is also met later in Ugric traditions: metal breastplates located on the costume of a dead woman as a six-starred Great Bear were found in a tenth-century Hungarian burial ground (Ashikhmina 1992a: 30).

Ancient Indian literature has references to a fantastic multi-legged animal *sharabkha*. As a rule it is described as a wild animal able to defeat large predators. Ancient Indians considered that the animal inhabited forests and snow-capped mountains and compared it with different animals, most commonly with the reindeer. It most likely that the elk, in Indian traditions the strongest representative of the cervidae inhabiting the forest zone, was a prototype of *sharabkha*. Some scientists believe that the ancestors of the Indians could have known the elk, an inhabitant of northern forests and forest-steppe, in their motherland (Bongard-Levin and Grantovsky 1983: 104–7), or, perhaps more correctly, in one of their motherlands. Munkachi has proposed a correspondence between the ancient Indian word 'sharabkha' and the name of the elk in the Ugric languages of West Siberia [Zauralya] – the Mansi and Khanty: 'shor(e)p', 'sharp', 'sarp' (see Bongard-Levin and Grantovsky 1983: 105–6).

INDO-EUROPEAN MIGRATIONS AND A KOMI LEGEND ABOUT PERA THE GIANT

Such massive migrations across the vast territories of the northern sub-Urals should be reflected in folk-memory. One hypothesis was that there should be connections between the Bronze Age population movements and the legends of Pera the Giant preserved among the southern Komi people (Ashikhmina 1993b: 74; 1993c). One legend speaks of the battle of Pera the Giant with the warriors of a southern Tsar, who could ride a 'wheel' and easily crush people with it. 'The Southern tsar himself could ride such wheels and defeat the soldiers of the Permian prince' (Ozhegova 1971: 59, [1]6).[3] In other variants of the legend Pera struggled with the 'wheel'. Most often the legend tells of a 'wheel' inside which sits a wonderful hero (Ozhegova 1971:63, [8]8) or which is 'rolled by a valiant knight and crushes people' (Ozhegova 1971: 61, [1]7). Evidently the episode of Pera's struggle with a 'wheel' reflects his fight against the warriors using 'wheels' in possession of steppe peoples, including the Abashevs, in the Bronze Age.

Investigators of the Seyma-Turbino bronzes noted the speed of movement and aggressive character of its representatives (Chernykh and Kuz'minykh 1989: 271–2). The very beginning of the Indo-European movement to the north-east of Europe may have been with the participation of the aggressive Seymins to judge by the situation reflected in folklore.

The name of the valiant knight possessing the functions of the God of Thunder is not only reminiscent of Slavonic Perun and Baltic Perkunas (Perkons) but may be related to the appearance on this territory of the Indo-Europeans and transplanting of the God of Thunder's functions onto the legendary valiant knight. Perun is the God of Thunder in Slavonic mythology. According to an Indo-European tradition the God of Thunder already had a military function and was considered a protector of a military troop and its leader. The main weapons of Perun were stones, arrows and axes. As a rule Perun was thought of as an oak or an oak grove and a mountain (Ivanov and Toporov 1982b: 306–7).

The features of the God of Thunder are also present in the legends of Pera the Giant. At the same time they seem to be reinterpreted; the stones are not always considered as the giant's weapons, but used to illustrate his force. For example, 'he played with stones as large as a bath-house as if they were balls' (Ozhegova 1971: 59, [1]6); 'he threw the stones very far' (Ozhegova 1971: 72, [1]12, 76, [1]17). 'Pera and Mizya giants played, threw axes and big stones to each other' (Ozhegova 1971: 99, [1]66); etc. Pera all the time uses a bow and arrows while fighting with a wood-goblin (Ozhegova 1971: 62,[1]7; 65, [1]8; 66; 69,[1]9). When he struggles with an enemy, the hero uses a beam as a peculiar club (Ozhegova 1971: 58, [1]5; 64, [1]8) which can be three-*sazhens*[4] long (Ozhegova 1971: 64, [1]32). He revenges himself on the 'wheels' quite simply, by raising them above his head and smashing them on the ground (Ozhegova 1971: 60, [1]6; 62, [1]7; 64, [1]8; 67, [1]9; 74, [1]16; 84, [1]35) or breaking them over his knee (Ozhegova 1971: 78, [1]21). The oak and oak-grove also correspond to the image of Pera. He either passes through the oak-grove and fells oaks for sledge runners (Ozhegova 1971: 68, [1]; 76, [1]17) or he may be rewarded by them for his force (Ozhegova 1971: 58, [1]5).

From numerous variants of the legends it is possible to discern some characteristics of the native inhabitants of the taiga. Pera speaks about himself: 'I am from remote frigid lands where blue rivers flow and take their start from the great Kama' (Ozhegova 1971: 68, [1]9). Being extremely strong the giant always goes to the war on skis on which he moves as quickly as an arrow (Ozhegova 1971: 58, [1]5); as a reward he asks for silk *teneta* − a net for a fox, marten, hare, bird or lake-fish (Ozhegova 1971: 62, [1]7; 64, [1]8; 68, [1]9; 71, [1]10; 73, [1]12; 76, [1]17; 81, [1]26; 82–3, [1]31–2) or a golden *kotochek-kochedyk* − an instrument for net and bast-shoe making (Ozhegova 1971: 73, [1]12; 78, [1]21–2; 81, [1]26); still being hungry after taking bread he asks for a large portion of boiled salt-moss from the forest (Ozhegova 1971: 55, [1]5), two *poods*[5] of couch-grass − 'grass growing under fir-trees' (Ozhegova 1971: 77, [1]21), a tub of dried oatmeal (Ozhegova 1971: 87–8, [1]40–1) or a bucket of fir-branches (Ozhegova 1971: 91, [1]44); he prefers to sleep not in a soft bed but in the *parma* (taiga) on the bed made of fir-branches with a birch-branch head of the bed near the *nodya* − a specially prepared fire (Ozhegova 1971: 62, [1]7).

In these legends there are also stories about Pera's struggle with the *Idolishche* (Idol). In some texts the image of the *Idolishche* is identified with a machine-wheel: 'The enemy had a machine, its name was *Idolishche*. This machine was a wheel' (Ozhegova 1971: 72, [1]12). But in other variants we read: '*Idolishche* is riding the wheels, everybody is looking'; 'There rushed the *Idolishche* on wheels' (Ozhegova 1971: 75, [1]17). One of the legends also suggests that the *Idolishche* is mounted on some machine, thus confirming the anthropomorphic nature of this folklore hero: 'The Russian giants assembled against the *Idolishche* . . . They met the *Idolishche* and fought with it and struggled. The *Idolishche* split and turned again . . . Then they threw the *Idolishche* over themselves and broke its legs and arms' (Ozhegova 1971: 73, [1]12).

Prior to Christianity, the East Slavs had their own traditional religion. Russian epics and folk-tales mention a creature called '*Idolishche Poganoe*' or '*Idolishche*'. The image of *Idolishche* is personified by a living Idol (Senkevich-Gudkova 1979: 118). In Indo-European mythology many of the gods are shown riding a chariot. Before important events a statue of the god to whom this event was dedicated was brought out on a chariot and before a battle there would be a statue of the appropriate god. At first Perun acquires the image of a horseman either mounted on a horse or on a chariot fighting with his enemy (Ivanov and Toporov 1982a: 302). Perkunas is also depicted as pursuing his enemy on a chariot (Ivanov and Toporov 1982b: 304).

In the legends of Pera the Giant there are traits characteristic both of an Indo-European deity and a local folklore character, illustrating the interaction between Indo-European and Finno-Ugrian peoples.

YIRKAP IN KOMI LEGENDS AND YIRKI IN HERODOTUS

The Komi people have preserved legends about the hunter Yirkap who hunted on very fast skis, one of which was made of magical wood. I. Vaskul (pers. comm.) hypothesizes a direct relationship between anthroponym 'Yirkap' and ethnonym 'Yirki' – peoples mentioned in Herodotus' *Histories*. According to Herodotus (IV: 22), the 'Yirki' people made their living hunting. He describes an unusual method of hunting characteristic of these people: 'A hunter sits in a hiding place in a tree, which grow all over the country. Everybody has a horse at call trained to lie down on its belly and a dog. As soon as a hunter sees an animal from the tree he is sitting in, he shoots, jumps on his horse and starts pursuit, with the dog following him.'

Judging by the description this takes place in the forest-steppe. Villages where the legends about Yirkap were recorded are currently situated in the taiga. Herodotus describes the Yirki as contemporaries of the Scythians and Sauromatians in the Early Iron Age. At that period the climate of the Vychegda river basin was much colder, and the kind of hunt described would have been impossible. But such hunting could have taken place earlier in the Bronze Age, about the middle of the 2nd millennium BC. This links with archaeological materials, e.g. discoveries of dwelling sites with ceramics characteristic of an alien Indo-European people. Palynological data also suggests climatic changes with a tendency to increasing temperatures.

We do not find the name of the Yirki people in Komi folklore, but the name of legendary hunter Yirkap may derive from this ethnonym, supporting the idea of Yirki presence in the Vychegda basin. Because the climate was getting colder, the phenomenon presumably took place in the last quarter of the 2nd millennium BC, when population migration from north-eastern Europe is observed (Khotinsky 1978: 13). The Yirki may have been Iranian-speaking, since the Tajik word '*yirk*' means 'race', 'family' or 'generation' (Matveev 1961: 137).

But the largest part of the Indo-Europeans, the Yirki included, migrated to the territory of the Volga–Kama, to the Urals and the areas behind the Urals. Some stayed in Vychegodsky region, as the anthroponym Yirkap preserved in Komi legends indicates. Complexes with mixed ceramics showing Abashevo, Fatyanovo and Pozdnyakovo features were found in these regions.

Pottery found in Late Bronze Age settlements demonstrates the absence of direct genetic links with Eneolithic ware forms. These vessels show strongly

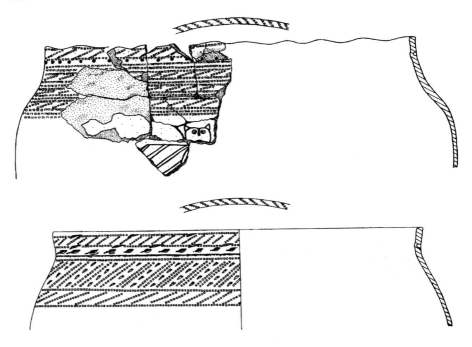

Figure 15.6 Ceramics of the Final Bronze (Lebyazhskaya culture) from the basin of the Vychegda river (dwelling site of Borganyel' 1).

transformed individual Abashevo and Fatyanovo traits. Pozdnyakovo traditions (Figure 15.6) are revealed much better, both in the shape and manner of pottery ornamentation (Ashikhmina 1993a).

From the fourteenth to sixteenth centuries BC the territories of the Middle Volga and Kama were inhabited by a population of Lugovskaya culture (according to Khalikov it is the Balymsko-Kartashikhinsky and Atabaevsky periods of Prikazan' culture), the pottery of which shows different cultural traditions affected by Srubno-Abashevo, Fodorovo-Cherkaskul', Alakul' impact (Figure 15.7). Similar pottery is found in the settlements in the basins of the Belaya river, Povolzhye and in Eastern Siberia, and the material can also be compared to the pottery of the Tazabagyabskaya culture in Middle Asia. As a rule, the appearance of groups with different cultures (of the Lugovskoe type) in the Middle Volga–Kama is explained by migration from East Siberia. But perhaps the Indo-Europeans who appeared in the Volga–Kama region in the eleventh to tenth centuries BC, and disturbed the Lugovskoe population, stimulated new migrations.

Settlements of the Late Bronze fifth to eighth centuries BC show groups of vessels of the Late Lugovskoe (Figure 15.7 – 8–13) and alien Maklasheevo population (Dubovogrivskaya II, Ikskaya I and III, Erzovskaya, Zayurchim-

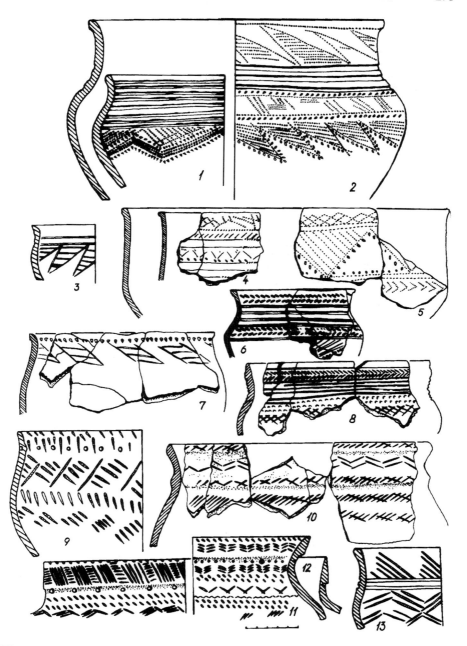

Figure 15.7   Ceramics of the Bronze Age (fourteenth to eleventh centuries BC) from the River Kama basin (Lugovskaya culture): Lugovskaya (1, 2), Zuevo-Kluchevskaya (3, 6, 8), Ikskaya I (7, 9) and II (12), Kumysskaya (10) and Dubovogrivskaya II (11, 13) dwelling sites.

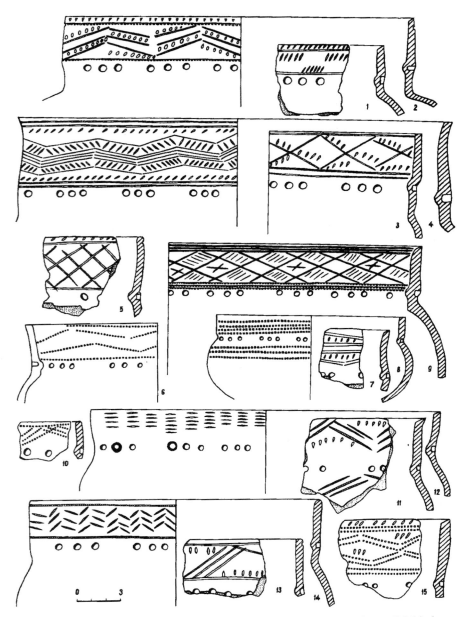

Figure 15.8 Ceramics of the Final Bronze Age from the Kama basin (Maklasheevo type): Dubovogrivskaya II (1–3, 8, 9) and Ikskaya III (4–7, 10–15) dwelling sites.

skaya, Byrgyndinskaya sites, etc.). Fatyanovo traditions are seen on Maklasheevo vessels, especially early ones. Vessels with a vertical neck (Figure 15.8
– 1–5, 7–15) almost at a right angle to a globular body with a sharp edge
on the interior are most frequent, while those with an everted neck are
rarer. Ornamentation is somewhat simplified, but very often a basic pattern
is set among bordering horizontal lines (Figure 15.8 – 1–6, 9, 13–15). From
Abashevo traits it is possible to distinguish an arch-like shape of the neck
(Figure 15.8 – 5, 10, 12, 15) and also a strongly everted vessel neck and a
slight globularity of the body.

ANCIENT IRANIAN HYDRONYMS IN CENTRAL RUSSIA AND THE URALS

Vessels of mixed traditions are found at Prygovskoe hillfort in the Middle
Urals (Figure 15.9) in the basin of the river Iset' (Gening and Pozdnyakova
1964, Tables III–VIII), dated to the Early Iron Age. There are sites with such
ceramics on the Tobol river and its tributary the Iset', recently dated to the
sixth to second centuries BC. Their appearance here is related to the penetration of the population using cross-ornamented ceramics (the Gamaun
culture) from the northern sub-Urals (Matveeva 1991). In this connection
attention should be given to the hydronyms of the South and Middle Urals
with initial p-. River names of this type are represented by two groups. One
group is the upper tributaries of the Chusovaya, Iset' and Pyzhma rivers, the
so-called the 'gates of the Urals' (*Rezh, Rezhik, Reshetka, Rechelga, Revda,
Revdel', Reft*). The other group of toponyms is in central Bashkiria (*Ryastok,
Ryaz', Rya, Revat*). A Bashkirian group of hydronyms with initial p- shows
some affinity with toponyms on 'p' of a Ryazan' type (compare *Ryaz',
Ryastok, Rya* and *Ryazan', Ryasa, Ryazhsk*) (Matveev 1961: 136–7).

Matveev (1961: 137) suggested an Iranian origin for these toponyms. The
most frequently applied topobases *Revd/Reft* and *Rezh/Resh/Rech* are
compared with the Tajik root *Rekhtan/Rez* meaning 'to flow, to pour'.
Hydronyms of this type can also mean '*flowing water, river*'. Ryazan' toponyms
with initial p- may also partly refer to Iranian sources. The origin of such
toponyms has a mixed Mordvinian, Iranian and Slavonic basis.

The hypothesis of an Iranian origin for some Uralic hydronyms is argued
by Muminov (1969). He refers to river names such as the Tura – a left
tributary of the Tobol river (ancient Indian – *turá-*; Persian, Kurdish – *tu:r*
'passionate'; Scythian – *tura* 'swift, strong') and the Utha, the right tributary
of the Belaya river (the Kama basin). This latter hydronym he connects with
ancient Iranian 'water' with the sound-change *a* to *o* and spirantization of *p*
to *f* in Scythian, supposing that *o* to *γ* took place in Turkic.

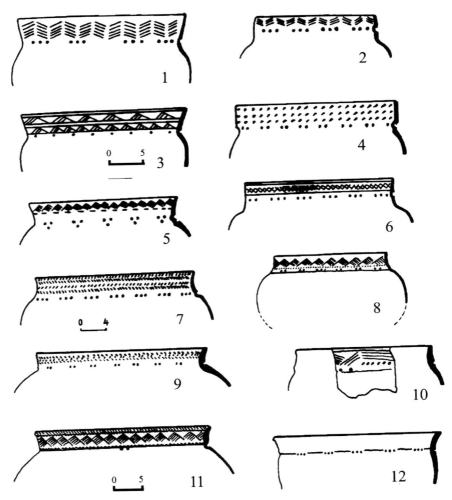

Figure 15.9 Some types of vessels with Fatyanovo, Abashevo and Pozdnyakovo traits from Prygovskoe hillfort.

WERE THE PEOPLES OF THE KURMANTAU CULTURE HERODOTUS' 'YIRKI'?

This affinity between Uralic and Ryazan' hydronyms is very suggestive. Toponyms of a Ryazan' type are found within the territories of the Fatyanovo, Abashevo and Pozdnyakovo cultures (Krajnov 1987: 60, map 5; Pryakhin and Khalikov 1987: 126, map 23; Bader and Popova 1987: 132, map 24). Some of these toponyms could have arisen in the Bronze and Early Iron Ages due

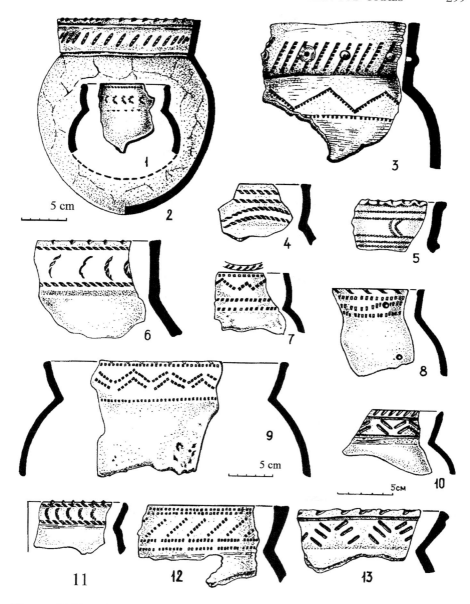

Figure 15.10 Ceramics of the Kurmantau culture from the settlements of the low stream Belaya river (1–4) and settlements from the middle Belaya river (5–12). Settlements of Kakry-Kul' (1, 2), Kushterak (3, 4), Duvanejskoe (5, 7), Birskoe (6), Kasyanovskoe (8–12).

to an influx of Iranian speakers. Evidently the Fatyanovo (Proto-Balts?) can be discounted, although some Fatyanovo ceramic traditions are very strong. It is difficult to say whether these hydronyms should be connected with the Abashevo or the Pozdnyakovo. The Abashevo population is more likely, if only because their traits are better characterized, but we cannot be sure.

Most probably the spread of Iranian hydronyms in central Bashkiria is connected with the Kurmantau culture which appeared in the basin of the River Belaya (left tributary of the Kama) at the end of the Bronze Age and lived there in the Early Iron Age (Ivanov 1982: 52–77). Ceramics of Kurmantau type (Figure 15.10) show both Fatyanovo and Abashevo-Pozdnyakovo features, but are so organically interrelated that in later complexes it is difficult to distinguish between them. Nevertheless, there is little doubt that this pottery reflects Indo-Europeans appearing in the Finno-Ugric-speaking regions around the middle of the 2nd millennium BC. Most Kurmantau sites are in the forest-steppe zone where the hunting methods typical of the Yirki are feasible (Herodotus IV: 22), and the population may conserve the Yirki ethnonym.

In connection with Kurmantau culture problem and the localization of the Yirki it may be relevant that among the numerous ethnonyms of the Dagestan peoples (in the Caucasus) the term 'Yirk' has been noted for the Rutul'sky dialect (Abdullaev and Mikhailov 1971: 17). Could this be a late echo of further movement of some part of the Yirki to the Caucasus? Abashevo, Fatyanovo and Pozdnyakovo traits are observed in the ceramics of a number of cultures of Late Bronze Age Siberia, apparent evidence of Indo-European migrations far to the east at the end of the Bronze Age. The ethnonym 'Yirki' may have been preserved and recorded on the Orkhonsky inscriptions from the monument to Kul' Tegin where a compound name 'Bayerku' and the 'Iir-Baiyrku' country are mentioned (Malov 1952: 34, 41). The hydronyms 'Indiga' (a river in the north-east of Europe flowing into the Barents sea) and 'Indigirka' (a river in East Siberia, flowing into the East-Siberian Sea) may signal Indo-European migration to north-east Europe and then to Siberia. If these hydronyms were analysable they might provide valuable clues to this process, although Komi linguists G.G. Baraksanov and A.I. Turkin (pers. comm.) assert that it is not possible.

THE 'ARCTIC HOME' OF THE INDIANS

At the beginning of the twentieth century the Indian politician Bal Gandkhar Tilak, in his book *The Arctic Home in the Vedas* presented his 'polar theory' of the origin of the Indians. Having analysed ancient Indian literature he concluded that the ancestors of the Indians inhabited Arctic regions in pre-glacial and mid-glacial epochs. As the climate became colder, about ten to eight thousand years ago, they moved south (cited by Bongard-Levin and Grantovsky 1983: 9).

Epic writings and holy stories of India refer to meteorological phenomena characteristic of Arctic regions but not of South Asia. These are the images of the fixed Polar Star, of a cold, long night lasting for half a year, and of a day of the same duration. In this fairy-land the sun rises only once a year and the constellation of Great Bear is seen high in the sky: 'the homeland of ten *apsars*' originating from the rainbow. These epic writings speak about 'captured' falling waters acquiring beautiful forms and many other things (Bongard-Levin and Grantovsky 1983: 7–8).

Could such phenomena, typical of polar regions, be observed and described in such picturesque detail unless at some stage an ancestral population had seen them with their own eyes? It is premature to assign a date for Indians inhabiting polar regions in the manner suggested by Tilak. However, the later period (the third and perhaps fourth quarter of the 2nd millennium BC) is sufficiently historical to be linked to these 'polar phenomena' and their reflection in the Veda. The Indo-Iranians remaining in the North can be connected to the formation of many of the cultures of the Late Bronze Age and Early Iron Age in the northern sub-Urals and Urals. Linguists have noted Indo-Iranian loanwords in Finno-Ugric languages that can be related to this period (Abaev 1981: 84–9; Gamkrelidze and Ivanov 1984: 921–34). Some characters in Finno-Ugric mythology can also be interpreted as of Indo-Iranian origin.

Bronze Age settlements with hexagonal half-mud huts are found in the subpolar regions. For example, the settlement of Ad'zva II, situated at the point where the river Ad'zva flows into the Usa (the right tributary of the Pechora river) is behind the Polar circle. The two opposite halves of hexagonal buildings, as well as the lunar calendar on the sanctuary-observatory (?) of Vomynyag, seem to represent or symbolize the 'scoop' of the constellation. The differing orientation of these constructions is of particular interest, especially if they can be shown to relate to the position of the constellation in the sky at the time of their construction. The last quarter of the 2nd millennium BC is characterized by a temperature decrease, and this may have induced the ancestors of the present-day Indians to leave these hostile northern lands. Some reached India recalling these conditions, and their narrations reminisce of this strange country and the six-legged *sharabkha* mentioned above.

THE COUNTRY OF 'THE BLESSED' HYPERBOREANS

One more legendary population might be related to this northern territory – the Hyperboreans. Researchers have located them in different regions (see Dovatur, Kallistov and Shishova 1982: 264–5, commentary 271). Herodotus in his *Histories* speaks about Aristey who reached the Issedons; above them lived the Arimasps, and still further north the Griffons guarding gold, and at the limit the Hyperboreans who lived at the sea's edge (Herodotus IV: 13).

The historian himself doubts the existence of the Hyperboreans (Herodotus IV: 32). The stories about this people formed a very old legend, far older than Aristey or Herodotus. The 'Country of the Blessed', or the land of the Hyperboreans, was situated in the far north beyond Scythia and the Ripeyskie mountains, which were thought to stretch in a latitudinal direction.

Bongard-Levin and Grantovsky, having summarized all the information presented by ancient writers, concluded that there were territories inhabited by real peoples known to the Scythians. Beyond them were located some frankly mythical tribes and fantastic creatures near the Ripeyskie mountains, and beyond them the Great Ocean, with its regions of 'polar' day and night and the country of the 'blessed' (Bongard-Levin and Grantovsky 1983: 36–8). They analyse the description of the country of the 'blessed' and compare it with epic poems of India and Iran describing the country situated behind the Great Northern mountains and its inhabitants (Bongard-Levin and Grantovsky 1983: 25–7, 45–7, 61–6).

Such similarities may result from the simultaneous appearance of the Hyperboreans with other Indo-Europeans. But the discovery of settlements with hexagonal half-mud huts, both in the subpolar regions and beyond the Arctic circle, suggests another version: Hyperborean could be the name for all the Indo-Europeans who had moved to the North by the middle or the third quarter of the 2nd millennium BC. Later all peoples living in the North were given this name.

Cattle-breeders who moved to new territories might have been able to continue their traditional occupations of cattle-breeding (Ashikhmina 1993c). Unfortunately, there are no finds of animal bones because the settlements were situated on pine grove terraces and bones are not preserved in sandy soils. An indirect proof that cattle-breeders continued their occupation is the presence of the remains of partitions or pillar holes found inside the hexagonal constructions and located parallel to the walls at a distance of 1.5–2 m. Sheds for cattle and a peculiar type of wall for dwellings, provided shelter for cattle retained for reproduction in severe winters.

THE GREAT PEOPLES' MIGRATION AND ITS POSSIBLE REFLECTION IN THE KOMI FOLKLORE

Significant migration to the northern sub-Urals has been dated to the end of the Iron Age: the fourth to sixth centuries AD (Figure 15.11). As a result of the 'Great Peoples' Migration' nomads appear – cattle-breeders with a form of barrow burial rite unusual for this region (Figure 15.12; Ashikhmina 1988). In Komi legends and traditional stories there are vague references to changes in the composition of the population or to a struggle between two groups of the Chud' (for discussion of the ethnonym Chud': Ageeva 1970: 194–203). Some of the legends and traditional stories can be reliably dated to this period.

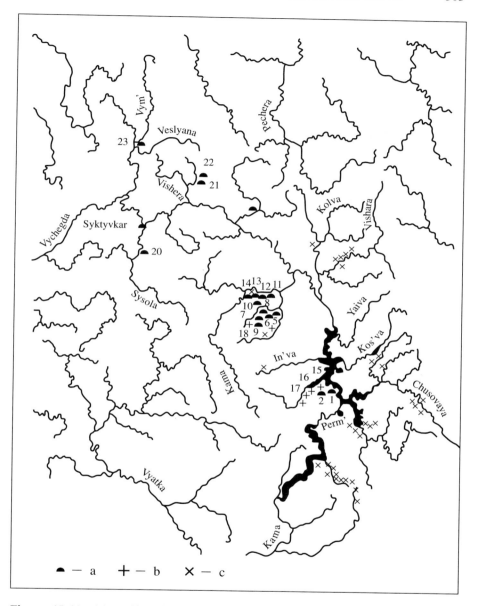

Figure 15.11 Map of burial mounds, fourth to sixth centuries AD, and steppe relicts distribution.

Conventional signs: a − burial mounds; b − sites; c − steppe relicts. *Burial mounds:* 1 − Burkovsry; 2 − Poludensky; 3 − Beklimishevsky; 4 − Bol'she-Visimsky; 5 − Chazevsky I; 6 − Chazevsky II; 7 − Peklaybsky I; 8 − Peklaybsky II; 9 − Mitinsky; 10 − Bel'kovsky; 11 − Agathonovsky; 12 − Kharinsky; 13 − Pyshtajnsky; 14 − Burdakovsky; 20 − Shojnayagsky; 21 − Yavanayagsky; 22 − Borganyel'sky; 23 − Veslyansky I; 24 − Vomynyagsky.

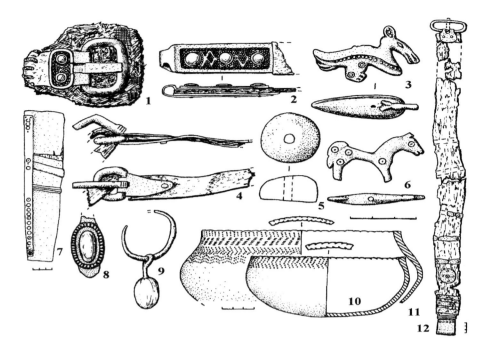

Figure 15.12 Grave goods of the fifth to sixth centuries AD from the burial mound of Borganyel' (the Middle Vychegda basin).

1, 2 – barrow VI/8; 3 – barrow VI/5; 4 – barrow V; 5 – barrow VI/7; 6 – barrow XI/2; 7 – barrow VI/3; 8, 9, 12 – barrow XIV/2; 10 – barrow IV/1; 11 – barrow II. *Material*: bronze – 3, 6; bronze, stone (chalcedony) – 9; bronze, gold, glass – 1, 2; bronze, leather – 4, 12; silver, wood, leather – 7; silver, amber – 8; amber –5; clay – 10, 11.

On the Vychegda river there is still a legend about the ancient road along which the people who previously inhabited this territory departed (Rochev 1984: 20). A legend of the struggle between the blue-eyed Chud' and under-sized black-haired Chud' (Rochev 1984: 149, commentary 4) has been recorded on the Vishera river (the basin of the Vychegda). The remains of a skeleton excavated under the barrows support the idea that the alien population was undersized. On the Mezen' river there is a legend about strong black-haired people; 'they were called the Chud' ... They cannot dance: first they bend their knees, then jump' (Rochev 1984: 18–19). The northern Udmurt use the word 'tetchany' for 'to dance', but its literal translation is 'to jump' (Vladykin and Churakova 1986). On the River Sysola (the Vychegda river basin) there are also fragmentary legends preserved speaking about burial customs: 'Dark, undersized, black-haired individuals found until now among the Komi people are supposed to be the ancestors of the Chud'' (Rochev

1984: 149, commentary 4). Also 'people . . . were buried in barrows' (Ashikhmina 1988: 17).

All these legends and traditional stories are interrelated with later layers connected with the Christianization of the Komi. They do reflect some population movement, quite probably an echo of the Great Peoples' Migration. The Komi-Permyak do not call themselves Permyak but *Komi-Utir* (Ozhegova 1971: 53, n. 1). The appearance of the ethnonym 'Utir' may date from this epoch and is probably connected with the arrival of separate groups of 'Utigurs' in the Upper Prikamje, a people well known from written sources.

CONCLUSIONS

An attempt has been made to relate archaeological materials to toponyms and folklore. This comparison helps to reconstruct migration processes as well as the ethno-cultural history of the population of the northern sub-Urals in the Bronze and Early Iron Ages. The conclusions are preliminary, and await future new information to support or reject them.

NOTES

1   The English text has been extensively rewritten by Roger Blench and occasional new sentences added to link sections. If the sense of the chapter has in some way been distorted by this process, he takes full responsibility. The editors would like to thank Paul Fryer for taking a draft to Komi for checking back with Dr Ashikhmina, and for help with the references.
2   Maps and illustrations presented in this chapter were made on the basis of material published by L.I. Ashikhmina, O.N. Bader, G.M. Burov, R.S. Gabyashev, O.C. Gadzyatskaya, V.F. Gening, R.D. Goldina, A.Kh. Khalikov, V.A. Ivanov, L.L. Kosinskaya, D.A. Krajnov, E.S. Loginova, A.K. Matveyev, N.P. Matveyeva, S.V. Oshibkina, M.G. Pozdnyakova, T.B. Popova, A.D. Pryakhin, P.N. Starostin and V.S. Stokolos.
3   Where oral literature texts are quoted in translation, the line number follows the page number in the text with a superscript 'one'.
4   *Sazhen* is a former Russian measure equal to two metres.
5   One *pood* = 20 Russian pounds = 18 pounds avoirdupois.

REFERENCES

Abaev, V.I. 1981. Doiistoria indoirantsev v svete ario-ural'skikh jazykovykh kontaktov. In *Ethnicheskie problemy istorii Tsentral'noj Asii v drevnosti* [Proceedings of the International Symposium. Dushanbe, October 1977], M.S. Asimov, B.A. Litvinsky, L.I. Miroshnikov and D.S. Raevsky (eds), 84–9. Moskva: Nauka.

Abdullaev, I. Kh. and K.Sh. Mikailov. 1971. K istorii dagestanskikh ethnonymov LEZG i LAK. In *Ethnografia imen*, V.A. Nikonov and D.D. Stratonovich (eds), 13–26. Moskva: Nauka.

Ageeva, R.A. 1970. Ob ethnonyme CHUD' (CHUKHNA, CHUKHAR'). In *Ethnonymy*, V.A. Nikonov (ed.), 194–203. Moskva: Nauka.

Ashikhmina, L.I. 1988. *Pogrebal'ny: obryad kurgannogo mogil'nika Borganel'*. Syktyvkar: Komi Nauchnyy Tsentr AN SSSR.

Ashikhmina, L.I. 1992a. Reconstruction of imaginations of the Tree-of-the-World in the population of the north sub-Urals in the Bronze and Early Iron Ages. In *Suomen Varhaistoria*. Tornion Kongressi 14, K. Julku (ed.), 23–34. Rovaniemi: Pohjois-Suomen Historiallinen Yhdistys.

Ashikhmina, L.I. 1992b. *Rekonstruktsia predstavleniy o mirovom dreve u naselenya Severnogo Priural'ya v epokhu bronzy i rannego zheleza*. Syktyvkar: Komi Nauchnyy Tsentr RAN.

Ashikhmina, L.I. 1993a. 'The Great Bear' in the world outlook of ancient people of the Urals region. In *Specimina Sibirica*, J. Pusztay and E. Saveljeva (eds), 5–19. T.VI. (Uralic Mythology. Papers of International Conference). Savariae, Szombathely.

Ashikhmina, L.I. 1993b. K voprosu o formirovanii lebyazhskoy kul'tury. In *Vzaimodeystviye kul'tur Severnogo Priural'ya v drevnosti i srednevekov'ye*. (Materialy po arkheologii Yevropeyskogo Severo-Vostoka, Vyp. 12), E. Savel'eva (ed.), 60–76. Syktyvkar: Komi Nauchnyy Tsentr RAN.

Ashikhmina, L.I. 1993c. Indo–Europeans and Finno–Ugrians: to the problem of ancient contact (2nd millenium BC). Paper read at the International Congress 'Historia Fenno–Ugrica' 14/8/1993. Oulu.

Bader, O.N. and T.B. Popova. 1987. Pozdnyakovskaya kul'tura. In *Arkheologia SSSR. Epokha bronzy lesnoj polosy*, O.N. Bader, D.A. Krajnov and M.F. Kosarev (eds), 131–5. Moskva: Nauka.

Bongard-Levin, G.M. and E.A. Grantovsky. 1983. *Ot Skifii do Indii. Drevnie arii: mify i istoria*. Moskva: Mysl'.

Burov, G.M. 1967. *Drevny Sindor*. Moskva: Nauka.

Burov, G.M. 1986. Kraynyy Severo-Vostok Yevropy v epokhu mesolita, neolita i rannego metalla. (Avtoreferat doktorskoy dissertatsii). Novosibirsk: Institut istorii, filozii i filosofii Sibirskoye otdeleniye AN SSSR.

Chernykh, E.N. and C.V. Kuz'minykh. 1989. *Drevnyaya metallurgia Severnoj Evrazii (Seyminsko-turbinsky fenomen)*. Moskva: Nauka.

Dovatur, A.I., D.P. Kallistov and I.A. Shishova. 1982. *Narody nashej strany v 'Istorii' Gerodota. Teksty. Perevod. Kommentarii*. Moskva: Nauka.

Gadzyatzkaya, O.S. 1992. Fatyanovsky komponent v kul'ture pozdnej bronzy (Volgo-Klyaz'minskoe mezhdurechje. *Sovetskaya arkheologia* 1, 122–40.

Gamkrelidze, T.V. and V.V. Ivanov. 1984. *Indoevropeyskiy yazyk i indoyevropeytsy*. Tom 2. Tbilisi: Izdatel'stvo Tbilisskozo Universiteta.

Gening, V.F. and M.K. Pozdnyakova. 1964. Prigovskoye gorodishche na r. Iseti. In *Voprosy arkheologii Urala*, Vyp. 6, V.F. Gening (ed.), 34–71. Sverdlovsk: Ural'skiy Gosudarstvennyy Universitet.

Herodotus. 1972. *Istoria*. Leningrad: Nauka.

Gondatti, N.L. 1888. *Predvaritel'nyy otchyot o poyezdke v Severo-Zapadnyy Sibir'*. Moskva.

Ivanov, V.A. 1982. Problema kul'tury Kurmantau. In *Priuralye v epokhu bronzy i rannego zheleza*, V.A. Ivanov and A.Kh. Pshenichnuk (eds), 52–77. Ufa: Bashkirskiy Filial AN SSSR.

Ivanov, V.V. and V.N. Toporov 1982a. Perkunas. In *Mify narodov mira*, Tom 2. S.A. Tokarev (ed.), 302–4. Moskva: Sovetskaya Entsiklopediya.

Ivanov, V.V. and V.N. Toporov. 1982b. Perun. In *Mify narodov mira*, Tom 2. S.A. Tokarev (ed.), 304–7. Moskva: Sovetskaya Entsiklopediya.

Khalikov, A.Kh. 1980. *Prikazanskaya kul'tura. Arkheologia SSSR. Svod arkheologich-eskikh istochnikov*. Vypysk V, 1–24. Moskva: Nauka.

Khalikov, A.Kh. 1987. Chirkovskaya kul'tura. In *Arkheologia SSSR. Epokha bronzy lesnoj polosy SSSR*, O.N. Bader, D.A. Krajnov and M.F. Kosarev (eds), 136–9. Moskva: Nauka.

Khotinsky, N.A. 1978. Paleogeograficheskie osnovy datirovki i periodizatsii neolitha lesnoj zony Evropejskoj chacti SSSR. In *Kratkie soobshchenia Instituta arkheologii*, Vyp. 153. I.T. Kruglikova (ed.), 7–14. Moskva: Nauka.

Kosinskaya, L.L. 1986. Keramika poseleniya Niremka I. In *Pamyatniki material'noy kul'tury na Yevropeyskom Severo-Vostoke*. (Materialy po arkheologii Yevropeyskogo Severo-Vostoka. Vyp. 10), E.A. Saveljeva (ed.), 35–44. Syktyvkar: Komi Filial AN SSSR.

Krajnov, D.A. 1987. Fatyanovskaya kul'tura. In *Arkheologia SSSR. Epokha bronzy lesnoj polosy SSSR*, O.N. Bader, D.A. Krajnov and M.F. Kosarev (eds), 58–76. Moskva: Nauka.

Loginova. E.S. 1993. Poseleniye Chudgudoryag. In *Vzaimodeystviye kul'tur severnozo Priural'ya v drevnosti i srednevekov'ye*. (Materialy po arkheologii Yeropeyskogo Severo-Vostoka. Vyp. 12), E.A. Savel'eva (ed.), 41–59. Syktyvkar: Komi Nauchnyy Tsentr RAN.

Malov, S.Ye. 1952. *Pamyatniki drevneturkskoy pis'mennosti*. Moskva–Leningrad: Izdatel'stvo Akademii Nauk SSSR.

Matveev, A.K. 1961. Drevneural'skaya toponimika i yeyo proiskhozhdeniye. In *Voprosy arkheologii Urala*, Vyp.1, V.F. Gening (ed.), 133–41. Sverdlovsk: Ural'skiy Gosudarstvennyy Universitet.

Matveyeva, N.P. 1991. O sootnoshenii gorokhovskikh i vorobyebskikh pamyatnikov v Srednem Priobolye. In *Istochniki etnocul'turnoy istorii Zapadnoy Sibiri*, N.P. Matveyeva (ed.), 148–64. Tyumen': Tyumenskiy Gosudarstvennyy Universitet.

Muminov, M.T. 1969. K voprosu ob iranskikh elementakh v substratnoy toponimike Srednego Zaural'ya. In *Proiskhozhdenie aborigenov Sibiri*, A.P. Dul'zon (ed.), 14–16. Tomsk: Izdatel'stvo Tomskogo Universiteta.

Oshibkina, S.V. 1987. Eneolith i bronzovy vek Severa Evropejskoj chasti SSSR. In *Arkheologia SSSR. Epokha bronzy lesnoj polosy SSSR*, O.N. Bader, D.A. Krajnov and M.F. Kosarev (eds), 147–56. Moskva: Nauka.

Ozhegova, M.N. 1971. *Komi-permyatskie predaniya o Kudym-Oshe i Pere-Bogatyre*. (Ucheniye zapiski Permskogo gosudarstvennogo pedagogicheskogo instituta. Vyp. 92). Perm': Permskiy Gosudarstvennyy Pedinstitut.

Pryakhin, A.D. and A.Kh. Khalikov. 1987. Abashevskaya kul'tura. In *Arkheologia SSSR. Epokha bronzy lesnoj polosy SSSR*, O.N. Bader, D.A. Krajnov and M.F. Kosarev (eds), 124–31. Moskva: Nauka.

Rochev, Yu.G. 1984. *Komi legendy i predaniya*. Syktyvkar: Komi Knizhnoe Izdatel'stvo.

Senkevich-Gudkova, V.V. 1979. 'Solotie ludi' v russkikh i finno-ugorskikh skaskakh. In *Otrazhenie mezhethnicheskikh protsessov v ustnoj proze*, E.V. Pomerantseva (ed.), 117–22. Moskva: Nauka.

Stokolos, V.S. 1988. *Kul'tury epokhi rannego metalla Severnogo Priuralya*. Moskva: Nauka.

Vladykin, V.Ye. and R.A. Churakova. 1986. Obryad-sëton v pominal'nom rituale Udmurtov. In *Muzyka v svadebnom obryade finno-ugrov i sosednikh naradov*, Kh. Ruytel' (ed.), 1–11. Tallin: Akademiya Nauk ESSR.

16   Oral traditions and the prehistory of the Ẹdọ-speaking people of Benin

Joseph Eboreime

LOCATION AND SCOPE OF STUDY

The Ẹdọ-speaking peoples occupy the forest and derived savannah extremities of the south-western region of Nigeria. The groups within this cluster include the Bini (Oredo, Orhiowmon and Ovia), the Etsako,[1] the Akoko, the Emai and Ora (of Ivbiosakon) and the Esan [=Ishan] (Figure 16.1). They fall largely within the boundaries of Ẹdọ State within the 30-state structure of Nigeria in 1996, and their principal town is Benin City.

The more southerly and linguistically differentiated cluster of Urhobo, Iṣẹkiri, Western Igbo and Ijọ peoples now constitute Delta State, with a headquarters in the Warri. With the creation of new States (1967, 1976, 1991) and the desire for more inclusive autonomies, the erstwhile sentiments and loyalties of the Delta peoples (except the Iṣẹkiri) to the Benin kingdom have waned considerably. Consequently, oral traditions have begun to undergo transformations to fit into present-day realities and identities (Eboreime 1992). In Ẹdọ State, the greater homogeneity of the Edoid languages has allowed such allegiances to be maintained.

This chapter[2] is concerned mainly with the oral traditions and prehistory of the Ẹdọ people who constituted the core of the ancient Benin kingdom, and still retain strong traditional ties and a religious loyalty to the monarch – the Oba of Benin, the symbol of Ẹdọ identity within the competitive ethnic political milieu of modern Nigeria. The Ẹdọ-speaking groups outside this core, whether north or south, are referred to as Edoid (following Elugbe 1986).

Much of what is published about the oral traditions of Benin, like her arts, has been from the dynastic point of view, underplaying the non-dynastic (peripheral) versions. Egharevba (1968, but editions go back to 1936) is the single most important expression of the dynastic myths of Benin. His account has been regularly expanded and re-edited over more than half a century to take account of changing political dynamics within the present ruling house. This chapter attempts to correct this imbalance by reinterpreting the

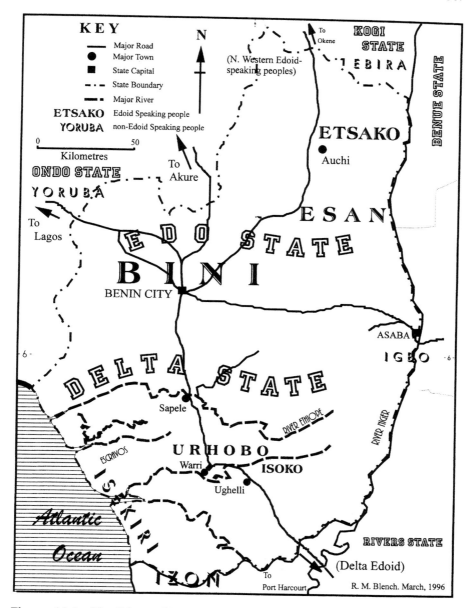

Figure 16.1 The Edo-speaking peoples.

prehistory and archaeology of Benin in the light of peripheral myths and traditions.

The date 1515 is significant as the period of a major war between Benin and the neighbouring Igala kingdom to the north-east. The Oba of Benin, Esigie, was said to have been helped to prosecute the war by Europeans. This is depicted in Benin bronze plaques and corroborated by written records (Ryder 1969). The date 1515 represents a point at which all types of evidence – oral traditions, art history and archaeology – can combine to throw light on the prehistory of the Ẹdọ-speaking peoples at both the core and periphery.

The Ẹdọ of Benin are bordered on the west by the Yoruba at Ife (Uhe in Ẹdọ) and Ọyọ. To the east and north-east are the Igbo and the Igala. North and north-west are the Ebira (Igbirra), and the Nupe around the Niger–Benue confluence area. South and south-west are the Ịzọn (Ịjọ) and the Isẹkiri. Igbo neighbours of the Bini refer to them as either Idu or Ado, from which the generic term Ẹdọ seems to have taken root.

THE ARCHAEOLOGY OF BENIN AND THE IMPLICATIONS FOR PREHISTORY

Summary of existing archaeological research

Archaeological research started in Benin City in 1954 with A.J.H. Goodwin, followed in 1959 by Frank Willet, Liman Ciroma (1960), Graham Connah (1961–4), and currently Patrick Darling who started work in the 1970s.

Archaeological evidence, from the polished stone axes of Late Stone Age origin commonly found in traditional Benin shrines, indicates that people were already inhabiting the Benin forest area well before the kingdom and the city came into existence. Connah (1975) posits that the Benin forest zone was inhabited by 3000 BC.

A survey of the elaborate Benin wall and ditch systems (Connah 1967; Darling 1974, 1976, 1994) throws light on how the city developed; initially a fusion of separate settlements owing allegiance to a central authority, in the fifteenth century Oba Ewuare constructed a true urban unit. The innermost city walls belong to a later period when the city was already becoming a distinct urban unit requiring a strong line of defence. Compared with the other earthworks, the inner walls are a defensive network in the fullest sense, as distinct from the outer walls of neighbouring Udo, Ohovbe and Ishan chiefdoms which were agricultural community boundaries (Connah 1975; Darling 1994).

Excavations at Benin City centre have uncovered remains of the early palaces of Benin extending back some 700 years. Radiocarbon dates for the earliest deposits at the Clerks' Quarters point to a thirteenth century AD date (Connah 1975). A chance discovery at another part of the Clerks' Quarters site revealed a ninth-century bronze caster's hoard of cast and sheet metal objects. An excavation at Usama, the palace site of the first four Obas of Benin, gave a thirteenth century AD date for the earliest deposits (Connah 1975). The Benin Museum site revealed evidence of occupation going back to at least the beginning of the fourteenth century. Potsherd pavements were already a feature of Benin architecture by that time. Such pavements are a well-known feature of ancient Ife and of a number of other places in West Africa.

Although there have been claims following a survey of the Benin rural earth-works (Darling 1995) for the start of large nucleated village settlements from 500 BC to AD 0, these are not generally accepted. The usual date for the devel-opment of the Benin centre of authority is immediately following those at Ife (i.e. *c.* AD 1000). Such a date would correspond well with existing dynastic oral traditions. This is far later than the genesis of the Ẹdọ-speaking peoples and presumably well after the formation of the Bini as an ethnic identity.

Typology of oral traditions and claims of origin

BINI TRADITIONS

Bini historical traditions explain their own origins and those of other groups by assuming the existence of a city *ab initio*, with the remainder of the Ẹdọ peoples migrating *from* Benin City (Egharevba 1968; Ryder 1969). This conflicts both with the suppressed non-dynastic myths in Benin City itself and with the material and linguistic evidence in peripheral villages and communities. First pro-dynastic ideological myths and non-dynastic traditions must be distinguished. Thereafter each corpus of tradition can be weighed against linguistic and archaeological data to obtain a balanced picture of the origins and development of Benin. We must, however, be careful not to mix up the origin of the present dynasty with the origin of the people as Egharevba has tended to do (Egharevba 1968).

NON-DYNASTIC MYTHS: AUTOCHTHONOUS TRADITIONS

Oral traditions from the Etsako, Esan and Ukpilla communities to the north widely acknowledge the pre-existence of autochthonous peoples who resided in the caves and shelters of the Kukuruku/Akoko hills. Five major groups of early settlers, pre-dating later waves of migrants from Benin, have so far been identified. They are said to have existed in these hilly areas during the LSA 5000–500 BC (Harunah 1986). Unlike Benin, no archaeological exca-vation has been conducted in the Northern-Ẹdọ country. The Akoko-Ẹdọ hills and rock-shelters offer a promising prospect for corroborative data through archaeology.

Three out of the five groups are said to be Edoid-speakers from the Akoko-Ẹdọ hills, while the other two were Igala and Ebira (respectively Yoruboid and Nupoid) (Harunah 1986). Migrations from Benin City in the sixteenth and seventeenth centuries, and the Nupe invasions of the nineteenth century, have tended to complicate the demographic and settlement patterns with consequent effects on the content of oral traditions (Omo Ananigie 1949).

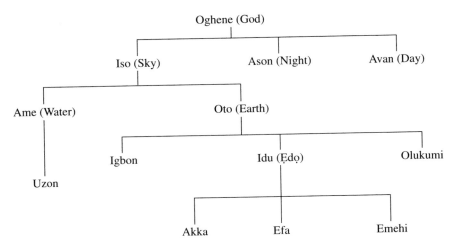

Figure 16.2 Traditional non-dynastic genealogy. Adapted from Omoregie's unpublished manuscript.

The myth of the pouring sky (Iso Norho)

The most popular surviving non-dynastic myth of a common Ẹdọ origin is that of Iso Norho, associated with the great flood that was occasioned by a heavy downpour as punishment for incest. It puts the emergence of the Benin and other Ẹdọ-speaking people in a primordial centre, Uhe, a place where problems are heaped before Oghene – the God of creation – which in remote times is said to have been near the Niger–Benue confluence (Ryder 1965: 25–39; Obayemi 1976). Uhe is said to have been occupied by Olukumi (Yoruba), Igbon (Igbo) and Uzon (Ịjọ).

The myth begins by naming Oghene (God) as the father of Iso (the Sky), Ason (Night) and Avan (Daylight) (Figure 16.2). Out of the three children of Oghene, only the eldest son, Iso (Sky), had children; Ame (Water) and Oto (Earth). The children of Oto were Igbon (Igbo), Olukumi (Yoruba) and Idu (Ẹdọ). Ame, the brother of Oto, gave birth to Uzon (Ịjọ). Oto had been banished by his father (Iso) for seducing and marrying his second wife, by whom he had had Igbon (Igbo). Iso used Ame (Flood) to punish Oto (Earth) for his incestuous acts. But Oghene did not want the children to suffer undue hardship. By means of a chain he poured sand on the flood water to form dry land for their habitation. Thus Uhe (i.e. old Ife) was formed by divine (Oghene's) providence.

In appreciation of this, Idu and his brothers established an altar dedicated to Oghene of Uhe. Idu bore the title of Oduduwa Oghene n Uhe (i.e. Oduduwa, the Oghene of Uhe). At Idu's death, his younger brother Olukumi assumed the office with a new title of Olofin (Omoregie n.d.). Olukumi became so high-handed that Idu's children (Akka, Efa, Emehi) had to migrate from Uhe to the present site of Benin City – then called Ubini – where they displaced a group of original settlers, Ivbirinwineko (dwarfs from the spirit world). Memories of these original settlers are preserved in Edọ songs and folklore.

For a long time afterwards Uhe remained a centre of pilgrimage for the Edọ. Similar migrations by a section of Yoruba also led to the founding of new Ife. But by the time of Eresoyen's reign (1735 and 1750) the Oghene shrine had been replanted at present-day Ife, in a spot where Oranmiyan is said to have left his mysterious walking stick – the stone monolith (Omoregie 1987).

This non-dynastic, collective myth also tries to account for the origin of other Edọ-speaking communities of Esan (Ishan) to the north of Edọ and Uhobo (Urhobo) to the South. Both Esan and Urhobo were said to be faithful disciples of Akka, the first of the three sons of Idu. Following Akka's death and burial at Irrua, Esan withdrew from the migrating groups and settled down to form the nucleus of the Ishan people. A disagreement between Uhobo and the other migrants resulted in the out-migration of Uhobo from Ubini to the Delta waters (Uworame). Efa and Emehi settled in the eastern and western side of Benin respectively. Each community was ruled by a body of elders (Edion) with the Odionwee (the most senior) as the head. From these, two new Edọ communities grew and developed.

PRO-DYNASTIC MYTHS

The pro-dynastic version of Benin history has outpaced the non-dynastic version (Bradbury 1957; Egharevba 1968). Egharevba traces the foundation of the Benin Empire/dynasty to AD 900, when the Ogiso (sky kings) were said to have ruled. He ascribes the origin of over one hundred villages in the old Benin division to different sons of the 'Sky Kings' who used to send their sons to rule over villages as Enogie (chiefs). So also the origins of other Edoid and Igboid groups as the Aboh and Onitsha are traced to this early dynastic phase of Benin history.

The last of the Ogiso kings, Owodo, was banished for misrule. Evian,[3] who was appointed as an administrator, attempted to perpetuate his lineage by appointing his son, Ogiamien, as his successor. The Bini people refused and instead appealed to the Oni of Ife, Odudua, to send one of his sons (Egharevba 1968: 6). It was in this circumstance that Oranmiyan was sent to Benin. He faced opposition from Ogiamien, but soon married the daughter of a Benin noble who bore him a son, Eweka. Shortly afterwards, Oranmiyan abdicated his office on the grounds that the land was a 'land of vexation' (Ile-Ibinu in Yoruba, an expression from which 'Benin' is said to derive). Oranmiyan established his son as the Alafin of Oyo before returning to Ife as the Oni (Egharevba 1968: 7). He ensured, however, that his son Eweka was named as the king (Oba). According to this tradition, the present Oba would be the twenty-eighth in the dynasty, whose beginning is variously dated from the twelfth to the fourteenth centuries. By this tradition, Oranmiyan never ruled in Benin but only established the dynasty.

During the coronation of 1978–9, another version which attempted to turn Egharevba's account on its head emerged (Eboreime 1985). This account gave an Ẹdọ interpretation and meaning to all the Yoruba names and culture heroes. Oranmiyan was renamed Omonoyan ('a pet child'), while Oduduwa became Izoduwa ('I have chosen a prosperous path'). The former was said to have been the son of the latter, who had earlier wandered from Benin. He found himself in Ife and corresponded to the Yoruba millennial expectation of a prince from the East. He was installed as the Oni of Ife. By 1992, another version had taken precedence:

> According to our traditional history this land of Ẹdọ is the origin of the world. It was founded by the first Oba of Benin who was the youngest son of the Supreme God. At that time (as the Holy Book came to confirm . . .) the universe was all water and no land.
>
> (Oba of Benin, quoted in Eweka 1992: 2)

This myth seeks to fuse the kingship, land and people into one corpus of tradition that rests on the divinity of kingship and marries non-dynastic and dynastic traditions.

Going by Egharevba's version, the first three kings lived at Usama, between the two city walls on the western side, where the installation of a new Oba still takes place (Bradbury 1957: 20). The fourth Oba, Ewedo, established himself at the present site after a successful battle with Chief Ogiamien. Oba Oguola is credited with building the main wall round the city, while brass casting is said to have been introduced from Ife (Uhe?). And by the time D'Avero visited Benin City in 1485 the accession of a new Oba had been approved by somebody he described as King Ogane (Oghene) who lived far away in the interior (Bradbury 1957: 20). Oba Esigie was said to have been aided by the Portuguese in prosecuting the Idah war around 1515.

THE ORIGINS OF THE BENIN EARTHWORKS

The origins of the *Iya* (Benin linear walls and earthworks) offer an excellent example of the phenomenon of feedback, as well as the conflict theory, which the dynastic traditions exemplify. The Benin dynastic tradition as recorded by Egharevba (1953, 1968) – has sought to legitimate the ruling dynasty by assigning the roles of city-wall builders variously to Oguola, Ewuare and Esigie. Egharevba's 1950 account asserts that by the order of Oba Oguola, all important towns and villages in Benin copied its example and dug similar moats and ditches round their villages. Such an account presents a rather illogical sequence of moat construction: the digging of outer walls (*Iya*) before the inner ones, which have no demonstrable unity (Connah 1975; Darling 1984). Reconciling the distribution patterns of settlements with Benin dynastic foundation claims and the *Iya* pattern is problematic (Darling 1984: 45). There are therefore few grounds for confidence in the claims by peripheral Benin villages that their walls were made by Oba Oguola, especially where the villages themselves claim later foundation dates.

In the same vein we should be wary of foundation claims by many Northern Edo groups that they migrated from Benin during the period of moat construction (Bradbury 1957: 65–7, 87–8, 101–31). While some of these claims may be true, others will reflect past political allegiances, the quest for prestige or political circumspection when Benin was at its most powerful (Darling 1984: 46).

Darling (1984) believes that the whole network of Benin Walls (*Iya*) and moats taken together 'represent a settlement distribution of a pre-dynastic Edo–Ishan culture, covering an area which was geographically similar but overlapped much of the later Benin and Ishan kingdoms'.

ORAL TRADITIONS IN PERSPECTIVE

For corroborative and comparative purposes, it is necessary to examine Ijo (Izon), Isekiri and Edo traditions of origin, to appreciate the uses to which prehistoric, historic and linguistic data are put by various interest groups in Nigeria.

Ijo myths trace their origin to about AD 600–1000 (Owonaro 1949). Ijo is said to be the first of four sons of Oduduwa (the Yoruba culture hero). Ijo became a rival of his father over the throne of the Ife kingdom. His father subsequently sent him to 'guard and protect the mouth . . . of the graceful Delta from foreigners' (Owonaro 1949: 4). He passed through the territory that was to become Benin, leaving some Ijo groups there as settlers, and then to the present site of Warri. It was there that the founder of the Isekiri invented a river craft, the canoe, with which the whole Niger delta was explored and conquered.

According to this account, the Ijo were already settled at Warri before the 'Isekiri' arrived encased in a mysterious box floating on water (Owonaro 1949: 9). Ijo gave out his young daughter in marriage to Isekiri, who produced many children. Isekiri and Ijo later fell out over the use of the latter's favourite granddaughter for ritual purposes and Isekiri fled back to Benin City.

Isekiri myths reveal that they have been closely connected with the Edo, Yoruba, Urhobo and Ijo through migrations, inter-marriage and trade connections. Isekiri have had longer and more continuous contacts with Europeans than any other groups in the Niger delta (Bradbury 1957: 177).

Whatever their shortcomings, oral narratives do point to the relationship between ecology, migration and history, and the outcome of interaction between contiguous peoples over space and time. Indeed, historical process is thus illustrated as a continuum in space and time.

The archaeological data suggests a common centre from which multi-directional movements of Edo, Igbo, Yoruba and other groups occurred in the pre-dynastic era of Edo history (Obayemi 1976: 200). But the dynastic myths of Edo origin and migration record conflict situations which resulted in the out-migration of groups from Benin. This has no present archaeological, linguistic or ethnographic basis.

By 500 AD, the following centres of civilization had emerged: the Niger–Senegal basin, the Niger–Bend, the Chad Basin, the Middle Nile Valley and the Niger–Benue (Central Nigeria) centre. The Nok culture (terracotta) has been tentatively dated to between 900 BC and AD 200; if so, it falls in the Nakuran Wet Phase (Jemkur 1992).

Both the non-dynastic myth of Ẹdọ origin and the linguistic evidence point to a northerly direction where the Ẹdọ, Yoruba, Igbo, Ịjọ, Igala and Idoma peoples interacted. Folklore and oral traditions talk of strong trade links between the Ẹdọ and the Idoma, where religious cults and oracles were also consulted. The Igala–Benin, Igbo–Igala relationships are indicative and instructive of these patterns of movements (Oguagha 1982/3). It must be stressed that the site of the Holy City of Ife (Uhe in Ẹdọ) has changed more than once in traditional times, and that its present location is the last of about six previous settlements (Williams 1974: 121).

Several towns and villages in present-day Nigeria are known as Ife, and Ife-type manufactures (such as stone carving and the famous potsherd pavements) occur at sites today distant from the Holy City. A northern connection of old Bini traditions, and those of a number of societies of the lower Niger, with Kanem-Bornu, have been suggested (Williams 1974: 127).

Obayemi (1976) observed that the Yoruba, the Idoma, Igbo, Nupe, Ebira and Gbari form a cluster of linguistic groups in the Niger–Benue confluence, from where a slow, steady population expansion and cultural differentiation took place, even as late as the nineteenth century. By the time the dynasties of Benin and Igala were inaugurated, the process of expansion and differentiation had been completed (Obayemi 1976).

A Benin cultural historian and specialist in Ẹdọ mythologies, Dr O.S.B. Omoregie has speculated that 'the *Iso Norho* myth' is a local interpretation of the Nakuran wet phase (850 BC to AD 500). It was during Olukumi's reign that the major emigrations started to take place – first the Uzon, then the Igbon, and finally the Idu. The sack of Uhe sometime between AD 1550 and 1735 brought the long Yoruba hegemony in Uheland to an end (Omoregie n.d.).

If Omoregie is correct in his claim, Idu reigned in the original Ife homeland in about the sixth century, and even after the migration of the Ẹdọ to their present site, they still maintained contact with the custodian of the Oghene (Ogane) shrine at Uhe which lay somewhere in the Niger–Benue confluence. Up to the seventeenth century the spiritual overlordship of Ogane (= Oghene) was said to have been felt at Benin, as well as the new Ife (Williams 1974: 126). The insignia of Ogane occurs on an important Tada bronze, on several Bini bronzes, and on a small bronze figure of the Ife School (Williams 1974). Despite this, Benin brass heads do not owe their major inspiration to Ife.

Obayemi (1976) has posited that the ancient Ile–Ife, described by archaeologists and art historians as classical Ife, was a mini-state made up of several settlements. This tallies with the non-dynastic oral traditions and the unpublished accounts of Omoregie which talk of separate acephalous communities living in contiguity at Uhe.

Speculative as this may seem, these re-evaluations are important:

(a) in redirecting the question of the Ife–Benin relationship before the sixteenth century and the unresolved question of the location of the Ogane's settlement;

(b) in understanding how intellectual traditions feed into oral traditions, and vice versa, in a unique and dynamic perspective among the Ẹdọ-speaking people.

LINGUISTIC EVIDENCE AND HISTORICAL INFERENCES

The Edoid languages show their greatest diversity in the hilly areas north-west of Benin City. Elugbe (1979) has suggested that this region is the original Edoid homeland. From this area Edoid speakers would have spread south-wards to the plains, and into the Delta area. The expansion of Ẹdọ culture from Benin City probably eliminated large numbers of Edoid languages with

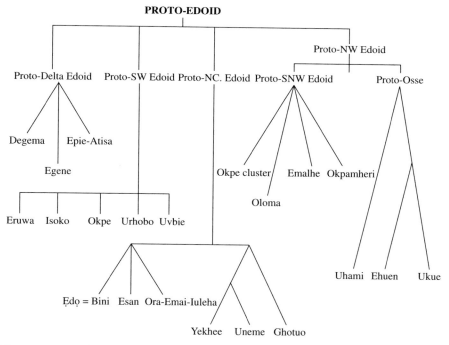

Figure 16.3 Classification of the Edoid languages.

Source: Elugbe 1986.

only a small number of speakers and left the remote Delta Edoid languages isolated south of the Bini area. Figure 16.3 shows the most recent classification of the Edoid languages, based on Elugbe (1986).

The linguistic evidence indicates an early dispersal from the north-western forest margin which distributed a Proto-Edoid belt from the north, to the extreme south and the far west, where they developed the dialectical features that now distinguish the Bini and Esan (Ishan) from the southern dialects.

An expansion of Igbo from east of the river into the Agbor region seems to be a later intrusion (Jones 1965, n.d.). The linguistic geography suggests that the Igbo communities may have eliminated a chain of peoples linking the North-Central and South-western Edoid speakers. The origin myths of the Niger Ẹdọ and Western Igbo communities indicate equally strongly an expansion from the Benin area towards the Niger to the north-east and east, particularly into the Ishan area which must have remained in very close contact with Benin. Claims of an Ife origin cannot be substantiated from the linguistic evidence; they apply to dynastic prototypes of the Oranmiyan genre who came to Benin as rulers (Elugbe 1979: 95).

The linguistic and oral evidence taken together presents a picture of an original dispersion of Ẹdọ-speakers to the extreme linguistic boundaries, followed by a later massive movement outwards from a major centre of expansion, the Benin kingdom.

Non-dynastic oral traditions provide alternative images of the prehistory of the Ẹdọ to the well-rehearsed dynastic myths. These myths relate to the present-day socio-political situation in Nigeria, where the invention of traditions and elaboration of myths have become strategic phenomena in ethnic competition, claims and counterclaims.

TOWARDS A THEORY OF ORAL TRADITION

Against this interdisciplinary background and analysis, hypotheses to account for the oral traditions of the Benin and Ẹdọ-speaking peoples can be set up. This can reveal patterns of relationships of varying degrees and interest between the centre and the periphery. The following categories of community and their attendant traditions can be distinguished:

(a) communities whose traditions seek to establish cultural links with Benin through myths of ultimate descent and migration (the Ora, other Ivbiosakon groups and Ishan);

(b) communities who, though politically involved with the Benin kingdom, look elsewhere for cultural affinities (the Igbo chiefdoms of Anioma, Ondo, Owo, Idoani Ikale);

(c) communities which construct relationships with Benin or claim autochthony according to prevailing circumstances (the pro-Islamic groups of Etsako, the Iṣẹkiri, Western Ịjọ);

(d) communities which seek to justify the present and ongoing socio-political transformations in Benin City.

The intense desire to gain more autonomy and thereby facilitate access to centrally controlled resources has given the invention and manufacture of oral traditions added impetus and colouring. Oral traditions have thus become manipulative tools for political bargaining in the hands of competing elites. For instance, the Northern Edo groups of Ora, Ishan and Etsako with their Akoko-Edo counterparts, are now demanding the excision of a new state (to be called AFEMESA) from the existing Edo State. The demand for this state develops from new linguistic findings, the rejuvenation of suppressed non-dynastic and autochthonous myths, as well as a revived appeal to Islamic-Nupe ties to strengthen their argument for marginalization.

It is fruitful to study the corpus of oral traditions over time and space, and relate them to changing interests – political, economic and social – as well as pattern of conflicts, competition and alliances within and between communities. Oral traditions should be viewed as dynamic and creative, as explanatory as well as coping models, adapted both to empiricist interpretation and the misuse of prehistoric and historical data.

NOTES

1 The numerous ethnic groups cited in this chapter are referred to by their standard reference names as found in Crozier and Blench (1992). However, where they occur in Edo traditions they often have lexically distinct names. The formula of equivalence is: Olukumi [Edo name] = (Yoruba) [Reference name].
2 This chapter has been rewritten in places by Roger Blench, who also redrew Figure 16.1 and expanded the section on Edoid languages. Unreferenced oral traditions are from Dr Eboreime's fieldwork, 1975–95.
3 To be distinguished from the French purveyors of mineral water, active in Nigeria.

REFERENCES

Ajayi, J.F.A. and M. Crowder. 1976. *A History of West Africa*. Vol. II. London and New York: Longman.
Beier, U. 1980. *Yoruba Myths*. Oxford: Oxford University Press.
Bradbury R.E. 1957. *The Benin Kingdom and the Edo-speaking peoples of S.W. Nigeria*. London: International Africa Institute.
Connah, G.E. 1967. New light on Benin City walls. *Journal of the Historical Society of Nigeria* 3, 593–609.
Connah, G.E. 1975. *The Archaeology of Benin*. Oxford: Clarendon.
Crozier, D. and R.M. Blench. 1992. *Index of Nigerian Languages* (2nd edn). Dallas: SIL.
Darling, P.J. 1974. The earthworks of Benin. *Nigeria Field* 39(3), 128–37.
Darling, P.J. 1976. Notes on earthworks of the Benin Empire. *West African Journal of Archaeology* 6, 143–9.

Darling, P.J. 1984. *Archaeology and History in Southern Nigeria: the ancient linear earth-works of Benin* (2 vols). Cambridge Monographs in African Archaeology 11. BAR International Series 215. Oxford.

Darling, P.J. 1994. World heritage sites for Nigeria. Manuscript. Leventis Foundation.

Darling, P.J. 1995. Surveys of Sungbo's Eredo, Ijebu-Ode. Manuscript prepared for the Nigerian World Heritage Committee, Lagos.

Eboreime, O.J. 1985. Coronation as drama: the installation of a Benin monarch as a study in the continuity of kingship: the transformation of tradition and the manu-facture of ethnic identity. *Cambridge Anthropology*, 10(2), 41–53.

Eboreime, O.J. 1992. Group identities and changing patterns of alliances in the Niger-Delta. Ph.D., Department of Social Anthropology, Cambridge.

Egharevba, J.U. 1953. *A Short History of Benin*. Benin: The author.

Egharevba, J.U. 1968. *A Short History of Benin*. Ibadan: Ibadan University Press.

Elugbe, B.O. 1979. Some tentative historical inferences from comparative Edoid Studies. *Kiabàrà* 2(1), 82–101.

Elugbe, B.O. 1986. *Comparative Edoid: phonology and lexicon*. Delta Series 6. University of Port Harcourt.

Eweka, E. 1992. *Evolution of Benin Chieftaincy Titles*. Benin: Uniben Press.

Harunah, H.B. 1986. A history of the autochthonous settlements in the pre-Etsako Territory. Seminar Paper for the Department of History, University of Lagos, Nigeria.

Jemkur, J.F. 1992. *Aspects of the Nok Culture*. Zaria: Ahmadu Bello University Press.

Jones, G.I. 1965. Time and oral tradition with special reference to Eastern Nigeria. *Journal of African History* 6(2), 15–160.

Jones, G.I. n.d. Tribal distribution in midwestern Nigeria: the Benin sphere. Unpublished manuscript.

Obayemi, A. 1976. The Yoruba and Ẹdọ speaking peoples and their neighbours before 1600. In *A History of West Africa*, J.F.A. Ajayi and M. Crowder (eds), 196–263. London and New York: Longman.

Oguagha, P.A. 1982/3. The conquest hypothesis in Igbo–Igala relations: a re-exam-ination. *West African Journal of Archaeology* 12, 55–61.

Omo-Ananigie, P.I. 1949. *A Brief History of Etsakor*. Lagos: Tokunbo Printers.

Omoregie, O.S.B. 1987. The theocratic monarch of Uhe. *Weekend Voice*, issue of 18–20 September, Benin City.

Omoregie, O.S.B. n.d. Benin under the Ogiso monarch: foundations of Ẹdọ civili-zation. Manuscript.

Owonaro, S.K. 1949. The History of Ijọ and her neighbours in Nigeria. Manuscript.

Ryder, A.F.C. 1969. *Benin and the Europeans 1485–1897*. London: Longman.

Williams, D. 1974. *Icon and Image*. New York: Routledge.

17   Oral traditions and archaeology: two cases from Vanuatu

José Garanger

Confronting data from oral traditions with archaeology is of scientific interest for both ethnology and prehistory, as well as being of practical and human interest both for the inhabitants of Oceania and for studying the general history of humankind.

In the nineteenth centuary and the early years of the twentieth, great hopes were placed in recording local traditions to uncover the Polynesian past, then considered to be of no very great time-depth. So, for example, in the case of New Zealand, Aotearoa was said to have been peopled by the canoes of the Kupe, Ngahue and the 'great fleet' that came from Hawaiki. More recent studies, especially archaeological, have revealed a more complex reality. Although we *might* be tempted to conclude, along with the well-known anthropologist Murdock (1959: 43), that native historical traditions '[form] the one type of historical information that is virtually valueless', this would be incorrect. In the Maori case, it was originally thought that the moas recorded in their traditions were mythical. After the discovery of *Dinornis*, it was originally suggested that these bird fossils should be dated to a geological era well before the presence of human beings, and that they had long disappeared by the time of human settlement in New Zealand. Eventually, however, archaeological research confirmed that the Maori and the moa were contemporaries, and indeed their eggs are found associated with human burials.

In the most acculturated regions of Oceania, oral traditions have lost their social function and are of limited interest, at least as far as they record a chronicle of past events. In the Vanuatu archipelago, which has interacted with the West less intensively and for less time than many other areas, oral traditions persist despite the trappings of modernity. Attempts have been made for the past thirty years to verify the historical truth of events occurring in the traditions of the centre of the archipelago, drawn from two cycles of myths, one linked to the other. We know from R.P. Michelsen, a missionary at Tongoa from 1879 to 1930, some details of the first one – that of Kuwae. However, the ensemble of oral traditions from central Vanuatu was systematically and exhaustively collected from 1958 onwards by the ethnologist Jean

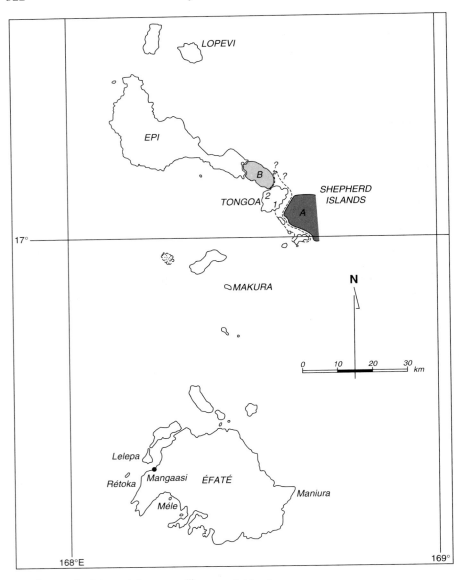

Figure 17.1 Efate and the north-central islands.

A = Limited of Kuwae caldera according to J.-J. Espirat (1964).
B = Kuwae Caldera according to J.-P. Eissen *et al.* (1994).
- - - = Speculative reconstruction of the boundaries of Kuwae.
? = Region of uncertainty (J.-J. Espirat 1964).
1 = Mangarisu.
2 = Panita.

Guiart. The collection was completed following a mission to the Shepherd Islands in 1963 (Espirat 1964; Espirat *et al.* 1973).

In the case of the second myth-cycle, that of the hero Roy Mata, Guiart noted that local informants were more reticent. This grew out of an internal political problem in relation to the colonial status of the islands, which were then a Franco-British condominium and whose population had aspirations to independence. However, the archaeological research carried out in 1964, 1966 and 1967 involved discussions between several local mythographers and thereby yielded a more precise and coherent body of information on Roy Mata.

The first myth concerns the legend of Kuwae which was destroyed by a volcanic cataclysm deliberately provoked by a young man named Tumbuk some twenty generations previously (in relation to the era of R.P. Michelsen). He was led by the people of his village to commit unwittingly an incestuous act with his mother, and so he decided to take vengeance by destroying the island with all its inhabitants. Of this shattered island only the small archipelago of the Shepherds still remains today (Figure 17.1). A study by a geologist, Espirat, confirmed the reality of such a cataclysm and indeed attempted to demarcate the boundaries of ancient Kuwae. Archaeological research (Garanger 1972, 1980, 1982) produced similar results; on the south coast of Tongoa a thick layer of erupted material covers several archaeological layers (ceramics, tools, hearths) of which the most ancient go back to the fifth century BC. The general stratigraphy confirms the oral tradition: earth movements, cave-ins and volcanic eruptions. Several C^{14} dates with similar results situate these events around AD 1450.[1] Espirat (pers. comm., 6/12/66) obtained a comparable date: AD 1460±37. In 1990, a new study undertaken by ORSTOM[2] researchers dated the climax of the cataclysm to AD 1452±1. They localized the caldera between Epi and Tongoa isles; not east of the Shepherds like Espirat. However, they were unable to explore the region north of Tongoa and, moreover, they concluded the situation was extremely complex; their researches continue. Whatever the case, the cataclysm at Kuwae was 'one of the seven most important volcanic eruptions in the world in the last ten thousand years' (Eissen *et al.* 1994; see also Monzier *et al.* 1994; Robin *et al.* 1994).

In the traditions, a young man escaped the cataclysm and sought refuge on a neighbouring island, Makura. Seven years later, he came back to what remained of ancient Kuwae (the small Shepherd archipelago) and organised its resettlement, calling back the former chiefs of Kuwae who had fled to Efate at the first premonitions of the cataclysm. The young man was made chief of the island he first reached, Tongoa, and took the title Ti Tongoa Liseiriki, derived from a spiny plant which was the first to grow on the soil of ancient Kuwae and which he spotted from Makura.

Both the place and the structure of his burial site are still remembered. It had to be on Tongoa on the territory of Panita, and not far from the place he first disembarked when coming back from Makura. I was told that it was

Figure 17.2 Tongoa (Shepherd Islands). A front view of the grave of Ti Tongoa Liseiriki between and at the foot of a standing stone. In front of him, to the right, the skeleton of a woman and that of another high up on the left. The bones are very poorly preserved (the grave is shallow and soil acid). The arc of conches can be clearly seen. Other skeletons (not so far excavated) are situated higher up at the left of the photo.

a collective grave: two women went with him to the country of the dead. Ti Tongoa Liseiriki would be recognizable by his central position at the bottom of a large standing stone and by the fact that he carried armlets of artificially deformed pig tusks (if the upper canines of a boar are removed the tusks develop a spiral form). Two armlets would be on the left arm and one on the right, the custom for chiefs of high rank who gave one of their armlets to whoever would be crowned following them. Finally, a circlet of shells, marine conches, would surround the grave-site. This was indeed found at the location indicated (Figure 17.2) and the layout was as in the oral traditions (except that there were five skeletons, not three). It was dated by bone collagen to AD 1475±85 which agrees well with the previous dates.

ROY MATA

The second mythic cycle concerns the 'civilizing hero' Roy Mata, who came in a canoe with several companions from very far away in a voyage whose stages are still recalled. They landed first on Efate at Maniura, where Roy

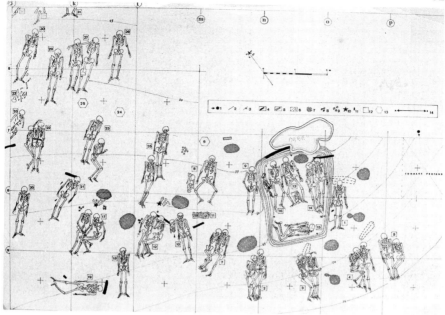

Figure 17.3 Retoka: collective burial of Roy Mata.

1 = Base level.
2 = Contour lines (at intervals of 5 cm).
3 = Bottom of the deep burial.
4 = Standing stones.
5 = Possible situation of a presumed former standing stone now lying on the upper layer of the burial.
6 = Indication of the location of basaltic prisms lying on the upper layer of the burial monument.
7 = Traces of hearths.
8 = Megapode egg-shells.
9 = Bivalve shells (*Codakia tigerina* Linn.).
10 = Pig-bones, either broken and charred or articulated.
11 = Stone, shell and coral tools.
12 = Numerical identifiers of burials. In the text, if this refers to a couple or to an association between 'primary' and 'secondary' burial, 'a' always refers to the individual placed to the east.
13 = Numerical identifiers of burials in Level I.
14 = Location of the stratigraphic section within the deep-level sample.

Mata crowned several chiefs. They then all departed to conquer central Vanuatu as far as Kuwae; this seems to have occurred long before its destruction. Roy Mata is remembered today as a pre-eminent chief and a true hero. He transformed the social structure of the region, organized a quinquennial peace festival and other things. On his death, he was buried on a small coral island near Efate: Retoka. The funeral ceremonies lasted several days with

Figure 17.4   Retoka: collective burial of Roy Mata. Southeastern area of Level II. The deep burial, in front of the two standing stones, has not yet been excavated.

dances and human sacrifices. Indeed several couples were buried alive, to represent the different clans who owed him allegiance and were voluntarily accompanying him to the land of the dead. The men were unconscious, drugged by a strong dose of kava (*Piper methysticum*), but the women were apparently fully conscious. Conches were placed inside and on the grave to allow the living to communicate with the dead and then Retoka was declared *fenua tapa*, a forbidden land, and indeed remains uninhabited to the present day.

Roy Mata is still remembered, not only for his social reforms, but also by the two large standing stones, the place and details of his burial, the songs of the enthronement ceremonies at Maniura of the different chiefs that he appointed, and the funeral chant of the ceremony at Retoka. A collective grave was found at the site indicated by tradition (Figure 17.3). There was an upper level, covered by 30 cm of more recent sediments, and marked by stone slabs, originally upright but later broken, and conches, all arranged in arcs centred on the two main standing stones.

The grave had two other levels; on the surface of the first lay some fifty individuals: eleven couples intertwined, arranged in the arc of a circle matching that of the upper level, with very rich decorations (necklets, pendants, and dance ornaments of pierced shells on the arms and ankles, bracelets in pig tusks or made from Trochus shell (*Trochidae* sp.) or conch shells). Other individuals, equally richly dressed, were set apart or accompanied by bundle or packet burials of complete skeletons (a form of secondary burial). In the centre was a bundle of the long bones of several individuals with their bracelets and dance ornaments still attached. What may be the rest of their skeletons were found in the north-west of the burial site. On the same compacted surface the remnants of dance ornaments were also scattered, with small hearths and other remains.

There was a different situation in the 8 sq. metres in front of the main standing stones: the soil was soft and without remains. By deepening the trench some 25 cm a rectangular pit was exposed. In it was a man, with a secondary burial (in a packet or bundle) between his lower limbs, with a couple at his left and a man at his right. In front of this group and at right angles to it the skeleton of a young woman is laid out. As with the grave of the chief studied at Mangarisu on Tongoa Island and of somewhat later date (Garanger 1972: 90–2), the man placed to the right is his *atavi*; in other words the one responsible for peace around the chief during his life and also in the country of the dead. The articulated skeleton of a pig was placed on the edge of the pit. We know from oral tradition (Espirat *et al.* 1973), as well as from the observations of former missionaries such as Turner (1861) and Codrington (1891), that this sacrificed pig was destined to be the guardian at the entrance of the undersea country of the dead (Layard 1942). The man placed at the centre, apparently very old, was certainly Roy Mata, wearing, among many other decorative items, the three pig tusk bracelets spoken of in relation to Ti Tongoa Liseiriki.

Figure 17.5 Retoka: collective burial of Roy Mata. Central area of the collective burial. Between the Level II burials the excavation has gone to the top of the deep burial.

The archaeological study of the site has confirmed the testimony of tradition but has also clarified, using spatial analysis, the stages of the mortuary
ceremony (Figure 17.5). The large number of people in this collective burial,
and the exceptional quantity of grave goods, is in accordance with the traditional importance accorded to Roy Mata. In terms of the mortuary ceremony
itself, a wide area must have been cleared by digging out the earth to a depth
of 30 cm and then a pit cut a little deeper at the centre where they placed
the chief, his *atavi*, an intertwined couple and a young woman at the feet
of Roy Mata at right angles to his corpse. Such an arrangement has already
been noted for an important grave at Mangarisu on Tongoa, and Glaumont
(1899) earlier reported that 'when a chief dies they put the body of one of
his wives below him so that the two bodies form a cross'. On the edge of
the pit where the guardian pig was placed, two large stone slabs were set
upright. The funerary ceremony took place all around this trench; to judge
by the broken ornaments and trampled soil there would have been dancing.
The trench was then closed on the volunteers who sacrificed themselves to
follow Roy Mata (the diversity of their ornaments suggesting that they represented different clans). These were couples and individuals alone or
accompanied by a secondary burial. After this there appear to have been
involuntary burials or human sacrifices, and finally the arc of conches
were put in place. Layard (1942) noted that conch shells played an important role in mortuary rites in central Vanuatu. Similarly, in the Banks Islands
'the dead person is taken to his last resting place to the sound of conches'
(Codrington 1891).

The place was filled with earth, and stones of different types were erected,
approximately above the couples and individuals arranged in an arc. Conches
were also placed in front of the two great standing stones of the deep grave.
They must have been used in the ceremonies for a final time before the
island was declared taboo and the survivors returned home. The burial has
been radiocarbon dated by collagen to AD 1275±140 which confirms that
the epoch of Roy Mata was 'well before the cataclysm of Kuwae' as tradition states. New AMS dating is in progress on the initiative of Matthew
Spriggs, using shells from ornaments collected from the grave in 1967.

In central Vanuatu, there is a major change in the material culture of all
sites in this same period (the thirteenth century). Pottery is abandoned (Lapita
and especially Mangaasi traditions), and the lithic toolkit of Melanesian type
is replaced by a shell toolkit characteristic of the atolls of the Polynesian
Outliers and of Micronesia. This underlines the importance of Roy Mata and
his group and suggests various hypotheses as to their origin.

The persistence of oral tradition over some seven centuries is remarkable,
but the explanation lies in the importance of the eruption and the reputation of a remarkable leader. It also explains the role played by oral traditions in maintaining social structures whose rules are codified in myths, the
intermingling of details preventing all deviations. For ethnologists, the archaeological results provide a time-depth to institutions recorded synchronically.

The social system (hierarchical relations, kinship) in central Vanuatu is different from other islands and corresponds exactly with the area of influence of Roy Mata. These differences must therefore go back to at least the thirteenth century. More generally, from the structuralist point of view, Levi-Strauss (pers. comm.) observes: 'It is certain that the structuralist analysis of myth would be strengthened if it were always the case, as thanks to you in the New Hebrides, that the point of departure is the historical kernel and the skin which covers it.' This step, bringing together oral traditions and archaeology, has been carried out successfully by several Oceanists from our team.[3]

Parallel to the support given by prehistory to ethnology, oral traditions can also guide the steps of the prehistorian. They can permit clarification of archaeological findings which would be otherwise uninterpretable, or which might be erroneously analysed. Another example from central Vanuatu is on Efate Island (the Mangaasi site) and the neighbouring islands of Mele, Lelepa and Retoka, where the orientation of burials is constant within each pre-contact site but varies between sites. The archaeologist might deduce that this was due to variation in mortuary customs, corresponding to different peoples – a plausible view in the light of the ethnic and linguistic diversity of local populations. As it happens, these different orientations all converge on a point in the sea near 'Devils' Point', in the north-east of Efate, named in tradition as the entrance to the undersea country of the dead: Bangona.

Ethnographic research, whether using oral tradition or the extant literature, will allow elucidation of, among other things, the real function in inter-island exchanges of prehistoric pottery in the Western Pacific, whether of Lapita or more recent periods. The recent thesis of Françoise Cayrol (1992) represents an interesting approach in this regard.

A double strategy, ethnological and archaeological, can also enlighten us on questions of traditional technology, at least for the more recent periods. Two final examples will demonstrate this.

In Micronesian and Polynesian atolls less in contact with the western world, old people retain the memory of technologies now more or less abandoned. Jean-Michel Chazine has been able to reconstruct ancient horticultural techniques adapted to these low fertility islets, while Eric Conte has studied the exploitation of traditional marine resources in the Tuamotus. The results of these studies relate to a relatively recent slice of the past, but they are also relevant for the future. The technical knowledge recovered can in fact help to re-establish self-sufficiency in these islands which are now over-dependent on the outside world. Thus scientific findings can also have practical value.

This association between ethnological and archaeological research holds another important interest for the people of the Pacific. Experience has shown that recovering history, especially in the least acculturated areas, is of interest to the direct inheritors of that history (as was the case in Vanuatu, where some sites were excavated at the request of the local population). Societies, like amnesiac individuals, can become sick when the roots of the past are cut away, and the result may be ethnodramas such as the cargo cults in various parts of Melanesia. Such detours may help people to live in the present, but they do not assure a stable future in the same way as a true knowledge of the past.

NOTES

1 Upper-case dates are all uncalibrated.
2 ORSTOM, Unité de Recherche 'Marges actives et lithosphere océanique' de Département 'Terre, Océan, Atmosphère'.
3 In particular the joint research project (ethnology B. Vienne, ORSTOM and D. Frimigacci, CNRS, LA 275) carried out on Futuna and Alofi since 1984. See Frimigacci (1990) and references therein. LA 275 is the reference number of the Laboratory associated with CNRS-Université de Paris I, called Laboratoire d'ethnologie préhistorique.

REFERENCES

Cayrol, F. 1992. La céramique en Mélanésie du Sud, fonction ou statut? Le Cas des Naamboi de Malekula: une approche ethno-archéologique. Thèse de Doctorat, Université Paris 1 (2 vols).

Codrington, R.H. 1891. *The Melanesians: studies in their anthropology and folk-lore.* Oxford: Clarendon Press.

Eissen J.P., M. Monzier and C. Robin. 1994. Kuwae, l'éruption volcanique oubliée. *La Recherche* no. 270, 1200–2.

Espirat J.-J. 1964. *Etude géologique de l'île Tongariki et observations sur la géologie des îles Shepherd.* Bureau de Recherches Géologiques et Minières (rapport de mission du 24 octobre au 7 novembre 1963), Nouméa.

Espirat, J.-J., J. Guiart, M.S. Lagrange and M. Renaud. 1973. *Système des titres électifs ou héréditaires dans les Nouvelles-Hébrides centrales, d'Efate aux îles Shepherd.* Museum National d'Histoire Naturelle, Mémoires de l'Institut d'Ethnologie no. X. Paris: Musée de l'Homme.

Frimigacci, D. 1990. *Aux temps de la terre noire.* Paris: Peeters.

Garanger, J. 1972. *Archéologie des Nouvelles-Hébrides, Contribution à la connaissance des îles du centre.* (Publication no. 30, Musée de l'Homme), Paris: Orstom et Société des Océanistes.

Garanger, J. 1980. Tradition orale et préhistoire en Océanie. In *L'archéologie aujourd'hui*, A. Schnapp (ed.), 187–207. Paris: Hachette.

Garanger, J. 1982. *Archaeology of the New Hebrides.* Translated by Rosemary Groube. Oceania Monograph, no. 24. Sydney: Oceania Publications.

Glaumont, G. 1899. *Voyage d'exploration aux Nouvelles-Hébrides.* Niort: Lemercier et Alliot.

Layard, J. 1942. *Stone Men of Malekula, the Small Island of Vao.* London: Chatto & Windus.

Monzier, M., C. Robin and J.P. Eissen. 1994. Kuwae (~1425 A.D.): the forgotten caldera. *Journal of Volcanic and Geothermal Research* 59, 207–18.

Murdock, G.P. 1959. *Africa, Its Peoples and their Culture History.* New York: McGraw-Hill.

Robin, C., M. Monzier and J.P. Eissen. 1994. Formation of the mid-fifteenth century Kuwae caldera (Vanuatu) by an initial hydroclastic and subsequent ignimbritic eruption. *Bulletin of Volcanology* 56, 170–83.

Turner, G. 1861. *Nineteen years in Polynesia and Researches in the Islands of the Pacific.* London: John Snow.

18   Puhi, the mythical paramount chief of Uvea and ancient links between Uvea and Tonga

DANIEL FRIMIGACCI

INTRODUCTION

Oral tradition in Uvea and Futuna can be classified into two main types, according to whether the form is free or fixed. On Futuna, free-form tales, such as the *Fanaga* (talking of many subjects) and the *Fakamatala* (on historical themes) are distinguished from those of fixed form like the *Mio* (generally on historic topics). Additionally, the words of certain dances have equally a fixed form – for example on Futuna with some *Tapaki* and *Takofe* (historical themes).

Tapaki and *Takofe* are dances accompanied by poetic chants to the glory of a hero. These dances can exalt the virtues of war but also evoke, as with the *Mio*, historical events or sometimes even an invocation to the gods. *Tapaki* and *Takofe* belong to a lineage or a village and are passed down without change.

The *Takofe* dance only exists on Futuna, and takes place in the open on the village square (*malae*) when there are major distributions of food (*Katoaga*). Sixty dancers carry a bamboo stick which represents the weapon of a warrior.

The *Tapaki* dance is not the exclusive prerogative of the Futunese; it is also performed in Uvea (Wallis) and Tonga. Occasions for it may be separate from food distributions; it also takes place in the open, involving some twenty participants. The dancers hold a very thin wooden paddle (*paki*) in one hand, which they twist and beat with their other hand to the rhythm of percussion instruments.

Tapaki, *Takofe* and *Mio* constitute invaluable sources for recording the history of these islands.

PASSING ON KNOWLEDGE THROUGH ORAL TRADITION

Are the words of these dances and chants really passed down without change? In 1932, E.G. Burrows collected some *Tapaki* and *Takofe* on Futuna, notably

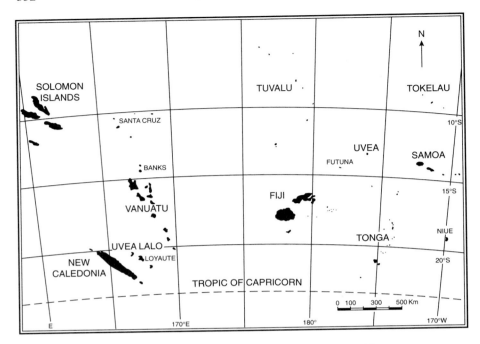

Figure 18.1   Location of Uvea (Wallis) and Futuna in the Pacific.

the *Takofe* of Fiua (Burrows 1936: 215; 1945: 11) and the *Tapaki* of Mauifa (Burrows 1945: 39). Burrows also recorded several parts of the *Takofe* of Alo (also known as the *Takofe* of Ono) and of the *Tapaki* of Sakumani (also called the *Tapaki* of Fiua), but no *Mio* were collected. It is interesting to compare Burrows's record and translations with ours.

Taking account of transcription methods, our version of the *Takofe* of Fiua collected fifty years on is exactly the same, except for line 6 which Burrows (1936: 215) transcribed and translated thus:

> *Tsio ki le kele, nga kuli ingoa*
> 'Look upon the earth, towards dog's name'.

Burrows explains in a note the meaning of *nga kuli ingoa* ('towards dog's name'); that is, 'its name is dog', an old expression meaning 'no food crops there'. The later version transcribes this line differently, which is perhaps the consequence of loss of the original phrase or simply a misunderstanding of the text by Burrows. We transcribe this phrase as:

> *Tio ki le kele na ku ligoa*
> 'Look at the land, it is deserted',

(*na ku ligoa* meaning '(the land) has been deserted'. This reading conforms better to the general sense of the text where we learn that the island of Alofi has only a small population and is rich, whereas the village of Fiua is over-populated and affected by want. This *Takofe* throws down a challenge to the Agaifo who live amidst abundance on Alofi. The famished people of Fiua threaten to make war on them, intimidate them and then pray to Lita, the goddess of fertility. This *Fakofe* is still spoken during feasts at Fiua, which is why the text has not undergone any significant changes. On the other hand this is not the case for the *Tapaki* of Mauifa which has not been performed for a long time. Our transcription of this shows some changes which, never-theless, do not alter the general meaning of the text. The order of the lines is not the same in the two versions. Two lines are missing in our version recorded in 1980, six in that recorded by Burrows. The translation of certain words differs from one version to the other. This can be explained by the fact that the language of the *Tapaki* is very archaic. All this suggests that these kinds of documents are not susceptible to major changes over time.

On Uvea, although the *Mio* and the *Takofe* dances are not performed, the same dual classification can be used. The *Fanaga* and the *Talanoa* (*Tala*/speech and *noa*/free 'oral traditions') contrast with the *Talatupua* (*Tala*/speech and *tupua*/world 'myths') and the *Talatuku* (*Tala*/speech and *tuku*/to let alone 'historical accounts'). The words of the dances (*Tapaki*, *Eke*, *Mauluulu*, *Lakalaka*) are equally stable.

Before archaeological excavations began on Uvea, I undertook, with Bernard Vienne (of ORSTOM), an inventory both of stratified sites and of surface monuments to link them with accounts from the oral traditions. Father Henquel had already recorded the key myths and oral traditions of Uvea between 1896 and 1908 in a manuscript written in Faka'uvea (the Uvean language) entitled *Talanoa ki 'Uvea nei* ('Stories of Uvea') deposited in the Bishopric of Lano. This document represents the most important corpus of Uvean oral traditions. In 1937, the ethnologist Burrows took the substance of his research from Father Henquel's manuscript. Sioli Pilioko and myself are publishing this manuscript in its entirety for the first time, in French and Faka'uvea (Henquel, in press). Oral traditions concerning the Tongan pres-ence on Uvea are very common, placing the Tongan arrival about the middle of the fifteenth century, during the reign of Takalaua, the twenty-third *Tu'i Tonga*, about AD 1450 on Gifford's chronology (1929: 50–5). Our research has been undertaken to complete the corpus of oral tradition, and particu-larly to locate on the ground the storied places mentioned in the *Talanoa ki 'Uvea nei*. Should the occasion arise, we will undertake excavation at such sites to confirm or disprove the oral accounts. This work has allowed us to establish the considerable reliability of oral tradition on Uvea. All of the recordings presented here were carried out in the field by Jean-Pierre Siorat (Museum of New Caledonia, Nouméa).

ORAL TRADITIONS: THE CHANT OF LAUSIKULA

Among the large corpus of oral traditions collected on Uvea, this example
is the ancient chant of Lausikula, first recorded by Father Henquel and again
in 1932 by Burrows (1937: 42, 90). This chant, it is said, was offered by the
priests on the occasion of the great annual first fruits ceremony:

> *Lausikula mo te Atuvulu*
> Lausikula and Atuvalu
>
> *Kote fakatahiaga o te Hau*
> it is the assembly place of the *Hau*[1]
>
> *Faitoka o Puhi mo Kakahu*
> Tomb of Puhi and Kakahu.
>
> *Ko vai tutulu e ke to*
> Vaituturu (?) will fall!
>
> *Fakaholo fagona kua hopo*
> Fakaholo Fagona[2] has already appeared.
>
> *Tama oio lava oio*
> Young man, oho! Conquered, oho!
>
> *Te fetu'u kua ti ki lalo*
> The stars fell down.
>
> *Tu'i Alagau fai ene aga*
> Tu'i Alagau acts as his wont is.
>
> *Afiafi pea taki te malama*
> In the evening he takes his torch,
>
> *Ko tona taume pe te polata*
> its wick is a Polata.
>
> *Tuusi te ulu ave ki tokaga*
> Cut the head and carry it to its proper place.
>
> *Pani kula ke malama*
> Head smeared with red that it may give light,
>
> *O mamata ai la e tagata*
> and that men may admire it.

This is an example of a category of oral tradition in the fixed form of a
chant interpreted by the priests of the ancient religion of Uvea. This chant
alludes to the 'tomb of Puhi and Kakahu', to 'the assembly place of the *Hau*
(Paramount Chief)' and to 'Tu'i Alagau' (old name of the chiefdom in the
western region of Uvea).

Traditions (*Talanoa*) on Uvea refer, under various guises, to the existence
of a *Hau* or Paramount Chief who would have reigned on Uvea before the

arrival of the Tongans, traditionally dated to the fifteenth century by Tongan and Uvean genealogies (Henquel, in press). This mythical chief, Puhi, rests with the goddess Kakahu on the summit of Lausikula ('leaf of the red *Cordyline terminalis*') Point, which towers a hundred metres high over the sea at the place called Atuvalu; that is to say, 'a line of eight (tombs)'. Puhi rests there beside the great warriors of Uvea. Long after the burial of Puhi, this spot would have been the privileged burial place of the first *Hau* of Uvea and of all great Tongan notables. The oral traditions referring to this site are often confused.

Various episodes of ancient history refer to its location. The chief Havea Fakahau (the third of the chiefly line according to Henquel's chronology) was buried here, as was Ohopulu, daughter of Kalafilia and the wife of the Tu'i Alagau. This princess gave birth to a son, named Alokuaulu, on the monument called Malamatagata ('light + man'). The moment of birth was illuminated by decapitated Tongans, transformed, it is said, into human torches. This is the real meaning of this part of the chant:

> Tu'i Alagau acts according to his custom. In the evening he takes his torch, its wick is a Polata.[3] Cut off the head and carry it to its proper place. A head smeared with red to give light, so that men may admire it.

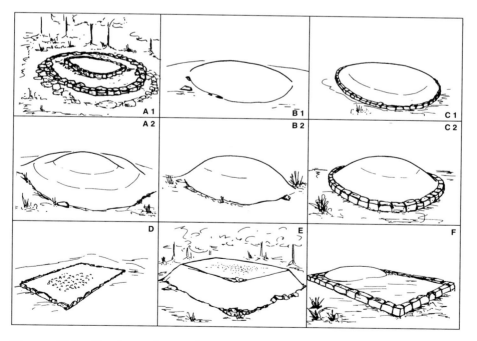

Figure 18.2 Typology of mounds on Uvea.

Finally, another oral tradition refers to the choice of Lausikula Point as a place to bury dead heroes, during the war of Molihina, a war with a sacred character because it pitted Tongan warriors against the brave 'local' chief of Hihifo, Maufehi Huluava. This war symbolizes the struggle of the Uveans against the Tongan oppressor. Other tombs on Lausikula Point can be linked, more generally, to the first Tongan chiefs who set foot on the island, those of the Ha'avakatolo lineage which occupied this part of Uvea.

ARCHAEOLOGICAL SITES

A typology of the monumental mounds on Uvea
Seventy-eight mounds were recorded on Uvea, of which seventy-six were funerary monuments. Mounds less than one metre high are labelled 'low', those greater than one metre in height are described as 'high'. The typology of these mounds, discribed below, is illustrated by Figure 18.2.

TYPE A MONUMENTS
Low earth mounds of round or oval shape, displaying two levels. This type can be further subdivided into two:

- Type A1: the mound is lined with a kerbing of stone blocks, delimiting each level (four cases).
- Type A2: the mound is of earth with no use of stone (two cases only).

TYPE B MONUMENTS
Earthen mounds of round or oval shape, without a kerbing of stone blocks. These are the commonest type. They can be further subdivided into two:

- Type B1: low mounds, slightly convex (fifteen cases).
- Type B2: high mounds, slightly convex or flat (nine cases).

TYPE C MONUMENTS
Earthen mounds of round or oval shape, with a kerbing of stone blocks. There are two subdivisions of this type:

- Type C1: low mounds, slightly convex or flat (nine cases).
- Type C2: high mounds, slightly convex (three cases).

TYPE D MONUMENTS
Rectangular earth mounds, flat-topped or slightly convex, lined by flat stone blocks set into the ground. Six mounds of this type have been recorded on Uvea.

TYPE E MONUMENTS

High earth mounds of rectangular form, flat-topped and sometimes marked by a kerbing of stone blocks. All mounds of this type are large, with a mean length of 20 metres. We have found four examples of this type.

TYPE F MONUMENTS

Earth mounds of rectangular shape, surrounded with stone kerbing and with a round raised mound in one corner of the rectangle. Two mounds of this type have been recorded. According to tradition, the most important person is buried in and under the raised mound, whilst the companions of his voyages overseas are buried some distance away within the rectangular mound.

Other monumental mounds have been noted on Uvea but they are in too bad a state of repair to be integrated into this typological scheme.

The tomb of the mythical chief Puhi

Lausikula Point, recognized by its eight tombs (Figure 18.3), brings together the tombs of the first paramount chiefs of Uvea (Frimigacci *et al.* 1984: 113–21). It is one of the most sacred places on the island. Oral tradition led us to Lausikula Point and to seek the grave of the mythical *Hau* Puhi. Among the eight tombs which were ranged along the crest, only tomb 'A' was situated on the highest point, in the centre of this impressive organized space. It is also the only one, apart from tomb 'I', down below and smaller, of type D, considered the most ancient type according to our enquiries. The other tombs there are of type B (Figure 18.2).

As all of the sacred ridge was arranged around this central tomb it was chosen for excavation as it might be the tomb of Puhi. The section through tomb A (Figure 18.4) shows that the platform of compacted red soil on which the tomb sits had been partly extended and enlarged by a massive addition of black clayey soil coming from the foothills. In addition to this, down the slope are two large pits (point B in Figure 18.4), another possible source for such clayey black sediments. The cross-section (Figures 18.3 and 18.4) of the site along the X–Y axis shows the two pits from where some of the soil used in refashioning the crest may have come. For these terracing works to be successful, the builders took care to construct small revetment walls in mid-slope (Figure 18.3). These major works suggest that they were constructed for the central notable who was laid in the middle of this extensive area on the ridge (Figure 18.5).

The excavation of Mound A showed that the grave area was strewn with small pebbles from the seashore. On the surface of the pebble layer were found twelve sherds of pottery, among which was a vertical handle from the side of a vessel. Ten centimetres below this surface, but still among the pebbles, were seven further sherds of undecorated pottery. This pottery, with a very hard volcanic temper, is characteristic of the recent pottery called Utuleve III (from the terminal period of ceramic use on Uvea).

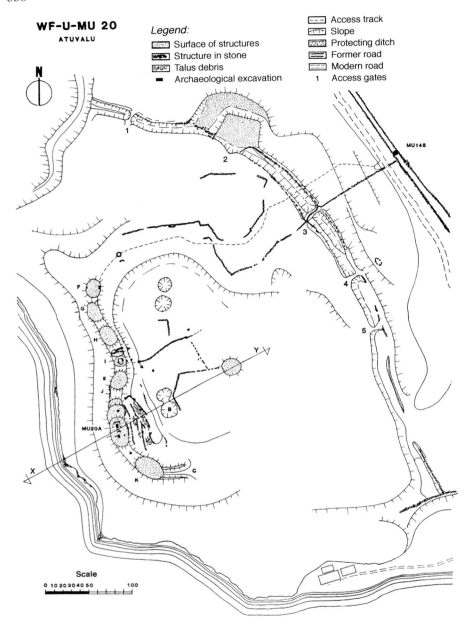

Figure 18.3 Plan of Atuvalu on the summit of Lausikula Point.

Figure 18.4 Cross-section of Atuvalu along the X–Y axis of Figure 18.3.

In the middle of the mound the excavation brought to light a couple, buried under a mean thickness of 0.25 m of pebbles (Figure 18.5). The man measured 1.94 m in height and was spread out on his back, lying on a bed of pebbles, with a pearl shell and a coral bead close to his neck, both symbols of power. The body had been covered with coarse coral sand and then with pebbles. The head of an adze (type 22A in Garanger 1972) was found in the sand at the level of his chest. In contrast, the woman who had been buried alive beside him had also been placed on her back, but on a bed of very fine marine sand, on top of pebbles similar to those on which the man was laid out. Her feet had probably been bound. After being placed in the grave, this sacrificial victim had raised her head and pebbles from above had fallen down and lodged themselves between the sand under her and her head. The woman had also drawn her legs up towards her body and the same pebbles which covered her had piled up under her left leg which she had raised.

The principal figure could well be the *Hau* Puhi. This tomb was placed at the centre of an enormous constructed area and was equipped with marks of authority. For example, a servant would be buried alive *only* with the holder of an important title. Dates obtained on bone samples placed this skeleton around the thirteenth or fourteenth centuries AD (Bone, ANU-7394A, 670±200 BP; Bone, ANU-7394B, 560±100 BP), clearly well before the construction of the large monuments characteristic of the arrival of the Tongans on Uvea, according to genealogical chronologies. However, the woman buried beside the principal figure would not be the goddess Kakahu, but instead a simple companion of the chief in death. Kakahu was a tutelary deity, who had fled, according to another oral tradition (Frimigacci 1990: 23, 65, 67ff), to Futuna where she took the name Finelasi (*Fine*, woman and *Lasi*, great).

RELATIONS BETWEEN TONGA AND UVEA

When did relations between Tonga and Uvea begin? The second part of the chant of Atuvalu refers directly to a Tongan presence on Uvea. Mahina

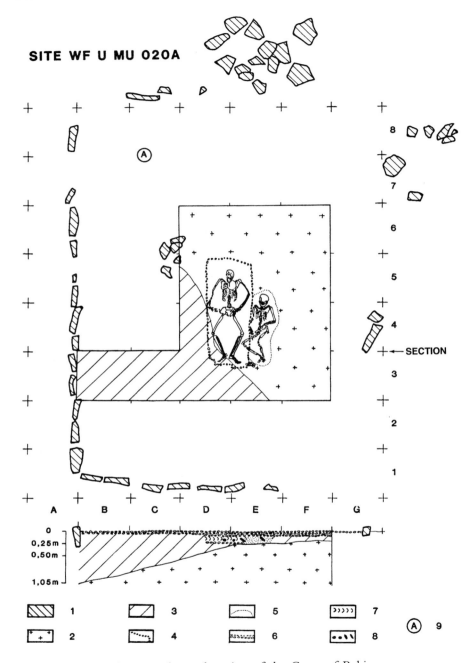

Figure 18.5 Schematic plan and section of the Grave of Puhi.

'Okusitino (1992) has worked extensively on documents gathered during the reign and under the authority of Queen Salote Mafile'o Pilolevu Tupou III and claims that relations between Tonga and Uvea could be very ancient. 'Aho'Eitu, the first *Tu'i Tonga*, had begun the process of unifying the Tongan archipelago, including also Uvea, Niuatoputapu and Niuafo'ou which were previously, according to this author, a unified grouping under Samoan domination. This group was detached from Samoan tutelage and again brought within the Tongan ambit. This is why some names of *Tu'i Tonga* who reigned immediately after 'Aho'Eitu could well be originally from Uvea and Niua, notably: Lihau, Kofutu, Kaloa, 'Apu'anea, 'Afulunga, Ma'uhau and Momo. It should also be recalled that 'Ilaveha, the mother of 'Aho'Eitu, came from Niuatoputapu.

The myth of Lo'au Tongafisifonua recounts that during the reign of Momo, Kae and Longonoa departed by canoe to seek the horizon. The canoe would have visited Ha'apai, Vava'u, Niuatoputapu, Samoa and Uvea (Gifford 1924: 43–54, 139–52).

Tongan oral tradition records that a little later the eleventh *Tu'i Tonga* Tu'itatui brought basalt rocks from Uvea for the construction of the royal tombs known as Langi Heketa and Langi Mo'ungafala, and even the coral uprights of the trilithon Ha'amonga 'A Maui (Bott 1982: 94). This is considered to be the period of expansion of the Tongan empire, about the year AD 1200 according to Tongan chronologies (Gifford 1929: 50–2).

Oral traditions of the first peopling of Uvea echo the Tongan stories. On Uvea, the figures of Maui Atalaga and Maui Kisikisi are associated with a great Tongan voyage, which could be identified with that of Kai and Longonoa in search of the horizon. The *Tu'i Tonga* Tu'itatui is also associated with the initial settlement of Uvea. Here is the tradition in question, recorded between 1896 and 1908 on Uvea by Father Henquel:

> 17. It is said that Maui Atalaga and Maui Kisikisi, father and son, had departed from New Zealand [*sic*] to search for a land of ease and had discovered Tonga and Uvea.
> 18. They arrived first at Tonga and then at Uvea and stated that these isles were henceforth inhabited. They departed again for Samoa and then returned to Tonga where they installed themselves on Vava'u at a place called Mataika. A little later they moved to Tongatapu to a place called Hamene'uli. The monument 'Ha'amonga a Maui' is the mark of their journey, constructed by the *Tu'i Tonga* Tu'itatui. Thus the island of Tonga was settled.
> 19. A lot later, two Tongans named Hauolekele and Ufi went to Uvea, and were joined there by a third Tongan, Lupelutu. These three Tongans and their wives were the origin of the Uvean people.

Thus, according to Uvean tradition, the first inhabitants were Tongans.

Finally, it appears that during the reign of the twenty-third *Tu'i Tonga* Takalaua, around the year 1450, Tongans came to Uvea and constructed a

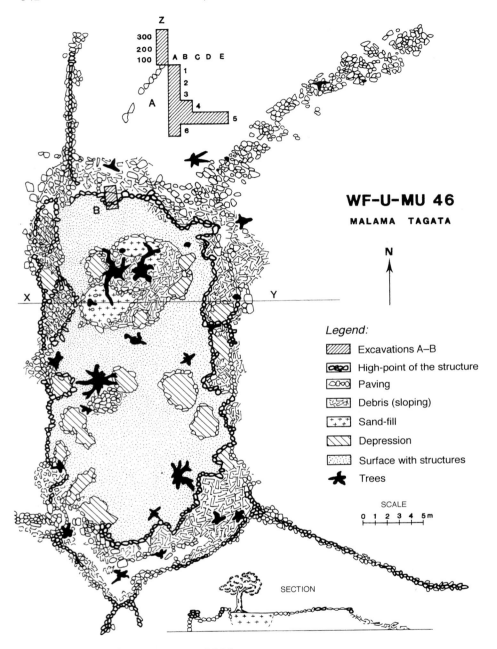

Figure 18.6 The monument of Malamatagata.

certain number of fortifications as part of a strategy of armed conquest of the island (Gifford 1929: 50–2). The chant of Lausikula also alludes to Tu'i Alagau and to the monument Malamatagata, related to the period of history on Uvea known as that 'of the forts'.

Oral tradition on Uvea records that a Tongan war chief named Ga'asialili landed in the south of the island, accompanied by Kalafilia and Folau-Fakate of the Ha'avakatolo and Ha'amea lineages originally from the region of Hihifo on Tonga. Having delimited their respective territories, they proceeded to construct a number of fortifications.

The monument of Malamatagata (Figure 18.6) is found below Lausikula Point, at Utuleve (Frimigacci et al. 1984: 98–112). This monument was built by Kalafilia for his daughter Ohopolu, in a union with Tu'i Alagau, to give birth on. Ohupolu, according to tradition, gave birth to her son Alokuaulu in particularly tragic circumstances. Ohupolu was about to give birth when she asked her father to show everyone that she was the daughter of highest rank. Kalafilia therefore constructed a monument close to her residence (or reconstructed an existing monument), on which the birth took place, illuminated by the light of Tongan men, decapitated and transformed into torches. From this comes the name *Malama* ('light') *Tagata* ('man') in other words, 'human torch' as has been discussed earlier.

The monument of Malamatagata was excavated. The surface of the structure is very irregular, owing to the many trees growing on it. There is, nevertheless, a well-paved area at the foot of a large tree in the centre of the monument. The hollows observed on the surface could be the traces of former trees. Human bones can be seen eroding out on the surface of the hollows, which are filled with marine sand, and the bones are said to be the vestiges of this macabre childbed. Charcoal taken from the base of the monument could date the latest occupation of the spot prior to its construction – that is to say at the end of the fourteenth century AD (ANU 4091, 600 ±300 BP, calibrated to AD 1317/1389 according to the program of Stuiver and Reimer 1987).

Excavations were undertaken in another monumental structure on Uvea, further confirming the presence of Tongans. This structure also belonged to the period 'of the forts', the structure in question being the fort of Kolonui with, inside it, the residence of Talietumu. It has now been restored (Frimigacci and Hardy, in prep.). This work has brought to light the successive rebuildings of part of the residence.

The platform on the north-west is defined in parts by stone slabs set in the ground. Excavation showed that these constructions covered a platform of much greater age than that belonging to the putative residence of Talietumu. This earlier platform was paved and is now covered by the basalt slabs contemporary with the residence. A Polynesian oven of *umu* type of the same age as this earlier platform dated its construction towards the end of the first millennium AD (ANU 9097, 1150 ±60 BP, calibrated to AD 714/1010).

This date from the ancient structure under the residence of Talietumu, as well as that from levels contemporary with the construction of Malamatagata, securely places the episode of Tongan presence on Uvea to the time of Momo and Tu'itatui, thus confirming the oral traditions collected from Tonga and Uvea. The *Hau* Puhi could be a noble Tongan chief of this long-ago mythical period.

NOTES

1 *Hau*: holder of the highest title (Paramount Chief) on Uvea, translated in French by 'Roi'.
2 *Fakaholo Fagona* could be a star which provides voyagers with a departure signal when it appears in the night sky, possibly the star which rises in the east, called *Fetu'u Folau* (star/voyage), the guiding star of voyagers. Burrows translated *Fakaholo Fagona* literally as 'Successive travelling parties'. Line 4 is correctly translated by Burrows, but it has been wrongly transcribed: *Ko vai-tutulu e ka to!* (Burrows 1937: 90).
3 Polata signifies 'an outside wrapper of a banana leaf', meaning 'human victim'.

REFERENCES

Bott, E., with the assistance of Tavi 1982. *Tongan Society at the Time of Captain Cook's Visits: Discussions with Her Majesty Queen Salote Tupou*. Polynesian Society Memoir 44. Wellington: The Polynesian Society.

Burrows, E.G. 1936. *Ethnology of Futuna*. Bernice P. Bishop Museum Bulletin 138. Honolulu: Bishop Museum Press.

Burrows, E.G. 1937. *Ethnology of Uvea (Wallis Island)*. Bernice P. Bishop Museum Bulletin 145. Honolulu: Bishop Museum Press.

Burrows, E.G. 1945. *Songs of Uvea and Futuna*. Bernice P. Bishop Museum Bulletin 183. Honolulu: Bishop Museum Press.

Frimigacci, D. 1990. *Aux Temps de la Terre Noire: Ethnoarchéologie des Iles Futuna et Alofi*. Langues et Cultures du Pacifique 7. Paris: Editions Peeters.

Frimigacci, D. and M. Hardy in prep. Talietumu, une Résidence Tongienne d'Uvea.

Frimigacci, D., J.P. Siorat and B. Vienne. 1984. *Inventaire et Fouille des Sites Archéologiques et Ethnohistoriques de l'Ile d'Uvea*. Document Provisoire, Diffusion Restreinte. Nouméa: ORSTOM.

Garanger, J. 1972. Herminettes Lithiques Océaniennes, Eléments de Typologie. *Journal de la Société des Océanistes* 27(36) 253–74.

Gifford, E.W. 1924. *Tongan Myths and Tales*. Bernice P. Bishop Museum Bulletin 8. Honolulu: Bishop Museum Press.

Gifford, E.W. 1929. *Tongan Society*. Bernice P. Bishop Museum Bulletin 61. Honolulu: Bishop Museum Press.

Henquel, J. in press. *Talanoa Ki Uvea Nei (Histoires d'Uvea)*. Texte de Tradition Orale, Traduit en Français, Annoté et Présenté par Daniel Frimigacci et Siolesio Pilioko. Paris: Editions Peeters.

Mahina 'Okusitino. 1992. The Tongan traditional history Tala E Fonua: a vernacular ecology-centred historicocultural concept. Unpublished MA thesis, Australian National University, Canberra.

Stuiver, M. and P.J. Reimer. 1987. University of Washington Quaternary Isotope Laboratory Radiocarbon Calibration Program, Rev. 2.0.

19 Traditions of extinct animals, changing sea-levels and volcanoes among Australian Aboriginals: evidence from linguistic and ethnographic research

MARGARET SHARPE AND
DOROTHY TUNBRIDGE

INTRODUCTION

Some chapters in this volume (Garanger, Frimigacci) highlight correlations between oral traditions and archaeological evidence from the Pacific area, an area where genealogies and persons of note have been important in the cultures. This chapter focuses on some actual and other possible correlations of myth and oral history about land (and sea) and fauna with palaeontological and archaeological data amongst Australian Aboriginal groups, where land and totemic relationship to fauna are of high cultural importance.

As with other pre-literate societies, there is in Australia a wealth of traditional stories accounting for origins, landforms, flora and fauna. Some such material correlates well – sometimes strikingly so – with the physical evidence. There is other evidence that appears to correlate with such data, but involves a certain amount of creative conjecture and perhaps an element of chance. To a large extent, and not surprisingly, these two categories of evidence relate to events in the comparatively recent past and events in the more distant past, the latter being the more open to conjecture.

Anyone investigating such correlations, which may be reflected in myths, stories, songs, hearsay and vocabulary, must be alert to the possibility of influence on these from white Australian 'knowledge', technology and influence on the environment, as well as the possibility of Aboriginal knowledge of fossil deposits, either in their own clan lands or reported to them from other areas and groups. For example, Tunbridge (1988: 44) records one story from the Flinders Ranges which includes as a character *gilanggila* 'galah'; the word is borrowed from another Aboriginal language and this bird was drawn down into this area by European introduction of certain seed grasses. In one origin story from north-eastern New South Wales, of three brothers and their coming to Australia, a recent version has the brothers arriving in a sailing ship rather than a canoe (Isaacs 1980: 13; Robinson 1977). It is even possible that stories can be changed *before* the 'first' outside contact, due to information (and misinformation) filtering to an 'untouched' group through other groups who

Figure 19.1   Sahul.

have been affected by white settlement or contact (Clark 1992). Elements in traditional stories can reflect the time of *telling* of the story as well as containing older elements.

It is established that Australia was initially colonized some 40,000–60,000 years BP. From what is now known of changing sea-levels and landforms, it is generally agreed that these migrations must have crossed some 50–100 km of water and would have needed some reasonably seaworthy forms of transport. At that time the land mass of Sahul (see Figure 19.1) included Papua New Guinea, Irian Jaya, and Australia (including Tasmania). Ocean levels fluctuated from time to time, sometimes quite extensively, and it was after 10,000 years ago that ocean levels rose to their present level, separating New Guinea from Australia, drowning many islands in the Indonesian Archipelago, and separating Tasmania from the mainland of Australia. Sahul and Australian fauna included a Giant Emu, the Diprotodon, a Giant Kangaroo, and the Thylacine (or Tasmanian Tiger), as well as other species that are now extinct or severely threatened. Other generally smaller species were once widespread but are now confined to more limited areas. Dating of fossil and sub-fossil evidence indicates that not all these fauna had reached extinction before the arrival of the first humans, and many became extinct quite recently. Fossil and sub-fossil remains of some of them occur in places where Aborigines could see them; other fossil and sub-fossil remains appear to have remained hidden until recently discovered by white researchers. Any of these species could possibly be attested in myth, art, song, or Dreaming sites. Volcanoes existed in Australia, the last only becoming inactive within the last 5,000–10,000 years, and some are claimed to feature in myth (cf. Isaacs 1980: 29–31).

This chapter examines myths related to changing sea-levels around Melbourne, Victoria, touches on volcanic activity and change of flora in north Queensland and on clan boundaries in the Gulf of Carpentaria, and recounts the search for evidence of no longer extant mammals among the Adnyama-thanha of the Flinders Ranges, South Australia.

CHANGING SEA-LEVELS, VOLCANIC ACTIVITY AND CHANGES IN VEGETATION

Stories of large floods are widespread, not only in Australian Aboriginal myths but elsewhere in the world, and although some may derive from times of temporary flooding, others may well have some of their origins in the rising of the seas at the end of the last Ice Age. Many Australian stories have the theme of rising sea-levels, sometimes with a story of land sinking into the sea, sometimes with a creator ancestor raising rocks to stop the sea. Around Melbourne, for example (see Figure 19.2), it is known that some land that was submerged later reappeared (for example, a narrow strip around the coast of Port Phillip Bay where Melbourne is situated, in the territory of the Woiworrung before the displacement white settlement brought). Many myths contain reference to hurricane and/or rain, and sometimes temporary inundation, often linked to some wrongdoing of one or more people, often young men, uninitiated or newly initiated. Other myths have reference to mountains belching fire.

CHANGING SEA-LEVELS

The stories connected with changing sea-levels and flooding in the Melbourne area seem (from the literature) to have very little probability of influence from established geological knowledge, and suggest an astonishing time-depth

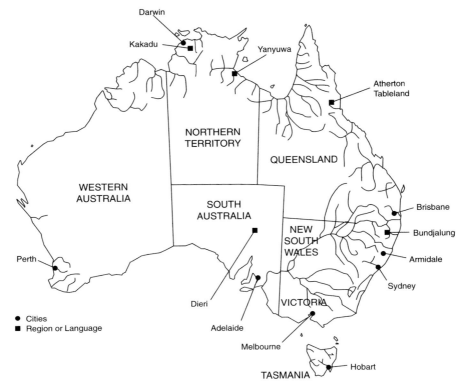

Figure 19.2 Australia, showing places and languages referred to.

of perhaps 10,000 years. At the time of early European settlement, one of the Woiworrung tribes claimed as their land a narrow strip around Port Phillip Bay. When compared with other tribal territories, this is an oddly placed territory, unless one sees it as a remnant of a larger territory when the sea-level was lower. Blake (1991), in his description of the Melbourne language, includes an account from the diary of Georgiana McCrae, who reported in her diary:

> Mr Robert Russell says that Mr Cobb talks to the blacks in their own language, and the following is an account, given by them, of the formation of Port Phillip Bay: 'Plenty long ago . . . *gago, gego, gugo* . . . along a Corio, men could cross, dry-foot, from our side of the bay to Geelong.' They described a hurricane – trees bending to and fro – then the earth sank, and the sea rushed in through the Heads, till the void places became broad and deep, as they are today.
>
> (McCrae (ed.) 1934: 176)

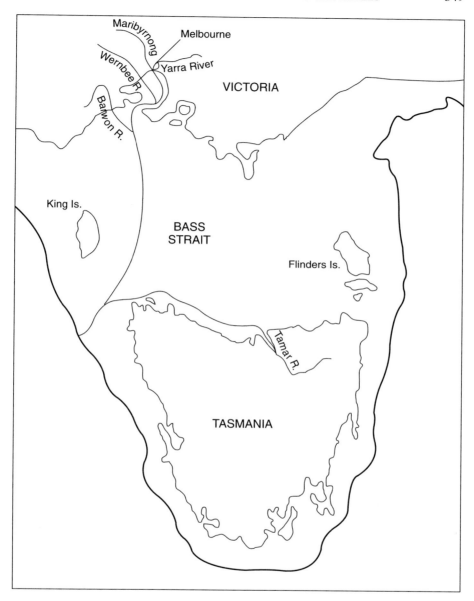

Figure 19.3 Southern Victoria and Tasmania, 18,000 BP.

Source: Blake 1991: 13.

Blake also quotes a Kulin account (Massola 1968: 47–8), which states that 'Port Phillip was once dry land and the Kulin were in the habit of hunting kangaroos and emus there.' Some little boys left in the camp upset a magic wooden trough containing water that unleashed a vast quantity of water that engulfed the land and threatened to drown everyone. However, the creator eagle Bunjil took pity on the people and placed rocks at Mornington and at the present heads of Port Phillip and told the water to run between them and meet the ocean.

Blake (1991: 34) reminds his readers that Aborigines had stories accounting for geographical features which existed well before human settlement, but the persistence of the flooding theme is compelling. The Kurnai of Gippsland told of how some children found a sacred object and showed it to some women. Straightaway the earth crumbled and the sea swept over it. The land to the south was gone forever, drowned under Bass Strait (see Figure 19.3) (Howitt 1904: 493; also Fison and Howitt 1880). Blake continues:

> The clinching evidence that Aborigines had an oral tradition that embodied memories of the cataclysmic events of 10,000 years ago is to be found in the following quotation from William Hull giving evidence on 9 November 1858 before 'The Select Committee of the Legislative Council appointed to enquire into the present condition of the Aborigines of this colony':
>
>> 'Murray, an Aborigine, assured me that the passage up the bay, through which the ships came, is the River Yarra, and that the river once went out at the heads, but that the sea broke in, and that Hobson's Bay [at the head of Port Phillip Bay] which was once hunting ground, became what it is.'
>>
>> (Blake 1991: 34)

This statement is now known to be accurate, and its early date rules out any possibility of it being influenced by European geological discovery. Ice Age theories accounting for fluctuating sea-levels were not accepted before the twentieth century.

It is also significant to note that the languages spoken in the Melbourne area are considered to belong to the Pama-Nyungan family, though as Evans and McConvell (Volume II) point out, there may be substrate languages in this part of Australia. If the recorded Melbourne area languages are Pama-Nyungan, these languages could be younger than the oral tradition by some thousands of years.

Volcanic activity and changing vegetation

The second example is from Dixon (1991) who collected a story in 1964 on the origin of the three crater lakes on the Atherton Tableland, North Queensland (Lake Eacham, Lake Barrine and The Crater) from George Watson, in the Mamu dialect of Dyirbal, very similar to one he reproduces in the Yidiny language, where two newly initiated men broke important taboos and so angered the rainbow-serpent, who then caused the earth to erupt, bringing about the formation of several deep lakes. Both texts (Dyirbal and Yidiny) provide a plausible account of a volcanic eruption.

After telling the story, in 1964, George Watson remarked that when this happened the country around the lakes was 'not jungle – just open scrub'. The volcanic eruptions that formed the lakes are said by scientists to have been at least 13,000 years in the past. George was saying that at this time there was no rain forest on the Atherton Tableland. In 1968 a dated pollen diagram from the organic sediments of Lake Euramoo by Peter Kershaw showed that the rain forest in that area is only some 7,600 years old. This suggests that the story of the volcanic eruptions may have been handed down from generation to generation for something like 13,000 years (Dixon 1991: 41).

However, although the evidence suggests the story is independent of and uninfluenced by any scientific findings on the changing vegetation, the date of its collection only precedes the date of establishment of the vegetation change by a small margin, and the possibility of some influence from recent speculation cannot be as firmly excluded.

Undersea clan boundaries

In the Gulf of Carpentaria, not only islands and mainland but also sea areas are traditionally owned by different clan groups (Baker 1989). The clan boundaries divide islands and sea in a mosaic that bears no prima facie correspondence with coastal outlines or changes in sea colour, yet the Yanyuwa are as confident in locating the sea clan boundaries as those on the land (Baker, pers. comm.). Further research is necessary to see if land and underwater boundaries follow similar geographical markers. Sharpe has not yet found any evidence among contemporary Yanyuwa people of stories accounting for the boundaries or linked to changes in sea-level.

EXTINCT MAMMALS IN THE FLINDERS RANGES, SOUTH AUSTRALIA

Tunbridge has studied Yura Ngawarla, the language of the Adnyamathanha, who inhabited the northern Flinders Ranges, South Australia (see Figure 19.4) at European occupation (1850s). During her work on the language she collected about a dozen language terms for mammal species which were no longer in existence. These terms had been orally transmitted in myth, song or story, or were simply remembered as a name one or other person could recall, something their predecessors had spoken of. Her search was in part triggered off by her senior adviser on the language, Annie Coulthard, who sang a lullaby about a girl who became lost at Martin's Well while wearing a long *urnda*-skin cloak. Coulthard, however, did not know what an *urnda* was, and was one of only a few people in Nepabunna who had even heard the word. Tunbridge felt it was important to attempt to identify what this name and others denoted, and used a number of complementary strategies and clues:

1   Ecological information on extant species was accurate, so the assumption was that ecological information on *extinct* species could also be accurate.

2   In songs and myths named species, except in speech being attributed to them, behaved as they did in 'real life', and occurred where they were found naturally. That is to say, there was an 'ecological rationale' to the mythology (cf. Newsome 1980).

3   Comparison of words with cognates in closely related languages provided possible identifications of species. Even though it is known that cognate names may be applied to different species by different language groups, they are usually applied to closely related species. Cognates could also provide information on the former distribution of these species. (For examples of comparative terminology, see Appendix at end of chapter.)

4   Study skins of animals were brought from the South Australian Museum in Adelaide for Adnyamathanha people to inspect.

5   Some older Adnyamathanha people had memories (sometimes passed down to them from parents or a previous generation) on diet, behaviour, habitat and appearance of specific fauna they had names for, sometimes with specific stories of encounters.

6   Some historical records from white settlers and families contained information on fauna.

7   Sub-fossil remains (no older than about 400 years) were collected and classified by an Adelaide science teacher, Graham Medlin, who focused his attention on owl pellets, inedible material regurgitated by the Barn Owl (*Tyto alba*). Such pellets are deposited around the owls' nesting sites, and pertain to food eaten by the owl over its range, estimated to be no more than 10 km.

Tunbridge collected a number of words for species the Yura Ngawarla team could name, but were no longer known in the area. These included *urnda, warda, yarlpu, idnya, urli, virlda, maiarru, urlka, pudkurra* and *yaliwarrunha andu*. Knowing very little about Australia's native mammals, Tunbridge set about trying to find out the identity of these mammals, when and why they became extinct, and what they had meant to the Adnyamathanha people. In the process, Adnyamathanha advisers taught her a great deal about mammals.

Although mammalogists generally begin their research with hard evidence – living mammals or mammal skeletal remains or skins, not with a set of words in an Aboriginal language – Tunbridge's method had certain advantages. Words survive after a species becomes extinct. If they are culturally significant, say if they occur in songs or Dreaming stories or place-names,

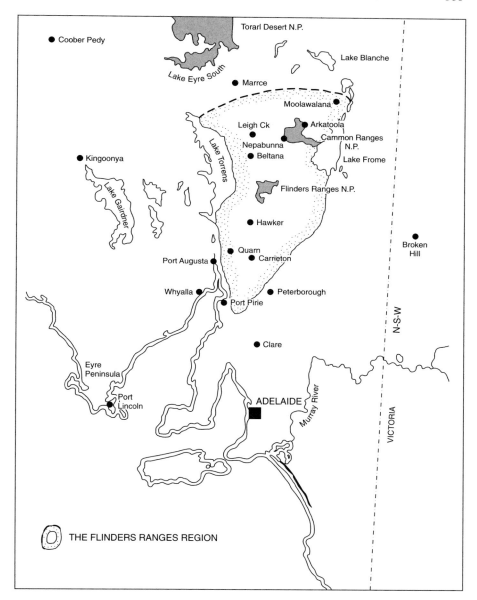

Figure 19.4   Flinders Ranges area.

Source: From Tunbridge 1988.

they could survive a hundred years or more. Therefore even if people do not know the specific meaning of a mammal word, they nevertheless may know something about the animal it represents. While skeletal remains and skins of long-extinct species alone could not recall to mind that knowledge, the use of both, together with other means, led to the identification of mammals which traditionally had sustained Flinders Ranges' Aboriginal people. Tunbridge's team built up a profile on each mammal. The elders were particularly knowledgable about mammal behaviour, and in response to questions they were often able to describe the diet of some species in considerable detail. The late Rufus Wilton recalled that his mother (born probably before 1880) used to sing the lullaby about the lost child, but because *urnda* died out before he was born (1909) she substituted the name *andu* in the song (*urnda* and *andu* are both wallabies). His father, he said, had described the *urnda* as a small, light-coloured wallaby, so the last sighting of *urnda* was approximately dated.

In 1985, from skins brought for viewing by the South Australian Museum, Rufus Wilton identified the Ghost Bat by its Yura Ngawarla name; and the team heard several people offer names for the 'black stuff' associated with stick-nest rat nests, and so on. The late Claude Demell picked out a Bilby skin and said his father had shown him a dead one of those some time before 1920 and named it *yarlpu*. In a deeply moving moment in Nepabunna Aboriginal School the whole community listened as the late Lynch Ryan, holding in his arms a Bilby skin and stroking it gently, told the children, 'This is my brother'. He went on to tell stories about this, his totem animal. No one would have guessed that this species was virtually extinct in the region when Ryan was born.

While collecting traditional stories for the community in 1986 (published in Tunbridge 1988), Tunbridge came upon a story about a woman who went mad hunting an *urnda*, a 'scrub wallaby', with her dog. The wallaby kept running into a hollow log at a place near Nepabunna, and just as the woman thought she had it trapped, it would escape out the other end. This story provided a good description of *urnda*'s habitat and behaviour. Les Wilton recounted another story in which some *urnda* were seen on the slopes of Mount Livingstone. He had also been told how the animal was skinned to make a waterbag. As well as *urnda*, long-extinct stick-nest rats and bandicoots had also walked across the stage of Dreaming history, as had the native cat and a large striped 'dog'.

More evidence was gleaned from comparative linguistic work: Yura Ngawarla was closely related to the (largely extinct) Aboriginal languages of the region around the two South Australian gulfs. Comparison with these showed that Yura Ngawarla had lost a word initial /k/. The Red Kangaroo was *urdlu* in Yura Ngawarla, and *kurdlu* in old language records of the Gulfs region; one stick-nest rat, *urli*, appeared as *kurli* on Eyre Peninsula. Words relating to bettongs, native cats, bandicoots and possums were also among those recurring throughout the region. In some cases the English translations in the word lists helped identify the species. Once a species was identified, the cognates provided information on the former distribution of these species.

The Yura Ngawarla word *urnda* turned up as *kurnda* elsewhere throughout the entire region. Its profile grew as the English meanings were noted. It was by now identified as a light-coloured 'brush' or 'scrub' wallaby; it was 'small' beside the Yellow-footed Rock-wallaby (*andu*); it lived both in the ranges and on the plains in scrubby country; it ran into hollow logs when chased; it was good for food and its fur made a good waterbag or blanket. And finally, it was described on Yorke Peninsula as the 'white-shouldered wallaby' – a description later confirmed by an Adnyamathanha man, Eric McKenzie, who had had it from his elders.

The most distinctively 'white-shouldered' wallaby known to have existed, the Crescent Nailtail Wallaby, was recorded historically only for Central and Western Australia. Could it have once lived in the Flinders Ranges? Zoologists wanted hard evidence, and there was none available at that time to locate this wallaby in either the Flinders Ranges or the Gulfs region to the south of the ranges. This led Tunbridge to comb through historical records with the help of mammalogists, one of whom, on the basis of his knowledge of desert species, had suggested she watch for this mammal.

Krefft, a nineteenth-century naturalist, had obtained mammal specimens from western New South Wales and even recorded their Aboriginal names. Tunbridge learnt that Wakefield reported in 1966 that one of Krefft's specimens lodged in the Victorian Museum had been incorrectly labelled, and was in fact a specimen of Crescent Nailtail Wallaby. This, along with a West Australian Museum record of sub-fossil remains from Maralinga in South Australia, now put the former range of this wallaby both east and west of the Flinders Ranges. Still without hard evidence, Tunbridge announced that the linguistic, cultural and scientific evidence together suggested that not only did the Flinders Ranges word '*urnda*' refer to the Crescent Nailtail Wallaby, but that this animal had lived throughout the entire Gulfs region.

Proof of the Crescent Nailtail Wallaby's former existence in the Flinders Ranges region finally came from Graham Medlin. Helped by his students over several years, he had amassed an extensive Flinders Ranges sub-fossil collection – thousands of bits and pieces of mammal remains, mostly (but not only) found in owl pellets. (The owl in question, the Barn Owl, *Tyto alba*, regurgitates inedible parts of its prey, such as hair, bones and claws; often skeletal remains in these pellets are comparatively intact, and indicate the presence of the particular prey in an area within the maximum flying circle of the owl from its roost.) Careful examination of a mammal fragment in his collection, now lodged at the South Australian Museum, showed that it indisputably came from an individual of this species. A further piece of evidence was Tindale's identification of 'kunda' (i.e. *kurnda*) as the Crescent Nailtail Wallaby in his original card file (1964 and 1975), though he used a different identification in his much earlier published version (1936). In 1995, Medlin located unpublished records of skeletal material of this species which confirm its former presence in almost all the regions represented by the related languages of the two Gulfs.

Not only confirming *this* species, Medlin's Flinders Ranges sub-fossil remains (believed to be no more than 400 years old) represented an important inventory of recent Flinders Ranges mammal species double the size of that previously recognized. By now Tunbridge and her team had already independently identified the species that her list of words referred to, and knew roughly when the extinct species were last seen. Almost all of these were represented in the remains, and many more smaller species besides, which were not distinguished by known Yura Ngawarla words.

All the evidence (Tunbridge 1991) indicated that there had been at least fifty-five native mammal species resident in the Flinders Ranges at the time of European settlement. Of around forty-five terrestrial mammal species which had sustained Aboriginal people for millennia, two-thirds vanished from the region virtually overnight – most *within the first 50 years of European colonization*. Only one species of bat disappeared as far as is known, the carnivorous Ghost Bat, which depended on small mammals for its survival. The historical record suggests that the worst damage was probably done in only three years, during the first prolonged dry period (1864–6). The effect on Aboriginal people's survival was devastating and irreversible.

THE THYLACINE (TASMANIAN TIGER)

Tunbridge also examines ethnographic evidence for other fauna known (or presumed) to have been extinct for much longer, including the Thylacine, which became extinct on the mainland after the introduction of the dingo some four thousand or more years ago, well after Tasmania became isolated from the rest of Australia; it was declared officially extinct in 1930 (although there is inconclusive evidence that it may still be alive in one part of Tasmania). The Thylacine had been attested in rock art, including an example in Kakadu, Northern Territory, and it existed within mythological memory in the Flinders Ranges. It may even have been alive there up to the end of the last century; there was a claimed sighting by a white settler around 1900, who identified it when he saw a Thylacine in the Melbourne Zoo (Tunbridge 1991: 48), and Coulthard stated that her grandfather (d. 1919) had seen and heard them around camps at night, and had warned adults to keep their children inside at night (Tunbridge 1991: 48).

The Adnyamathanha had a term, '*marrukurli*' for an animal described as dog-like and *marlkamarlkanha* 'striped' by Coulthard (Tunbridge 1991: 48). Dreaming sites of the *marrukurli* coincide exactly with places in the Flinders where sub-fossil Thylacine remains have been found. The claimed sighting suggests the animal's complete extinction on the mainland may have been within the last 150 years. While the presence of sub-fossil remains could trigger the invention of myths, it is unlikely that the striped coat or the habits would be 'invented' so accurately.

MEGAFAUNA IN MYTH

There are numerous myths in Australia featuring giant animals. Myths of a similar ilk occur all over the world and, given the very human propensity for 'the one that got away' to grow in size, need to be treated cautiously.

Tunbridge reported that after bones of the Diprotodon were unearthed by white scientists in the Flinders Ranges region, the Adnyamathanha 'recognized' these bones as those of the *yamuti*. Historical records show that some Adnyamathanha had previously seen the bones, and in fact had led Europeans to the site (Mincham 1983: 81), although present-day Adnyamathanha did not know that. Elsewhere, stories of giant animals are often linked to sites where bones of extinct megafauna are found. This may well be the case here: stories of the giant *yamuti* were the subject of Adnyamathanha myth, and associated sites were within 160 km of the bone sites. As well as general agreement that *yamuti* was bigger than any native mammal known today, and that its neck was such that it could not look up, there is disagreement on its form and habits. It is described by some as a type of *marlu* (spirit kangaroo), and by others as a sort of large wombat. Most accounts depict it as a dangerous carnivore (eating humans if nothing else!), but some depict it as herbivorous, with *yandhana* (*Hakea edniana*) being one of its favourite foods (Tunbridge 1991: 72). The Diprotodon was in fact a wombat-like creature about the size of a rhinoceros; it was herbivorous, and purportedly was not able to raise its head to look up. A question to be considered is: Did the bones give rise to the stories – this would explain the 'errors' in the mythology – or had the stories been kept alive for millennia, perhaps even aided by the presence of the bones?

The 1890s explorer and geologist J.W. Gregory was told a story associated with giant bones revealed in the desert, among the Dieri tribe. The story also tells of a time when the climate of the desert was different. The vegetation was lush and green, as could have been the case before the end of the last Ice Age (Isaacs 1980: 15). Isaacs also quotes Aranda stories of well-watered country and lush vegetation in the MacDonnell Ranges and Alice Springs (1980: 15). At different times during the Ice Age this may have been true, although desert areas were more extensive at times, and also traditional hunting and gathering had less severe impact on the flora and fauna than is typical today.

Extinction of the Diprotodon (and other of the 'giant' fauna) is put at 5,000–15,000 years BP at the most recent; however, most researchers believe extinction occurred much earlier, in the range 30,000 to 50,000 years BP. The Adnyamathanha stories suggest that at this time-depth there is considerable likelihood for distortion or 'embroidering' of the facts, or 'blending' of different fauna in resultant myths. It is more likely that the myths arose to explain fossil bones. Even in this case hunter-gatherers would be likely to make informed evaluations as to whether the remains were of carnivores or herbivores on the basis of tooth form.

It is possible to regard some myths of a past 'golden age' of lush vegetation as due to a very human propensity of viewing the past with happy nostalgia. But the Aborigines of eastern Australia, where food animals and plants were always in abundance, also remembered the land as more plentiful before the white invasion. As the traditional lifestyle was geared to limit population to that which was sustainable in the worst seasons (in contrast to much white management), this perception is understandable.

CONCLUSION

As White and O'Connell (1982: 20–1) remind us, ethnographic material, in the form of myths or alleged histories, must be viewed with considerable caution. Stories may be altered by influence of other cultures and their 'knowledge'; stories may also be lost, or sections omitted or changed, as species die out and landforms change. None the less, valuable evidence on the past seems to be retained in much of the data, and suggests such stories are worth investigating. They may not always lead to the types of discovery Tunbridge's work did, but they may at least inform us on attitudes to landscape and fauna held by indigenous Australians. And as our knowledge of the prehistoric past is increased from geological, palaeontological and archaeological work, we may gain a better appreciation of myth and its sometimes tenuous, sometimes close, connection with the 'real' past.

APPENDIX 1: SOME EXAMPLES OF COGNATE MAMMAL TERMINOLOGY

Table A.1 compares Yura Ngawarla terminology with that of some genetically related languages/dialects of the southern region of South Australia around Spencer Gulf and the Gulf of St Vincent. This list is a sample only, and is compiled from data presented in Tunbridge (1991) and linguistic research in 1995 by Tunbridge.

To recognize correspondences in the table it is necessary to note the following. Terms in plain print are as they are spelt in the literature, having been recorded without the input of modern linguistics. Terms in asterisked ***bold** are reconstructed phonetic forms. Terms in **bold** (only) are phonetically correct (personally recorded). Note that the languages other than Yura Ngawarla probably did not make a voicing distinction at the phonemic level.

Table A.1 Examples showing correspondences in the mammal terminology of genetically related languages

Mammal species		Yura Ngawarla	Ngadjuri		Barngarla		Narunga		Kaurna	
Scientific name	Common name	(Northern Flinders Ranges)	(S. Flinders/N. Mt Lofty Ranges)		(Eyre Peninsula)		(Yorke Peninsula)		(Adelaide)	
Dasyurus prob. *geoffroii*	Quoll, prob. western	**idnya**	***ngaku-idnya**	akuindji	**idnya**		***dhidnya**	didinya	***mabu**	mabu
Macrotis lagotis	Bilby	**yarlpu**			***yarlbu**	yalbu	***bingku**	bingku	***pingku**	pingko
Lasiorhinus latifrons	Southern hairy-nosed wombat		***wartu**	watu	***wartu**	warto	***wartu**	warto	***wartu**	warto
Trichosurus vulpecula	Common brushtail possum	**virlda**	***birlda**	bilda	***birlda**	pilla	***birlda**	birlta	***pirlta**	pilta
Bettongia penicillata	Brush-tailed bettong	**urlka**			***kurlka**	kulka			***kurlka**	kurka
Onychogalea lunata	Crescent nailtail wallaby	**urnda**	***gurnda**	gunda	***kurnda**	kunna†	***kurnda**	kunda	***kurnda**	kunda
Macropus robustus	Euro	**mandya** (old: **yudu**)	***yudu**	juru	***yudu**	**yudu**	**waluwaru**			
Macropus rufus	Red kangaroo	**urdlu**	***gurdla, tharnda**	gudla, tanda	**gurdlu**	kurdlu/			***tharnda *kurdlu**	tarnda(m) kurlo(f)
Macropus eugenii	Tammar		***wadlha**	wadla	**yumbala**		**wadlha**	wadla	***wadlha**	wadla
CHIROPTERA	Bats	**mika**	**mika**			miltyinye	***matyu-(ma)-tyu**	matyityu	***matyu-matyu**	maityo-maityo
Leporillus conditor	Greater stick-nest rat	**urli**			***kurli**	kulli				

† There is some evidence that in the original record two records, *kunna* and *kunda*, were mixed, hence the reconstructed form ***kurnda** (see Tunbridge 1991).

Yura Ngawarla does not distinguish between the pairs n/rn or l/rl when they occur before either p/b or k/g. (It is not known whether the related languages did or not.) Reconstructed forms are written for each language with the retroflexed form of the nasal and lateral in that phonetic environment. Note also that Yura Ngawarla initial $\#p$-/$\#b$- underwent a sound change to $\#v$- in the early post-European era. Perhaps around that time, or earlier, Yura Ngawarla lost its initial $\#k$-/$\#g$- sound, and its initial $\#th$-/$\#dh$- sound dropped before the vowel i.

REFERENCES

Note that the references include not only those within the text but all the data sources used to compile the Appendix Table.

Allen, J., J. Golson and R. Jones (eds). 1977. *Sunda and Sahul: Prehistoric States in Southeast Asia, Melanesia and Australia.* London: Academic Press.
Baker, R.M. 1989. Land is life: continuity through change for the Yanyuwa of the Northern Territory of Australia. Ph.D. thesis, University of Adelaide, Adelaide.
Berndt, R.M. and T. Vogelsang. 1941. Comparative vocabularies of the Ngadjuri and Dieri tribes, South Australia. *Transactions of the Royal Society of South Australia* 65(1), 1–10.
Black, J.M. 1920. Vocabularies of four South Australian languages – Adelaide, Narrunga, Kukata and Narrinyeri – with special reference to their speech sounds. *Transactions of the Royal Society of South Australia* 14, 76–93.
Blake, B. 1991. Woiworrung, the Melbourne language. In *The Handbook of Australian Languages Vol. 4: The Aboriginal language of Melbourne and other grammatical sketches*, R.M.W. Dixon and B.J. Blake (eds), 91–122. Sydney: Oxford University Press.
Clark, I.D. 1992. 'That's my country belonging to me': Aboriginal land tenure and dispossession in nineteenth century Western Victoria. Ph.D. thesis, Monash University, Melbourne.
Davidson, A.G. 1992. *Ice Age Earth: Late Quaternary geology and climate.* London: Routledge.
Davidson, I. 1991. Archaeologists and Aborigines. *The Australian Journal of Anthropology* 2(2), 247–58.
Davis, J. and C. Edwards. pers. comm.
Dixon, R.M.W. (ed.) 1991. *Words of our Country.* St Lucia: University of Queensland Press.
Dixon, R.M.W. and B.J. Blake (eds). 1991. *The Handbook of Australian Languages Vol. 4: The Aboriginal language of Melbourne and other grammatical sketches.* Oxford University Press, Australia.
Evans, N and P. McConvell in press. The enigma of Pama-Nyungan expansion in Australia. In *Archaeology and Language II*, R. Blench and M. Spriggs (eds). London: Routledge.
Fison, L. and A.W. Howitt, 1880. *Kamilaroi and Kurnai.* Melbourne: George Robertson. (Reprinted by Oosterhout N.T. 1967).
Howitt, A.W. 1904. *The Native Tribes of South East Australia.* Melbourne: Macmillan.
Isaacs, J. 1980. *Australian Dreaming: 40,000 years of Aboriginal history.* Sydney: Lansdowne Press.
Johnson, J. 1899–1905. Vocabulary of Lower Yorke Peninsula. Manuscript, Mitchell Library.

Jones, R. 1977. Man as an element of a continental fauna: the case of the sundering of the Bassian Bridge. In *Sunda and Sahul*, J. Allen, J. Golson and R. Jones (eds), 317–86. London: Academic Press.

McCrae, H. (ed.). 1934. *Georgiana's Journal: Melbourne a hundred years ago* [Diary of Georgiana McCrae]. Sydney: Angus & Robertson.

Martin, P.S. 1989. Prehistoric overkill: the global model. In *Quaternary Extinctions: A Prehistoric Revolution*, P.S. Martin and R.G. Klein (eds), 354–403, Tucson: University of Arizona Press.

Martin, P.S. and R.G. Klein (eds). 1989. *Quaternary Extinctions: A Prehistoric Revolution.* Tucson: University of Arizona Press.

Massola, A. 1968. *Bunjil's Cave: myths, legends and superstitions of the Aborigines of south-east Australia.* Melbourne: Lansdowne.

Mincham, H. 1983. *The Story of the Flinders Ranges.* Adelaide: Rigby.

Mountford-Sheard Collection. 1940. The Ngadjuri tribe, northern South Australia. Field notes (ms).

Newsome, A.E. 1980. The eco-mythology of the red kangaroo in central Australia. *Mankind* 12, 327–33.

Robinson, R. 1977. *The Man Who Sold His Dreaming.* Sydney: Currawong.

Ryan, J.S.R. (compiler and ed.) 1964. *The Land of Ulitarra: early records of the Aborigines of the mid-north coast of New South Wales.* Armidale: Mid-North Coast Regional Office, Department of University Extension, University of New England.

Schürmann, C.W. 1844. *Vocabulary of the Parnkalla Language Spoken by the Natives Inhabiting the Western Shores of Spencer's Gulf.* Adelaide: George Dehane, Morphett Street.

Teichelmann, C.G. and C.W. Schürmann. 1840. *Outlines of a Grammar, Vocabulary and Phraseology, of the Aboriginal Language of South Australia, Spoken by the Natives in and for Some Distance Around Adelaide,* Adelaide: Thomas.

Tindale, N.B. 1936. Notes on the natives of the southern portion of Yorke Peninsula, South Australia. *Transactions of the Royal Society of South Australia* 60, 55–70.

Tindale, N.B. 1964 and 1975. Manuscripts. South Australian Museum, Adelaide.

Tunbridge, D. 1986. Barngarla cultural knowledge. Unpublished report to Aboriginal Heritage Branch, Adelaide.

Tunbridge, D. 1988. *Flinders Ranges Dreaming.* Canberra: Aboriginal Studies Press,.

Tunbridge, D. 1991. *The Story of the Flinders Ranges Mammals.* Sydney: Kangaroo Press.

White, J.P. and J.F. O'Connell. 1982. *A Prehistory of Australia, New Guinea and Sahul.* Sydney: Academic Press.

Williams, W. [1839] 1933. A vocabulary of the language of the Aborigines of the Adelaide district and other friendly tribes of the Province of South Australia. In *A Vocabulary of the Languages of the Aborigines of the Adelaide District, and Other Friendly Tribes, of the Province of South Australia.* Parkhouse 1933 (of 1933–35) (ed.). [Parkhouse's retranscribed version of Williams's manuscript], Parkhouse 1933 (ed.), 55–70. Adelaide: A. McDougall.

Wyatt, W. 1879. Some account of the manners and superstitions of the Adelaide and Encounter Bay Aboriginal tribes, with a vocabulary of their languages, names of persons and places. In *The Native Tribes of Australia*, J.D. Woods (ed.),157–81.

20   The lost languages of Erromango (Vanuatu)

JERRY TAKI AND DARRELL TRYON

INTRODUCTION

Erromango is the largest island within the southern district of Vanuatu, known also as the TAFEA area (an acronym for the five constituent islands: Tanna, Aneityum, Futuna, Erromango and Aniwa). The islands of the TAFEA area extend between 180° 37′ S and 200° 16′ S. The island of Erromango, the main focus of this discussion, has an area of 902 square kilometres.

Melanesia is one of the most diverse areas in the world in terms of numbers of languages per head of population. Over 1,200 distinct languages are spoken in the area comprising Papua New Guinea, the Solomons, Vanuatu and New Caledonia.

ARCHAEOLOGICAL RESEARCH

There has been very little archaeological research carried out on Erromango until recently. In 1964 research was carried out by Richard and Betty Shutler (1966), who discovered six caves with cultural deposits, but details and locations are not mentioned in their report.

In 1972, Les Groube made a two-week archaeological survey of Erromango, which remained unpublished. In 1983 Matthew Spriggs carried out further survey work and made test excavations on the island. In 1988 Spriggs surveyed the area of Happylands village near the west coast of the island (Spriggs 1988). More recently, Spriggs and Roe (1989) undertook a cultural resources study of Erromango which synthesized all the information on sites surveyed from 1972 until 1988.

Spriggs and Wickler report (1989: 73–4) that sites surveyed to date include limestone caves and shelters, some of which were used as war refuge caves as late as 1900. They also report on burial caves, caves with rock paintings and petroglyphs, as well as extensive petroglyph sites. There are also natural features such as rock formations of great cultural importance to the people of Erromango.

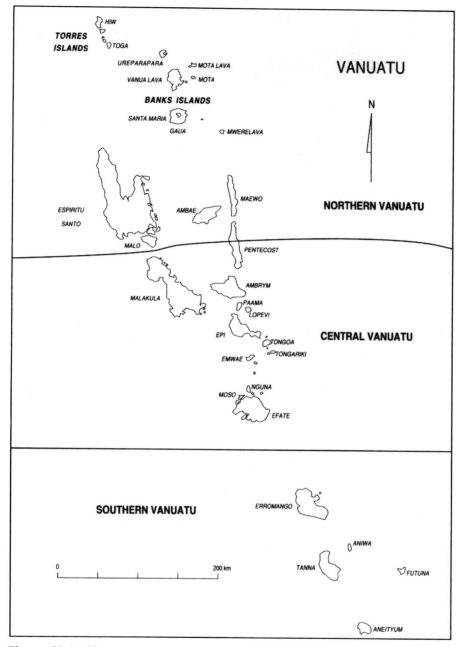

Figure 20.1 Vanuatu.

Spriggs and Wickler (1989) also report that seven of the early sites on the Imponkor Limestone area yielded pottery, all near past reef passages or at river mouths and concentrated on beach ridge formations. Two of these sites, Naen and Ifo, were excavated in 1983, and a further site, Velilo, was also tested. Most of the pottery is probably a regional variant of the Mangaasi tradition with some Lapita sherds present. Mangaasi probably represents either an intrusive population which replaced/absorbed the previous Lapita pottery-using inhabitants of island Melanesia, or the culture of the original pre-Lapita inhabitants reasserting itself after a brief Lapita migration stopover in the area. Spriggs and Wickler note also that pottery-making appears to have died out on Erromango and elsewhere in the TAFEA region some 2,000 years ago.

LINGUISTIC EVIDENCE

Much of the reconstruction of the culture history of Erromango and the other islands of southern Vanuatu will depend not only on the material culture records recovered by archaeologists but also on the linguistic reconstruction of the early Erromangan world. This can be clarified by a better under-standing of the position of the languages of Erromango within Austronesian.

To set Erromangan in context, the languages of Melanesia are members of two large and distinct families. The first group, Papuan, is spread throughout the highlands of New Guinea (Irian Jaya in Indonesia and Papua New Guinea). Papuan languages are also spoken on some of the smaller islands in Indonesia, for example Alor and Pantar, as well as in parts of Timor and Halmahera. East of Papua New Guinea they spread down the Melanesian chain for some distance, to New Britain, New Ireland, Bougainville and the Solomons, where six Papuan languages are spoken out of a total of sixty-two. There are some 750 Papuan languages (Tryon 1994). Within the Melanesian area there are a further 550 Austronesian languages. This language family has its homeland in Asia, spreading from there to the Pacific about 4–5,000 years ago.

THE LANGUAGES OF VANUATU

All the 120 languages of Vanuatu are Austronesian: approximately one language per 1,500 people, since the total population of Vanuatu is roughly 150,000 (Tryon, Volume III). The position of the languages of Vanuatu within the Oceanic region is illustrated in Figures 20.2, 20.3 and 20.4.

Within Austronesian (Figure 20.2), the languages of Vanuatu are all members of the Oceanic sub-group, which includes all of the non-Papuan languages of the Pacific lying east of Geelvink Bay in Irian Jaya, east of a north–south line a 130° 00′ E. The classification of Oceanic is shown in Figure 20.3.

Within Oceanic, the languages of Vanuatu belong to the Remote Oceanic sub-group – a sub-group including the languages of Te Motu province in

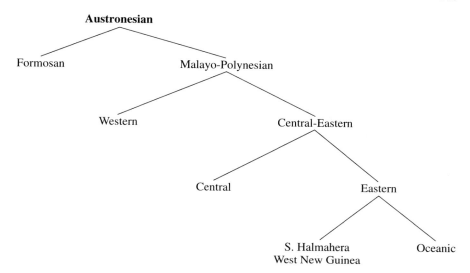

Figure 20.2   Austronesian.

the Solomon Islands, the languages of Micronesia, Vanuatu, New Caledonia, Fiji and Polynesia. The position of the languages of Vanuatu within Remote Oceanic is illustrated in Figure 20.4.

Figure 20.4 shows that the languages of Vanuatu (see Figure 20.1) fall into two major sub-groups: North-Central and Southern Vanuatu. There are currently nine languages in the Southern Vanuatu sub-group (five on Tanna and one on Aneityum), plus two languages on Erromango. In addition, a Polynesian Outlier language, West Futunan, is spoken on the islands of Futuna and Aniwa in southern Vanuatu.

On Erromango today only one language, Sie, is spoken throughout the island, by a population of approximately 1,000. A second language, Ura, is remembered by only a handful of elderly speakers. However, at the time of first European contact there were almost certainly six languages spoken on Erromango (see Figure 20.5). These were as follows:

1   Ura (north–west)
2   Novul Amleng (north–east)
3   Utaha (north–west)
4   Yoku (south–west)
5   Uravat (north–east)
6   Sorung (south–east)

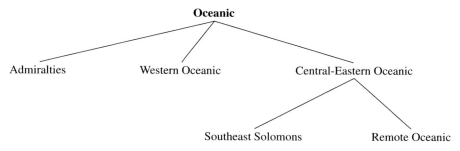

Figure 20.3 Oceanic languages.

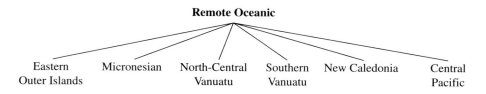

Figure 20.4 Remote Oceanic languages.

Lynch (1983) has summarized the available information on these languages
and their status, and Spriggs and Wickler (1989) have provided additional
oral testimony.

Any discussion of the languages of Erromango should refer to the decim-
ation of the population, due mainly to the introduction of European diseases,
such as measles and whooping cough, in the early and mid-nineteenth century.
McArthur and Yaxley's (1968: 4) estimates of the population figures for
Erromango are shown in Table 20.1.

The consequence of the depopulation of Erromango was not only
the tragic loss of human life, but also the disappearance of a number of
languages. The first records of Erromangan were made by the Presbyterian
missionaries who concentrated on the language spoken around their headquarters at Dillon's Bay on the west of the island. In his 'Sketch of Eromangan
Grammar' (1889: 61–84), the missionary J.D. Gordon lists the following
languages/dialects and approximate populations for the late 1860s–early 1870s:

1 Yoku *or* Enyau (1,000?).
2 Sorung *or* Sie (2,000?).
3 Ura (500?).
4 Utaha (50?).
5 Novul-Amleng (extinct).

Yoku, Enyau and Sorung are all terms meaning 'mine, my'; Sie means 'what?'.

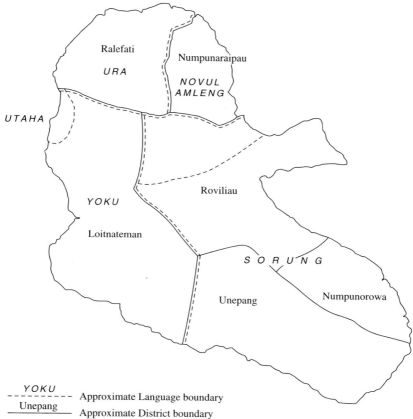

Figure 20.5 Erromangan districts and languages, mid-nineteeth century.

Source: amended from Lynch 1983, map 2.

Humphreys (1926) lists six speech-forms spoken on Erromango as follows:
(1) Eniau, (2) Etio (=Utaha), (3) Adiau (=Ura), (4) Sorung, (5) Seimo, (6) Tanempenum. Lynch (1983: 4) remarks that Humphreys provides no linguistic evidence
as to the identity of Seimo or Tanempenum, nor to the seventh possible dialect
whose name Humphreys suggests had been lost at the time he was writing.

Table 20.1 Population figures for Erromango

Year	Pop.	Year	Pop.	Year	Pop.
1850	5,000	1893	1,000	1927	463
1860	6,000	1898	1,500	1929	439
1865	4,000–5,000	1910	800	1930	421
1872	1,000–2,000	1921	484	1931	381
1875	2,000	1924	513	1967 (Census)	595
1889	2,550	1926	474	1979 (Census)	945

How different were the Erromangan languages from one another? Were they distinct languages or just dialects of the same language? We have modern evidence for Sie (formerly known as Yoku) and Ura which shows that they are certainly distinct languages (Tryon 1976; Lynch 1983). The Utaha wordlist published in Gordon (1889) shows that Utaha was linguistically distinct from both Sie (Yoku) and Ura. Grammatical information available on these three speech-forms also confirms that we are indeed dealing with three distinct languages. While little information is available on Sorung, what there is suggests that it too was significantly different from the other Erromangan speech-forms – so different as to be considered a separate language. Gordon reports that Novul Amleng was extinct by the early 1870s. This means that at the time of European contact there were at least five distinct languages spoken on Erromango. Spriggs and Wickler (1989) report yet another speech-form whose name, Uravat, is still remembered today by elderly Erromangans. This would bring the original language total to six.

The relationship between the various Erromangan languages is not clear, but based on the evidence available today all of them were fairly closely related, almost certainly more closely related to each other than to any languages outside Erromango. Ura, Uravat and Novul Amleng were considered to be very close, while Yoku and Sorung were quite close, so much so that with depopulation and regrouping Sorung had a marked influence on Yoku or Sie (as it is better known today).

The geographical distribution of the current and former languages of Erromango is set out in Figure 20.5. Spriggs and Wickler (1989) note that language and political district boundaries at contact did not necessarily coincide. Yoku and Utaha were spoken within the Loitnateman district; Sorung was spoken in Unepang, Numpunorowa and the southern part of the Roviliau district; Uravat was spoken in the northern part of Roviliau; while Ura was limited to the Ralefati district and Novul-Amleng to Numpunaraipau.

THE LINGUISTIC SITUATION TODAY

Two languages are spoken on Erromango today – namely Sie (Yoku), the sole language for all practical purposes, spoken by approximately 1,000 speakers, and Ura, remembered only by a handful of very elderly individuals. Novul Amleng and Uravat had disappeared by the 1870s, while Utaha probably became extinct by the turn of the twentieth century. Yoku and Sorung were the major languages of Erromango in the nineteenth century, and were apparently quite distinct languages which today have somehow merged. This probably occurred through the establishment of a major Christian village, Nuru Navosavos (Happy Land), where Yoku and Sorung speakers came together. Sorung (h) has replaced Yoku (s) in many words, but certainly not all. As Lynch remarks:

In modern Sie, contrast between /s/ and /h/ has indeed been lost, and although Sie-speakers still appear to retain [s] in some words and [h] in others, [h] appears to be gaining ground. A comparison of earlier Yoku forms with forms in modern Sie shows a strong tendency for earlier /s/ to become Sie /h/ initially and medially.

(Lynch 1983: 7)

Despite this, Sie does not appear to be a continuation of the old southern language Sorung, although it has been strongly influenced by it. Today very little Sorung material remains, but what does is quite sufficient to show that modern Sie can be identified with Yoku rather than Sorung, as the examples in Table 20.2 show. In addition, one of the two alienable possessive paradigms in Sie derives from Sorung, the other from Yoku (Gordon 1889: 80).

Table 20.2   Sorung/Yoku/modern Sie word comparison

Sorung	Yoku	Modern Sie	Gloss
sat	sat, ur	ur	'bad'
siklim	sukrim	sukrim	'five'
vilik	virog	virog	'small'

THE ERROMANGO CULTURAL ASSOCIATION

The Erromango Cultural Association, of which Jerry Taki is a member, was set up to record what remains of the five Erromangan languages lost over the past hundred years. The Association has trained its own fieldworkers to interview the last elderly speakers of these languages, especially Ura. It is the intention of the Association to research and publish a wordlist in as many of the languages as possible, to record the remaining oral traditions and songs of Erromango, and to reconstruct the culture history of the island.

The Association has established a team of four local researchers who began work with elderly Erromangan men and women in 1993. The project has completed the first stage of its linguistic research, and at present the Erromangan Cultural Association has turned its attention to work on the prehistory of the island in collaboration with members of the Division of Archaeology and Natural History at the Australian National University and under the general supervision of the Vanuatu National Cultural centre.

By bringing together archaeology and comparative linguistics much of the detail of the early culture history of Erromango may be salvaged, provided that research can be carried out before the passing of the elderly Erromangans who are the last custodians of much linguistic and cultural knowledge.

ACKNOWLEDGMENTS

The present study reports on a project currently being undertaken by the Erromango Cultural Association which is attempting to record and reconstruct the culture history of the island under the auspices of the Vanuatu National Cultural Centre. We are being assisted in this endeavour by a grant from the Australian South Pacific Cultures Fund. The Erromango Cultural Association project comes also under the umbrella of the Australian National University's TAFEA Culture History Project.

REFERENCES

Gordon, J.D. 1889. Sketch of the Eromangan Grammar. In *South Sea Languages Vol. 1*, D. MacDonald (ed.), 61–84. Melbourne: Melbourne Public Library.

Humphreys, C.B. 1926. *The Southern New Hebrides: an ethnological record*. Cambridge: Cambridge University Press.

Lynch, J.D. (ed.). 1983. *Studies in the Languages of Erromango*. Pacific Linguistics, Series C, No. 79. Canberra: RSPACS.

McArthur, N. and J.F. Yaxley. 1968. *Condominium of the New Hebrides: a report of the first census of the population, 1967*. Sydney: New South Wales Government Printer.

Shutler, R. and M.E. Shutler. 1966. *Oceanic Prehistory*. Menlo Park: Cummings.

Spriggs, M.J.T. 1988. Cultural resources of the proposed Erromango Kauri Reserve and adjacent areas. FAO Working Document 1 (27 pp.). Program VCP/VAN/6755. Rome: FAO.

Spriggs, M.J.T. and D. Roe. 1989. Planning for preservation: a general evaluation of the cultural resources of Erromango. Report prepared for Moores and Rowland. Canberra: National Heritage Studies.

Spriggs, M. J.T. and S. Wickler. 1989. Archaeological research on Erromango: recent data on southern Melanesian prehistory. *Indo-Pacific Prehistory Association Bulletin 9*, 68–91.

Tryon, D.T. 1976. *New Hebrides Languages: an internal classification*. Pacific Linguistics, Series C, No. 50. Canberra: RSPACS.

Tryon, D.T. 1994. The Austronesian languages. In *Comparative Austronesian Dictionary*. Vol. I, Part 1, D.T. Tryon (ed.), 5–44. Berlin: Mouton de Gruyter.

Tryon, D.T. in press. Dialect chaining and the use of geographical space. In *Archaeology and Language III*, R. Blench and M. Spriggs (eds). London: Routledge.

Oral traditions, archaeology and linguistics: the early history of the Saami in Scandinavia

INGER ZACHRISSON

INTRODUCTION

Oral traditions concerning early history are especially important for a people without a writing tradition, like the Saami, one of the main indigenous populations in northernmost Europe. Their oldest history therefore has been orally transmitted, and traditions about their immigration into Scandinavia are recorded from the eighteenth century onwards by others. We hear the voice of the losers of history. Around 1700, the Saami came under increasing pressure from the national states of Scandinavia,[1] with Christian missionaries trying to extinguish the Saami indigenous religion as well as much of their culture. Even the Saami in the far north were soon looked upon as Christianized, in spite of their native religion living on in secret, with its sacrificial sites and shaman drums (Rydving 1993: 1).

This chapter considers the status of Saami oral traditions, and how they can be compared with evidence from archaeology, linguistics, history and other sources, such as genetics.

SAAMI ORAL TRADITION: 'MYTH'

Pehr Högström in Sweden, a tolerant missionary, wrote in 1746 that 'some Saami state that their ancestors in the old days owned all Sweden; but that our forefathers have conquered them and reduced them more and more' ([1747] 1980: 39). On the origin of the ancestors of the Saami, he got the answer that

> Saami and Swedes were one people from the beginning, brothers; but a violent storm grew and one of them got afraid and tried to hide under a board. His offspring became Swedes, and God turned the board into a house. But the other, who was more fearless and did not want to flee, became the ancestor of the Saami, who still live under the open sky.
>
> (Högström [1747] 1980: 48)

The Norwegian missionary Knud Leem in 1767 stated that the Saami said that they were the first inhabitants of Scandinavia, driven further north by a people coming in later on (Leem [1767] 1975: 3, note 2).

The dean Jacob Fellman in Finnish Lapland in 1831 had the long epic poem *Sámieatnama álgo-olbmuid birra* ('About the first inhabitants of Saamiland') recited to him. His informant had heard it sung *c.* 1805 by a Saami in Finnmark in northern Norway. Then, however, it was much longer and more elaborate. According to this *joik*, time among the Saami was divided into three periods. During the first time period, the Saami came to northern Scandinavia after a long migration, hindered by large rivers. There was already another people, who did not speak the Saami language, living there. They were driven away, the last members living at the Tana River in northern Norway. The Saami learned from the banished people the skills of living in the cold country, which many others had tried to reach before without succeeding. The Saami made tools of stone for hunting. During the second time period, other Saami groups with a more developed culture came. After a while yet another group of Saami arrived from the south-west, with reindeer. With them the shaman drum is said to have been introduced. After a period of serious conflict, they found that they were all relatives; the groups were reduced to one, of which today's Saami are the offspring. The third time period begins with the Saami coming under the rule of 'kings' (Lundmark 1979: 60–7, 87–98; Gaski 1993: 23f., 28–44, 86–8).

Some of the epic poems told by the Saami clergyman Anders Fjellner, contemporary with Fellman, also describe how the Saami came into existence. The famous epic 'The Sun's sons' tells how the son of the sun sails far away to ask the giant's daughter to become his wife. She gets diminished and turns into a Saami woman, giving birth to sons of the sun. Saami and giants are depicted as having similar culture and language (Lundmark 1979; Gaski 1993).

Fjellner also wrote down the following tradition, generally known among Saami in Härjedalen and adjacent parts of Norway and confirmed by shorter variants from the Saami in the Torne district. The Saami lived long in a south-eastern land (Himalaya), before enemies parted them. Some Saami, without reindeer, stayed to fight; others, owning reindeer, fled and emigrated with their animals in two directions – one southerly and the other more northern. The southern group passed Gaukasi ('the gaping, astounding') and Alpasa ('mountains with peaks like lynxes'), over Jutas-, Datjas- and Skane-tjålme (the two Danish and the Danish-Swedish sounds). They travelled over these sounds in small leather boats, with their goods on sewn-together, blown-up reindeer hides, drawn by swimming reindeer. Thus they arrived in Scandinavia; after a long time they wandered northwards in the totally barren, uninhabited land. They found Vinerjaure ('the bewildering lake'; Lake Vänern), large as the sea, Vättarjaure ('the lake surrounded by hills'; Lake Vättern) and Melejaure ('the lake possible to pass on rafts'; Lake Mälaren). They wandered around for a long time, also into Norway. But other people came, troubling the Saami, who were driven northwards, some along the coast of the Baltic, as far north as the Tana River; still others kept to the Norwegian mountains. When they travelled along the mountains and came as far north as the sources of Rive Ume, they met other people, whom they did not know. Their language had some likeness with their own, but was heavier and harder. But after some time they recognized the Saami who had emigrated northwards, 'on their looks, their songs, their traditions, their customs and their faith' (von Düben [1873] 1977: 372ff.; Lundmark 1979: 60–98).

Another famous Saami informant, Johan Turi, says that nobody has heard that the Saami came from anywhere ([1917] 1987: 5). Earlier, when they lived by the coast, there were no other inhabitants there; the Saami also once lived all over Sweden. There were no farmers there then; the Saami did not know that any people other than themselves existed.

'MYTH' AND 'HISTORY': A QUESTION OF IDENTITY

How then should we look upon and estimate the veracity of oral tradition as a whole? Oral tradition ought to have as great a value as written sources. 'Whereas historical records so far have been the only acceptable evidence of history, recollections now re-enter the scene as equally valid material for the reconstruction of the past' (Hastrup 1987, 1990; Vansina 1985). Hastrup (1987) says that 'myth represents the history of oral culture, while history is the myth of literate culture. – While earlier, myth and history were firmly distinguished, present day scholars conceive of a dynamic interrelationship between them.' She also stresses that these 'two modes of recollection are equally faithful to the past', and that a sense of shared 'history' is necessary to the making of both ethnicity and a collective identity. According to Hastrup the traditions referred to above should be called 'myth', and the research discussed below, 'history'.

ARCHAEOLOGY, LANGUAGE, WRITTEN SOURCES, GENETICS: SAAMI EARLY 'HISTORY'

Archaeological investigations of ancient monuments indicate that human settlement followed the retreat of the inland ice c. 13,000–7,000 BC from all sides into what is now Scandinavia. The oldest-known finds from northern Sweden have connections with other objects along the Norwegian coast, in their turn pointing southwards (Knutsson 1993). The coast of northernmost Norway may have become ice-free as early as the coast of south Norway (Sandmo 1989).

Norwegian archaeologists look upon the Saami as the original population in northernmost Scandinavia (Olsen 1994, cf. 1986). The same should be the case for central Scandinavia, which later became a 'two-culture area' for a long period, with Saami and Scandinavian/Germanic peoples living in a state of symbiosis. The picture of the ethnic situation of the area has, however, been heavily influenced by the general view of the late nineteenth century, characterized by Social Darwinism, nationalism and ethnocentrism, and Saami presence here has been called into question. Ten years' study of this region has made it possible to discern the interaction between the members of the two main ethnic groups in archaeological material and in written sources from the period AD 0–1350 (Zachrisson 1993, 1994, cf. 1995).

Linguists have recently presented a number of new interpretations of Scandinavian history. Pekka Sammallahti is returning to the general view of the early nineteenth century, that the first people in the whole of northern Europe, even in northern Germany, spoke Uralic language(s), like Saami, and that present-day Saami are the last trace of that culture. He also assumes that the Saami language was once spoken over a much larger area at its south-western and south-eastern extremes (Sammallahti 1993, 1989: 7; cf. Larsson 1992 and Makkay 1990). The earlier suggestion that the Saami once completely changed their language seems to have little support today.

Another view is that the Germanic languages (Indo-European), were not the earliest languages in Scandinavia; Colin Renfrew, combining archaeology with philology, has reached the conclusion that the Indo-European languages as a whole – and the culture connected with them – did not arrive in Europe until *c.* 6000 BC (Renfrew 1987).

'Finn', is the ancient Scandinavian/Nordic name for 'Saami'. Place-names with 'Finn-', as well as traditions about Saami, are to be found not only in central but also in southern Scandinavia. At the beginning of the last century, scholars saw this as one of several proofs of the Saami being the original population in all Scandinavia. They also recorded traditions about how the ancestors of the Germanic people were met on their arrival by a wild forest people, *trollen*, with differing language, customs and religious conceptions, who 'owned the whole country' (Hyltén-Cavallius [1863–4, 1868] 1972). In the West Nordic literature from *c.* AD 1100–1350 there are many parallels between Finnr, dwarfs and giants.

Written sources from *c.* 550 and later give much information about Finnr (i.e. Saami), in northern as well as central Scandinavia. The only known recorded tradition of the early Germanic/Nordic population's view of the original immigration into Scandinavia is in the Icelandic chronicler Snorre Sturlasson's Edda, written down in the thirteenth century. He relates the tradition that when the *asar* (the foremost of the Nordic gods) arrived in Scandinavia, there were others there before them.

Lars Beckman (1959, 1979) has been able to see clear differences between Saami and non-Saami in today's Sweden through analyses of blood groups. He states that all studies of the origin of the Saami neglect their relationship with other known populations, and that the Saami very rightly call themselves the aboriginal population. His map also shows relatively high values of 'Saami characteristics' inland in southern Sweden as well as on Gotland.

Research on bear migration patterns has also been helpful; an investigation of the genetics of bears in all of Europe found that the bears in Scandinavia fall into two kinds – one in the northern part and another in the central. Those in the north relate to the bears in Finland and Russia, while those in the centre relate to those further south in Europe. The difference is interpreted as the result of two separate immigration routes into Scandinavia after the melting of the inland ice (*New Scientist*, London, 1994), and may also indicate the main immigration routes for human beings.

CONCLUSION

The picture of early Saami history given in their oral traditions is ambiguous. There are, however, accounts of several Saami 'immigration waves' into Scandinavia, mostly from the south, but also from the north. The views of the archaeologists are contradictory, especially concerning the ethnic affiliation of peoples of northern and central Scandinavia. Philology seems to have reached further, especially when combined with archaeology, and worked more on giving an overall view of the processes of history. The philologists' very interesting contributions to the debate have, however, scarcely been given the importance that they deserve in today's archaeological debate in Sweden. The most fruitful way to proceed must be through collaboration between all relevant disciplines.

NOTE

1   This chapter concerns the Scandinavian peninsula, i.e. Sweden and Norway. Also, there are still Saami today in Finland and Russia (for Saami myths from the Kola peninsula, see Terebikhin 1993).

REFERENCES

Beckman, L. 1959. *A Contribution to the Physical Anthropology and Population Genetics of Sweden*. Lund: Hereditas.
Beckman, L. 1979. Distributions of genes in time and space. Theoretical considerations and examples derived from northern Sweden. Reports from a Symposium in Umeå, Sweden, June 1977. In *Time, Space and Man. Essays on Microdemography*, J. Sundin and K. Söderlund (eds), 35–43. Stockholm: Almqvist and Wiksell.
Gaski, H. 1993. *Med ord skal tyvene fordrives. Om samenes episk poetiske diktning* (2nd edn). Karasjok: Davvi Girji o.s.
Hastrup, K. 1987. Presenting the past. Reflections on myth and history. *Folk* 29, 257–69.
Hastrup, K. 1990. Worlds apart. Comprehending each other across time and space. *Acta Borealia* 1990(1), 14–24.
Högström, P. [1747] 1980. *Beskrifning öfver de till Sveriges krona lydande Lappmarker*. Facsimile. Norrländska skrifter nr 3. Red. R. Jacobsson. Umeå: Två Förläggare Bokförlag.

Hyltén-Cavallius, G.O. [1863–4, 1868] 1972. *Wärend och Wirdarne. Ett försök i Svensk Ethnologi.* Del 1–2 (3rd edn), N.-A. Bringeus (ed.). Lund.

Knutsson, K. 1993. Garaselet-Lappviken-Rastklippan. Introduktion till en diskussion om Norrlands Äldsta Bebyggelse. *Tor* 25, 5–51.

Larsson, L.-G. 1992. Gemeindelappen und Schweden. In *Finnisch-ugrische Sprachen zwischen dem germanischen und dem slavischen Sprachraum.* Vorträge des Symposiums aus Anlass des 25-jährigen Bestehens der Finnougristik an der Rijksuniversiteit Groningen 13–15. November 1991, 97–110. Groningen.

Leem, K. [1767] 1975. *Beskrivelse over Finmarkens lapper 1767. Efterord av A. Nesheim.* Facsimil. København: Rosenkilde & Bagger.

Lundmark, B. 1979. *Anders Fjellner – Samernas Homeros – och diktningen om solsönerna.* Acta Bothniensia Occidentalis 5. Umeå: Västerbottens Musem.

Makkay, J. 1990. New aspects of the PIE and the PU/PFU homelands: contacts and frontiers between the Baltic and the Ural in the Neolithic. In *Congressus Septimus Internationalis Fenno-Ugristarum,* 55–73. Sessiones Plenares/Dissertationes. Debrecen.

Olsen, B. 1986. Norwegian archaeology and the people without (pre-)history: or how to create a myth of a uniform past. Archaeology and politics. *Archaeological Review from Cambridge* 5(1), 25–42.

Olsen, B. 1994. *Bosetning og samfunn i Finnmarks forhistorie.* Oslo: Universitetsforlaget.

Olsen, L. 1995. *Stadnamn og kulturlanskapet.* Deb 7. Nasjonale konferansen i mane-gransking. Blindern 19, November 1993. M. Harsson and B. Hellelland (eds). Avdeling for namnegransking. Oslo: Universitet i Oslo.

Renfrew, C. 1987. *Archaeology and Language. The puzzle of Indo-European origins.* Cambridge: Cambridge University Press.

Rydving, H. 1993. *The End of Drum-Time. Religious change among the Lule Saami, 1670s–1740s.* Acta Universitatis Upsaliensis. Historia Religionum 12. Uppsala: University of Uppsala.

Sammallahti, P. 1989. A linguist looks at Saami prehistory. *Acta Borealia* 2, 3–11.

Sammallahti, P. 1993. Suomalaisten ja saamelaisten juuret ['The Roots of the Finns and the Saami']. *Kieliposti* 1, 3–4.

Sandmo, A.-K. 1989. Stilistisk variasjon og tidlig postglasial bosetting i Troms. In *Fremskritt for fortida i nord. I Povl Simonsens fotefar,* 59–73. Tromsø: Tromsø Museum.

Terebikhin, N.M. 1993. Cultural geography and cosmography of the Sami. *Acta Borealia* 1, 3–17.

Turi, J. [1917] 1987. *Muittalus Samid Birra. En bok om lapparnas liv,* E. Demant Hatt (ed.). Swedish translation S. Karlén and K. B. Wiklund. Lapparne och deras land. Skildringar och studier utg. av Hjalmar Lundbohm VI. Facsimil. Umeå: Två Förläggare Bokförlag.

Vansina, J. 1985. *Oral Tradition as History.* London-Nairobi: University of Wisconsin Press.

von Düben, G. [1873] 1977. *Om Lappland och lapparne, företrädesvis de svenske. Ethnografiska studier* (2nd edn). Stockholm: Gidlunds.

Zachrisson, I. 1993. A review of archaeological research on Saami prehistory in Sweden. *Current Swedish Archaeology,* 1, 171–82.

Zachrisson, I. 1994. Herdalir i Finnland – Finnlendinga i Herdala. In *Odlingslandskap och fångstmark. En vänbok till Klas-Göran Selinge,* 337–45. Stockholm: Riksantik-varieämbetet.

Zachrisson, I. 1995. Archaeology and politics: Saami prehistory and history in central Scandinavia. *Journal of European Archaeology* 2, 361–8.

Index

Abashevo culture: ceramics of 287,
15.2; *see also* northern sub-Urals
Aborigines: colonization of Australia
346–7; extinct species recorded in
Aboriginal myth 351–8; sea-level
changes recorded in Aboriginal myth
347–8, 350; vegetational changes
recorded in Aboriginal myth 350–1;
volcanic activity recorded in
Aboriginal myth 350–1
Africa: crabs, discussion of the
treatment of in the major language
phyla of 168, **A.2a**; crabs, similarities
of the associations of in African
languages with the lexemes applied
to crabs in Indo-European languages
170–2; cultural salience of crabs,
frogs and turtles 172, 173; frogs and
toads, discussion of the treatment of
in the major language phyla of
168–9, **A.3a**; ideophones in the
languages of 170; lexemes, discussion
of the lack of change in the lexemes
applied to turtles, crabs and frogs
169–70; phonoaesthemes in the
languages of 170; riverine adaptations
and their relationship with the
language phyla of 172–3; turtles and
tortoises, discussion of the treatment
of in the major language phyla of
168, **A.1a**; *see also* Bantu, Benin,
Edo
Afroasiatic language phylum:
distribution of and agricultural

dispersals, discussion of the
relationship between 86–7
agricultural dispersals: critique of
Renfrew's theory of 76, 80; and the
distribution of Bantu languages 86;
and the distribution of the Indo-
European language phylum 86–7;
and the distribution of the Afroasiatic
language phylum 86–7; and language
replacement, discussion of the
relationship between 84–6; models of
84; process of, discussion of its
relationship with linguistic dispersal
82–9, 123; *see also* linguistic dispersal
Anatolian model: discussion and critique
of its account of Indo-European
origins 109–11, 115; *see also* Renfrew
archaeology: archaeological correlations
with the mythology of Vanuatu,
discussion of 323–9, **17.2**, **17.3**,
17.4; cognitive archaeology,
definition of 43; correlation of
archaeological data with cultural
reconstructions derived from lexical
analysis, discussion of 155–6;
epistemological and methodological
framework for the recognition of
writing systems in prehistory,
discussion of 55–61; historical
linguistics, role of in generating
hypotheses for archaeology 10–11;
and linguistics, discussion of the
history of the relationship between
1–11, 13–15; oral traditions,

recorded in Aboriginal myth 350–1; volcanic activity recorded in Aboriginal myth 350–1; Yirkap, discussion of the myth of 293; *see also* oral traditions

network structure: characterization of the network structure of speech-community event 215, 217, **13.3**; *see also* social network model

New Ireland: linkage rejoining in 230, **13.14**

northern sub-Urals: Abashevo culture, discussion of the ceramics of 287, **15.2**; Fatyanovo culture, discussion of the ceramics of 284, 287, **15.2**; Great People's migration 302, 304–5; hexagonal dwelling structures in, discussion of the archaeological evidence for 287, 289–90, **15.4**, **15.5**; hexagonal dwellings, Indo-European symbolic associations of 290–1; Hyperboreans, discussion of the myth of 301–2; Indo-European migrations into, discussion of the archaeological sequence for 283–4, 287, 293–4, 297, 301; Indo-European migrations into, discussion of their reflection in folk memory 291–3; Indo-European traits in the mythology of 290–3; Iranian hydronyms, discussion of the presence of in 297–8, 300; Iron age migrations into, discussion of the myths of 302, 304–5; Kurmantau culture, discussion of the ceramics of 300, **15.10**; Lugovskaya culture, archaeological evidence of 294, 297; Pera the Giant, discussion of the myth of 290–3; Pozdnyakovo culture, discussion of the ceramics of 287, **15.2**; Yirkap, discussion of the myth of 293

Nostratic theory: chronology of 70–1; definition of 65, 70–1

Old Frisian: modelling language similarity of to Later North-west Germanic 272–3; Probabilistic Finite State Automaton derived from modelling similarity of Later North-west Germanic to Old Frisian **14.5**

Old High German: Probabilistic Finite State Automaton derived from modelling similarity of Later North-west Germanic to Old High German **14.6**

oral traditions: archaeological correlations with the oral traditions of Uvea 337, 339; collection of 26; cross-generational transmission of oral traditions on Futuna 331–3; Edo oral traditions, characterization and discussion of 308–19; Indo-European migrations into the northern sub-Urals, discussion of their reflection in folk memory 290–93; persistence of 26; Sami oral tradition, discussion of the veracity of 370–75; Uvea, typology of oral traditions of 331; value of to archaeology, discussion of 24–5, 27; *see also* myth

orthography: conventions of xx

Pacific Pigdin: history of 252, 253

palaeolinguistics: *see* historical linguistics

Palaeolithic: evolution of thought during, discussion of the evidence for 75–6; Indo-Europeans, discussion of the evidence for the Palaeolithic origins of 74–6, 80–1; language evolution, discussion of the evidence for during 75–6; regional differentiation in Eurasia during, discussion of the evidence for 74–5

Palaeolithic art: Grotte de Gargas, discussion of the morphological variation in painted hands at 56–8; as a writing system, discussion of the evidence for 55–6

Pera the Giant: discussion of the myth of 290–3

PFSA: *see* Probabilistic Finite State Automaton

Philippines: *see* Tasaday

phonetics: conventions of xx